Sharī'at and Ambiguity in South Asian Islam

Sponsored by the
JOINT COMMITTEE ON SOUTH ASIA
of the
SOCIAL SCIENCE RESEARCH COUNCIL
and the
AMERICAN COUNCIL OF LEARNED SOCIETIES

Sharīʿat and Ambiguity in South Asian Islam

EDITED BY
Katherine P. Ewing

UNIVERSITY OF CALIFORNIA PRESS
Berkeley • Los Angeles • London

University of California Press
Berkeley and Los Angeles, California
University of California Press, Ltd.
London, England

Printed in the United States of America
1 2 3 4 5 6 7 8 9

Library of Congress Cataloging-in-Publication Data

Sharī'at and ambiguity in South Asian Islam.

Papers from a conference held at the Pendle Hill Conference Center in Pennsylvania, May 22–24, 1981.
"Sponsored by the Joint Committee on South Asia of the Social Science Research Council and the American Council of Learned Societies"—P.
Includes bibliographies and index.
1. Islam—South Asia—Congresses. 2. Islamic law—South Asia—Congresses. I. Ewing, Katherine Pratt. II. Joint Committee on South Asia.
BP63.A4S646 1988 297'.14'0954 86-25055
ISBN 0-520-05575-6 (alk. paper)

Contents

Illustrations and Tables

Map

Figures

Tables

Preface

The papers in this volume were originally prepared for the conference "South Asian Islam: Moral Principles in Tension," which was held May 22–24, 1981, at the Pendle Hill Conference Center in Pennsylvania. The conference and resulting volume have been sponsored by the Social Science Research Council/ American Council of Learned Societies' Joint Committee on South Asia, as part of a larger effort sponsored by the Joint Committee to understand moral values and sources of authority in South Asian Islam. It is the successor to a previous conference and volume (Metcalf 1984) which focused on the concept of *adab* (proper behavior) as a way of exploring core values of Islam. During discussion of *adab* at the first conference, the issue of alternative ways of ordering experience emerged. Papers were solicited for a second conference that examined the actual processes by which Muslims resolve the tension among what are perceived as alternative values and traditions.

In addition to contributors to this volume, there were several participants at the conference whose contributions enriched our discussions and added valuable perspectives on the material. Khalid bin Sayeed and Peter Bertocci presented papers that are, unfortunately, not included in the present volume. Vincent Crapanzano and Dale Eickelman acted as discussants for several of the papers and gave us stimulating observations made from their perspectives as experts on quite a different part of the Muslim world. Ira Lapidus and Barbara Metcalf, who were also present as discussants, have been involved in this project at every stage of planning and execution and have offered their constructive criticisms of earlier drafts of this manuscript. Warren Fusfeld, who presented a paper, also made local arrangements for the conference at Pendle Hill. I cannot give enough thanks to Sandria Freitag, who, in addition to providing a paper, acted as gadfly, copy editor, word processor, and my most persistent and constructive critic. My husband Thomas DiPrete also carefully read and commented on the manuscript, as well as giving me encouragement at crucial moments. David Szanton of the Social Science Research Council was generous with his support, guidance, and patience during the long process of organizing the conference and preparing the papers for publication. Finally, though my thinking was greatly stimulated by the papers, conference discussion, and comments on the manuscript, responsibility for the formulations and conclusions presented in the introductory chapter rests with me.

KATHERINE P. EWING
Chicago
September 1985

Contributors

AKBAR S. AHMED is currently Commissioner, Sibi Division, in Baluchistan. Between 1976 and 1980 he was Political Agent in the Orakzai and South Waziristan Agencies of the Northwest Frontier Province and has served in various other capacities in the Pakistani government. He received his Ph.D. in anthropology from the School of Oriental and African Studies, London University, in 1978. He has been a Visiting Professor at the Institute for Advanced Studies at Princeton and at the Department of Anthropology and Institute of International Development, Harvard University. His publications include numerous books and articles about Pakistan and Muslim society, focusing particularly on the Northwest Frontier Province.

RAFIUDDIN AHMED is Professor and Chairman in the Department of History and Dean of the Faculty of Arts at the University of Chittagong, where he has taught since 1968. He received his doctorate in modern history at Oxford University in 1977. His publications include *The Bengal Muslims 1871–1906: A Quest for Identity* and numerous journal articles. He has edited two volumes, *Islam in Bangladesh: Society, Culture and Politics* and *Bangladesh: History, Society and Culture*. He is presently working on a new book, *Symbols and Social Mobilization: The Muslim Masses of Bengal in Politics 1905–1935* and preparing a chapter for the *Encyclopedia of Asian History*.

CATHERINE B. ASHER received her Ph.D. in 1984. She has written extensively on Indo-Islamic architecture, including her dissertation, which focused on the architectural patronage of Sher Shāh Sūr. Currently she is completing a book on Mughal architecture. She teaches at the University of Minnesota and Carleton College.

KATHERINE P. EWING received her Ph.D. in anthropology from the University of Chicago in 1980. In addition to articles in journals and edited volumes, she has just completed a book on Sufi saints and their followers in Pakistan. She has been Instructor in the College of the University of Chicago and is a Research Candidate at the Institute for Psychoanalysis in Chicago.

SANDRIA B. FREITAG received her doctorate in modern South Asian history from the University of California, Berkeley, in 1980. Currently she is an

Adjunct Lecturer in the History Department and a research associate at the Center for South and Southeast Asian Studies at the University of California, Berkeley. She recently completed a monograph on community identity and the development of communalism in north India. She now is working on the definitions and approaches to criminality developed in that area in the nineteenth century, and editing a volume on the popular culture of Banaras.

WARREN FUSFELD received his Ph.D. in history from the University of Pennsylvania in 1981. He was a Lecturer in History at the University of Pennsylvania between 1981 and 1983, and has done post-doctoral work in the field of Law and Islamic Studies at the Law School of the University of Pennsylvania, while also obtaining a J.D. At present he is an attorney at the firm of Wolf, Block, Schorr, and Solis-Cohen in Philadelphia.

DAVID GILMARTIN teaches in the Department of History at North Carolina State University. He has done research in Pakistan on twentieth-century Muslim politics in the Punjab and has published several articles on Punjab politics. He received his Ph.D. in history from the University of California at Berkeley.

RICHARD KURIN received his Ph.D. in anthropology from the University of Chicago, and has done extensive research in Pakistan and India over the past fifteen years. Specializing in the study of kinship, social structure, cultural change, and folk conceptual systems, his publications on South Asian Islam have appeared in *Asian Survey, Middle Eastern Studies, Human Organization, Contributions to Indian Sociology, Natural History*, and in numerous edited volumes. He is currently Deputy Director of the Office of Folklife Programs at the Smithsonian Institution and a professorial lecturer in the School of Advanced International Studies at Johns Hopkins University.

DAVID LELYVELD, a historian, is currently Dean of Students, School of General Studies, Columbia University. His book *Aligarh's First Generation: Muslim Solidarity in British India* (Princeton, 1978) is a study of the experience of English-style education in the lives of north Indian Muslims in the late nineteenth century. Since that time he has been working on a social history of Urdu and its relation to South Asian Muslim identity. He has done research in India and Pakistan and was formerly Associate Professor of History and South Asian Studies at the University of Minnesota.

AZIM NANJI is Professor of Religious Studies and Director of the Center for Global Studies at Oklahoma State University. He specializes in Ismā'īlī studies and in the cultural history of Islam in Africa south of the Sahara. His publications include *The Nizari Ismaili Tradition in the Indo-Pakistan Subcontinent* (1978), *The Religious World: Communities of Faith*, co-author (1982), and *Religious Values and Cultural Change in African Contexts* (forthcoming); and articles and chapters on Ismā'īlism and on religious and cultural change in Africa.

CARROLL McC. PASTNER is Associate Professor of Anthropology at the University of Vermont. Her teaching and research interests focus on social organization, gender roles, and ideology, particularly in the Middle East. She received her Ph.D. from Brandeis University in 1971 and has twice (1968–69 and 1976–77) worked in Pakistan among the Baluch. Her publications include chapters in *Women in the Muslim World* and *Pakistan: the Long View* and in the journals *Ethnology*, *Journal of Anthropological Research*, *Signs*, and *Human Organization*. Presently she is comparing the ideology of sexuality and pollution beliefs in Islam and Judaism on both ethnographic and textual (*sharī'at* and *talmud*) levels.

STEPHEN L. PASTNER, Associate Professor of Anthropology at the University of Vermont, received his Ph.D. in anthropology from Brandeis University in 1971. Both with Carroll Pastner and alone, he conducted fieldwork among the Baluch tribes of Pakistan in 1968–69, 1976–77, 1979, and 1982. He has also carried out research in the Caribbean, in Ethiopia, and, most recently, in Israel. His articles on the Baluch have appeared in such journals as *Anthropological Quarterly*, *Man*, *International Journal of Middle East Studies*, and *Journal of Asian and African Studies*, as well as in numerous edited volumes. He is the co-editor (with Louis Flam) of *Anthropology in Pakistan* (Cornell South Asia Monograph Series).

CAROL PRINDLE received her Ph.D. in anthropology from the University of Chicago in 1982. Her dissertation, "Rank among Muslims in Chittagong, Bangladesh," was based on twenty-two months of research in Bangladesh and India. She has taught anthropology and South Asian studies at the University of Wisconsin, Madison.

JUDY F. PUGH is Assistant Professor of Anthropology at Michigan State University, where she teaches in the Department of Anthropology and the College of Human Medicine. She holds a Ph.D. in anthropology from the University of Chicago (1981). Her papers have appeared in a number of scholarly journals, and she is the co-editor of *South Asian Systems of Healing*, a special issue of *Contributions to Asian Studies* (1984). She has just completed a book on divinatory counseling and ethnopsychiatry among the Hindus and Muslims of Banaras. Currently she is engaged in research on Islamic medicine (*yūnānī ṭib*) and on Urdu cinema.

WILLIAM R. ROFF, M.A. (New Zealand), Ph.D. (Australian National University), is Professor of History at Columbia University, New York, where he has taught since 1969. Author of several books and numerous articles on Islam and society in Southeast Asia, he has also made comparative studies of Muslim peoples in South Asia and the Middle East. He is editor of the volume of essays *Islam and the Political Economy of Meaning: Comparative Studies of Muslim Discourse*.

Note on Transliteration

The system of transliteration used in this volume is based on that used for the Urdu language by John T. Platts in his *A Dictionary of Urdu, Classical Hindi and English* (1977, reprint of 1884 edition; Delhi: Oriental Books Reprint Corporation). The list of consonants, in Urdu alphabetical order, is as follows:

b, p, t, ṭ, s̤, j, ch, ḥ, k͟h, d, ḍ, ẕ, r, ṛ, z, zh, s, sh,
ṣ, ẓ, t̤, z̤, ʻ, g͟h, f, q, k, g, l, m, n, ṅ, w, h, y, ʼ

Arabic words used in other languages, such as Malay and Bengali, have also been transliterated according to this system, except where otherwise indicated.

INTRODUCTION

Ambiguity and *Sharī'at*: A Perspective on the Problem of Moral Principles in Tension

KATHERINE P. EWING

The relationship between codes for behavior derived from Islamic principles and codes derived from other sources is the focal point for these essays on South Asian Muslims. In introducing this collection, I would like to suggest that the uses of ambiguity, the tendency for groups of Muslims to define boundaries when placed under stress, and the new role of ordinary people in defining appropriate codes of behavior are central issues uniting the case studies that follow.

The relationship traced here may be seen as an interplay between the integrative role of ambiguity, on the one hand, and the decontextualized emphasis on consistency supplied by the *sharī'at* on the other. Generally the ambiguities of everyday life obscure inconsistencies in a society's organizing principles. It is not only that, during periods of relative stability, members of a community know how to apply implicit codes and rules for behavior that (though generally agreed upon) are contextually specific and mutually inconsistent. More than simply tolerating ambiguity, community members value and exploit it. Even if they have engaged in conflict over these codes, they implicitly agree on the rules about how conflict should be conducted and resolved, about the limits of discourse (e.g., C. Pastner, this volume). But rapid social change—during which lines of authority, styles of leadership, and boundaries of community are being challenged—can cause actors to question fundamental rules and limits of discourse and to reexamine basic organizing principles of the society. It is at such moments of transition that organizing principles can be clearly discerned. Consistency becomes important as actors closely examine contradictions and carefully define terms and symbols (cf. Geertz 1965; Silverman 1977). Even the lives of ordinary people may come under political scrutiny. Indeed, the recent inclusion of ordinary people in such discussions has changed the ways in which the Muslim community has integrated alternative codes for behavior with those based on Islamic organizing principles.

For the most part, then, the relationship between Islam-derived and alternative codes can be characterized by its ambiguity. We can see other characteristics of the relationship as well. Traditionally, hierarchy has been central to the process by which such alternative codes are incorporated. A Muslim understanding of hierarchy as an organizing principle rests on a concept of center (the prototypical center being God and the Prophet) and on the premise that those who are closer to the center are morally and / or socially superior.

In addition to this hierarchical ordering, the limits of acceptable behavior for Muslims are expressed in terms of the concept of *sharī'at*—the canon law of Islam, which has been given by God and which is the basis for judgment of actions as good or bad. *Sharī'at* regulates the external relations of men to Allāh and to their fellow men. It is concerned with the fulfillment of prescribed duties. The *sharī'at* consists of guidelines for judging actions; these guidelines have their roots in the Qur'ān and in accounts of the life of the Prophet. From this perspective, Islam can be seen to provide constraints, rules, and limits of discourse.

Sharī'at is thus a way of demarcating the boundaries of the community. The concept of "*kāfir*" (infidel), which is used to describe those who have been declared or defined as being outside the community, is associated with the idea of a Muslim community whose social relations are ordered in terms of *sharī'at*, however *sharī'at* is articulated and defined at a particular time and place. The term *kāfir* has been used to designate non-Muslims, but, as sects have developed in Islam over the centuries, it has also been used to castigate Muslims of different opinion (see Fusfeld, this volume), members of other sects, and individuals who violate the *sharī'at*—and even to express rivalry among tribal or ethnic groups (see S. Pastner; A. Ahmed, this volume). This label is used when boundaries are being clearly drawn, and when alternative values and practices are explicitly rejected.

Ambiguity as a Reconciling Rhetoric

To investigate how people reconcile conflicting values and codes for conduct involves examining the pragmatic social functions of specific actions. This is the traditional domain of rhetoric, defined in its broadest sense by Burke (1969) to mean the alignment of social groups through communication, identification, and persuasion. A focus on the pragmatic functions of speech and behavioral acts is in contrast to the consideration of the decontextualized referential meanings of salient cultural categories such as "*adab*" (proper behavior) and "*sharīʿat*," the latter being analogous to the relatively timeless grammar and lexicon of a language.

Ambiguity is at the heart of rhetoric. Though culture as an organizing system of postulates and categories allows room for ambiguity in the definition and articulation of these categories, especially when concepts and symbols have not been self-consciously systematized, it is only in specific historical contexts that we can observe the ways in which particular ambiguities are socially significant. Individuals rely on ambiguity as they strategically use language and other cultural media in specific social situations, maneuvering to achieve their social goals. Utterances and actions can be multifunctional, and ambiguity derives from the possibility of pragmatic indeterminacy: the same act can be interpreted (and thus can constitute social relationships) in many different ways (Silverstein 1967:47). In a stable social environment, these pragmatic meanings, though "criss-crossing, frequently contradictory, ambiguous and confusing" (Silverstein 1967:54), can be interpreted in terms of culturally established, often implicit, rules of use, with reliable criteria for determining the appropriateness of specific acts and interpretations in a particular social situation.

The conflict over honor among tribal Baluch analyzed by C. Pastner provides an example of pragmatic indeterminacy and the strategies used to support a contested goal in a situation of everyday life. In this case, the conflict did not involve a debate over the rules about how to argue; both men and women, the protagonists, agreed on the principles by means of which one must justify one's argument. The conflict was articulated in terms of the concept of honor (*ʿizzat*), and all agreed that honor was to be defined and discussed in terms of the fulfillment of obligation (*ḥaqq*), the maintenance of Baluch customs, and obedience to the tenets of Islam. Custom and Islam were not clearly distinguished. Though from our perspective (or from a reformist's perspective) the

Map of South Asia Showing Locations Discussed by the Authors

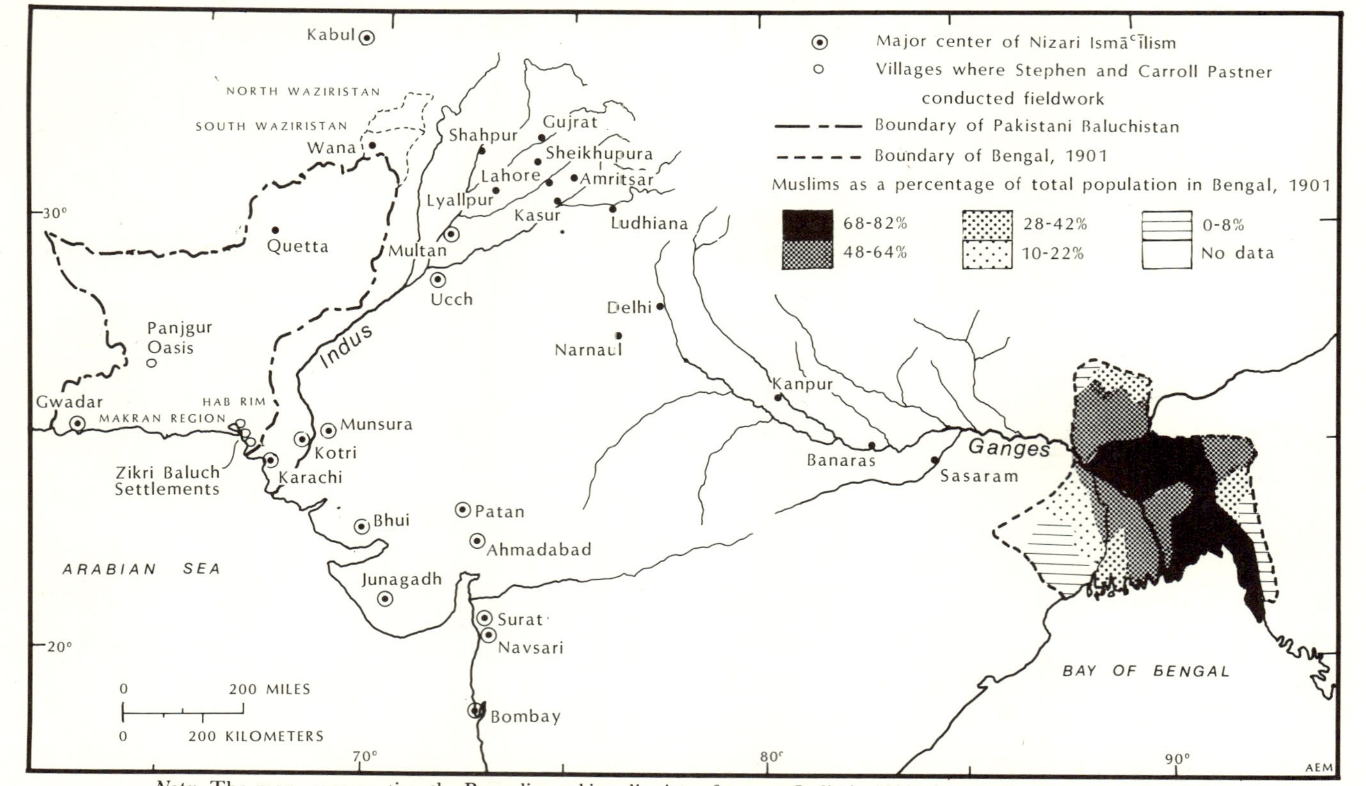

Note: The map, representing the Bengali-speaking districts of eastern India in 1901, shows the distribution of Muslims in the region and is based on a map published in the *Census of India* 1901, vol. VI:I, p. 156.

principles of *ḥaqq, riwāj*, and Islam may be seen as values which must be reconciled and maintained, the Baluch do not focus on discrepancies, but rather use these principles as rules for proper discourse. Since the specific goals of the men and women were different in this situation, they applied these principles differently when articulating the significance of specific actions. The resolution of the conflict, like much of daily living, demanded accommodation and compromise.

During major social upheavals involving the structure of political power, authority, and the form and level of political participation, actors may perceive implicit pragmatic messages to be no longer tolerably ambiguous, but rather disorganized or inappropriate. This disorganization or discrepancy may become manifest at a moment of crisis or confrontation, when a previously routine activity becomes a focus of conflict and the polarization of groups (see Geertz's analysis of a ritual that failed [1973]; Freitag, this volume). A typical reaction to such a situation is debate (see Silverman 1977; Geertz 1965; as well as essays in the present volume, especially Roff, R. Ahmed), during which participants articulate implicit pragmatic rules and systematize them by providing a rationale for these rules vis-à-vis the core values and concepts of the culture, or by eliminating certain activities that are defined as being inconsistent with these core values and concepts. During this process, the core values and concepts are themselves systematized and may be redefined, thus eliminating another source of ambiguity.

Among the core values and concepts of Islam that have periodically been redefined and systematized are *sharīʿat* and *adab* (proper behavior; in its plural form, rules or codes for behavior). *Adab* was the focus of the first conference and collection of papers (Metcalf 1984), which explored the concept as a shared ideal based on values common to all Muslims.[1] A comprehensive cultural concept, *adab* addresses all domains of life and expresses the Muslim goal of bringing all of society into consonance with a common core of values. Though domains of activity can be distinguished and expectations for specific roles vary, the concept of *adab* reinforces the understanding that all Islam is ultimately one (Metcalf 1984).

1. The essays in that volume examined standards of moral responsibility as set out in manuals of *adab* written for kings, sufis, teachers, judges, musicians, family heads, and women. Among the conclusions drawn there were that (1) there are common moral expectations for those occupying all social positions; and (2) a fundamental basis for authority in Islam is the exemplification of moral qualities, ultimately represented by the Prophet Muḥammad.

The papers and the ensuing discussion at that conference established that codes of *adab* were elaborated and systematized particularly during the twelfth to fourteenth, and again in the eighteenth to twentieth, centuries—that is, when the political system was in crisis and there was a concern with guarding the Muslim tradition. Many articles in the present volume concentrate on such moments of tension and change. In these situations, rules for actions that were previously taken for granted are no longer consistently applicable and therefore are challenged and redefined. In the process, core symbols and categories such as *adab* and *sharīʿat* are also redefined and systematized. During the period of Muslim rule, *sharīʿat* was implicitly understood to be a symbolic system tied to the state, a conception of ordering the world under the unity of Islam. The ruler and elites represented Islam; the position of peasants and indigenous populations in the system did not require of them strictly proper behavior. The elites assumed, rather, that the population was simply *be-adab* (incapable of proper behavior). The last two centuries have been a time during which this hierarchical perspective has been questioned; and thus the ability of Islamic principles to deal with alternative codes has been tested.

These articles reveal situations of striking transition. Where ambiguity in the relationship between everyday behavior and the doctrines of Islam once blurred lines of social division, many community leaders began to feel it necessary to establish boundaries by invoking the principle of *sharīʿat*. The Muslim loss of political control to the British in India has been the context in which this reexamination of the organizing principles of the Muslim community has occurred. With the loss of power, Muslims also lost their identity as a community defined in terms of adherence to *sharīʿat* as an ideal, with primary responsibility for approaching that ideal hierarchically located in the ruling elite and in public observance. Several essays included in the present volume examine instances of debate over a potential stimulus that had previously gone unnoticed in the course of everyday activity (i.e., a locus of activity potentially definable as being in violation of *sharīʿat*, such as a small mosque [Freitag], dog saliva [Roff], customary law [Gilmartin]). The activity became a center of controversy when a broader challenge used that activity as a focus. The stimulus then became an emotionally charged issue in terms of which the rules and limits of discourse for the entire community were articulated. We began by noting that in such circumstances groups often move from ambiguity to careful definition of symbols and terms. The historical context forces attention to lines of authority, styles of leadership, boundaries of community, and even the styles of living practiced by ordinary people.

Hierarchy as an Incorporating Principle

From a Muslim historical perspective, religious and political centers as loci of authority in the Muslim community have, since the leadership of the Prophet Muḥammad, never again been in perfect congruence. A world view expressed in the traditions and attributed to Muḥammad himself is that the Muslim community would steadily become worse after its golden age in the time of the Prophet and His Companions, until the coming of the *mahdī*. Muslim societies understood *sharīʿat* to be an unattainable ideal and accepted the divergence of everyday practice from this ideal. The *sharīʿat* continued to claim unconditioned theoretical acknowledgment, and everyone who failed in this respect was to be considered an infidel (*kāfir*); but at the same time, *sharīʿat* could not be enforced in practice and thus actual observance was not expected (Schacht 1974:527). This principle left room for ambiguity in the relationship between the declaration of oneself as Muslim and the everyday practice of Islam. Such a declaration was primarily a statement of one's place in an ideal social order which rested on a principle of hierarchical ordering with God unambiguously located at the apex, separate from his creation.

Thus *sharīʿat* was a system of symbols and values ambiguously tied to the state. Eaton (Metcalf 1984) pointed out in the first conference that mediation was the basis of organization in both religion and politics: Islam was the overarching system to which peasants had access through religious functionaries such as *pīrs* (saints), who were expected to adhere more strictly to Islamic rules of conduct articulated in the *sharīʿat*. The primary need of rulers prior to the end of the eighteenth century had been to establish the legitimacy of their regimes, which represented a narrow elite governing a mass of people, a point made by Lapidus at the second conference in his discussion of Asher's paper about the sixteenth-century ruler Sher Shāh Sūr.

In previous centuries, then, some kind of hierarchical ordering had been one way that alternative values and practices were incorporated into the Islamic tradition. With a shift of focus from the perspective of the first conference (which emphasized the referential content of the concept of *adab* as a system of values), *adab* can be seen pragmatically as a way of expressing and indexing a hierarchy of social relations within the community (see Silverstein 1967:53). *Adab* is one of a number of concepts which Muslims use in this way. We argued above that this Muslim understanding of hierarchy rests on a concept of center, with those closer to the center perceived as morally and / or socially superior. Thus, the peasant or tribesman who professes Islam but is ignorant of even the most basic tenets is not called an infidel (*kāfir*) by the leaders and more educated members of the Muslim community. Simply *be-adab*, he is a Muslim brother nonetheless.

There are other concepts which rest on a similar assumption about the nature of social hierarchy. For instance, the *ashraf* (of good, noble family) can be distinguished from *'ām lōg* (ordinary people) by virtue of their descent from the Prophet. A similar distinction is expressed in the relationship between *k͟hāliṣ* (pure) and *rōz-marra bōlchāl* (everyday speech), pure speech originally being Arabic, the language of the Qur'ān (see Lelyveld's essay, this volume). Moreover, persons and even whole social or ethnic groups can be hierarchically ordered in terms of the extent to which their actions are thought to be guided by reason (*'aql*) or dominated by *nafs* (the soul associated with demands of the flesh), guidance by *'aql* bringing one closer to God, and also higher on the social scale. Similarly, the distinction made in Sufism between exoteric (*z̤āhir*) and esoteric (*bāṭin*) knowledge is a way of distinguishing a spiritual elite (the saints and their disciples) from the masses who go to the shrines to ask for amulets and blessing. Each of these characteristics moves such persons away from the center of the hierarchy. Like the opposition between *adab* and *be-adab*, these are terms that are used in many different social contexts, and the distinctions can often be correlated so that, for instance, a tribal or peasant may be regarded as *be-adab*, dominated by *nafs*, and incapable of using pure speech.

Yet, as Kurin notes in his essay, those who from an Islamic perspective are dominated by *nafs* are also acting in terms of a different set of values, "women, wealth, and land" in the case of Punjabi villagers. The categorizing of persons according to hierarchical criteria is therefore also a way of incorporating diverse peoples and practices within the community of Islam, subsuming them in terms of a distinctively Islamic notion of hierarchy, which acts as a fundamental organizing principle. Ordinary people, thus, have been defined in terms of *adab*, that is, distance from the center, rather than being declared in violation of *sharī'at*, which would have placed them outside of the political order altogether.

Among the tribal Baluch there is a model for exemplary conduct expressed in a pan-Islamic vocabulary which shapes consciously articulated expectations that the Baluch have about the proper behavior of the *sardār* (tribal leader) and the *pīr*. S. Pastner suggests, however, that in practical terms the ideal qualities of the political leader, "readiness to protect honor, shrewdness, and strength," are analogous to the rural Punjabi values of "land, wealth, and women," examined by Kurin in his essay. The Baluch declare that they expect their *pīr*s to renounce the pleasures of this world and to act altruistically by warding off misfortune and acting as arbiters in disputes. Such a model of exemplary conduct coincides with the broader Muslim paradigm for proper behavior elaborated in the first conference: control of the *nafs* in the service of spiritual development. Nevertheless, the *sardār* and the *pīr* demonstrate and exercise their power in surprisingly similar ways. The stories about *pīr*s which the Baluch recount are replete with contests of power, demonstrating that *pīr*s are attributed spiritual power (*barakat*) only after validating it in the competitive arena, just like *sardār*s. Any discrepancy between indigenous values and an Islamic model of *adab* is ignored, because guiding principles have not been codified and juxtaposed. Within the wider Islamic state, these tribal peoples are unquestioningly accepted as Muslims, despite any divergences from an Islamic model of proper behavior.

This process illustrates a strategic application of the concept of *adab* in the ordering of social relations. The labeling of villagers or tribal peoples as "*be-adab*" removes everyday behavior from the political realm; personal practice is not a political statement, nor need it be of particular concern for the organization of the state as a Muslim community.

In another situation, everyday behavior, including ritual detail, may be interpreted as a political act, marking an individual as a member of a particular party or sect. A political leader may thus take advantage of the ambiguity inherent in the pragmatic rules for applying and interpreting concepts such as *sharīʿat* and *adab* in order to mobilize a following.

That *sharīʿat* was accepted as the (unattainable) ideal prompted tension in the relationship between Muslim rulers and the ideals of Muslim community embodied in the *sharīʿat*. The problem for all Muslim leaders has been to synthesize the principles of Islam with conflicting goals dictated in part by specific historical circumstances and in part by other standards for actions such as Persian courtly *adab*. Rulers established their image as good Muslim rulers by acknowledging their intention of administering the state in accordance with *sharīʿat*. Strategies for reconciling this intention with other political goals have included seeking rulings (*fatāwā*) that stress that *sharīʿat* does not pronounce a specific situation reprehensible and taking advantage of the discrepancies and ambiguity inherent in the *sharī'at* itself. Though expressed as a single, overarching concept and serving as a vehicle for expressing the unity of Islam, the *sharī'at* incorporates conflicting rules, expressed in terms of four schools of law (*maẕhab*).

Moreover, political leaders have often used the discrepancy between political and religious spheres to their advantage by highlighting ambiguous symbols. As noted, ambiguity about the "center" in terms of which hierarchy is being expressed—characteristic of Islamic discourse—can be seen in the use of language, in the distinction between *k̲h̲āliṣ* and *rōz-marra bōlchāl*, discussed by Lelyveld in his essay. In religious discourse, Arabic is the language of God, the vehicle of communication between God and the Prophet. Learning Arabic is an important part of a religious education. Yet Persian became the language of the political elite, and then Urdu. Closer to Arabic than the everyday speech of the indigenous population of India, Persian actually represented courtly ideals (*adab*) that were at many points at variance with the values of Islam.

The discrepancy between political and religious authority (between *dīn* [religion] and *dunyā* [the world]) may be masked by highlighting parallels in symbols of authority in the religious and political spheres, such as the use of turban and *dargāh* and title "*shāh*" by both rulers and saints (especially those saints with a wide following who also played the role of political mediators between the tribes and Mughal rulers). For example, the sixteenth-century ruler Sher Shāh Sūr's use of architecture helped to establish the legitimacy of his rule. Asher in her essay discusses the public monuments he created as reminders of the power of the center, and as a way of distinguishing his lineage from the rest of the population. He used the language of political elites (big tombs, forts) and drew on *adab* texts as models. He also used the symbols of Islam. By building a tomb for his grandfather in a location that would encourage its association with a popular saint and by establishing the use of the tomb as a religious school, he implicitly attempted to locate his grandfather in the hierarchy of saints, the religious elite, thus simultaneously using Islam to separate himself from the masses and to bring himself into contact with them as an ideal ruler. He played on the ambiguity of the significance of tombs to establish his legitimacy as a political and spiritual leader.

Though leadership styles have changed, ambiguity—especially in the expression of one's religious status and relationship to Islam, as well as to other sources of legitimacy—is still a device frequently used by modern political leaders. Now, however, such ambiguity is only one option used by political leaders; another option has been to focus on the *sharīʿat* through debates over how it should be expressed or redefined in contemporary terms.

The rhetorical strategies of Zulfikar Ali Bhutto, prime minister of Pakistan during the 1970s, represent an example of efforts to maintain as much ambiguity as possible in his claims to being a Muslim leader and in the relationship between specific policies and the principles of Islam. Bhutto's election slogan of "Islamic socialism" suggested social revolution in the name of Islam. At the conference, Khalid bin Sayeed argued that this idea of Islamic socialism had no systematic thought or legislative plans behind it. One likely reason for his failure to develop a systematic Islamic ideology was the perception that aligning socialism and land reform with Islam too explicitly would have had the effect of declaring the landlords and others with an interest in the perpetuation of a hierarchical social order to be in violation of the fundamental principles of Islam, which would have been politically unwise. Declaring a group in violation of Islam is a way of drawing social boundaries between groups, which Bhutto did not want to do. Bhutto, like many leaders before him, thus left his connection with Islam ambiguous.

The tribal leader in Swat, described by A. Ahmed in this essay, provides us with another example of a political leader of modern Pakistan. He drew on several different sources of legitimacy and used a variety of strategies to consolidate his power and mobilize the Wazīrs, a tribal group, behind him. He, like Bhutto with his vaguely defined Islamic socialism, used ambiguity as a tool to allow him to maneuver between secular political and religious, charismatic paradigms, though in this case the locus of ambiguity was in his self-definition rather than in his articulation of Islamic principles to achieve political ends.

Debate and Redefinition

The organization of the Muslim community changed dramatically after the displacement of Muslim rulers by the British. No longer could the public practices of the ruler be the measure of the implementation of *sharīʿat* in the community. There were no longer Muslim rulers in a position to employ men learned in Islamic law, patronize religious education, and supervise religious charities. Freitag in her essay, drawing on earlier work done by Metcalf, points out how, after the loss of Muslim political power, the *'ulamā* took on a new role in guiding Muslims in their everyday life and shifted focus to the personal observance of *sharī'at* by all members of the community in all spheres of activity. The limits of *sharī'at* were thus redefined, and a new criterion for adherence became the actual practice of the masses; emulation of the Prophet and His Companions was stressed as a way to live everyday life.

A basic reaction of South Asian Muslims to loss of political power to the infidel British was to question Muslim practice, to attribute this loss of power to weakness brought about by the straying of the Muslim community from the proper practice of Islam. The dominance of the British needed to be justified in terms of a Muslim world view. One powerful explanation, which has colored Muslim scholarly views of modern history and has been a stimulus to reformist activity throughout the Muslim world, was that the decline of the Muslim community could be attributed to the failure of Muslims to live up to the standards established and exemplified by the Prophet and His Companions. What was perceived as an increasing gap between everyday practice and *sharī'at* needed to be closed.

Thus many Indian Muslims have attributed the political, social, and economic disaster which struck the Muslim elite community in the colonial situation to degeneration of the Muslim community. Yet this position presupposed the existence in premodern India of a pure Islamic order which, in fact, never existed. For Bengali Muslims, on the contrary, as R. Ahmed points out in his essay, Islamization of the average Muslim in Bengal began only with the nineteenth-century revivalist movements.

The emergence of this presupposition of degeneration from a pure Islamic order can be identified as a moment when *sharī'at* was redefined. Ambiguity in the relationship between everyday practices and *sharī'at* was replaced by debate and efforts at systematization of values and practices. This form of debate over the proper interpretation of tradition, especially those aspects of tradition concerned with ritual detail, can be seen as a characteristically Islamic cultural response to stress.

Debate thus arose among Muslims over what the proper practice of Islam was to be. At the conference Roff characterized this debate over the proper interpretation of *sharī'at* as being about how leaders should derive their authority for establishing properly Islamic behavior in a changing world and about what the proper mechanisms are for change and renewal. He emphasized that a fundamental aspect of the debates intended to clarify these principles has been argument over how to argue. In the most extreme reformist doctrines, *ḥadīs̤* (the Tradition of Sayings of the Prophet and His Companions) has been eliminated altogether as a guide for argument and for action, and *sharī'at* has been equated only with the Qur'ān and *sunnat* (the practices of the Prophet). There was a proliferation of sects, often marked by the accusation that traditional beliefs and practices were *shirk* (worshiping others alongside God, thus violating the principle of the unity of God). This accusation was made by reformists who were against the practices associated with saints and shrines, which they considered to be folk practices that made it difficult to distinguish Muslims from their Hindu neighbors.

One can see this phenomenon of debate over *sharī'at* in material presented both by Fusfeld and by Roff. They describe heated debate which, from our perspective, was clearly stimulated by the impingement of Western influences and power (the focus of the Malay debate discussed by Roff was a European dog) but which, from the perspective of the participants, was concerned with determining proper procedures for interpreting *sharī'at*.

For instance, debates between the Sufi Shāh Aḥmad Sa'īd and anti-Sufi reformists, Fusfeld tells us, occurred at a time of intellectual ferment among the Delhi Muslim elite. Yet Shāh Aḥmad Sa'īd made only casual mention of the foreigners and no mention at all of Hindus in his writings. What mattered for him was the Muslim community, especially other Muslim Sufis and sects with whom he disagreed. Focus in *fatāwā* and debates was on asserting the correctness of details of ritual. Even groups claiming the same source of legitimacy, in this case the traditions of the Naqshbandī Sufi order, were vehemently opposed. To support his position Shāh Sa'īd used two rhetorical strategies which we see evident in several papers presented at the conference: (1) he instituted changes by asserting that he was simply embodying tradition, a powerful legitimating device; and (2) he defined the limits of belief and debate by asserting the infidelity of his opponents. (We can see in A. Ahmed's essay that this latter strategy is still powerful today.)

Couched in terms of duties prescribed by the *sharī'at*, the problem of boundaries of permissible behavior are addressed in Roff's case study. This 1937 debate argued whether or not the act of keeping a dog should be declared polluting because it was in violation of the *sharī'at*. But, Roff suggests, a more fundamental issue was the establishment of ground rules in terms of which *sharī'at* itself is to be defined. Ultimately, the debate was between, on the one hand, those who were pushing for change and reform by arguing that one could draw on any one of the four schools of law when interpreting the *sharī'at* in a specific situation, and, on the other hand, those who used bureaucratic and legal forms borrowed from the British to reinforce (paradoxically) a conservative approach to the *sharī'at* based on conformity to a single school of law.

A similar phenomenon of debate within the Muslim community can be seen among the nineteenth-century Bengali Muslims described in R. Ahmed's essay. One reaction to the British was an intensification of debate among various branches of reformists and between them and traditionalists. This debate was carried to the rural population, and, though it could not shatter the traditional structure of indigenous belief, it led to a new communication between the elite and the rural population coupled with the emergence, for the first time, of a sense of Muslim community and identity—the paradoxical outcome of bitter rivalry and debate.

Debate and controversy within the Muslim community were given further stimulus by the court system, bureaucratic procedures, and political institutions created by the British. They provided new forums, models, and rules for debate over the definition and boundaries of Muslim community and identity. Conflicts which emerged as consequences of British administrative policy are discussed by both Nanji and Gilmartin. British policy allowed no room for the ambiguity that had traditionally facilitated the coexistence of divergent values and behavioral orientations. This policy was based on the nineteenth-century "social sciences" world view that saw every social phenomenon as a bounded entity which could be categorized and labeled. What had previously been left ambiguous was challenged directly in the context of British rule, and there was a new articulation of conflict and identity.

A dispute within the Nizārī Ismā'īlī community developed because certain groups of Ismā'īlīs had formerly practiced *taqīya* (pious dissimulation), either continuing Hindu practices or identifying themselves as Sunni Muslims. Nanji shows us that under "Anglo-Muhammedan" law it became necessary in 1865 to establish the relationship of the Nizārī Ismā'īlī community to Muslim law; those practicing *taqīya* were forced to be explicit about their identity as Shī'ī Muslims once the Aga Khan, leader of the community, had opted for identification as a Shī'a group. This explicit definition of the community led to changes in ritual practice and doctrine. Once the community had explicitly redefined its identity as Shīʿa, efforts were made to eliminate Hindu practices, to ground everyday practices in Shīʿa personal law, and to downplay those parts of the religious texts which referred to Hindu figures. Nanji's essay is one of several in this volume which illustrate the emergence of a reformist orientation in Islam associated with a shift from syncretism to boundary definition and the elimination of ambiguity.

Similarly, "tribal" structure and customary law took on new meaning and then became unacceptable under the British. Gilmartin discusses British attempts to codify customary law and enforce it through the court system, tying the British legal system to an indigenous tribal foundation on which colonial rural administration was based. Customary law thus stood in opposition to the *sharīʿat*, as it had not done previously. The association of customary law with the state made it increasingly difficult, even for Muslims who supported the British, to defend customary law on moral grounds in overt opposition to the *sharīʿat*. Though material presented in other essays makes it clear that there have been internal forces within the Muslim community pushing for the articulation and clarification of the organizing principles of the community, the cases presented by Nanji and Gilmartin demonstrate that British policy was also a stimulus that made accommodation through ambiguity impossible in many cases.

A twentieth-century case of the emergence of new political and communicative processes, resulting from the direct challenge to Muslim identity posed by British rule, is presented by Freitag. There was a growing discrepancy between the emergence of a shared Muslim consciousness (traced in other essays focusing on nineteenth-century conflicts) and the development of a national public structure for the Muslim community. Freitag examines the Kanpur riots of 1913 and 1931 as moments in which a new expression of Muslim community identity erupted into violence. She argues that the riots fused the public and personal exercise of Islam. Personal acts such as wearing shoes in the washing place of a mosque became the symbolic focus for mass protest and violence, having been interpreted as threats to the integrity of the Muslim community as a whole. Everyday behavior had become a political act.

These debates, which used modern forums such as mass publications and new educational and organizational structures as well as traditional forums such as Friday prayers at mosques and the issuance of *fatāwā*, generated a potential common language for Muslims that drew on traditional symbols. The use of classical "high cultural" vocabulary was popularized by the *'ulamā* in proselytizing their visions of the personal practice of Islam to the masses, but in the twentieth century, a new concern for protecting the public aspects of Islam reemerged. Roff's essay is also concerned with the emergence of a new public expression of Islam in relation to the post-colonial state. Leaders used bureaucratic and legal forms derived from the British to reinforce their position as authorities on how *sharī'at* should be interpreted.

A New Style of Synthesis

Despite reformist efforts to translate *sharī'at* into personal practice, alternative values were not simply eliminated. But a new style of synthesis developed. Both Nanji and R. Ahmed discuss in their articles how syntheses of Islamic and indigenous beliefs and practices in previous centuries had involved incorporating Hindu symbols and drawing equivalences between Hindu and Muslim practice. The outcome of debate and reform was a sharp delineation of Hindu and Muslim. Ideologically, the reform effort involved rooting out all Hindu practices as one strategy for drawing a clear boundary around the Muslim community, in order to reinforce Muslim identity. Examination of specific cases presented at the conference, however, suggests that everyday practices of Muslims changed less than did their way of conceptualizing and labeling these practices. Now more self-conscious about their personal practices, which they accepted as defining their identity as Muslims, ordinary people were concerned about articulating their values and practices within the limits of discourse defined by *sharī'at*.

Illustrations of a relatively un-self-conscious synthesis of indigenous values and Islam, still possible today in a tribal setting, are provided by Stephen and Carroll Pastner's studies of Pakistani Baluch. Such a synthesis rests on the ambiguity possible when the principles of Islam are understood in a very general, abstract sense. This arrangement stands in sharp contrast to Gilmartin's discussion of the way in which indigenous Punjabi practices that had previously been unproblematic came into direct conflict with the *sharī'at* as these systems were juxtaposed, examined, and codified.

The modern rural Punjabis discussed by Kurin are aware of the discrepancy between their values and practices—a stress on ties to the land and pre-Muslim genealogy—and those of the urban Urdu-speaking elite, but their perceptions are nevertheless rooted in a shared Islamic vocabulary for talking about persons. They use an Arabic vocabulary of *rūḥ* (spirit), *nafs* (lower soul), and *'aql* (reason) shared by Muslims throughout the world. Indeed, the Punjabi villagers whom Kurin describes are self-conscious about their identity as Muslims in an Islamic state.

Rural Bengali Muslims have also adopted an Islamic vocabulary for talking about themselves, their beliefs, and their practices: R. Ahmed points out that Hindu surnames have been replaced by names perceived to be Arabic and that rituals involving divination and amulets are now accompanied by incantations in Arabic. Nevertheless, these changes depend on historical context, having emerged when stimulated by the growing awareness of Muslim identity created by nineteenth-century debates and when the general population experienced pressure by elites, both modernist and traditionalist, to regard themselves as Muslim instead of Bengali. Beneath the intermittent adoption of Islamic practices and even claims of foreign descent, there is a fundamental difference between the Urdu culture of the elite and the Bengali culture of the rural population. R. Ahmed suggests that among Bengali Muslims, identity became increasingly tentative, as demonstrated by a phenomenal rise in those claiming foreign descent.

The problem of redefinition of indigenous practice was important in an era when the boundary between Hindu and Muslim provided the focus of articulation and strife, and when *sharī'at* had been defined in terms of the personal practices of all members of the community rather than in terms of overarching political relationships. In a more recent setting the problem of redefinition has been addressed by Pugh. Her analysis of Muslims in the modern urban milieu of Banaras confirms R. Ahmed's suggestion that the process of Islamization often involves a replacement of Hindu practices with overtly similar Arabized ones.

In her discussion of the use of astrology in everyday life, *sharī'at* defines the limits of discourse, and Muslims use certain principles based on the *sharī'at* to define which practices are acceptable and which are not. What may appear to the observer as a mere relabeling of certain practices in Arabic terms is culturally distinctive and is perceived as the maintenance of the proper hierarchical relationship between God and Man. The limits on proper behavior are established by condemning certain folk practices as black magic, for in black magic men attempt to usurp powers that are reserved for God, or they draw on other powers instead of turning to God. If, however, similar ends can be achieved in

God's name, then the practices used to achieve these goals can be defined as within the bounds of *sharī'at*. The replacement practices, such as selecting auspicious days on the basis of the Islamic lunar month instead of on the basis of the influence of the planets, systematically maintain the proper boundaries of human knowledge and of man's relationship to God and to other powerful beings. Thus the replacement practices permit Banarsi Muslims to stay within the bounds of *sharī'at* while continuing local practices they consider significant.

The accusation of practicing black magic is not limited to Muslims concerned with differentiating themselves from Hindus but recurs in many contexts. It is a strategy for declaring that an enemy has violated the *sharī'at* and is therefore outside the boundary of the Muslim community. This strategy is frequently used by one ethnic or tribal group against another. In the case of tribal warfare in Swat, presented by A. Ahmed, the Mahsuds, who had been branded *kāfirs* by the *mullā* organizer of the rival Wazīrs, attempted to undermine the *mullā*'s legitimacy as a holy man by attacking his character. They accused him of homosexuality, debauchery, and the practice of black magic. Similarly, in S. Pastner's description of the tribal Baluch, we see Sunni Muslims attacking the rival Zikri *pīrs* in almost identical terms: labeling them black magicians and declaring them sexually unnatural (saying that their babies have pubic hair).

A. Ahmed's article clearly illustrates the strategy of delimiting a boundary by invoking *sharī'at* in a tribal setting. In this case, the Wazīr *mullā* used two rhetorical strategies to accomplish his political and economic goals at the expense of a rival tribe: (1) he damned the Mahsuds, the rival tribe, as *kāfirs*, declaring a *jihād* (religious war) against them; and (2) he gave sermons and issued *fatāwā* declaring his Wazīr struggle to be an Islamic one. He thus expressed tribal rivalry (and rebellion against the central government) in a religious idiom, simultaneously invoking the *sharī'at* as a boundary-setting device and exploiting the ambiguity of political and religious sources of authority. He used the term *kāfir* to justify the aggression of one tribal group against another. Once they were declared infidels (*kāfir*), outside the pale of the community (*ummat*), then *jihād* was ostensibly justified.

The Bengali Muslims discussed by Prindle further demonstrate how the tenets of Islam constrain the way in which everyday practices are talked about, in this case the articulation of hierarchy. Prindle worked among modern Bengali Muslims who, like most post-Partition Muslims, have been concerned with distinguishing themselves from Hindus and with bringing personal practice within acceptable limits defined by *sharī'at*. Such concerns have been manifested in an uneasiness about social hierarchy, which has been identified with the caste organization of the Hindus. These Muslims have stressed the emphasis in Islam on the equality or brotherhood of all men. Prindle provides us with a description of strategies used by Bengali Muslims to reconcile social inequality in everyday life with the emphasis in Islam on the equality ("brotherhood") of all men. One basic strategy is to distinguish between social and religious frames of reference. This distinction is a traditional one in Islam, the distinction between religion (*dīn*) and the world (*dunyā*), which allows ambiguity in the application of *sharī'at* and the organization of the Muslim community. Chittagonian Muslims refer to this distinction in terms of community ("*sāmājik*") and religious ("*dharmik*") modes of discourse. Though in religious terms all Muslims are regarded as equal, there is an elaborated social hierarchy that informants today associate with Hindu influences. ("Hindu influence" is thus another way of explaining the inconsistency between ideals and action.) But the social hierarchy is also regarded as necessary to the organization of the community. Prindle discusses how Chittagonians use the ambiguity inherent in the distinction of two modes of discourse to figure relations of rank among people. One strategy is to delimit the hierarchical distinctions to refer only to wealth, not to human qualities. Another strategy draws explicitly on the acceptable model of hierarchical family relations. This metaphor also provides rules of proper behavior for social unequals, within the limits of discourse prescribed by Islam.

From the religious perspective, all men are equally capable of being good or bad persons, without reference to social status. In practice, however, it appears that, especially in the context of asserting pride in their identity as Chittagonians with a high valuation of the successful, independent businessman, the social and religious bases for evaluation converge. Just as Sher Shāh Sūr, the sixteenth-century Muslim ruler discussed by Asher, exploited the ambiguity of markers of high status in religious and social spheres to enhance his position at the center, Chittagonians similarly blur the distinction between piety and wealth.

We may ask what "equal" means for these Bengali Muslims. Along with the redefinition of *sharī'at* which has occurred over the past century, the concepts of equality and hierarchy have also changed. An important aspect of many of the reform movements was the rooting out of practices that reinforced hierarchical distinctions previously central to the organizing principles of the Muslim community. The reformist and politician Maulānā Maudūdī, for instance, strove to eliminate distinctions such as that traditionally made between esoteric (*bāṭin*) and exoteric (*ẓāhir*) knowledge, a distinction central to Sufi thought. He argued that this distinction implied a spiritual elite in possession of knowledge to which ordinary people do not have access and asserted that such a doctrine is in violation of the egalitarian spirit of Islam (Ewing 1980).

This replacement of the dichotomy of elite / uninitiated with an enlarged role for ordinary people is reflected in several of the essays, but particularly in the discussion of the changing cultural role played by language. The changing styles and uses of language, and how leaders have asserted themselves linguistically from the late eighteenth through the twentieth centuries, are examined by Lelyveld through the evolution of poetry, oratory, and Urdu films. Poetry was the vehicle of elites associated with the ruler and court. Poets used Arabic, which was accessible only to the learned, as their model. This model was extended to Persian and ultimately to Urdu. Lelyveld argues that language indexes social relations: language removed from everyday speech signifies refinement, marks elite status, and reinforces claims to political authority.

For serving these functions, the referential content of the utterances is less important than the fact that the linguistic code being used is a restricted one, thus indexing the superior status of the speaker (Geertz 1960:248; Silverstein 1967). A basic organizing principle that has persisted throughout South Asian Muslim history has been the use of two languages to index social relationships, a point articulated at the conference by Lelyveld and Lapidus. In many situations, this use of two languages is associated with social hierarchy, one language marking the speaker as being closer to the moral and political center(s) of the society and the other, local language, being the vehicle for communicating with the masses, who are considered to have strong non-Muslim roots.

In the twentieth century new speech contexts or situations have overlaid such established uses. These include political speech making and the mass media. In general discussion triggered by Asher's essay on the social and political relationships that are expressed through an architectural idiom, Lelyveld pointed out that changes in the political process can also be seen in the changing uses of public architecture. Today, for instance, the Taj Mahal is maintained by the Archeological

Survey and is accessible to all. Modern monuments such as that built in honor of the Qā'id-i Aʿẓam, founder of Pakistan, reflect a continuity with the past but also maintain an aura of accessibility to the general public. By downplaying the notion of a religious elite associated with the saints in favor of an emphasis on the connections between leader and the general public, the new architecture thus highlights a very different aspect of Islamic tradition. Similarly, the goal of political language is no longer to express legitimacy through separation from the masses, but rather to express solidarity with the masses and to serve as a direct vehicle of communication between elites and masses.

Bhutto, as leader of the Pakistan People's Party, exemplified this rhetorical style. Bhutto's response to critics—who accused him of personal violations of the *sharīʿat* such as drinking in order to discredit him and his leadership—represented, in A. Ahmed's words, a dividing line in the history of Urdu when he acknowledged personal violation of the *sharīʿat* with such statements as "I drink, but I do not drink the blood of the people." In drawing on the political power of the people in this way, he appealed to what they valued most highly—not the spiritual "faith, unity, and discipline" associated with the Urdu-speaking elite, but the "women, wealth, and land" associated with the worldly but honest concerns of the villager. We could say, then, that he was expressing the values of the Pakistani peasant (described by Kurin in his essay), for whom the dominance of *nafs* is a sign of vitality and power. The villager can never match the city dweller in the development of *ʿaql* and *rūḥ*, in personal adherence to *sharīʿat*, but if *nafs* and land become the basis of politics, the peasant is well-qualified to participate.

Ultimately, Bhutto was ousted by leaders rhetorically espousing a return to a strict adherence to *sharīʿat* at both the state and personal levels. We can thus see a continuation of the struggle over how *sharīʿat* is to be interpreted and administered, the relationship of *dīn* and *dunyā*.

Examination of the articles in this collection suggests, then, that there may be two basic strategies for dealing with divergent values and practices. On the one hand, ambiguity is highlighted, leading to the incorporation of diversity. On the other hand, purification and systematization are stressed, leading to debate, articulation, and the exclusion of values that are felt to challenge the integrity of Islam. These essays illustrate the ways in which, when ambiguity is valued, actors use rhetorical strategies to take advantage of this ambiguity, reconciling what would otherwise be opposing values. The essays also illustrate, however, that when articulation and systematization are of concern, *sharī'at* is called into play. With the urge for consistency come characteristically Islamic strategies, forums, and limits for debate, all ultimately connected to the definition and interpretation of *sharī'at*.

References

Burke, Kenneth
1969 *A Rhetoric of Motives*. Berkeley: University of California Press.
Ewing, Katherine
1980 "The Pir or Sufi Saint in Pakistani Islam." Ph.D. dissertation, University of Chicago.
Geertz, Clifford
1960 *The Religion of Java*. New York: The Free Press.
1965 *The Social History of an Indonesian Town*. Cambridge: MIT Press.
1973 "Ritual and Social Change: A Javanese Example." In *The Interpretation of Cultures*. New York: Basic Books.
Metcalf, Barbara Daly, ed.
1984 *Moral Conduct and Authority: The Place of Adab in South Asian Islam*. Berkeley: University of California Press.
Schacht, Joseph
1974 "Shari'a." In *Shorter Encyclopaedia of Islam*. H. A. R. Gibb and J. H. Kramers, eds. Leiden: E. J. Brill.
Silverman, Martin
1977 "Making Sense: A Study of a Banaban Meeting." In *Symbolic Anthropology: A Reader in the Study of Meanings*. Janet Dolgin, David Kemnitzer, and David Schneider, eds. New York: Columbia University Press.
Silverstein, Michael
1967 "Shifters, Linguistic Categories, and Cultural Description." In *Meaning in Anthropology*. Keith Basso and Henry Selby, eds. Albuquerque: University of New Mexico Press.

PART ONE

Sharī'at, Custom, and Legal Change: Debates over the Institutionalization of Islamic Principles

1

Whence Cometh the Law? Dog Saliva in Kelantan, 1937

WILLIAM R. ROFF

Considerable public and academic interest is again being expressed in the processes of change—ideational and pragmatic—which seem to characterize Islamic societies.[1] This interest is not new, but it seems to present itself anew in each generation, partly perhaps because it is something that has concerned Muslims themselves for most of the fourteen centuries that have elapsed since the religion of Islam was proclaimed afresh and finally, by the Prophet Muḥammad, in 622. These societies—of those who regard themselves as "*muslim*," acceptors of the revealed law or "way" (*sharī'at*) of God—are not alone in being required to see life as ideally governed by an unchanging set of rules which must be understood and conformed to. This much is true of many other systems of belief which rest upon transcendent authority. It is sometimes held, however, that of all such believers in a transcendent moral law, Muslims have an especially hard time in bringing life as (and where, and under what other cultural constraints) it is led into conjunction with the enjoined ideal. This is principally (it may be and often is said) because the definitive law—the *sharī'at*—was revealed once and for all in what became an especially restrictive way: in a particular time and place (seventh-century Arabia), expressed in the

1. This chapter was originally published as "Whence Cometh the Law? Dog Saliva in Kelantan, 1937," in *Comparative Studies in Society and History*, vol. 25, no. 2 (April, 1982) and copyrighted by the publisher, Cambridge University Press. It is reprinted with the permission of the author and the publisher.

prophetic revelation (in the Arabic of the day) of God's injunctions to humankind (embodied later in the text of the Qur'ān), and as made manifest in the life (the practices and sayings) of His Prophet, recorded at the time or reliably recollected thereafter.

Established procedures for elucidating the meaning of the Qur'ānic utterance and of the traditions about Muḥammad, where they were not plain, and of applying them to situations and questions not (apparently) foreseen, could lead as much to disputation and difference as to certainty. And jurisprudential questions concerning the discovery of the law aside, there exists for the Muslim community, it has been argued, as for other communities of the kind, the problematic that inasmuch as the *sharī'at* is an ideal way, it can always be only approximated and striven after in this world, never realized or actualized. In consequence it may be said that the history of the Muslim peoples, severally and jointly, has been characterized throughout by an incessant and necessary dialectic between that which ought to be (and its discovery) and that which is.

It is this dialectic, then, and the need for it, that acts as one impulse for change, both ideational and actual, within Muslim societies. Assuming this, a principal task of the historian who wishes to grasp the inwardness of such change must be to attend to the dialectic (to listen to the discourse that marks it), in an effort to understand how it has operated (and perhaps now operates), according to what conventions and rules, under what constraints of place, time, and culture, through what kinds of men and institutions, at and between what levels of society.

This is what I have tried to do in the following essay, which, even though it concerns, as detailed studies must, one group of Muslims at one particular moment of time, seems nevertheless to call into play the intellectual and cultural resources of an altogether wider Muslim world, in an almost paradigmatic way.

Authority and Conflict

This is a case study of conflict over authority, tribunal, and decision in Malay Islam. The dramatis personae (except for the final court of appeal) were all Malay, though most had had significant periods of education outside Kelantan, the natal state of the majority. The two sides and their respective groups of supporters are shown in the following diagram, which also indicates their place of training and, when relevant, their ascriptive or achieved status (see figure 1.1).

Figure 1.1
Alignment of Principals and Their Supporters in the Dog Saliva Debate

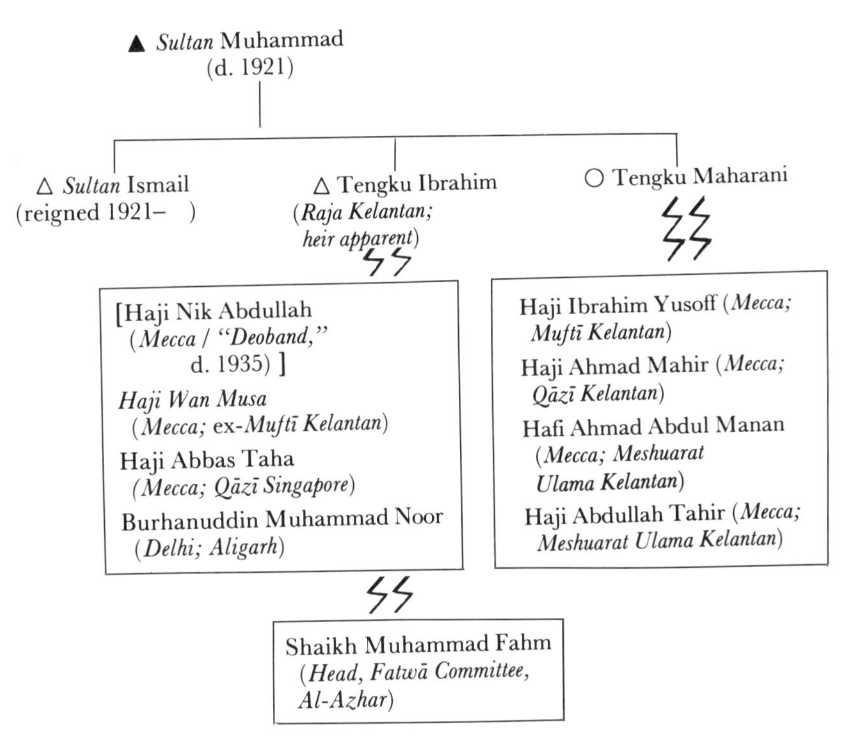

Note: Place of training and, where relevant, status are indicated in italics.

The conflict on which the case centered concerns a dog—a Dalmatian hound kept domestically by Tengku Ibrahim, the Raja Kelantan, heir apparent and younger brother of the Sultan of Kelantan, on the east coast of peninsular Malaya, in the mid-1930s. Ibrahim's sister, Tengku Maharani, lived separately in the state capital of Kota Bharu but was accustomed to visiting her brother's household. She objected to dogs in general, as do most Malays, and to this one in particular, as defiling and polluting according to the *sharī'at*, especially should one be contaminated by their saliva. Ibrahim sought a ruling in the matter from a young scholar (*'ālim*) newly returned from studying in Mecca, Nik Abdullah, son of a controversial ex-*muftī* (jurisconsult) of the state, Wan Musa b. Wan Abdul Samad. Abdullah ruled in favor of Ibrahim—that it was permissible to keep a dog—but the ruling was strenuously contested by other scholars (*'ulamā*) in the state.

The issue became a matter of public disputation, and eventually Ibrahim called a public council of debate (*majlis muzākara*) to discuss it. On the side of Ibrahim, the participants were the ex-*muftī*, Wan Musa (whose son had died unexpectedly), and two *'ulamā* from Singapore, Haji Abbas b. Muḥammad Taha, who was a religious magistrate (*qāẓī*) there, and a long-time "modernist," and Burhanuddin b. Muhammad Noor, a young Malay recently returned from study in Delhi and Aligarh. On the side of Tengku Maharani were ranged the *muftī* of Kelantan, Haji Ibrahim b. Haji Yusoff, chief *qāẓī* Haji Ahmad b. Ismail, Haji Ahmad b. Abdul Manan, and Haji Abdullah Tahir b. Ahmad (the last two being leading teachers, and members of the state *'ulamā* committee [Meshuarat Ulama]). The *majlis muzākara*—held in public at one of the state palaces in January 1937—was attended by more than two thousand people, the largest public gathering then known in Kelantan, according to reports. The result of the debate was inconclusive inasmuch as the two sides held firmly to their opinions, supported by argument and text (*naṣṣ*) from the Qur'ān, the traditions of the Prophet (*ḥadīṣ*), and commentators. Following the *majlis*, the matter was referred to Cairo, to the Shaikh al-Azhar. The latter gave a legal opinion (*fatwā*) in May of 1937, in favor of dog keeping. There the matter seems to have rested.

As this brief summary suggests, a wide range of explicit and implicit sources of authority was deployed in the dog saliva debate, from the ascriptive authority enjoyed by the Kelantan ruling class to the authority conferred by office within a state religio-judicial bureaucracy (as *muftī*, *qāẓī*, or member of Meshuarat Ulama), the authority flowing from learning acquired in Kelantan, Mecca, Deoband, Cairo, Aligarh (even Singapore), and the authority derivable by appeal to law schools (*maẕhab*) other than that of the Shāfi'ī school exclusively followed in Kelantan. Analysis of the dispute and its background may contribute to an understanding of the way in which Muslim societies confronted with behavioral—and by extension moral—principles in tension may seek to resolve them.

Kelantan in the 1930s was a large agrarian state centered on the deltaic rice plain of the river that gave the state its name, densely settled with peasant farmers and coastal fishermen, and almost entirely Kelantan Malay in population (for general background see Roff 1974). Since 1909 it had been under British "protection" and subjected accordingly to British administrative systems, though less intrusively and intensively than had the west coast states of the peninsula. Nonetheless, the incidence of British rule had been sufficient to prompt reaction, in the form of an episode of rural rebellion in 1915, and later in the same year, of the creation, at the instance of members of the Kelantan ruling aristocratic and religious elites combined, of a state Islamic Religious Council (Majlis Agama Islam) to reassert for Islam its central place in Kelantan life. While each of the Malay sultans in the peninsula was held, within his domain, to be God's vice-caliph and responsible for defending the faith and protecting the *sharī'at*, only in Kelantan was this responsibility given institutional form. The Council, an appointive body enjoying the delegated authority of the sultan, was accorded extensive jurisdiction over the administration and adjudication of all matters Islamic throughout the state (Roff 1974:101–52). The Council in turn established (in 1917) an *'ulamā* committee (Meshuarat Ulama) whose role it was, among other things, to issue through its head, the state *muftī*, authoritative *fatāwā* on matters referred to it. At the time of the dog saliva dispute, the president of the Council was dog owner Tengku Ibrahim, the Raja Kelantan. That he did not refer the dispute to the *'ulamā* committee is, as will appear, more an indication of the probable decision there than of concern over possible conflict of interest, or of other ascertainable reluctance to mobilize the available machinery. In fact, the Council and its associated *'ulamā* committee, though formally uninvolved in the dispute, played an important role in validating the right of some of the parties to it to express authoritative opinion.

Though the debate of 1937 was certainly about dog saliva, it was about a good deal else as well, not least the much larger question of how one should, and might, derive one's authority for properly Islamic behavior in a changing world. Kelantan, like many other Muslim states, was caught up in processes of change not of its own choosing or direction, as colonial rule and commercialization of agriculture, and their attendant social and economic transformations, impinged increasingly on ordinary life and customary relationships. In the 1930s, Kelantan was perhaps not much advanced in this process—compared, say, to the west coast Malay states, to Muslim India, or to Egypt—but it was embarked upon it, and concern at the actual and incipient loss of control over the changes taking place, and disagreements over the remedy, as well as over how to grasp the new opportunities afforded, were real and strongly felt. Nor was there lacking a universe of discourse in which such matters might be discussed.

The northeastern Malay states were often seen and spoken of by outside observers as isolated and remote, cut off—as a result of the absence of modern communication systems—from the rest of the world. So they were, when viewed in British or west coast Malayan terms of reference. But these states also existed in quite another context, that of the wider Muslim world of which they were an integral part. Kelantanese in considerable number regularly made the *ḥajj* to Mecca, and a significant proportion remained to study for long periods before returning home. Kelantanese scholars taught in Mecca, and also in Patani (southern Siam), Cambodia, and other parts of Southeast Asia, as well as in their own state, where Islamic boarding schools (*pondok*) flourished. *'Ulamā* from elsewhere in the Muslim world came frequently to Kelantan to teach, and in many cases to reside. Far from being isolated, the Kelantan delta and its people were part of a complex network of Islamic learning and exchange that knew no state boundaries.

As an indication of what this could mean, we may instance two visitors to Kelantan in the early twentieth century. The first, Shai<u>kh</u> 'Abū Ḥasan Azaharī, arrived from Mecca around 1914. Noted especially as a *shai<u>kh</u>* of the Aḥmadiyya-Idrīsiyya Sufi order (*ṭarīqa*), he attracted large numbers of pupils and gained the patronage of the *muftī*, Wan Musa, who established an endowment (*waqf*) for his maintenance (Abdul Aziz 1977: 71). Wan Musa himself, prior to his return in 1908 from many years in Mecca, had been a member of the Aḥmadiyya order, and may indeed (though the sources do not suggest this) have been instrumental in bringing Shai<u>kh</u> Azaharī to Kelantan. The order had some history of controversy in the state, since its introduction in the late 1890s by a west coast Malay *shai<u>kh</u>* who had been a pupil in Mecca of Ibrāhīm al-Rashīd, one of the successors to the founder of the order, Aḥmad b. Idrīs.[2] At that time the then sultan, complaining of public discord arising from the order's teachings, addressed a series of written questions concerning them to a noted Patani Malay *'ālim* in Mecca (described by Snouck Hurgronje as "a great savant"), Ahmad b. Muhammad Zain al-Fatānī.[3] In 1917, the Aḥmadiyya again became a center of controversy, and Shai<u>kh</u> Azaharī was expelled from the state at the behest of the recently formed Majlis Agama Islam, because of "misleading" teachings that, according to the *'ulamā* of the Majlis,

2. Abdul Aziz (1977:45); and cf. al-Attas (1963:33). On the order at this time, see Trimingham (1971:120–21), and Le Chatelier (1887:96–97).

3. Part of the text is reproduced in Abdul Aziz (1977:219); Snouck's comments on Ahmad appear in Hurgronje (1931:286–87).

conflicted with the *sharī'at*.[4] Wan Musa, who had resigned as *muftī* the previous year as a result of differences of his own with the sultan and certain of the *'ulamā*, was unable to prevent this and indeed had to leave the country for a time himself.

What was at issue here? In a measure this conflict too, like that over dog saliva later, related to change and pressure for change. Aḥmad b. Idrīs, the founder of the Aḥmadiyya-Idrīsiyya order, was brought up, it has been said, "in the formal Sufi tradition grafted on to the legal tradition" (Trimingham 1971:114–15). He based the order's practice strongly on the Qur'ān and the *sunnat* (the Traditions), rejecting, under Wahhābī influence, the accretions of *ijmā'* (consensus) and the *'ulamā*, though this laid him open to the contumely of the latter. This configuration was continued by his successor Ibrāhīm al-Rashīd, who similarly came into conflict with the *'ulamā* of Mecca. In Kelantan, at the turn of the century, and again in 1917, though the charges against Aḥmadiyya teachings are not made explicit, it seems likely that the issues were similar, and arrayed a "reformist" *ṭarīqa* against "scholastic" *'ulamā*. Wan Musa's involvement seems to support this interpretation, for he above all Kelantan *'ulamā* at this time sought to reconcile the Sufi path with the Law, and to pursue teachings that would lead to the unity in Islam of intellect (*akal*; Arabic: *'aql*), intuition (*hati*) and emotion (*nafsu*; Arabic: *nafs*) (Muhammad Salleh b. Wan Musa 1974:160).

Wan Musa became at least as closely associated with the second visitor of this period who should be noted, Abū 'Abdullāh Sa'īd Ḥasan b. Nūr Ḥasan b. 'Umar al-Tukkī al-Ghilāzī, better known in Kelantan as To' Khorasani. To' Khorasani, whose toponymic suggests western Iranian origins, is said to have come to Kelantan from either Afghanistan or "Pakistan" in 1915 or 1916, as a cloth merchant and teacher. He rapidly found a leading place among Kelantan scholars as a specialist in *ḥadīṣ* literature, and as an exponent of *talfīq* (selective and combinative employment of the schools of law) or perhaps more properly *takhayyur* (choice). To' Khorasani had studied at the Dār al-'Ulūm, Deoband, where he had been a pupil of Maḥmūd al-Ḥasan, the noted "Shaikh al-Hind," with whom he had studied the writings of Shāh Walīullāh of Delhi. It was from Walīullāh, clearly, that the decisive characteristics of his teachings sprang, emphasizing especially the controlling role of *ḥadīṣ* in interpretation and juridical employment of the compendious rulings of the four principal law schools. To' Khorasani taught from his own

4. Kelantan State Records, Pejabat Menteri (KPM) File 79/1917; and cf. KPM 28/1922 and Mahkamah (KM) File 14/1922, National Archives of Malaysia.

home and, from 1928 (it is said at the invitation of Sultan Ismail), in the central mosque in Kota Bharu. Among his many pupils were Wan Musa's son Nik Abdullah, and the young Ahmad b. Ismail, later to be chief *qāẓī* of Kelantan. When Abdullah went to Mecca in 1926 to continue his studies, he came in due course (after working with several other teachers) to be a pupil for four years of 'Ubāyd-Allāh al-Sindhī. 'Ubāyd-Allāh, a contemporary of To' Khorasani at Deoband and later an emissary of Maḥmūd al-Ḥasan, was a leading exponent of Deobandī theological ideas, as well as a noted political agitator on behalf of Muslim Indian anticolonialism (see, e.g., Aziz Ahmad 1967:195–201). While in Mecca, Nik Abdullah himself taught many students from Malaya, Indonesia, and Cambodia, and his reputation at home spread. It is said that the chief minister of Kelantan, Nik Mahmud, who had been one of the prime movers in 1915 for the establishment of the Majlis Agama Islam, tried unsuccessfully to persuade Wan Musa to have his son removed to Cairo from Mecca, away from the influence of 'Ubāyd-Allāh al-Sindhī—though whether for primarily doctrinal or political reasons is unclear.

Nik Abdullah's return to Kelantan toward the end of 1934 met with both enthusiasm and caution—enthusiasm among those students and teachers who, on the basis of reports from Mecca, saw him as likely to be a vital force for renewal in Kelantan Islam, and caution among those who thought his views and teachings wrong-headed and misleading. The Raja Kelantan was of the first group, saw Nik Abdullah often privately, invited him to teach al-Bukhārī to public gatherings at his palace—and sought from him a ruling about the permissibility in Islam of keeping a dog.

Filth—pollution—is not in general a paramount concern of Malay Muslims, any more than of most Muslims, except in relation to ritual prayer. Dogs, however, seem to have been regarded within many Muslim societies as especially dangerous in this respect, and the impurity (*najas*) associated with them and with their secretions as something that had to be expunged by ritual cleansing, seven times with earth and water.[5] One consequence was that dogs were (and on the whole still are) seldom kept by Malays, who indeed saw no utilitarian purpose for them. In the first known account of Kelantan by a European, in 1889,

5. For a spirited tenth-century defense of dogs from within the Islamic tradition, see Marzuban (1978). On the question of differences between *mazhab* over dogs, see Ebied and Young (1977:251–62); and cf. also Allen and Smith (1975:114–15 and associated citations).

the writer remarked that "Kota Bharu . . . [has] rather an appearance of a small Arab town, and the only difference is, that no dogs are seen straying about."[6] What possessed the Raja Kelantan in the 1930s to acquire and harbor domestically a dog is unknown. Possibly it seemed to him "modern," after the fashion of the ruling Europeans who increasingly set the tone in his state and elsewhere. Certainly, as a Malay, and as a Muslim (in consequence) of the Shāfi'ī school, he was aware of Shāfi'ī strictures upon dog pollution, and in seeking a ruling was actively seeking to vary the source of authority.

It is a matter of historical accident that the Shāfi'ī school had come to prevail in Southeast Asian Islam, but the consequence for most Malays was clear—that one was obliged, by the rule of *taqlīd* (unquestioning adoption), to follow Shāfi'ī doctrine, both in itself (as set out in Shāfi'ī's *Risāla* and the commentators) and as against that of the other three main schools. One's *mazhab* was, indeed, inherited, not chosen, and in a state such as Kelantan where all save a negligible number of Muslims were in this manner Shāfi'ī, it was expected that *qāẓīs* and other authorities would apply Shāfi'ī doctrine. In the Straits Settlements and elsewhere, with Muslims adhering to other schools present in some numbers, the principle of giving judgment according to the school of the litigant was accepted, but though recognized in Kelantan this practice had little relevance and no practical application.

In response to the Raja Kelantan's request for a ruling about his dog, Nik Abdullah—relying not on Imām Shāfi'ī but on Imām Mālik—said that it was indeed permissible to keep dogs, for household security and similar purposes, without being obliged to undergo special ritual cleansing in consequence of coming into contact with them. In justifying his ruling, and his departure from Shāfi'ī doctrine on the matter, he adduced the principle of *talfīq* (or combination of *mazhab*) in modification of that of *taqlīd*—holding at the same time that in so doing he remained an unquestioning follower (*muqallid*) with respect to the four orthodox *mazhab* as a whole. When Nik Abdullah's ruling, and his reasoning in support of it, became known, it was widely contested by other *'ulamā*, but Abdullah shortly thereafter died suddenly (in May 1935), and the matter lapsed. When it was reopened in 1936, Nik Abdullah's place was taken by his father, Wan Musa, who restated Abdullah's position in a private discussion of the issue with *muftī* Haji Ibrahim, chief *qāẓī*

6. "Abstract of journal kept by Mr. C. F. Bozzolo . . .", October 1888 (printed copy in Conf. Despatch, Governor, Straits Settlements, to Colonial Office, Jan. 31, 1889; Colonial Office File 273/157, Public Records Office, London), p. 10.

Haji Ahmad b. Ismail, and two others at the Raja Kelantan's palace. Not long after this discussion (which was inconclusive) Wan Musa had occasion to go to Singapore, to send one of his children to Mecca. There he met, or went to see, Haji Abbas b. Muhammad Taha, a long-time modernist polemicist, and a young man called Burhanuddin b. Muhammad Noor, who had recently returned from Aligarh Muslim University in India. It was as a result of this meeting, and the interest displayed by Abbas and Burhanuddin in the outcome of the dog saliva issue, that the two were invited to Kota Bharu to take part in a *majlis muzākara* to debate it publicly (Abdul Aziz 1977:128–29; and cf. also Abdul Aziz 1979–80:175).

Of the protagonists in the debate, those "in favor of dogs" were by background and career distinctly modernist, though in varying ways. Wan Musa, while in Mecca at the turn of the century, had become a member of a Sufi *ṭarīqa* noted for its "Wahhābī" and irenic beliefs, had later sponsored the *ṭarīqa* in Kelantan, and had then become closely associated with the unificationist or synthesist ideas of the Deoband school, through To' Khorasani and his own son. Abbas Taha, Singapore-born in 1885 and educated as a young man in Mecca, had a more directly Egyptian-derived intellectual lineage, having spent several years on his return to Singapore as assistant editor and editor of the influential Malay-language reformist journals *Al-Imām*[7] and *Neracha* (1911–15), for which the terms of discussion were largely set by Muḥammad 'Abduh and Rashīd Ridzā (Roff 1965:56ff). Burhanuddin, aged only twenty-five or twenty-six in 1937, is a less clearly defined quantity. Educated for a time at the modernist Madrasa al-Mashhur in Penang, he had gone in 1928 to India, where he took a homeopathic medical degree at the Ismā'īliyya Medical College in Delhi, and later attended Aligarh Muslim University. Returning to Malaya in 1935, he had taught at a Singapore religious school (*madrasa*) and published in 1936 a single issue of a journal called *Taman Bahagia* which, banned by the British (for reasons unknown), earned him a brief jail sentence.[8]

Abbas Taha represented the kind of mainstream reformism that had been present in Malaya since shortly after 1900, which focused on rather general attacks on unwarranted innovations (*bid'at*), on

7. This journal (1906–8) was modeled directly on the Cairo *Al-Manār*.
8. This information is culled from a number of sources, some conflicting. Burhanuddin's later career—as Dr. Burhanuddin al-Hilmi, radical political activist and president of the Pan-Malayan Islamic Party—has distracted attention from his early life. A note in Abbas Taha's *Risalah* on the dog question states that the publication was not able to include a separate *risāla* by Burhanuddin (Abbas b. Muhammad Taha 1937:115).

traditionalist *'ulamā* and *taqlīd*, and on a number of specific issues—the best known of which related to the practice of *talkin* (Arabic: *talqīn*; here, giving instruction to the dead before burial) and *niat* (Arabic: *nīyya*; here, controversy over the formulation of intention before prayer, whether aloud or inwardly). What Nik Abdullah and Wan Musa seem, in effect, to have done in Kelantan in 1936–37 was to shift the modernist emphasis from broad assertions that blind *taqlīd* and *bid'at* were to be avoided and expunged, to the more exact proposition that there existed mechanisms for change and renewal, not simply (though this first) in terms of returning to the Qur'ān and the *sunnat*, nor through potentially uncontrolled exercise of individual reason in *ijtihād*, but by the employment of reason within *taqlīd* on the basis of choice (*takhayyur*) between *mazhab*, or—as they more often put it—of *talfīq*, selective and combinatory use of *mazhab* rulings. It was this that provided the central argument in the debate that then ensued.

The Debate

It took place on the evening of 5 January 1937, in the audience hall of the Seri Chemerlang Palace, before more than two thousand spectators, and in the presence of the sultan and numerous dignitaries.[9] The occasion has a legendary character in Kelantan history, and until a few years ago it was not difficult to find people who recalled it or knew of its occurrence, whether or not they were present. It appears to have acted as one of those junctures in the life of a state or community from which other events and processes can be dated, a simultaneous confluence and separation of ways, a coming together of interests and tendencies as well as a demarcation of lines and boundaries.

On the opposite side from Wan Musa, Abbas, and Burhanuddin were four men whose background and training did not markedly differ from theirs. Ibrahim b. Haji Yusoff, the *muftī*, was a year younger than Wan Musa. Like Musa he had been taken to Mecca as a child and had grown up there; they had many of the same teachers, and it seems probable that Ibrahim too became a member of the Aḥmadiyya-Idrīsiyya *ṭarīqa*. He had returned to Kelantan probably during the First World War, became head teacher of the Malay school established by the Majlis Agama Islam in 1917, and in 1928 was appointed state *muftī*. Ahmad b. Haji Ismail, who was chief *qāẓī* in 1937, had actually been

9. *Al-Hikmah* (Kota Bharu), 14 Jan. 1937, vol. 3, no. 122, p. 10, has a brief descriptive account.

born in Mecca, in 1905, son of a well-known Kelantan *'ālim*, and came first to Kelantan at the age of eleven. After five years with local teachers (including To' Khorasani), he studied jurisprudence (*fiqh*) at Al-Azhar for three years, was in Mecca again during the late 1920s, and returned to Kelantan in 1931 as Inspector of Education for the Majlis Agama Islam. He became editor of the Majlis's journal *Pengasuh* in 1933, and was appointed chief *qāẓī* in 1935. Ahmad b. Abdul Manan, aged fifty-three in 1937, had spent many years in Mecca before returning to Kelantan to open a *pondok* school. He taught at the central mosque in Kota Bharu, and became a member of the Majlis's *'ulamā* committee, as did the fourth member of the group, Abdullah Tahir. Born in 1897, Abdullah had studied with local religious teachers before going to Mecca in 1926, where his fellow students included Nik Abdullah and Ahmad Haji Ismail. Returning to Kelantan, he founded in 1931 what became in time the largest *madrasa* in the state, at Bunut Payung, just outside Kota Bharu.

What distinguished the one side from the other, given their many similarities in background, education and experience, and career? Of them all, Burhanuddin was nearest to odd man out, for we know least about him and his intellectual development at this time, and it is hard to say what his contribution to the discussion of the issues was. Abbas Taha, though like Burhanuddin not a Kelantanese, nevertheless shared with Wan Musa and all the others lengthy residence in Mecca (the three eldest had overlapped between 1895 and 1905, the three youngest between 1926 and 1931), and had made his living thereafter as a purveyor of religious authority and opinion. What seems most to set apart the "anti-dog" group, then, is that they enjoyed employment in the service of the state, through the Majlis Agama Islam. (True, Abbas Taha was a *qāẓī* in Singapore, and Burhanuddin according to one source was assistant secretary to the Muslim Advisory Board there,[10] but these were community-derived offices given a mere imprimatur by the British, who strove to remain detached from religious affairs, and the Straits Settlements were notoriously hospitable to Islamic dissent.) On the face of it, then, there is a clear association between office in the service of the Islamic bureaucracy of the sultanate state of Kelantan and a conservative view of the issues. Ibrahim Yusoff, head teacher at the Majlis school from 1917, had been *muftī* since 1928; Ahmad Mahir b. Ismail (who had gained the sobriquet "*māhir*," "skilled," while at

10. *Al-Hikmah* (Kota Bharu), 7 Jan. 1937, vol. 3, no. 121, p. 20, describes him (in Malay) as "assistant secretary to the Council of Ulama" in Singapore.

Al-Azhar) was successively Inspector of Religious Education, editor of the Majlis's journal, and chief *qāẓī*; Ahmad Abdul Manan and Abdullah Tahir, though operating their own *pondok* schools, were both members of the state *'ulamā* committee (of which Ibrahim and Ahmad Mahir were, respectively, chairman and secretary). One might, in fact, be able to press this kind of argument a little further, for by the 1930s (and to some degree from the outset) the Majlis was an important instrument of patronage and power, less for the sultan (whose delegate it was) than for the ruling aristocratic group in Kota Bharu, centered residentially on that part of the town known as Atas Banggul, and headed by the autocratic chief minister, Nik Mahmud.[11] Not all of the connections are clear, but Ahmad Mahir was certainly a favorite of Nik Mahmud and the *muftī*, Ibrahim, though descended from an immigrant Sumatran family settled at Kamuning, outside the town, now lived in Atas Banggul. Further inquiry would be necessary to establish more certainly the nexus between conservative opinion, office, and the dominant socio-political group in the state, but there can be no question that position within the Majlis structure was an important part of the Kelantan authority system.

It is not to my purpose here, even were it possible or desirable, to offer a detailed exegetical account of the *majlis muzākara* itself. For those interested, it is possible to follow the arguments put forward by the "pro-dog" group in the *risāla* published by Abbas Taha shortly after the event (Abbas 1937). This sets out, in considerable detail, in Arabic and Malay, the texts employed by his side. It argues at the outset (Abbas 1937:2) that, Islam not being an oppressive or restrictive (*haraja*) religion but an easy and facilitative (*yasara*) one (as evidenced *inter alia* by sura "Al-Baqara" of the Qur'ān, verse 286: "God imposes no burden upon a soul except in so far as it can bear it," and verse 185: "God desires for you ease and does not desire for you hardship"), and Islam being, moreover, divinely blessed by disagreement (*ikhtilāf*) within the community[12] (as stated by the Prophet in a *ḥadīṣ* attested to by Ibn Hajar), it is incumbent upon all conforming members of the faith (*ahl al-sunnat wa'l-jamā'at*) to employ reason (*'aql*) in order to know and understand the *sharī'at* (Abbas 1937:6). And just as Al-Sha'rānī, in his *Mizan*, says that Imām Shāfi'ī himself held that where there exist both a strong opinion and a weaker opinion one is free to choose between them (Abbas 1937:7), so we may follow one *maẕhab* in certain circumstances

11. On Atas Banggul and its significance, see Kessler (1978:48–49).
12. Abbas (1937:10); cf., on this maxim, Schacht (1964:67).

and another *mazhab* in other circumstances (Abbas 1937:11). Though there are differences between *mazhab* regarding the kinds of impurity (*najas*) and the necessity of their riddance before prayer, notably in the present instance with respect to dogs (Abbas 1937:20ff), we may, if circumstances require, follow Imām Mālik in the matter in preference to Imām Shāfiʿī, by employing the principle of *talfīq* within *taqlīd* (Abbas 1937:70ff). And Imām Mālik states that dogs are (in the relevant sense) not unclean and may be kept in circumstances that require their use.

These arguments, thus summarily presented here but developed at great length in the *risāla*, give a clear enough view of the position taken by Wan Musa, Abbas, and Burhanuddin. In the absence of a similar contemporary source for the other side (beyond a restatement of Shāfiʿī) it is less easy to know with exactitude what their views were. It appears, however (Abdul Aziz 1977:133), that they relied principally on three contentions: that the "constitution" (*perlembagaan*) of Kelantan required adherence to the Shāfiʿī school, most particularly for those in the service of the state; that the concept of *talfīq* must be opposed because all Kelantanese were adherents of the Shāfiʿī school; and that *talfīq* must be opposed because, if persisted in, it was liable to encourage the growth of new *mazhab* from the resulting mixtures.

With respect to the first of these arguments, though Kelantan did not at this time possess a formal constitution, written or other, the processes of institutionalization and bureaucratization of Islam which had been taking place during the first two decades of the century (culminating in the establishment of the Majlis Agama Islam and its associated bureaucracy) had resulted in the reduction to writing of instruments setting out the jurisdiction and authority of *muftī*, *qāzī*s, *sharīʿat* courts, and the issuance of *fatāwā*, some of which instruments did indeed refer to *mazhab*. For instance, a legal *notis* (notice) of 1917 (enacted by the sultan in State Council, a procedure introduced under the British),[13] provided that no *fatwā* on any question of *fiqh* might be given by anyone without the prior approval of the Majlis Agama, and that all *fatāwā* issued to applicants of the Shāfiʿī school must follow Shāfiʿī doctrine, save when given by the *muftī*, who must in such exceptional cases provide text and authority for his variant decision. At about the same date, the earliest extant *surat kuasa*s or *tauliyat*s (letters of authority, commissions) issued to *muftī*s and chief *qāzī*s require the latter to decide cases "following the Muhammadan *sharīʿat* or administrative regulation (*siasat shariah*)," all

13. Notis 45/1917, copy encl. in File KM 218/1917.

decisions to be made in accordance with the most approved Shāfi'ī opinions ("*qaul yang mu'tamad pada mazhab shāfi'ī*"), and in the interests of the governance of the state ("*yang jadi maslihat bagi perentahan negeri*"). The *muftī* similarly is directed to use "the books of the Shāfi'ī school except where the public interest is not met by them, when he may seek and pronounce opinion from the books of other *mazhab*."[14]

While there was no reason to suppose the sentiments embodied in these instruments to be foreign to Kelantan society, the force given to them by their enactment into (or contingent upon) positive law was innovatory, supplying new sanctions against nonconformity as well as strengthening the ideology of conformity by casting it in additional, extra-Islamic, legal forms. In appealing to statutorily determined status—within the *sharī'at* courts system and the Majlis Agama Islam—and on statutorily defined, limited, and legitimated procedures, office-holders such as the *muftī* and the chief *qāzī* in particular, and members of the Meshuarat Ulama perhaps not much less so, could see themselves, if they wished, as obliged or permitted to take a "strict constructionist" view of matters at issue. That in addition the individuals here concerned did indeed feel strongly on the matter of *talfīq* is also probable.

At the conclusion of the *majlis muzākara*, Sultan Ismail "gave no decision, but directed the people of Kota Bharu in particular and Kelantan in general to follow the opinion of either Haji Wan Musa or Mufti Haji Ibrahim" (Abdul Aziz 1977:130), and to all intents and purposes the matter was closed. But not quite, for the Raja Kelantan proceeded to address a request for a *fatwā* to the Fatwā Committee of Al-Azhar. Drafted by Wan Musa, it sought to know (1) whether the keeping of dogs for household security was permissible or not; (2) whether, when licked or touched by a dog, one might follow Imām Mālik on limited ablution, in combination with Imām Shāfi'ī on other aspects of ritual prayer, by applications of *talfīq* to the two *mazhab*; and (3) whether Māliki opinion regarding the (relative) cleanliness of dogs controverted the religion of Islam or not. A reply was in due course received from the head of the Fatwā Committee, Shaikh Muḥammad Fahm, giving an affirmative response to the first two questions and a negative one to the third.[15] And there the matter did end. Except that

14. *Kuasa Kathi Besar*, 20 April 1920, and *Kuasa* [*Mufti*] 6 March 1921, copies encl. in KM 71/1921.

15. The text of the request and of the resulting *fatwā* are given, in Arabic and in Malay translation, in Abbas (1937:97–99); and a slightly different translation appeared in *Al-Hikmah*, 6 May 1937, vol. 4, no. 138, p. 10.

for some time afterward there circulated throughout Malaya, in the public prints and elsewhere, photographs of Haji Abbas Taha, Haji Wan Musa, and the Raja Kelantan, proudly sitting with, indeed clutching, the Raja Kelantan's handsome spotted dog.

Conclusion: Arguing about How to Argue

It was suggested at the outset of this essay that the events and processes described illustrate conflict over authority, tribunal, and decision in Malay Islam—a conflict precipitated by changing circumstances and modes of thought. One might more briefly say that the dog saliva dispute was an argument about how to argue. In content and occasion it has been seen to be not very different from numerous other confrontations, in Malaya and elsewhere, between "reformist" Islam and an entrenched order. If, in Kelantan in 1937, it had not been about dogs, it might have been (as indeed it was also) about eating peacocks, practicing *talkin* (instruction to the dead before burial; Arabic: *talqīn*), wearing trousers at prayer, *riba'* (usurious interest), the performance of *ẕikr* (recollection of God), or any one of a host of other issues that have from time to time agitated Muslim communities since the death of the Prophet Muḥammad. In the course of the nineteenth and twentieth centuries, for reasons complex in their etiology but cumulatively well-known, most Islamic peoples came under tremendous pressure from without (from alien systems of belief, values, and rule) and from within (through the exertions of some Muslims to confront and deal with these pressures). Kelantan, far from being an exception (of which Muslim community can this be said?), was deeply involved in both the Islamic and non-Islamic precipitants of this kind of conflict.

The centrality of the *sharī'at* to the conflict is important. Wan Musa is said to have sought to bring up his sons "to become meticulously and juristically well-versed scholars of the *sharī'aṭ*, capable of responding to the challenges of modern times" (Muhammad Salleh 1974:161). The statement has its triteness, but the challenges, in the colonial situation, were real, and no one—whether pro-dog or anti-dog—was prepared to relinquish the importance attached to "writ." Differences arose only in the realm of whence writ should be derived, how the *sharī'at* should be known and employed, how the rules of argument about such questions should themselves be determined. The sources of learning, and therefore of writ, were as we have seen numerous, but the variables relatively few; the significant one appears to have been the intrusion into an otherwise standard configuration of argument (for Malaya, though not for Malaya alone) of the influence of the Deoband school (possibly reinforced by Aḥmadiyya-Idrīsiyya Sufism), with its emphasis on *talfīq*, and hence on principles of selective combination of writ which seemed to threaten the very basis of existing disputation.[16]

Talfīq most expressly threatened the new validator of authority and source of writ in Kelantan, the Majlis Agama Islam. Embodying a restatement of two essentially Islamic constituents—temporal authority (*sulṭān*) over a Muslim community, in conjunction with proper consultation (*shūrā*) with the learned—the Majlis nonetheless partook also of bureaucratic and legal forms borrowed from the British. Established in the name, and ostensibly as the delegate, of the sultan's vice-caliphal responsibility, it reflected principally the patronage interests of the state's ruling aristocracy and those of the *'ulamā* allied with them. In contesting the resort by the "dog group" to a selective or combinatory use of *maẕhab* in order to adapt to (or facilitate) change, the establishment *'ulamā* chose to appeal not simply to their own, quite traditional, view of the *sharī'at* but to a supposed obligation, validated extra-Islamically by another form of writ (statute or positive law and its instruments), to derive the *sharī'at* in a particular way (solely through the Shāfi'ī *maẕhab*).

The Kelantan case was, in effect, adjourned *sine die*, and the argument, in one form or another, will certainly be resumed. Indeed, arguments about how to argue, arguments about how one may properly construct meaning and order from the materials available and subject to the given constraints of culture, place, and time,[17] seem to lie close to the heart of many and perhaps most processes of change (ideational and actual) within societies that regard themselves as and desire to be *muslim*. If so, it makes sense to listen carefully to the discourse and its dialectic, to the clash of argument—in short, to the *dīn*.

References

Abbas b. Muhammad Taha, ed.
1937 *Risalah Penting Pada Mas'allah Jilat Anjing Di-atas Empat-empat Madzhab*. Singapore: Ahmadiah Press.

16. A similar point emerges strongly from Rafiuddin Ahmed's discussion of rural *baḥaṣ* (religious disputations) in late nineteenth-century Bengal, in Krishna (1979:92–94). On *talfīq* and related procedures in the context of modernist disputation in Egypt and elsewhere in the Middle East, see, e.g., the references to the writings of Muhammad 'Abduh and Rashīd Ridzā in Hourani (1962:152–53, 236–37); and to those of al-Tahtāwī and al-Kawakebī in al-Husry (1966:26, 62).
17. See, in this connection, Yengoyan (1981:326–27).

Abdul Aẓiz b. Nik Hasan
1977 *Sejarah Pergerakan Ulama Kelantan*. Kota Bharu: Pustaka Aman Press.
1979–80 "Perbahasan Tentang Jilatan Anjing: Suatu Perhatian." *Jebat* (Bangi) 9: 173–80.

Ahmad, Aziz
1967 *Islamic Modernism in India and Pakistan, 1857–1964*. London: Oxford University Press.

Allen, M. J. S., and G. R. Smith
1975 "Some Notes on Hunting Techniques and Practices in the Arabian Peninsula." *Arabian Studies* 2: 108–47.

Attas, Naguib al-
1963 *Some Aspects of Sufism as Understood and Practiced among the Malays*. Singapore: Malaysian Sociological Research Institute.

Ebied, R. Y., and M. J. L. Young
1977 "An Unpublished Legal Work on a Difference between the Shāfiʿites and Mālikites." *Orientalia Loviensa Periodica* 8:251–62.

Hourani, Albert
1962 *Arabic Thought in the Liberal Age*. London: Oxford University Press.

Hurgronje, C. Snouck
1931 *Mekka in the Latter Part of the Nineteenth Century*. Leiden: E. J. Brill.

Husry, Khaldun S. al-
1966 *Three Reformers: A Study in Modern Arab Political Thought*. Beirut: Khayats.

Kessler, Clive S.
1978 *Islam and Politics in a Malay State: Kelantan 1838–1969*. Ithaca, N. Y.: Cornell University Press.

Krishna, Gopal, ed.
1979 *Contributions to South Asian Studies*. Vol. 1. Delhi: Oxford University Press.

Le Chatelier, A.
1887 *Les Confréries Musulmanes du Hedjaz*. Paris: E. Leroux.

Marzuban, Ibn
1978 *The Book of the Superiority of Dogs over Many of Those Who Wear Clothes*. G. R. Smith and M. A. S. Abdel Haleem, trans. and eds. Warminster: Aris & Phillips.

Muhammad Salleh b. Wan Musa
1974 "Theological Debates: Wan Musa b. Haji Abdul Samad and His Family." In *Kelantan: Religion, Society and Politics in a Malay State*. William R. Roff, ed. Kuala Lumpur: Oxford University Press, pp. 153–69.

Roff, William R.
1965 *The Origins of Malay Nationalism*. New Haven: Yale University Press.

Roff, William R., ed.
1974 *Kelantan: Religion, Society and Politics in a Malay State*. Kuala Lumpur: Oxford University Press.

Schacht, Joseph
1964 *An Introduction to Islamic Law*. Oxford: Clarendon Press.

Trimingham, J. Spencer
1971 *The Sufi Orders in Islam*. Oxford: Clarendon Press.

Yengoyan, Aram L.
1981 "Cultural Forms and a Theory of Constraints." In *The Imagination of Reality: Essays in Southeast Asian Coherence Systems*. A. L. Becker and Aram L. Yengoyan, eds. Norwood, N. J.: Ablex Publishing Co., pp. 325–30.

2

Customary Law and *Sharī'at* in British Punjab

DAVID GILMARTIN

> The most fundamental basis for the division of the population in this part of India is tribal rather than religious, and should rest, not upon community of belief or ceremonial practice, but upon ancestral community of race, in which, whether it be genuine or only supposititious, the claimants of a common origin equally believe.
>
> Sir Robert Egerton,
> Lieutenant-Governor of the Punjab, 1878

> Let the idols of race and caste be destroyed!
> Let the old ways that fetter men fast be destroyed!
> For this only is victory, this the Faith's power,
> That among the world's peoples true union should flower!
>
> "To the Punjab Peasant,"
> by Muhammed Iqbal, 1936

The conflict between the commitment to "race" and "tribe" and the commitment to Islamic solidarity was put in stark terms in the Punjab in the decade preceding the creation of Pakistan in 1947. Perhaps none put it so succinctly as the prominent English-educated Muslim League politico, Mumtaz Daultana. "Thirteen hundred years ago our Prophet taught us that all Muslims are one," he said, "that they have one culture, one organization, one interest, that Islam which is based on religious culture is the exact opposite and the most determined enemy of tribal factionalism" (Daultana 1944:21).

But what was the root of this opposition? The notion that Islam was in its very origins based on a challenge to "tribal" solidarity is one that has sometimes found expression in Western writing on Islam. In the view of one recent sociologist, for example, early Islam represented from the start "a partial triumph" of urban over tribal norms. "The universalism of the new Islamic community (*ummat*) based on faith rather than blood cut right across the particularism of the tribal system" (Turner 1974:35–36). Implicit in such a view has been the assumption that the morality of Islam, derived from divine revelation, challenged by its very definition an earlier morality based on the obligations of blood relationship—of "tribal" kinship.

To see the roots of the conflict between "tribal" and Islamic identity solely in this light, however, would do little to help us understand the particular pressures which led to the widespread articulation of this conflict in twentieth-century Punjab. Though a latent tension between the moral obligations of the faith and the moral obligations of blood may indeed be inherent in Islam, as in any religion based on divine revelation,[1] there is little to suggest that before the twentieth century this tension had been a critical element in the history of Punjabi Islam. On the contrary, Islam had provided in Punjab, as elsewhere, a "repertoire" of concepts and styles of authority which had served to encompass potentially competing values—including the values of tribal kinship—within a common Islamic idiom (Metcalf 1984). In this sense, Islam had traditionally represented less a challenge to tribal identity than what might be called an idiom of integration. In the countryside in particular, the dominant forms of Islamic authority and organization, particularly those associated with Islamic shrines, had served to articulate the way in which tribal groups fit into the Islamic cosmos.

To understand the emergence of a publicly expressed conflict between "tribal" and "Islamic" authority, therefore, we must look not just to inherent tensions in Islam, but to the peculiar cultural and political context in which these conflicts were played out. This was a context shaped fundamentally by the structure of British colonial rule. As J. C. Heesterman has suggested, the most telling crisis experienced by colonial Indian society was one of cultural integration, a crisis brought about by the inevitable cultural isolation of the colonial state from the rest of society. With the state in a domain "taken out and set apart from society," society itself had lost under the British "much of its diffuse but effective coherence." It had become, in spite of its rationalized administrative structure, "more parochial and fragmented" (Heesterman 1978:54). It was this, more than any inherent conflict in Islam, which was responsible for the increasing tensions under the British in Punjabi

1. The tension between kinship and sense of community in European Christianity, for example, is discussed in Bossy (1973). I would like to thank Keith Luria for this reference.

Islam. But more specifically, the character of the conflict between "tribal" and "Islamic" identity was a product of the particular form which this crisis of integration took in the Punjab, a crisis shaped by the distinctive character of British policy in the province.

The British and Customary Law

In this essay I would like to look at the conflict between *sharīʿat* and customary law in the twentieth century as an example of the wider, perceived conflict between "Islamic" and "tribal" identity. In a sense, the contrasting systems of *sharīʿat* and customary law embodied two systems of morality: that derived from revelation, on the one hand, and that derived from the obligations of "tribal" kinship, on the other. As the *Observer* of Lahore suggested in 1915, these two moral systems were in sharp opposition: "Most of the provisions of custom run counter to and are diametrically opposed to the expressed and binding injunctions of Muslim law," the newspaper declared.[2] In practice, however, opposition between these two sources of law was by no means clear cut. Nevertheless, the conflict between *sharīʿat* and customary law was shaped and sharpened in the nineteenth and twentieth centuries by the development of the law within the colonial order.

To understand the evolution of the law under the British, we should begin by looking at the relationship between the structure of Punjabi kinship and the British colonial state—a relationship which reflected the peculiar ideological requirements of the British as alien, colonial rulers. From a relatively early date, the British attempted, as a matter of policy, to tie their rural administration to the structure of rural kinship as they perceived it. For many British administrators, this was a policy of administrative necessity, a policy little different from that followed by rulers before them. But for others, it represented an effort to find for themselves indigenous ideological sources of legitimacy. As one official put it, "it is through the tribe and clan that Government can gain its firmest hold on the inclinations and motives of the people" (Tupper 1881, vol. 1:17). This was particularly important since the British, by the very nature of their position as culturally alien rulers, could make little claim to legitimate authority on the basis of religion. For some at least, identification of the Government with kin-based loyalties was thus a conscious alternative to an appeal to political solidarity based on

2. *Observer* (Lahore), 25 Sept. 1915. Excerpted in *Report on Newspapers and Periodicals in the Punjab for the Year 1915*, no. 40.

religion. "If you weaken the sense of tribal fellowship," the same official thus noted, "the only thing that could be put in its room would be religion, not a polytheistic indifferentism or a contemplative philosophy, but a religion like that of the Sikhs or Muhammadans, that by inspiring enthusiasm would generate a sense of brotherhood; and here," he added pointedly, "the British Government could take no part" (Tupper 1881, vol. 1:19).

British administration in rural Punjab was closely tied to local units of administration (most notably *zail*s, consisting of roughly ten to forty villages) which were intended to encapsulate extended rural kinship structures within the British administration—structures which the British liked to refer to as "tribes." In fact, the term "tribe" was an extremely vague one as the British used it, referring generally, as Lieutenant-Governor Egerton had suggested, to any group claiming a patrilineally reckoned "ancestral community of race."[3] As even most British administrators realized, the structure of "tribe" in this context provided little solid foundation for the organization of rural administration. Most "tribes" were dispersed in innumerable villages and possessed little indigenous political organization. In choosing *zail* leaders, or *zaildār*s, for example, the British found few existing "tribal" leaders in the *zail*s. As the system developed, *zaildār*s tended to emerge under the British not only as "the leading men of a particular tribe or section of the country" but also, and more important politically for the British, as "the representative[s] of Government" in the *zail*s.[4] The structure of "tribal" leadership recognized by the British was thus to a large extent artificial, adapted to serve the administrative needs of the British as much as to reflect an indigenous "tribal" structure. But the recognition of leadership in terms of "tribal" loyalties and solidarities was nevertheless of critical significance in an ideological sense, for it provided the British with an indigenous idiom, the idiom of *barādarī*, *ẕāt*, and *qaum*, in which rural administrative authority could be articulated.[5]

3. Letter from Sec. to Govt, Punjab to Sec. to Govt of India, Dept. of Revenue, Agriculture and Commerce, 24 August 1878. Printed in Tupper (1881, vol. 1:225–26).
4. Letter, E. A. Prinsep, Settlement Commissioner, Punjab to Secretary to Financial Commissioner, 27 June 1871 and Proceedings of the Lieutenant-Governor, 29 February 1872. Punjab Board of Revenue, File 61/142.
5. The relationship between British and indigenous terminology was often very vague. The settlement officer of Jhelum suggested that the population of his district was "clearly sub-divided into tribes (*qaum* or *ẕāt*), having a common name and generally supposed to be descended from a traditional common ancestor by agnatic descent" (Talbot 1901:2). The term *barādarī* appears less often in British records, but was frequently used, at least in the twentieth century, to describe the political solidarity based on a claim to common descent.

It was in this context that the development of the system of customary law was significant. As the British elaborated their administration, they developed a system of personal law in Punjab which was tied, not to the law of Hinduism or Islam as in many other provinces, but to a system of "customary law" or, as some British officials put it, "tribal custom." Like "tribes" themselves, these customs varied widely throughout the Punjab. But British officials sought to systematize custom by collecting and compiling district records of "tribal" customs. Such records were originally included in the village records of rights, or *wājibu'l-'arz*. But after 1873 they were compiled into separate volumes, or *riwāj-i 'ām*, for each district—volumes which were prepared at the time of settlement operations on the basis of oral questionnaires administered to local gatherings of influential "tribal" or village leaders (Gledhill 1962:135–37). The "tribal" character of the customs recorded was, as even some British officers realized, often open to question, since the answers given by the "tribes" to these questionnaires were frequently influenced by "the convenience of their influential members" (Noon 1925:1). This was particularly true since many of the questions applied to hypothetical situations in which little in the way of concrete example could be cited. But though the concept of "tribal" custom, like that of "tribe" itself, proved to be a vague one, it nevertheless served a critical ideological purpose for the British in the structuring of their rule. This was clearly understood by at least one British official, C. L. Tupper, who prepared the first provincial questionnaire for ascertaining custom and attempted in his 1881 provincial compendium of customary law to outline general principles underlying nearly all "tribal" custom in Punjab—principles which, as Tupper saw it, allowed the customary law to be developed by the British as a comprehensive, state-supported legal system. Such principles served the critical purpose of tying the British legal system to an indigenous, "tribal" foundation, even as that system was structured and controlled by the British Government. "It necessarily happened," Tupper wrote, "that the view I had been led to form of the character of customary law in great part suggested to me the feasibility of using it for public or political ends" (Tupper 1881, vol. 1:22).

The political importance of customary law in this context derived largely from its definition, in legal terms, of the system of kinship to which the British tied their administration. In this the central element was the law of landed inheritance. The key to the analysis of custom lay in the link between the pattern of inheritance in rural Punjab and the pattern of marriage. In spite of considerable diversity in detail, customary inheritance patterns recorded by the British tended to show widespread uniformities. In Tupper's analysis, this was a result of the predominance of a pattern of marriage which fostered geographically widespread kinship linkages. This was the system of clan and village exogamy so common throughout northern India. Daughters in this system were married, as Tupper put it, "outside the closely drawn limits of the clan, but within the looser, but still remembered circle of the tribe or race of origin" (Tupper 1881, vol. 2:70). The pattern of marriage was thus responsible for the prevalence in rural Punjab of geographically wide-spread, or, as many British put it, "tribal" identities based on extensive, presumed ties of kinship.

The pattern of marriage thus helped to define what Tupper saw as the "tribal" pattern of kinship to which the British had tied their rural administration, and customary law had helped in this context to give the structure of kinship a legal form. Customary inheritance practices, as Tupper analyzed them, had developed in Punjab's predominantly agrarian society with a view in particular to the protection of family property within the context of this exogamous marriage network. Since daughters normally passed by marriage out of their clan or village of origin, inheritance customs were, despite variations in detail, almost universal in denying a regular share in landed inheritance to women. This denial was of positive importance in the preservation of Punjab's kinship system; it was, for Tupper, a rule which took on normative significance. Though such a normative view of custom was not held by all, it nevertheless played a critical role in the subsequent evolution of customary law. As customary law developed under the British, it came eventually to rest on the fundamental assumption, recognized by most British jurists and administrators, that "as a rule, daughters and their sons, as well as sisters and their sons, are excluded by near male collaterals."[6] In political terms, the enunciation of such an underlying rule of inheritance, in spite of its roots in kinship structure, helped to define the indigenous foundations of customary law as a rationalized system of law supported by the colonial state.

The evolution of customary law along these lines, however, was not without its ambiguities. Though Tupper's "principles" of customary law were formulated after wide observation of Punjabi society and the extensive recording of customs, they could by no means subsume all the varieties of Punjabi kinship. Tupper's view of Punjabi marriage patterns, for example, though generally characteristic of the dominant Jāt and

6. J. Boulnois and W. H. Rattigan, *Notes on the Customary Laws of the Punjab* (1867), quoted in Tupper (1881, vol. 2:80).

Rājpūt clans of Punjab was, as his own evidence showed, by no means universal. Many Muslims of western Punjab in particular did not marry outside the village as Tupper suggested, but tended to prefer marriages "of close affinity within the clan" (Tupper 1881, vol. 2:200). In fact, as one western Punjab Settlement Officer suggested in 1901, "Muhammadan Law," though generally ignored in matters of inheritance, had "had such a strong effect as regards the question of intermarriage of relations that it has entirely abrogated the rule forbidding intermarriage of agnates, and such intermarriages are everywhere very common; indeed it is thought preferable that a man should marry his cousin" (Talbot 1901:3). In such circumstances, the rigid exclusion of daughters from inheritance was naturally not so ubiquitous as legal theorists like Tupper felt on principle that it should have been.

Such ambiguities added considerable complexity to the system of customary law, but they did not, in the end, alter the basic principles of the law that Tupper had identified, nor did they lessen the political importance of these principles for the British. Though the practical diversity of custom helped to prevent the law's codification,[7] the principles of customary law identified by Tupper served nevertheless to provide a foundation for the development of the law as it evolved through the more flexible mechanism of case law precedent in the courts. Interpretation of inheritance law in the courts came increasingly to be guided in the late nineteenth century by what was known as the "agnatic theory" of inheritance, which was elaborated by several high court justices, notably Sir Meredyth Plowden and Sir Charles Roe. This theory was based on the legal assumption that the exclusion of daughters in favor of male collaterals, no matter how distant, should always be taken as a basic judicial presumption in the absence of positive proof of custom to the contrary. Though exceptions to the rule of female exclusion were recognized, the "agnatic theory" thus came increasingly to guide the evolution of custom through the development of case law.[8] In

7. The history of the complicated debate on the issue of the codification of the customary law is traced by Watson, and by Worsley, in *Report on the Punjab Codification of Customary Law Conference* (1915:51–59).

8. Naturally, the decisions of the courts tended over the long term to affect the views of the people themselves on what their "customs" actually were. For officers in the field who were collecting customary law, this could on occasion engender considerable confusion. As one Settlement Officer commented in 1910 on one point of custom, "Answers to enquiries on this point were vague and being generally based on the experience of the various tribes in the law courts cannot be considered reliable evidence of customary law" (Kitchin 1911:14).

practical fact, of course, the relative importance of this theory is difficult to judge without an extensive study of specific cases. But the degree to which the "agṇatic theory" had by the twentieth century come to influence deeply the workings of Punjabi inheritance law is indicated by the comments in 1915 of the well-known Punjabi lawyer, Sir Muhammad Shafi. As Shafi saw it, daughters had, under the operation of the "agnatic theory," sometimes been excluded from inheritance by male collaterals whose relationship was so distant that it was beyond the range of Punjabi kinship terminology. "There is no Punjabi word," he pointed out, "for an ancestor beyond a great-great-grandfather" (*Report on the Punjab Codification of Customary Law Conference* 1915:19). In such cases, the application of the "agnatic theory" indicated clearly the degree to which the operation of customary law had transcended altogether the workings of local custom and had come to serve as an ideological instrument for the state.

The development of a system of customary law had thus proved critically important. Though variations in kinship were recognized, an idiom of kin-based solidarity was used by the British as a legitimizing foundation for their own legal policy. While not denying the particularistic power of the idiom of "tribal" solidarity, the British sought to transcend that particularism not by an appeal to transcendent religious principles, but rather by identifying a universal structural logic underlying Punjab's system of "tribal" kinship. In this sense, the idiom of kin-based solidarity for the British had become itself an idiom of integration. The structure of kinship had provided not only a foundation for the structure of the administration but also, through the elaboration of the law, an indigenous idiom manipulated by the British for the support of the state.

Customary Law versus *Sharī'at*

It is in light of this close connection between customary law and the colonial state that the reaction against both custom and "tribal" loyalties in twentieth-century Punjab can perhaps best be understood. The development of a self-conscious Muslim identity in twentieth-century Punjab was, at least in part, the result of cultural opposition to colonial domination, and such an identity was for many Muslims closely tied to the public avowal of the *sharī'at*. As Geertz has written in *Islam Observed*, the European colonizers, whatever else they might be, could never be Muslims (Geertz 1968:62–65)—a fact which the British themselves had recognized clearly in their policy in the Punjab. For those, like the *'ulamā*, who were primarily concerned with Islamic norms, the maintenance of Muslim identity in the colonial setting thus required an increasing emphasis on the presentation of these norms in self-conscious, public terms. That adherence to the inheritance law of *sharī'at* should be emphasized in this context is hardly surprising. As one Muslim meeting resolved in urging public support for the recognition of the inheritance rights of daughters under *sharī'at*, "He who does not believe in the Quran and the Prophet cannot be a Muhammadan."[9] Adherence to the *sharī'at* had thus become, in this context, a critical element in the preservation of personal Muslim identity.

But to understand the particular character of the tension between "tribal" and Islamic identities, we must understand the law's broader political implications. The development of customary law under the British had aroused opposition in Punjab not only because it was a system supported by the colonial regime but also because it reflected a special view of the role of localized kin-based loyalties in the construction of the political order. The development of the law, in this sense, was closely related to the development of the colonial system in general. In organizing their rule, the British had developed in Punjab a system of political integration in which the idiom of "tribal" solidarity had played a central role.

The system of customary law was thus just one part of the larger colonial political fabric. In the twentieth century the integration of Punjabi society came increasingly to depend on the development of the province's diffuse "democratic" electoral structure, a system whose underlying principles were, significantly, in some ways strikingly similar to the principles underlying the customary law. Though the introduction of institutions of "democratic" politics in Punjab was gradual and complex, the establishment of an elected Provincial Council in 1920, and later of a more broadly based Provincial Assembly, suggested a fundamental British view of society as based on local units of social cohesion linked together through their incorporation into a common, provincial institutional framework. Though the units of representation for the Council and Assembly were generally not "tribal" but territorial and communal (religious), the appeal to divine guidance in the selection of representatives for the legislature was overtly discouraged; in fact, the invocation of "divine displeasure" in electoral contests was

9. *Zamindar* (Lahore), 6 December 1915. Excerpted in *Report on Newspapers and Periodicals in the Punjab for the Year 1915*, no. 50.

specifically a corrupt electoral practice (Swarup 1936:55). The foundations of the electoral system were thus based on the expression of local interests, which were, as many British officials saw it, very frequently "tribal" interests.[10] Rural elections tended to revolve, in British eyes, around the formation of local "tribal" factions.

More important, however, the articulation of authority in a "tribal" idiom was strongly encouraged with the passage of the Punjab Alienation of Land Act of 1901. Though passed primarily as a means of slowing the alienation of land from agriculturalists to moneylenders, the provisions of the Act directly encouraged the definition by rural leaders of common economic interests defined largely in "tribal" terms. Under the Act's provisions, the key structural units of rural society were defined as Punjab's "agricultural tribes"—units within which the ownership of land was to be protected. Alienations of land were thus barred under the Act from members of statutorily defined "agricultural tribes" to those who were not members of these "tribes." Subsequently, for many agriculturalist leaders themselves, the Land Alienation Act came to be seen as the "Magna Carta of their political and economic life."[11] It not only helped to protect their lands from alienation, but, more importantly, it also conferred on them, as leaders of the "agricultural tribes," a special political status by identifying these "tribes" as the foundation of the agrarian order. Whatever the actual roots of their local authority, rural leaders thus tended to an important degree to articulate their claim to influence at the provincial level in terms of "tribal" leadership. This tendency found concrete expression in the 1920s with the formation in the Provincial Council of the Punjab Unionist Party. As a party of primarily Muslim (and some Hindu) rural leaders, it served in the 1920s and 1930s as a provincial platform for the expression of local interests as defined in the Land Alienation Act. As one of the Unionist Party's critics declared in the 1930s, "the Unionists seem to believe that the Land Alienation Act is to them what the Vedas and the Holy Quran are to the Hindus and Mussalmans."[12]

10. The "tribal" foundation of elections was clearest at the most local level. District Board constituencies were frequently drawn by the British with "tribal" representation in mind. As Olaf Caroe noted on the subject in 1921, "in the west of the Province the tribal system is strong. We ought surely to preserve and not disintegrate it." Punjab Civil Secretariat Archives, Local Self-Government/Boards, A proceedings, File 30, August 1923.

11. Statement of Sir Fazli Husain, *Punjab Legislative Council Debates*, 1928–29, vol. 12:709.

12. Raja Narendra Nath in the *Tribune* (Lahore), 28 April 1936.

For those who attacked customary law and supported *sharī'at*, therefore, the issue in the 1920s and 1930s was not simply one of personal identity and personal adherence to the law, but rather of the definition of the cultural foundations for the state and for the integration of society. In personal terms, most urban supporters of *sharī'at* already adhered to the inheritance rules of *sharī'at* in any case, and these rules were generally enforced in the courts. Since customary law had never been codified, it was even open to prominent agriculturalist families to renounce the "un-Muslim provisions of the Punjab custom"[13] if they so desired, and to announce, at the revision of the *riwāj-i 'ām*, their adherence to *sharī'at*. For most supporters of the *sharī'at*, however, the question involved broader issues concerning the role of the state in defining theoretical principles for the integration of society. In this context, the support of *sharī'at* in opposition to customary law was less a matter of personal identity than a matter of the cultural identity of society as a whole.

These issues were clearly evidenced in debates over the subject in the Provincial Council. Criticism of British reliance on customary law was nothing new in the early 1930s, but at that time a bitter debate on the subject was touched off by a bill brought into the Council on behalf of one of the most prominent and powerful landowners of the Punjab, Sir Umar Hayat Khan Tiwana of Shahpur District. The bill called for the establishment of the legal impartibility of Sir Umar Hayat's important estate, in spite of the conflict of this principle with the inheritance rules of the *sharī'at*. Sir Umar Hayat's motives for the introduction of this bill are not completely clear, since according to the Tiwana *riwāj-i 'ām*, succession by primogeniture was already well established for "Tiwana chiefs." The real issue may have been the definition of Sir Umar Hayat's own position as a "tribal chief," since his political power derived not so much from "tribal" tradition as from his extraordinary influence in the British army and administration, and from his control of one of the Punjab's largest and most profitable landed estates.[14] His own peculiar perception of his role as "tribal" leader may have been indicated by his formation of a Tiwana tent-pegging and polo team with which he toured the cantonments of the Punjab, attempting to bring "the name of the Tiwana clan and his district to the fore."[15] Whatever

13. *Observer* (Lahore), 25 Sept. 1915. Excerpted in ***Report on Newspapers and Periodicals in the Punjab for the Year 1915***, no. 40.
14. Sir Umar Hayat descended from a cadet branch of the main Mitha Tiwana lineage. For a history of the family see Griffin and Massy (1910, vol. 2:167–83).
15. "A Brief Account of the Career of Captain the Hon'ble Malik Umar Hayat Khan, Tiwana, C.I.E., M.V.O.," included in Punjab Board of Revenue, File 301/1406.

the precise character of his "tribal" position, however, the establishment of the impartibility of his estate was undoubtedly an issue of long-term political significance for his family. The object of the bill as argued by the mover was "simply [to secure] the sanction of this House to put the custom on a stronger foundation so that in future the family may be saved any further trouble with respect to litigation."[16] In this sense, Sir Umar Hayat's goal was to secure, through the intervention of the Provincial Council, the position of his family as "tribal" leaders within the framework on which the British administration rested.

In assessing this bill, Muslim leaders in the Council were initially in sharp opposition as regards its implications for the definition of Muslim identity. It is clear that for Sir Umar Hayat the bill involved no personal conflict with religion. Sir Umar Hayat was himself a *murīd* of the influential reformist *pīr*, Sayyid Mehr Ali Shah of Golra, and he prided himself on his close associations with many of "the Mohammadan spiritual leaders, saints and pirs" of his district, for whom he sometimes mediated with the Government. His "knowledge of Islam and its tenets" was, he wrote to Government, "in no way inferior to that of the saints and pirs of the Muhammadan public."[17] To introduce a bill relating to the succession to property within his family—a subject long governed by custom—was thus for him not a matter of religion at all, but of "tribal" politics. For Shaikh Muhammad Sadiq, on the other hand, an urban Kashmiri Council member from Amritsar, the issue appeared in a far different light. The bill represented, in his eyes, a clear violation of Islamic law, and he cited *fatāwā* of leading *'ulamā* to prove it. "Islam has strict injunctures against any procedure of this kind," he said, "and when you take such a step you utterly run counter to the wishes of God and the Holy Prophet." In Shaikh Muhammad Sadiq's view, Sir Umar Hayat had certain personal obligations as a Muslim. Granted, he admitted, that Sir Umar Hayat's family did not, even before the introduction of the bill, "strictly follow Shariat," but still, he said, "they are at least born as Muhammadans."[18]

For most rural Muslims in the Council, however, the real debate was not about whether Sir Umar Hayat would or would not distribute his property according to *sharī'at*, since the customs for the distribution of

16. Speech of Shaikh Abdul Ghani, *Punjab Legislative Council Debates*, 1931, vol. 19:791.
17. "A Brief Account of the Career of . . . Malik Umar Hayat . . ." Sir Umar Hayat stated that he had played a critical role in arranging for the participation of many of the *pīrs* of Punjab in the Delhi Durbar of 1911.
18. Statement of Shaikh Muhammad Sadiq, *Punjab Legislative Council Debates*, 1931, vol. 20:61–66.

Tiwana property were already fixed by customary law, subject only to the interpretation of the British courts. The debate was rather about whether the Legislature itself could or should give official sanction to such a procedure—a question related intimately to the principles on which the Muslim members of the Council perceived their moral claim to legislate for the province. At root, the real issue was thus the moral foundation for the integration of society. The moral dilemma for many Muslim members in this context was expressed clearly by one rural member, Chaudhri Shah Muhammad of Sheikhupura.

> *Chaudhri Shah Muhammad*: . . . If Sir Umar Hayat Khan wants to assure of his property remaining intact, the Rivaj-i Am in his own family can stand him in good stead. Then where lies the necessity of mutilating the law of the Prophet of Islam? Why should the zamindars of this Council be forced to enact a measure contrary to the Shariʿat?
>
> *The Hon'ble Captain Sardar Sikander Hyat Khan*: The zamindars do not follow Islamic law.
>
> *Chaudhri Shah Muhammad*: That does not matter. . . . We cannot murder the Islamic law with our own hands. . . . If this Bill had been passed without inviting us to give our opinion, I for one, would have raised no objection.[19]

For Chaudhri Shah Muhammad, the central issue was not what law was followed by rural leaders, whatever the *fatāwā* of the *ʿulamā* might say.[20] Rather, the issue for Muslims in the Provincial Council was how society as a whole was to organize its affairs. Implicit in Chaudhri Shah Muhammad's remarks, and those of many others who opposed the bill, was a tacit rejection of the principles of integration on which the British had tried to organize and legitimize their own rule, principles derived from the "tribal" organization of society. They seemed to be saying that, as a moral basis for the integration of society beyond the locality, the only truly legitimate principle was revelation. As Shaikh Muhammad Sadiq put it, "the shares [of inheritance] which the Quran has fixed, this Council has absolutely no right to alter."[21] Such arguments were not enough to sway the majority of the Muslim members of the Council, who, under the influence of Government and the Unionist Party, voted to pass the bill. Many were no doubt embarrassed by the debate and

19. Statements of Chaudri Shah Muhammad and the Hon'ble Captain Sardar Sikander Hyat Khan, *Punjab Legislative Council Debates*, 1931, vol. 20:199.
20. This is not to suggest that Chaudri Shah Muhammad was not influenced by the *ʿulamā*, for his comments suggest that he was. Rather, it appears that his political concerns went beyond those embodied in the *fatāwā* of the *ʿulamā*.
21. *Punjab Legislative Council Debates*, 1931, vol. 20:64.

chose, as Mian Nurullah charged in opposing the bill, to absent themselves from the Council during a speech in which important *fatāwā* against the bill were quoted. "Unfortunately this Bill relates to one of the most powerful zamindars of the province," Nurullah said, "and nobody has the courage of conviction to rise to the occasion and say that the Bill should not receive our support."[22]

But the political and moral issues involved in the debate in fact ran far deeper than the influence of one powerful rural leader. The continuing political importance for many rural Muslim leaders of the principles of integration on which the colonial system had been built was indicated by reactions to a subsequent bill proposed in response to the passage of Sir Umar Hayat's bill. This was a bill submitted by Malik Muhammad Din of Lahore city, which called on the Council to set the record straight by sweeping away the British system of customary law altogether and by endorsing the *sharī'at* in its place as the personal law of all Muslims. In practical terms, this bill stood no real prospect of passage, for the Government and the Unionist Party leadership opposed it. But the opinions solicited when the bill was circulated to the districts for comments indicated, if perhaps in somewhat rough form, the political and moral dilemmas rural Muslims faced at this time in dealing with the issue.

These comments revealed that, whatever the basis for debate in the Council, personal adherence to *sharī'at* in matters of inheritance was on the increase. Though application of the *sharī'at* in inheritance matters had long been widespread in the towns, by the 1930s the spread of education had begun to lead, as the Commissioner of Multan Division suggested, to an increasing awareness and acceptance of *sharī'at* in the countryside. This tendency was particularly noticeable in the more commercialized parts of the province, such as Lyallpur District, where connections between town and countryside had expanded rapidly and where the power of British administrative intermediaries was weakest. "There is a marked tendency among the Muslim agriculturalists to give up their personal laws in favour of the Muhammadan Law," one Lyallpur *taḥṣīldār* remarked. "The idea is gaining ground and has come to stay" and was even gaining increasing recognition in the British courts.[23] There was even a tendency, noticed by a few, for changes in the

22. Statement of Shaikh Muhammad Sadiq, *Punjab Legislative Council Debates*, 1931, vol. 20:70.

23. Statement of M. Abdur Rahman, *taḥṣīldār*, Jaranwala. Punjab Civil Secretariat Archives (PCSA), Home Judicial, File 20, October 1936.

law to be related to changes in the exogamous marriage patterns to which Tupper had attached so much importance. As one Lahore District *zaildār* suggested, the spread of "education and propaganda" might itself lead to changes in Muslim marriage patterns, encouraging more intensive marriage within the family, and thus facilitating the disappearance of customary law and the more general acceptance of *sharīʿat*.[24]

Whatever the general trend in marriage patterns, however, most of the responses to the bill indicated that, all in all, adherence to *sharīʿat* in matters of inheritance in rural Punjab was still extremely limited. For the overwhelming majority of the Muslim population in the rural areas, where the rate of illiteracy remained at over 90 percent, the impact of the spread of education was still very slight, and the political and economic logic supporting customary law retained undeniable significance. For most rural leaders, the introduction of *sharīʿat* was thus seen as a challenge to the basic structure of authority in which their local and provincial power had been articulated. As one Muslim *taḥṣīldār* of Gujrat District declared, "To abrogate the tribal law altogether by one stroke of the pen and thereby substitute the Muhammadan law instead would not only be impossible under the circumstances but would completely disintegrate the homogeneity of the agricultural tribe."[25] Sardar Mohammad Shahbaz Khan of Kasur was even more pointed. "Strangers will freely intermix," he said, "and their presence would lead to the disruption of tribes, giving rise to all kinds of disputes."[26]

In fact, the degree to which such "tribes" possessed the social cohesion to control the inheritance of their members is highly questionable, for intensive litigation over inheritance had long been endemic under the system of customary law. But the claim for the protection of "tribal" rules of inheritance related to more than the problematic character of local "tribal" solidarity; it was also tied closely to the assertion by these rural leaders of a claim to political power and status at the provincial level. The most frequently cited drawback to *sharīʿat* in this connection was the fear that in abrogating the customary law, introduction of *sharīʿat* might also undermine the Land Alienation Act. As the Government's Legal Remembrancer pointed out, the application of customary

24. Statement of M. Hidayat Ali, *zaildār* of Gharyala (Lahore). PCSA, Home Judicial, File 20, October 1936.

25. Statement of M. Ahmed Khan, *taḥṣīldār*, Kharian. PCSA, Home Judicial, File 20, October 1936.

26. Statement of Khan Bahadur Sardar Muhammad Shahbaz Khan, Honorary Magistrate of Kasur. PCSA, Home Judicial, File 20, October 1936.

law had helped to guarantee that land was always "protected by the Punjab Alienation of Land Act" since it prevented land from passing through inheritance by daughters out of the agnatically defined "agricultural tribe."[27] Many agriculturalist leaders seemed to attach critical importance to this. As the Deputy Commissioner of Ludhiana District put it, "If as a result of the passing of the bill the protection afforded by the Punjab Alienation of Land Act will be automatically withdrawn, then the Muslim agriculturalists are opposed to the introduction of the bill."[28] The linking of the system of customary law to the Land Alienation Act was thus a signal of the continuing concern of these leaders with the system of law as a cultural and political prop for that system of integration in which their power had developed under the British.

The real dilemma, however, was that despite the continuing political importance of customary law, it had become increasingly difficult by the 1930s to translate this support for custom into moral terms. Though the idiom of "tribal" kinship had in fact been effectively adapted by the British as an indigenous idiom for the articulation of authority in Punjab's political system, the very process of political integration under the British had for many weakened the "tribal" idiom's moral power. Even for those who strongly supported the system of customary law, therefore, it was increasingly difficult to deny the moral authority of the *sharīʿat* as a symbol of incorporation in God's wider community. As one Muslim *taḥṣīldār* expressed it, it was hard for anyone, in giving opinions on Malik Muhammad Din's bill, to withstand publicly "the stigma of opposing the introduction of law sanctioned and sanctified by the Holy Quran."[29] Even so powerful a figure in rural Punjabi politics as Nawab Fazal Ali of Gujrat District thus felt compelled to express his own strong opposition to the bill and his support for customary law in terms, ironically, drawing on the moral authority of the *sharīʿat*. Since the "agricultural tribes" had already legitimized customary law by their willingness to follow it, he said, "the existing practice (Rivaj) has the sanctity of the will according to Shariat."[30]

Such an appeal was perhaps too ingenious for most rural Muslims, but even more telling, as an indication of the growing search for an

27. Statement of the Legal Remembrancer. PCSA, Home Judicial, File 20, October 1936.
28. Statement of DC, Ludhiana. PCSA, Home Judicial, File 20, October 1936.
29. Statement of M. Sultan Bakhsh, *taḥṣīldār*, Gujrat. PCSA, Home Judicial, File 20, October 1936.
30. Statement of Khan Bahadur Chaudhri Fazal Ali, O.B.E., M.L.C., PCSA, Home Judicial, File 20, October 1936.

Islamic justification for customary law, was the appeal by supporters of custom to the authority of the traditional religious leaders of rural society. For the backers of customary law the support of these "saints and *pīrs*" was particularly important since these were leaders whose religious authority had traditionally derived not from their knowledge of the Qur'ān or the classical law, but from their local mediation between cultures of the rural population and the transcendent power of God. Many of these religious leaders in fact followed local, "tribal" inheritance customs with regard to their own property. As a Jāt *zaildār* of Gujrat put it, "most Muslim religious leaders, being themselves zamindars, have been following this custom," and for many, this in itself gave religious authority to the workings of custom. "Custom is not against religion," the *zaildār* thus declared.[31] Such support for customary law was particularly important in the case of men like Makhdum Murid Husain Qureshi, *sajjāda-nishīn* of the shrine of Bahā' al Ḥaqq Zakariya (d. 1263) at Multan, who had long been influential in provincial politics and active in the Unionist Party, and whose local prestige gave powerful religious legitimacy to the opposition of the acceptance of the inheritance rules of *sharī'at*.[32]

But such opposition in the end did relatively little to bolster the moral position of those who argued for the retention of customary law at the provincial level. Though the moral influence of leaders like Makhdum Murid Husain was doubtless still considerable in local affairs, the moral character of their authority was of necessity altogether different at the provincial level, where the conflict between customary law and *sharī'at* was increasingly debated as a question of state policy. These men served in the Provincial Council, like other "tribal" leaders, as representatives of local interests within a system of political integration devised by the British. At election time, *pīrs* like Makhdum Murid Husain drew their support not from a special relationship with God, but from the local ties of *parti* ("party," i.e., faction) based on alliances of local "tribal" leaders.[33] In ideological terms, they could thus do little at the provincial level, in spite of their religious prestige, to answer the call

31. Statement of Chaudhri Bahawal Bakhsh, president, Zamindara League, Gujrat. PCSA, Home Judicial, File 20, October 1936.
32. Makhdum Murid Husain was reported by the Deputy Commissioner of Multan to be in opposition to Malik Muhammad Din's bill. PCSA, Home Judicial, File 20, October 1936.
33. In Multan District, local electoral politics revolved around two factions or *partis* centered on the Gilani and Qureshi families. These were the two most influential families of religious leaders in the district.

for adherence to the *sharīʿat* as a symbolic statement of the commitment of society as a whole to an Islamic moral order.

The crisis in the conflict between customary law and *sharīʿat* was thus, in the end, a crisis of cultural integration under the British—a crisis which became increasingly acute as British rule drew to a close. As Muslims gained a growing share of political power, the tension between custom and *sharīʿat*, between "tribal" and "Islamic" political idioms, permeated Punjabi Muslim politics. The call for the rural population to forget the bonds of "tribe" and to remember only the name of Islam became the common coin of the Pakistan campaign in the 1940s. The Muslim League called for the recognition of a transcendent Islamic morality as the foundation for a new, independent state. Muslims were told to abandon the claims of "*barādarī, rishtadār* and *ẕatī taʿalluqāt*,"[34] as one appeal put it, since "tribal" and Islamic loyalties were, in the words of Daultana, "exact opposite[s]." Such appeals were, in fact, nothing new in Punjab, for they had long been made by urban supporters of the *sharīʿat*. But in the years just before 1947, these appeals were made not just by the advocates of strict personal adherence to Islamic law, but by many rural leaders as well—men who had in some cases long followed custom in their own families. For some of these men, the contradictions in this position were overwhelming, since the rules of customary law had played an important part in the maintenance of their own local power under the British administration. But in 1946 and 1947, it was not local power, but the construction of a new political and moral order, which was at issue.

With the creation of Pakistan, the attempt to ground the Punjabi political system in a new Islamic idiom thus came to fruition. As a symbol of the new state's cultural foundations, the *sharīʿat* was adopted in 1948 as the official system of personal law supported in Punjab by the new Islamic state.[35] But even in Pakistan, the conflict between *sharīʿat* and the idiom of local, kin-based authority persisted. For many of those rural leaders who had supported the creation of Pakistan, the official adoption of the personal law of *sharīʿat* signaled little more than the official definition of a new Islamic idiom for the integration of the old agrarian order. But for others, particularly among the *ʿulamā*, the adoption of *sharīʿat* in Pakistan represented much more. For them the

34. "Brotherhood, relatives, and personal connections." *Inqilab* (Lahore), 11 Nov. 1945.

35. The personal law of *sharīʿat* superseded customary law in nearly all cases by the West Punjab Personal Law (Shariʿat) Application Act of 1948.

law was not just a symbol of the state's cultural foundations; it represented in addition a program for individual religious commitment and reform, a rejection of the primacy of the local loyalties on which the British had built their authority. As Pakistan constructed its own political system, the political role of the law continued to be a subject of intense controversy.

References

Bossy, John
1973 "Blood and Baptism: Kinship, Community and Christianity in Western Europe from the Fourteenth to the Seventeenth Centuries." In *Sanctity and Secularity: The Church in the World.* Derek Baker, ed. Oxford: Oxford University Press.

Daultana, Mumtaz Muhammad
1944 "Address." Punjab Muslim Students' Federation. Fourth Annual Session. Lahore: Punjab Muslim Students Federation.

Geertz, Clifford
1968 *Islam Observed: Religious Development in Morocco and Indonesia.* Chicago: University of Chicago Press.

Gledhill, Alan
1962 "The Compilation of Customary Law in the Punjab in the Nineteenth Century." In *La radaction des coutumes dans le passé et dans le présent.* John Gilissen, ed. Brussels: Institut de Sociologie de l'Université Libre de Bruxelles.

Griffin, Lepel, and Charles Massy
1910 *Chiefs and Families of Note in the Punjab.* 3 vols. Lahore: Civil & Military Gazette Press (revised edition).

Heesterman, J. C.
1978 "Was There an Indian Reaction? Western Expansion in Indian Perspective." In *Expansion and Reaction.* H. L. Wesseling, ed. Leiden: Leiden University Press.

Kitchin, A. J. W.
1911 *Customary Law of the Attock District.* Lahore: Civil & Military Gazette Press (revised edition).

Metcalf, Barbara Daly, ed.
1984 *Moral Conduct and Authority: The Place of Adab in South Asian Islam.* Berkeley: University of California Press.

Noon, Mohammad Hayat Khan
1925 *Customary Law of the Pakpattan and Dipalpur Tahsils of the Montgomery District.* Lahore: Government Printing Office.

Report on the Punjab Codification of Customary Law Conference
1915 Lahore: Government Printing Office.

Swarup, Krishna
1936 *The Punjab Elections Manual.* Lahore: Upper India Scientific Works.

Talbot, W. S.
1901 *General Code of Tribal Custom in the Jhelum District of the Punjab*. Lahore: Civil & Military Gazette Press.
Tupper, C. L.
1881 *Punjab Customary Law*. 3 vols. Calcutta: Government Printing.
Turner, Bryan S.
1974 *Weber and Islam*. London: Routledge & Kegan Paul.

3

Sharī'at and *Haqīqat*: Continuity and Synthesis in the Nizārī Ismā'īlī Muslim Tradition

AZIM NANJI

The study of the spread and development of Nizārī Ismā'īlism in South Asia from the thirteenth century onward reveals two important features about the movement. First, in contrast to previous Ismā'īlī movements that had led to the emergence of the Fāṭimid Caliphate (909–1171) and later to the establishment of a Nizārī state in Iran (1904–1256), it was apolitical. Second, the movement sought consciously and selectively to integrate indigenous traditions into its vision of Islam, as reflected in the *ginān* literature preserved among the Nizārī Ismā'īlīs and in the pattern of ritual and cultural life that evolved among them. Both of these features were to have major implications for the community in its transition to modernity.[1]

This brief study, based on field work in India and Pakistan and on an analysis of the *ginān*s, seeks initially to establish a context for understanding the mode of synthesis of thought and ritual practice established in South Asian Ismā'īlism. It then proceeds to relate this mode of thought and practice to an altered context, beginning in the late nineteenth century, which forced the community to review questions of authority and self-identity. Finally, it outlines some of the ways in which the community has sought to resolve, since the early part of this century, questions related to continuity and change in its religious heritage.

1. For a history of Ismā'īlism in the Subcontinent, see Nanji (1978), chapters 2–5. A general introduction to Ismā'īlī history can be found in Madelung (1971) and in Esmail and Nanji (1977).

The *Ginān* Tradition: Symbolic and Ritual Aspects

The word *ginān* refers to the indigenous literary heritage that was developed and preserved among the Nizārī Ismāʿīlīs of the Subcontinent. The origin and composition of the *ginān*s is attributed to various Ismāʿīlī scholars, called *pīr*s or *sayyid*s, who undertook the work of conversion and preaching in India from the fourteenth to the nineteenth centuries. The recording of the *ginān*s was done in the Khojki script, an adaptation from Devanagari; some of the surviving *ginān*s represent early forms of Sindhi, Gujarati, and Punjabi as well. Over the period of some six centuries, thirty *pīr*s and *sayyid*s are believed to have composed *ginān*s of differing lengths, of which approximately eight hundred have survived. Internal evidence in the existing manuscripts of *ginān*s suggests that a practice of recording *ginān*s and establishing uniform texts began in the sixteenth century, if not earlier (Nanji 1978:9–17).[2]

In the mid-nineteenth century, groups of the Indian Ismāʿīlī community were to be found in Sind, Gujarat, Punjab, and other centers in northern and western British-ruled India. After the migration of Imām Ḥasan ʿAlī Shāh (Aga Khan I) from Iran to India, and the eventual establishment of his headquarters in Bombay in 1848, several changes took place in the organization of that community. One result of the change was the systematization and stabilization of the *ginān* corpus, and its eventual publication. The *ginān*s continue to this day to play a vital role in the daily religious and devotional life of Nizārī Ismāʿīlīs of Indo-Pakistani origin.

From the point of view of literary categories, the *ginān*s may best be defined as "anagogic," that is to say, "mystical or esoteric in the broadest sense" (Strelka 1971:1). Like the esoteric *haqā'iq* literature of classical Shīʿa Ismāʿīlism, they thrive on the use of hermeneutical interpretations whose function it is to penetrate to the inner (*bāṭin*) signification of the Qur'ān and Islam rather than being confined to the mere external (*ẓāhir*) aspects. On this basis, the *ginān*s comprise a whole system of hermeneutics, in which the inner meaning of religious acts has greater primacy and in which conformity to the *sharīʿat* is a step toward a deeper understanding of the meaning of such acts. In the *ginān*s such a process is referred to as *satpanth*, the "Right Way." Though *satpanth* has connotations similar to those of *sharīʿat*, its significance includes the idea that the individual is led through the *ṭarīqat*, a process of ritual,

2. The linguistic background and influences are discussed in a recent doctoral dissertation by Asani (1984).

intellectual, and spiritual initiation beyond the *sharī'at*, to the truths of esoteric Islam, the *haqīqat*.[3]

Preserved among the *ginān*s are a set of narratives which trace the arrival and establishment of Nizārī Ismā'īlism in India. The literal testimony of the narratives is valuable for historical purposes and, in conjunction with other available epigraphic and archaeological evidence, permits one to reconstruct the main phases of this history. It is, however, by studying the internal structure of the different accounts that we find revealed an iterative pattern of thematic development that illustrates the symbolic nature of the *ginān*s (Nanji 1978:50–55). If each sequence in the action of the narratives is treated as an episode, then the plot reveals the following pattern:

1. anonymous arrival at a well-known Hindu or Muslim religious center or city;
2. performance of a miracle to draw attention of the leaders or rulers of the area and to win over disciples;
3. confrontation with a local saint or religious figure and triumph over him;
4. conversion of the people in the city;
5. departure.

The *ginān*s use already-existing Hindu or Indo-Muslim hagiographic materials to transform the narratives into vehicles of Ismā'īlī teaching. Such a process is best defined as mythopoesis, that is, a re-creation that reflects "a critique of the existing social norms and points to a futuristic order which is envisaged as integrating the valuable residues of the past and the present" (Slochower 1970:34). The prototype of the narratives, containing the iterative pattern and stereotypical features, symbolizes the goals of the *da'wat* (preaching). It is significant that one of the narratives contains reference to meat in a "raw" state that must be cooked and tasted before the truth of the preaching and the identity of the *pīr* can be realized: transformation is at the heart of the symbolic import of such *ginān* narratives.

This form of literary mythopoesis in the *ginān*s is complemented by the development of ritual processes. After the *pīr*, by his preaching, gained converts to Ismā'īlism from among the Hindu population, he initiated the converts into Islam through a ceremony called *ghaṭ-pāṭ*.[4] As described in the *ginān*s and observed in a continuing tradition of practice,

3. For a discussion of the esoteric aspect of Ismā'īlism see the collection of essays of the late Henri Corbin (1983) and Nanji (1985).
4. For the ceremony, see Nanji (1978:175n21).

the ceremony was devised for new converts. These converts participated in a group ritual where they drank a sip of sacred water after having given up the traditional *jane'ū*, the sacred thread they had worn as practicing Hindus. Such a ceremony continued to play an important part in the religious centers of the community (*jamā'at-khāna*) and is still current, a fact we shall have occasion to return to in a discussion of the modern situation of the group.

The term *ghaṭ-pāṭ* is a compound derived from two Sanskrit words, *ghaṭ*, a vessel for water, and *pāṭa*, denoting a low, long, dais-like table on which vessels are placed. Among the community, the ceremony was also referred to in Persian as *āb-i shifā* (Water of Healing). The water placed in the vessel was generally mixed with that obtained from the well of *zamzam*, with small clay tablets obtained from Shī'a holy places such as Karbala, or during visits to the headquarters of the *imāms* (which were in Iran at that time). In this way the sacred character of the water was established. The vessels used during the ceremony were also cleansed ritually through recitation of prayer and the use of incense. Within the community, a link was established between this ceremony and the practice of the Prophet Muḥammad, who is said to have performed initiatory rites for the early converts to Islam. Parallel traditions, of course, also existed among many Sufi groups in the Subcontinent and elsewhere in the Muslim world.

The communal drinking of *āb-i shifā* was related to both Muslim and Samvat calendars and was held on Fridays, the night of the new moon (*chandrat*) and other major festival occasions, when a larger congregation was present. The ceremony followed the completion of a form of esoteric prayer, called *du'ā* among the Nizārī Ismā'īlīs; individuals lined up behind each other in front of the *pāṭ* and drank from a small cup into which the *āb-i shifā* had been poured from a larger vessel. The members of the congregation were also given an offering of sweet food after having completed the ceremony. In the *ginān*s, reference is made to this offering and particular emphasis is placed on the symbolism of the five ingredients that are used for making it—milk, sugar, clarified butter, wheat flour, and water. Each of these ingredients is said to signify a moral or spiritual trait such as purity, generosity, a spirit of cooperation, moral strength, and spiritual seeking. The vessels used in the ceremony are made of earthenware and are always white in color, emphasizing the above qualities.

There are several aspects of the total ceremony that need to be considered, first, in their initial context as representing a transition from a Hindu world view to a Muslim one; and second, in a modern context as establishing a continuity and adaptation of past practice. In the context of the larger process of conversion in medieval times from Hinduism to Islam in the community, the ceremony fulfilled several important functions. It affirmed a notion of purity but also revised it, through a ritual form that had indigenous Indian roots. In the new and changed order, however, purity and impurity were projected as representing a new order which sought to integrate a number of castes and which related their allegiance to an external figure, the Shī'a Ismā'īlī *imām*.

The sources of the water, the well of *zamzam* in Mecca or the sacred places in Karbala, reinforced the symbolic and ritual link with Shī'a Ismā'īlī Islam. The *ginān*s also include many references which link the ceremony to Qur'ānic descriptions of the spring of al-Kawthar (sura 108). Classical Ismā'īlī works include ritual purity (*ṭahārat*) among the traditional pillars of faith. Thus an overarching frame of Islamic and Ismā'īlī metaphors was used to establish the new religious and social order within which the ritual was seen to have significance. Several other functional characteristics of the ceremony may also be identified as elements that reinforced a new religious and social identity and also consolidated allegiance to the *imām* as the pivotal figure of authority in bonding the followers into a community.

It is, however, at the level of its esoteric and symbolic significance that the ceremony affords an opportunity for analyzing a synthesis between Hindu and Muslim religious experience. The ceremony of *ghaṭ-pāṭ*, interpreted in its esoteric (*bāṭinī*) aspects, enabled the individual follower to participate in one of the profoundest religious experiences possible in Indian Ismā'īlism. As described in various *ginān*s, in terminology analogous to that of Sufi literature, the drinking of the sacred water was symbolic of the heart being illuminated by divine light (the Qur'ānic *nūr* of sura 24). At one level, the ritual merged the individuals into the new community; on another, they were able to transcend the merely structural or *ẓāhirī* aspects of ritual, enabling them to experience the dimension of *bāṭin*, the interior religion, through which an individual quest for spiritual knowledge and understanding was attained (Nanji 1982:105–7).[5]

I have dwelt on what might be called the interior aspects of the *ginān*s and of Ismā'īlī ritual, in order to establish the context for discussing

5. The comments of Victor Turner (1974) bear an interesting comparison with the esoteric aspects of this Ismā'īlī ritual.

how a similar process of tension, followed by adaptation and reintegration, may be discerned in modern times, when different structures were brought to bear and alternative responses had to be devised in the community to meet changing needs and circumstances.

Changing Contexts: The Transfer of the *Imāmat* to India

In 1866 public attention was drawn by a case in the Bombay High Court that came to be known as the "Aga Khan Case." A certain minority section of a group from among the Nizārī Ismāʿīlīs was seeking to obtain a decree of the court to remove the Aga Khan from his position and authority as spiritual head and hereditary *imām*. After passing judgment in favor of the Aga Khan, the judge described the Ismāʿīlīs as "a sect of people whose ancestors were Hindu in origin, which was converted to and has throughout abided in the faith of the Shia Imami Ismailis and which has always been and still is bound by ties of spiritual allegiance to the hereditary Imams of the Ismailis" (Fyzee 1965:545).[6]

This dramatic event in the community's modern history highlights the particular social and historical context that created the need for a re-evaluation of the community's identity and future direction. I want to focus on two aspects of this problem, the question of authority and the issue of self-identification. The Aga Khan Case revealed a tension regarding the position of the *imām* and his absolute spiritual authority. The *imām* in question, Shāh Ḥasan ʿĀli Shāh (Aga Khan I), left Iran in 1841, and the headquarters (*dar-khāna*) of the *imām* eventually came to be situated in India. What had been a symbolic link for Indian Ismāʿīlīs now became a physical presence. Though the history of the group had not been without small schisms and seceders from the mainstream, the actual physical presence of the *imām* among the community raised immediate questions among some Ismāʿīlīs about his authority and power.

The second issue, regarding the confluence of Hindu and Muslim traditions in the community, was also highlighted by the Aga Khan Case. Ismāʿīlīs, as other Shīʿas in general, have often had to face persecution. This led to the development of a practice called *taqīya* (pious dissimulation) to guard against oppression. One of the forms that this

6. The issues involved in the case and the subsequent judgment can be found on pp. 504–49.

took among the Ismā'īlīs in India was a continuation of Hindu cultural patterns in matters of dress, food, inheritance laws, and, on occasion, funerary customs. When it became necessary to establish under "Anglo-Mohammedan" Law the relationship of the group to Muslim Law, the *imām* affirmed the group's identification as Shī'a Ismā'īlī Muslims. In the face of this need for a specific commitment and self-identification with Ismā'īlī Islam, a minority felt strongly about the loss of their earlier ambiguous status. Conflict ensued; some people who resisted the *imām*'s position filed for litigation, wishing either to be recognized as Sunni Muslims or, in some cases, as Hindus. It was these two issues that provided a *casus belli* for the case. The judgment in favor of the Aga Khan established clearly the Ismā'īlīs' total self-identification with Shī'a Islam, and a discarding of the use of *taqīya*. One interesting result—which I was able to trace among certain sections of the community in Gujarat and Punjab—was a series of open declarations of being Ismā'īlī by such groups, who had hitherto regarded themselves as covert (*gupt*) Ismā'īlīs, and an increasing interaction with Ismā'īlīs living in other centers of British India.

Thus the impact of the judgment in the Aga Khan Case on the future development of the community was immense. It clarified the position of the *imām* and his relations with his followers, affirming his hereditary right to make decisions on communal planning, property, and legal aspects related to matters of religious and daily life. The Aga Khan and his successors, Aga Khan II (d. 1885) and the well-known international figure Aga Khan III (d. 1957), adopted in subsequent years a program of reorganization and modernization of the community's structure which sought to establish continuity with past tradition even while creating connections with institutions and patterns of economic life under the British.

Overall, the strategy adopted by the *imām*s for effecting change in the community was to introduce modern administrative and educational institutions into the community and to relate these changes to an interpretation of the role of Ismā'īlī Islam and the *imām* as a transforming agent. The key to this process was the mobilization and reorientation of traditional values. If, as it is generally maintained among Ismā'īlīs, their transition to modernity has been a successful synthesis of religious continuity and adaptive capability, then it is to their traditional institutions and values that one must look for clues as to how they perceive this to have been achieved.

Toward Resolution: Congruence of Authority and Development in a Religious Community

In 1905 Aga Khan III began the process of reorganizing administrative structures in the community. In order to do this he established a Constitution. Since that time the Constitution has been periodically revised and updated, the latest one having been revised during the *imāmat* of Aga Khan IV, Shah Karim, who became *imām* in 1957. The preamble to the Constitution laid down clearly the legal and traditional position of the *imām* as defined by the 1866 Case. It stated that the rules had been conceived within the "spirit of Islam" and that "nothing therein contained shall affect the Absolute Power and Sole Authority of the Imam of the time to alter, amend, modify, vary or annul at any time, or to grant dispensation from the Constitution or any part thereof."[7] The *imām*'s authority in spiritual and material affairs thus came to be affirmed clearly. The Constitution also provided for the establishment of councils in matters relating to the economic, educational, and social development of the community, and also provided for rules and regulations in matters of personal law, rooting them within Shīʿa Ismāʿīlī Muslim tradition and eliminating Hindu practices. The Constitution, incidentally, was welcomed by the British, who preferred, in the context of their colonial administration in India, to reduce their difficulties by dealing with a well-organized framework of leadership. The apolitical nature of the community's history also harmonized with this pattern of relationship, the more so as Aga Khan III's nonsectarian role on the behalf of Indian Muslims in the early era of British Indian politics became more pronounced. After Partition, this pattern continued with the governments of the two newly independent countries through broader efforts to build bridges with fellow citizens as well as with the Muslim *ummat* at large.

Between the early part of the century and the Second World War, the community's institutions developed rapidly under the guidance of the *imām*. The councils were augmented by educational institutions (the community tried to build and staff its own schools) and by the establishment of economic institutions such as an investment trust company, an insurance company, and various cooperative ventures to unify trading interests. In addition, medical institutions were built in major centers.

7. Preamble to *The Constitution of the Shia Imami Ismaʿilis in Pakistan* (Karachi: 1962). Papanek (1962) explores some of the changes that eventually took place.

It is worth noting that financial resources for such projects were generated in part by the staging of major symbolic events in the thirties and the forties to mark the Golden and Diamond Jubilees commemorating, respectively, fifty and sixty years of the *imām*'s stewardship. If one were to simplify and pinpoint the areas within which the community saw its future at this stage, the emphasis would undoubtedly be on development, by way of modernizing education and socio-economic life; education as a means of ensuring the future of the community within a changing political and social framework; and trade and economy as the fields in which the historical entrepreneurial talents of the community lay. Changes were brought about primarily through newly created institutions and meetings of various community leaders with the *imām*, who during the war had moved his residence to Europe. The *imām* also sent religious guidance (*farmāns*) on a regular basis that were read in all the *jamā'at-khānas*. It is impossible to say how many such *farmāns* were actually made during this period, but from the materials still preserved, it is evident that *farmāns* addressed a wide variety of subjects including health, economy, migration, daily and personal life, and specifically religious matters.

The various councils and organizations, seen against this constitutional and structural development, thus emerged as extensions of the *imām*'s authority and the instruments by which his guidance and vision for the community were effected. At local levels, however, these extensions were coordinated to involve as many Ismā'īlīs as possible at varying levels of organization. Hence, though the main thrust came from the *imām*, it was actually the community, by its voluntary involvement in the day-to-day workings of the system, that assured the implementation of the programs. All of this continued to be cemented together by the religious life of the *jamā'at-khāna*.

The interplay of all these factors is best illustrated by considering how the "spirit of Islam" was incorporated into changes of ritual and religious life. Over the years several practices and elements from the *ginān*s were allowed to gradually lapse as the need for *taqīya* was eliminated. Hindu customs in birth, betrothal, and marriage ceremonies, the practices associated with visits to the shrines of various *pīr*s, and even the observance of traditional *muḥarram* practices, lapsed. Part of the rationale for the change was sought in a closer identification with classical Ismā'īlī practices, a de-emphasizing of *taqīya* as reflected in past Hindu practices, and also a dissociation from certain practices specific to Twelver Shī'ism to affirm the central role of the living *imām* in

Ismā'īlism. An often-quoted *farmān* from Aga Khan III mirrored this emphasis:

From time to time as the circumstances change, some new things come up and fresh issues arise. At different times, new difficulties crop up. The world also changes. The conditions of the world prevailing thousands of years ago were different than the present times and will radically change in the years to come. There have always been great transformations in the world. It is on account of this that the Imam of the time is always present to guide you according to the changed times. My firmans in years to come will be quite different from the present ones. Therefore you should obey the Firmans of the Imam of the time. (*Precious Pearls* 1954, no. 12)

But certain ritual practices were retained and modified and even acted as agents of change in the movement toward greater self-identification with modern Ismā'īlī Islam. The use of one of the *ginān*s traditionally associated with many rituals—the *dasā avatāra* (ten descents or manifestations, a key element in the mythopoesis of the doctrine of *imāmat*)—was limited to the final section on the tenth manifestation (i.e., of 'Āli and his descendants, the *imām*s), and the references to the first nine (the traditional Vaishanavite figures) were curtailed. This further dissociated the Ismā'īlīs from Hindu antecedents, placing greater emphasis on self-identification with their antecedents within the Islamic tradition.

As is well known, the Ismā'īlīs, like other Shī'as in general, have evolved through Muslim history their own framework for implementing the *sharī'at*.[8] The above process indicates a re-establishment of the fundamental practices with reference to that historical framework and a realignment of practices that were congruent with past practice as well as with the normative Ismā'īlī traditions among its communities in other parts of the world such as Syria, Iran, Central Asia, and East Africa. These communities were also going through similar periods of transition, albeit at a differing pace and within varying historical circumstances.

This process of change was given even wider application in the social context, as illustrated in the ceremony of *ghaṭ-pāṭ*. Younger members of the *jamā'at* were now encouraged to lead the prayers and play a more significant role in ritual practice. The *imām* also encouraged women to participate actively in the public performance of prayers. When studying

8. The classical Ismā'īlī formulation is contained in the work of al-Nu'mān (1951–60). It must be noted, however, that such a formulation, in the Ismā'īlī view, is not restrictive; as in subsequent periods, further elaborations, based on the living *imām*'s guidance, could and did take place.

the community in a comparative context, one finds the role of women in public practice more pronounced among Ismāʿīlīs of Indo-Pakistani origin than perhaps among other Muslim groups; the wider role envisaged for women by the *imāms* was facilitated and prepared for in part by their growing role in the religious life of the community. Certain rituals thus played a crucial role as agents of social change and were linked to the overall policy of the community in encouraging education among girls and indeed in creating a stronger role for them in the modernized institutions of the community. When viewed diachronically, Indian Ismāʿīlī rituals may be very useful tools for analyzing in more detailed fashion how patterns of belief and community organization are interdependent, and may provide significant clues to how a religious community adapts its symbols and concepts in new or changed situations.

Conclusion

In any general analysis of the process of resolution of moral tensions as evidenced among the Nizārī Ismāʿīlīs, one must ask two basic questions. The first concerns the specific ways in which changes are effected, while the second relates to the adherents' perception of the type of society these changes have produced, and of their own self-image as Muslims.

These questions need to be addressed in terms of the process by which transformation and change come about in Ismāʿīlī Islam. The role of the *imām* has traditionally been perceived as embracing the totality of development within the community, in both the material and spiritual spheres of Muslim life. The two realms are seen to be complementary: the *sharīʿat*, encompassing the formal sphere of human action, provides the basis for developing an inner spiritual orientation, which in turn leads to an understanding of the *haqīqat*, the esoteric dimension of Islam. In his capacity as custodian of these two foci, the *imām* acts to sustain this vision of Islam. When circumstances have been favorable, and the case of the Fāṭimid and Nizārī Ismāʿīlī states are cited as past examples, an attempt was made to realize and implement these goals. According to Ismāʿīlī history, overt assertion of this vision of Islam has not always been feasible, given the vicissitudes of the Ismāʿīlī situation. But in modern times, the *imāms*, it is argued, can play a more direct role in promoting development in both material and spiritual spheres.

Hence, new boundaries of activity, particularly in the elaboration of the *sharīʿat*, have been evident. There has been a closer identification with the Muslim *ummat* as a whole. There has also been a widening of the sense of Ismā'īlī identity. The enlarged boundary is no longer restricted to the immediate Indo-Ismā'īlī context or to its past history, but rather reaches beyond them to encompass other periods and places of Ismā'īlī history and activity. In fact, a new phase has emerged within a wider global context, since Ismā'īlīs of South Asian origin have migrated in modern times not only to other areas within the Subcontinent, but also to other countries in Asia, Africa and, in recent times, to the West.

The emergence of the nation-state has also raised additional questions about identity for Ismā'īlīs, as for other Muslims in South Asia. The creation of new boundaries associated with the nation-state has been accompanied by notions of secularism as alternative modes of defining and relating religious and moral stances to issues of daily life and development. Some of the responses and changes evident among Ismā'īlīs reflect the interplay of historical context and moral concerns central to the Ismā'īlī tradition. In this encounter with its changing patterns of relationships and authority, there is, I would argue, no single response or synthesis that can be regarded as normative; rather, the process of resolution among Ismā'īlīs reflects an affirmation of its traditional cosmology and an awareness of its potential to stimulate new approaches to guidance in equilibrating the tensions and stresses created by change.

If one wishes to identify any one emphasis in the process of resolution, then it appears to lie in the wider approach of integrating within the Ismā'īlī framework alternative codes and of creating syntheses. Where historical ambiguity has been recognized, it has been transcended and overcome, if not entirely eliminated. In this process, the principles of *ẓāhir* (outer) and *bāṭin* (inner) as tools for defining *sharī'at* and *haqīqat* become the means for comprehending and assimilating change at both individual and communal levels of understanding.

Finally, as Clifford Geertz (1983:225–26) has observed in his reflections on what he calls "an hermeneutics of legal pluralism," Western academic discourse faces the challenge of formulating "standards of cogency" that take into account how the legal world is construed within a tradition. In a discussion of *sharī'at* and its centrality in the quest for resolution of questions of community organization among Muslims, the need for such an attitude is urgent; in the case of the Ismā'īlīs, where *sharī'at* is linked to an internal hermeneutical system, the attitude is sine qua non.

References

Aga Khan
1954 *Memoirs*. New York: Simon & Schuster.

Algar, H.
1969 "The Revolt of the Aga Khan Mahallati and the Transference of the Ismaili Imamate to India." *Studia Islamica* 29:55–81.

Asani, Ali
1984 "The Bujh Niranjan: A Critical Edition." Ph.D. dissertation, Harvard University.

Corbin, Henri
1983 *Cyclical Time and Ismā'īlī Gnosis*. London: Kegan Paul International, in association with Islamic Publications, Ltd.

Esmail, Aziz
1972 "Satpanth Ismailism and Modern Changes within It." Ph.D. dissertation, University of Edinburgh.

Esmail, Aziz, and Azim Nanji
1977 "The Ismā'īlīs in History." In *Ismā'īlī Contributions to Islamic Culture*. Seyyed H. Nasr, ed. Teheran: Iranian Academy of Philosophy.

Fyzee, Asaf Ali Ashgar
1965 *Cases in the Mohammedan Law of India and Pakistan*. Oxford: Clarendon Press.

Geertz, Clifford
1971 *Islam Observed: Religious Development in Morocco and Indonesia*. Chicago: University of Chicago Press.
1973 *The Interpretation of Cultures*. New York: Basic Books.
1983 *Local Knowledge: Further Essays in Interpretive Anthropology*. New York: Basic Books.

Hodgson, Marshall G. S.
1964 "Islam and Image." *History of Religions* 3:220–60.

Horton, Robin
1971 "African Conversion." *Africa* 41:85–108.

Madelung, W.
1973 "Ismailiyya," in *Encyclopaedia of Islam*. Vol 3. Leiden: E. J. Brill (new edition), pp. 198–206.

Nanji, Azim
1974 "Modernization and Change in the Nizari Ismaili Community in East Africa—a Perspective." *Journal of Religion in Africa* 6:123–39.
1978 *The Nizārī Ismāl'īlī Tradition in the Indo-Pakistan Subcontinent*. New York: Caravan Books.
1982 "Ritual and Symbolic Aspects of Islam in African Contexts." In *Contributions to Asian Studies*. R. C. Martin, ed. Leiden: E. J. Brill, pp. 102–9.
1985 "Towards a Hermeneutic of Qur'ānic and Other Narratives in Ismā'īlī Thought." In *Approaches to Islam in Religious Studies*. R. Martin, ed. Tucson: University of Arizona Press, pp. 164–73.

Nasr, Seyyed Hossein, ed.
1977 *Isma'īlī Contributions to Islamic Culture*. Tehran: Iranian Academy of Philosophy.

al-Nu'mān ibn Muḥammad, Abū Hanīfa
1951–60 *Da'ā'im al-Islām*. 2 vols. Asaf Ali Ashgar Fyzee, ed. Cairo: Dār al-Ma'ārif.
Papanek, Hanna
1962 "Leadership and Social Change in the Khoja Ismā'īlī Community." Ph.D. dissertation, Harvard University.
Precious Pearls
1954 (A brief collection of the *farmāns* of Imam Mowlana Sultan Mohamed Shah.) Mombasa: Ismailia Association.
Slochower, Harry
1970 *Mythopoesis*. Detroit: Wayne University Press.
Speeches of His Highness Karim Aga Khan
1963–64 Parts 1 and 2. Mombasa: Ismailia Association.
Strelka, Joseph, ed.
1968 *Perspectives in Literary Symbolism*. University Park: Pennsylvania State University Press.
1971 *Anagogic Qualities of Literature*. Vol. 4. University Park: Pennsylvania State University Press.
Turner, Victor
1974 "Metaphors of Anti-structure in Religious Culture." In *Changing Perspectives in the Scientific Study of Religion*. A. W. Eister, ed. New York: John Wiley & Sons.
1975 "Symbolic Studies." In *Annual Review of Anthropology*. B. Segal et al., eds. Palo Alto: Annual Review.

PART TWO

Changing Idioms of Political Discourse: Religious Legitimacy, Leadership, and Popular Mobilization

4

Legacy and Legitimacy: Sher Shāh's Patronage of Imperial Mausolea

CATHERINE B. ASHER

Architecture may seem an odd place in which to examine moral principles, much less their conflict, but it is both possible and useful to do so, and perhaps nowhere more so than in the architecture erected under the patronage of Sher Shāh Sūr. The Sultan Sher Shāh ruled north India for a brief period, from 1538 to 1545, yet posterity remembers him as a vigorous patron of architecture. Through the evidence of extant buildings, inscriptions, near-contemporary histories, and local tradition, it is known that Sher Shāh extended his patronage to four major types of construction: public works, defensive works, religious edifices, and mausolea. His motivation in doing so, as I shall indicate below, is based on *adab*, or moral, ethical behavior.

Architecture and the Ideal Ruler

According to most of the near-contemporary accounts of Sher Shāh's rule, such as 'Abbās K͟hān Sarwānī's *Tārīk͟h-i Sher Shāhī* or Badāyūnī's *Muntak͟hab al-Tawārīk͟h*, this sultan was actively engaged in the construction of public and defensive works ('Abbās K͟hān 1964:168–74; Badāyūnī 1973:472–73; 'Abd Allāh 1969:127–28; Aḥmad 1936:174–75). The authors of these and other extant texts commonly credit Sher Shāh with building four major tree-lined highways that connected the principal cities of his empire from east to west. Such texts relate that Sher Shāh constructed a serai for the welfare of travelers every five miles. These serais were complexes providing a number of facilities, including a well with separate water arrangements for Hindus and Muslims, and a brick-constructed mosque. Some texts such as the *Tārīkh-i Sher Shāhī*, the history of Sher Shāh's reign written at Akbar's command, state that food and fodder were provided at the government's expense, thereby preventing the despoliation of the peasants' land by imperial troops. This is a standard notion put forth in *adab*-type texts such as Niẓām al-Mulk's *Siyāsat Nāma* and Sa'dī's *Gulistān* (Niẓām al-Mulk 1960:102; Sa'dī 1964:96). There is evidence, although not material, that at least some of these serais actually existed: the Bhaṭhiyārās or Muslim innkeepers of Uttar Pradesh claim descent from a line of Sūrī serai keepers (Ansari 1960:42). In addition, Badāyūnī claims that traces of Sher Shāh's serais were still extant when he wrote his *Muntakhab al-Tawārīkh*, some fifty years after their construction (Badāyūnī 1973:473).

Massive forts, too, were erected at strategic locales across north India. Some of these extant forts, such as Rohtas in the Jhelum District, Pakistan, and Shergarh in Rohtas District, Bihar, are stone- or brick-constructed (for Rohtas Fort, see 'Abbas Khān 1964:172; for illustrations see Hayauddin 1954:44–47; for Shergarh Fort see Kuraishi 1931:193–96); others, simply mud-constructed, have disappeared, but their name, Shergarh, has been left behind as a likely Sūrī legacy.[1] In addition, Sher Shāh appears to have developed his reputation as a patron of military architecture so successfully that even some fortifications not built by him are popularly credited to this sultan. For example, when the local inhabitants of Rajgir (Gaya District, Bihar) were asked in the early nineteenth century who built the mighty stone fortifications, which archaeologists date to the sixth century B.C., their unanimous response was Sher Shāh (Buchanan-Hamilton 1925:129). In addition to buildings, forts, and public works, Sher Shāh is also credited with building many mosques and providing them with a caretaker, *mu'azzin*, and an *imām* ('Abbās Khān 1964:157–92). However, only one of these mosques—the Qal'a-i Kuhna in Delhi's Purānā Qal'a, Sher Shāh's imperial citadel—remains.[2]

Ostensibly, Sher Shāh's pragmatic outlook explains the erection of

1. An example is a village named Shergarh, eight miles from Chatta (Mathura District, U.P.), where today only the foundations of an old fort remain. However, according to Growse, in the nineteenth century a large fort with six towers and four gates stood here which, according to local tradition, was built by Sher Shāh (Growse 1883:378).
2. For the significance of this mosque, see Asher 1981:212–17. For a published description of this mosque, see Brown 1968:86–87.

these structures. All of these buildings were highly utilitarian and therefore a practical expenditure. The corpus of these structures was built to serve the subjects directly or built for them by serving Islam; in none of these architectural complexes, including the forts, are there any buildings whose function was not of a strictly utilitarian nature.[3] This contrasts notably with the less practical patronage provided by many of Sher Shāh's predecessors and successors. For example, the first Mughal, Bābur (1526–30), built his many *chār-bāghs* (four-part garden) as a counter to his personal dislike of the arid landscape of Hindustan (Bābur 1970:531–33), and Jahāngīr (1605–28) built a very expensive hunting lodge for his personal comfort at the grave site of a favorite deer (Jahāngīr 1968:182).

What might explain Sher Shāh's evident predilection for pragmatic architecture? This question can probably best be answered by examining the monarch's attitude toward kingship. 'Abbās Khān Sarwānī, Sher Shāh's first posthumous biographer, depicts this sultan as an ideal Islamic ruler, deeply concerned with justice and the welfare of his subjects ('Abbās Khān 1964:157–92). Other biographers agree with 'Abbās Khān, including several writers such as Mīrzā 'Azīz Koka and Niẓām al-Dīn Aḥmad (Athar Ali 1978:39; Aḥmad 1936:175). This is particularly significant, since writers loyal to the Mughal rulers demonstrated blatant antipathy toward the earlier Afghan ruling houses (for example, Abū al-Faẓl 1972:343). Even in Sher Shāh's own time, the Awadhī poet Malik Muḥammad Jāīsī, in the preface to his *Padmāvatī*, proclaimed Sher Shāh an extraordinarily just ruler whose reign was marked by peace and prosperity (Jāīsī 1944:12). Since the poet Jāīsī did not enjoy Sūrī patronage, and 'Abbās Khān wrote his *Tārīkh* at the behest of Akbar (not for the Sūrī house), there is reason to rely on the integrity of their statements ('Abbās Khān 1964:1).

Thus it appears that Sher Shāh was attempting to adhere to the image of an ideal sultan. That the image was of the type portrayed by Persian *adab* texts intended for the edification of rulers is indicated by

3. Sher Shāh's forts consisted largely of defensive outer walls, lacking for the most part the elaborate domestic and administrative structures found in both Tughlug and Mughal forts. While interior structures within the perimeters of Sūrī defensive walls do exist, these are usually later Mughal additions. For example, the residential structures in the Rohtas fort (Jhelum District, Pakistan) were built during the Akbarī period (Hayauddin 1954:45). The fort at Shergarh (Bihar) contains extensive interior buildings; however, these buildings are neither elegant nor elaborate. It appears that nonpermanent architecture such as tents, highly appropriate for a military regime constantly on the move, formed the bulk of the structures in Sher Shāh's forts.

the fact that some texts of this sort, such as Sa'dī's *Būstān* and *Gulistān* and Baranī's *Fatāwā-i Jahāndārī*, were known during the Sūrī period.[4] For example, both 'Abbās and Badāyūnī tell us that Sher Shāh read the *Būstān* and *Gulistān* ('Abbās K͟hān 1964:9 and Badāyūnī 1973:467). The availability of others such as Niẓām al-Mulk's *Siyāsat Nāma* or al-Dawwānī's *Ak͟hlāq-i Jalālī* is less certain; however, it is clear from a study of statecraft practiced in Sultanate India that the nobles and rulers were cognizant of the general sentiments expounded in these texts.

While *adab* texts on kingship differ on minor points, they all stress the need for justice and state that benevolence toward subjects will result in contented citizens, well-regulated institutions, and a prosperous domain. In addition, the sultan was to uphold Islam.[5] Sher Shāh's purpose in patronizing utilitarian architecture thus becomes more apparent. That is, structures such as those he built contributed to the contentment of his subjects. Public, defensive, and religious architecture thus became a tangible manifestation of ideal rule, evidence of a monarch dedicated to serving his subjects. The reasons behind Sher Shāh's patronage of utilitarian architecture may seem obvious and indeed may appear to be the obligation of a royal leader. But it is significant that extensive public architecture had not been erected on a regular and systematic basis under his predecessors—for example, Humāyūn, Bābur, and even the last Lodī sultan. Indeed, Khwānd Amīr's descriptions of Humāyūn's elegant and frivolous floating bazaars (Khwānd Amīr 1940:36–37), built for the amusement of the court, stand in pointed contrast to Sher Shāh's highly pragmatic buildings.

The Mausolea of Sher Shāh

Seemingly different from Sher Shāh's patronage of public, defensive, and religious architecture, is his construction of a fourth type: mausolea. The image evoked by a sultan who spent vast sums of money upon royal tombs might appear to contradict that of an ideal ruler. Thus we must

4. While there is no textual statement that Baranī's works were read during the Sūrī period, there is good reason to suggest that they were. According to 'Abbās K͟hān, Sher Shāh was well acquainted with the lives of earlier kings ('Abbās K͟hān 1964:9). In addition, many of Sher Shāh's administrative reforms reveal a specific awareness of the practices of 'Ala'al-Din K͟halji. It is through Baranī's writings that most of these practices are known, indicating that Sher Shāh had access to these texts. For discussions of this K͟halji influence upon Sher Shāh, see Qanungo (1921:393–94) and Asher (1981:213–14).

5. For some typical texts, see Niẓām al-Mulk (1960) and Kai Kā'ūs (1951); for a secondary analysis, see Rosenthal (1968:81–83).

Fig. 4.1 Tomb of Ibrāhīm Sūr Narnaul

ask the obvious: why did Sher Shāh erect three monumental tombs, one each for his grandfather, his father, and himself? The answer is interestingly related to the concept of moral principles in tension.

In 1542, some fifty years after Ibrāhīm Sūr died in 1488 ('Abbās Khān 1964:7),[6] Sher Shāh erected a large domed tomb, approximately nineteen meters square, over the grave of his grandfather in Narnaul, Mahendragarh District, Haryana[7] (figure 4.1). This was the site of his grandfather's *jāgīr* ('Abbās Khān 1964:6).[8] The tomb, situated on a high plinth, appears to be two-storied from the exterior, but in reality the interior is simply a vast, unbroken space. The façade is covered with pink and gray dressed stone; the intricate carving upon it foreshadows the complexity of much Akbarī architecture.

In Sasaram, now in modern Rohtas District, Bihar, Sher Shāh built

6. 'Abbās Khān gives no actual date but states that Bahlūl Lodī was still on the throne when Ibrāhīm died, and this sultan too died shortly thereafter.
7. For an illustration and discussion of the inscriptions on the tomb, see Asher (1985:268; plates 264–66).
8. While it has been argued that the term *jāgīr* was not yet current during this period, I am following 'Abbās Khān, who uses "*jāgīr*" rather than "*iqta'*."

Fig. 4.2 Tomb of Ḥasan Sūr Sasaram

two tombs—one over the grave of his father, Ḥasan Sūr, and another for himself. Just as Narnaul had been the site of Ibrāhīm Sūr's *jāgīr*, so Sasaram was the seat of Ḥasan Sūr's *jāgīr* as well as Sher Shāh's own ('Abbās Khān 1964:39). Ḥasan Sūr's tomb is a three-storied octagonal structure, measuring thirty-four meters in diameter and situated in a low-walled enclosure complete with a mosque[9] (figure 4.2). In lieu of carved dressed stone as at the Narnaul tomb, Ḥasan Sūr's mausoleum was veneered with stucco, traces of which remain bearing intricate incised geometric patterns. Inscriptions on the tomb's interior indicate when the monument was constructed. The titles ascribed to Sher Shāh, *Farīd al-Dīn wa al-Dunyā Abū al-Muẓaffar Sher Shāh Sulṭān*, the patron, imply that this tomb was built sometime after 1538, when Sher Shāh assumed the title of Sultan throughout eastern India.[10] Moreover,

9. For a full description of this tomb, including measurements, inscriptions, and illustrations, see Kuraishi (1931:185–86).
10. Two coins of Sher Shāh that would appear to indicate his accession to the throne of Bihar in 1535/36, two years earlier than customarily believed, have been published recently (Misra 1969:39–47; Farid 1976:115–21). However, the evidence they yield is by no means certain. I have examined the coin published by Farid; it does not bear an early

Fig. 4.3 Tomb of Sher Shāh Sūr Sasaram

historical and stylistic evidence indicate that his tomb was not commenced until 1541 at the earliest, but surely before Sher Shāh's death in 1545.[11]

The third and final mausoleum built under Sher Shāh's patronage was his own (figure 4.3). Situated in the middle of an artificial lake, Sher Shāh's monumental three-storied octagonal mausoleum evokes an image of paradise, so fitting for the tomb of a sultan.[12] At the time of its construction, Sher Shāh's tomb was the largest tomb in all India, measuring forty-one meters in diameter. Even today, it remains the

---

date, as claimed, but rather one equaling A.D. 1545. No photograph of the other coin has been published, and though supposedly in the collection of the Aligarh Muslim University, the staff was unable to find it or any record of it during my visit to examine the coin. Moreover, epigraphic evidence such as an inscription dated to 1536 in Bihar, his stronghold, refers to the monarch as Sher Khān, and no coins of 1537 that are considered authentic are known. Coins referring to Sher Shāh as sultan, however, are known in great numbers from 1538 and commence a series uninterrupted until his death in 1545. Furthermore, even if Sher Shāh had become sultan in 1536, the arguments pertaining to architecture remain unaltered.

11. For a more complete discussion see Asher (1977: 295–97).

12. For a detailed description see Asher (1977:273–93).

second largest, surpassed in size only by that of Sultan Muḥammad in Bijapur (Cousins 1976:100). Historical and stylistic considerations indicate that Sher Shāh's tomb was commenced after 1540, although epigraphical evidence indicates that Islām Shāh, Sher Shāh's son and successor, completed this tomb in 1545, only three months after the Shāh died. All scholars agree that the majority of it was designed and built during Sher Shāh's own lifetime (Brown 1968:84; Goetz 1938:97–99).

The Sūr background explains many of the reasons behind the construction of these three tombs. The Sūrs were a minor Afghan tribe originally from the mountainous regions of Roh ('Abbās Khān 1964:5). Sher Shāh's grandfather, Ibrāhīm Sūr, whose Narnaul tomb is described above, was a horse trader.[13] He immigrated to India as did many Afghan tribesmen from Roh in response to an invitation from Sultan Bahlūl Lodī (1451–88) ('Abbās Khān 1964:5). He arrived in India with the last wave of Afghan émigrés, and was granted the rank of forty *suwār* (horse) and some villages in the *pargana* (district) of Narnaul. Never advancing further in rank, Ibrāhīm Sūr died about 1488. His son, that is, Sher Shāh's father, Ḥasan Sūr, obtained greater favor under the Lodīs. According to 'Abbās Khān, Ḥasan Sūr rose to a rank of five hundred *suwār*, obtaining Sasaram and Khaspur-Tanda in Bihar as his *jāgīr*; he maintained both of these until his death in about 1525 ('Abbās Khān 1964:8, 31).[14] While Ḥasan Sūr's rank of five hundred *suwār* was a great advancement over the forty *suwār* held by Ibrāhīm Sūr, he did not belong to the upper echelons, for ranks as high as thirty thousand *suwār* are recorded during this period (Siddiqi 1969:37). Many nobles held ranks above a thousand (*hazārī*) *suwār* (Siddiqi 1966:70, 75). But it must be noted that no member of the Sūr tribe ever was awarded a high-ranking position under the Lodī sultans. Moreover, in no extant inscription or text referring to Sher Shāh's father is he distinguished as a noble or anything other than Ḥasan Sūr or Miyān Ḥasan.[15] This reinforces the argument that his rank was relatively low. After Ḥasan

13. Abū al-Faẓl (1972:326) underscores Ibrāhīm Sūr's lowly origins by adding "nor had he any distinction among the crowd of tradesmen."

14. The exact date of Ḥasan Sūr's death is not given, but historical evidence suggests that it was shortly before the defeat of Ibrāhīm Lodī at the battle of Panipat in 1526.

15. For inscriptions containing Ḥasan Sūr's name see Ahmad (1973:125, 141) and Nicholls (1906:33). The term *miyān* is affixed to the name of many Afghan *amīrs* and religious personages. This term appears to be used as an expression of respect or affection, but does not indicate a specific rank as would the title "Khān" following a name. In addition, it is only on Ḥasan Sūr's tomb that he is called Miyān Ḥasan, and by 'Abbās Khān, who in his history of Sher Shāh sought to idealize this sultan's rule.

Sūr's death about 1525, Sher Shāh gained control of the *jāgīr* of Sasaram; he quickly acquired additional territory until he controlled all eastern India. Just before defeating the Mughal Humāyūn at the Battle of Chausa in 1539, Sher Shāh had crowned himself sultan in 1538. In 1540, Sher Shāh took command of Delhi, and, by his death in 1545, he had included most of north India under Sūrī control.[16]

The acerbic Badāyūnī, whose attitude toward Sher Shāh is unusually favorable, says in his opening words on this ruler, "Inasmuch as he . . . rose from the rank of *beg* [petty officer] to royal dignity, it is essential to give a brief account of his career" (Badāyūnī 1973:466). Implicit in Badāyūnī's words is the view that Sher Shāh's rise to power was *be-adab*: for a man of his background to assume the name of sultan transcended the codes of conduct established for princes. For example, in the *Akhlāq-i Naṣīrī* by Ṯūsī, one of the many texts written as advice for princes, good descent is listed first among the seven vital qualities needed for any ruler (Naṣīr al-Dīn Ṯūsī 1964:227). While it is not known if this text was read in Sūrī India, similar views on the virtues of high birth are reflected by works such as the *Gulistān* and the *Fatāwā-i Jahāndārī* (see Sa'dī 1964:77–80; see also Habib and Khan 1961:997–99). These texts, it is known, were widely studied in India during this period. Tracing his lineage to a low-ranking, untitled father and a grandfather who was a horse dealer, Sher Shāh hardly possessed this quality. According to Badāyūnī and 'Abbās Khān, this sultan was conversant with popular *adab*-type texts for princes ('Abbās Khān 1964:9), and thus he must have been poignantly aware of his social inadequacy.

In addition, other accounts of Sher Shāh's character underscore unsavory aspects of his nature, thus implying that his claim to the throne was not proper. One such account, found in Abū al-Faẓl's *Akbar Nāma*, states that, in his youth, the future Sher Shāh breached all levels of acceptable social etiquette by offending his father with "his arrogance and evil-disposition," and practiced "theft, robbery and murder" (Abū al-Faẓl 1972:327–28). According to 'Abbās Khān and most other writers, it was Ḥasan Sūr who mistreated Sher Shāh, his eldest son; it was not Sher Shāh who was in error ('Abbās Khān 1964:8–9). Whether Sher Shāh did indeed practice robbery, as is artfully justified by one modern historian (Qanungo 1965:33–34) is irrelevant. These stories—given the greatest stress by Jauhar and Abū al-Faẓl, who were hostile to Sher Shāh—were related in order to underscore the belief that Sher

16. For a detailed account of Sher Shāh's rise to power see 'Abbās Khān (1964) and Qanūngo (1965).

Shāh was indeed unsuitable for kingship. Similarly, accounts that Sher Shāh frequently resorted to treachery and deceit to obtain victory and power imply his unsuitability for a royal role (see, e.g., Aḥmad 1936:160–68; Jauhar 1970:141–42). Sher Shāh's capture by treachery of the fort of Rohtas in Bihar, considered pivotal in his sudden rise to power, was well known and caused such outrage that 'Abbās K͟hān in his *Tārīk͟h-i Sher Shāhī* attempted to counter what he called, "that commonly known story" (1964:79). His arguments, however, are hardly convincing. But the attempt was essential in order to make Sher Shāh's actions appear acceptable, even to posterity, for *adab* texts such as the *Fatāwā-i Jahāndārī* and the *Qābūs Nāma* constantly warn against such unscrupulous behavior on the part of kings (Habib and Khan 1961:67; Kai Kā'ūs 1951:138).

Thus dual images of Sher Shāh appear. Neither is totally reconcilable with the other; together they imply a crisis of the sort to which this present volume is dedicated. On the one hand is Sher Shāh, who became sultan through cunning and treachery rather than as the result of the customary and expected good birth or high-ranking lineage. On the other hand, he sought to overcome this by projecting his image as ideal sultan—just and concerned with the welfare of his subjects. His utilitarian architecture conveyed an important part of that image, implying that in reality, if not in theory, he was indeed suited for kingship.

His patronage of tombs served a similar purpose. That is, they served to elevate his lineage, by posthumously glorifying his deceased ancestors, and thus to indicate his suitability for kingship. Indeed, Sher Shāh took special steps to ensure that the name of the tomb's occupant as well as his patronage of the monument would be publicly proclaimed and preserved for posterity. This he did by inscriptions, on the doorway in the case of his grandfather's tomb at Narnaul and on the *miḥrāb* in the case of his father's tomb at Sasaram (Asher 1981; Kuraishi 1931). This stands in marked contrast to customary practice among his predecessors; the name of the principal occupant of most royal Sultanate–period tombs in north India is known only by tradition and not by any inscriptional evidence. For example, the tombs commonly identified as those of Iltutmish, Muḥammad Shāh Sayyid, Bahlūl Lodī, and Sikander Lodī are so identified by tradition alone, and not by any epigraphical evidence.

Further evidence that Sher Shāh sought to gain honor for his own name from the patronage of tombs may be gleaned from Ni'mat Allāh's

Tārīkh-i Khān Jahānī. According to this chronicle the dying Sher Shāh, lamenting that he had been unable to build a tomb at Panipat for a predecessor from another Afghan dynasty, Ibrāhīm Lodī, is said to have uttered the following words:

I have four desires . . . which still remain without accomplishment. . . . the last one is to have raised a tomb for Ibrāhīm Lodī . . . with such architectural embellishments, that friend and foe might render their tribute to applause—and, that my name [*nām-i man*] might remain honored upon earth until the day of resurrection. (For the Persian text see Ni'mat Allāh 1960:336; for the English translation see Ni'mat Allāh 1873:107–9).

If his desire to enhance the Sūrī name was Sher Shāh's principal motivation, why did he build the tombs exclusively in the provincial cities of Narnaul and Sasaram? One large dynastic mausoleum in Delhi, the traditional burial site of most north Indian sultans, might have seemed more prestigious. It was well within standard Islamic and Indo-Islamic tradition for one of the first sultans of a line to establish a dynastic burial ground with elaborate mausolea. But usually this was done at a single site in or near the ruler's capital city. For example, the Timurids established the Gur-i Amīr in Samarqand (Hoag 1976), and the Lodīs built mausolea in the Bāgh-i Jūd in Delhi ('Abd Allāh 1969:21; Ni'mat Allāh 1960:228).[17] In the case of Sher Shāh's family, a dynastic burial ground could have been established by shifting the graves of his father and grandfather; there was Indo-Islamic precedent for doing so (Nath 1974:151). If Sher Shāh had simply wanted to perpetuate the names of his predecessors at such a dynastic burial ground, a single monument would have sufficed.

Instead, Sher Shāh erected splendid tombs over the graves of his father and grandfather: an unprecedented act, both because these predecessors were low-ranking and because they had long been dead. There is no textual or historical evidence to suggest that Sher Shāh had any strong personal attachment to his grandfather, for this reputed horse trader died about 1488, when Sher Shāh was approximately two years of age. So personal affection alone cannot explain the reason Sher Shāh erected the magnificent Narnaul tomb almost a half century later. Similarly, Sher Shāh had little personal attachment to his father, Ḥasan Sūr; texts repeatedly state that tremendous animosity existed between them ('Abbās Khān 1964:28; Badāyūnī 1973:466; 'Abd Allāh 1969:109–10). In this case, too, fondness cannot explain why Sher Shāh

17. The text here reads *wujūd*; however, it is generally agreed that the correct name is Jūd.

provided his father with this mausoleum some fifteen years after Ḥasan Sūr's death.

Their size and shapes, however, provide an explanation for the construction of these tombs and Sher Shāh's own mausoleum: to enhance Sher Shāh's image. The sultan's own tomb at Sasaram was octagonal, a type usually reserved for royalty (Brown 1968:26), but it is much larger and placed in a more spectacular setting than any earlier tomb. This, together with the fact that it was built as the largest tomb in India, suggests that the patron, the ruler himself, wished to be remembered in some extraordinary manner.

The tombs of both Ḥasan Sūr and Ibrāhīm Sūr seem excessively impressive for their low-ranking occupants. The square tomb of Ibrāhīm Sūr appears to be a grander, more elaborate, and much more carefully crafted version of the type generally reserved for high-ranking nobles of the Lodī period. For example, the small tomb of Mubārak Khān in Delhi (1481, South Extension I), a high-ranking noble in the reign of Bahlūl Lodī, is only made of roughly hewn stone covered with a stucco veneer (Nath 1978:plate 78; Sharma 1964:73); by contrast, the tomb of Ibrāhīm Sūr, a horse trader who held only the rank of forty *suwār* during the reign of the same sultan, measures nearly nineteen meters square, and is made of finely carved masonry. Similarly, Ḥasan Sūr, who never attained a rank of over five hundred *suwār*, is buried in an octagonal tomb, a type usually reserved for royalty during this period.[18] In contrast is the typical, small, two-storied tomb of Sultan Sikander Lodī in Lodī Gardens (Delhi), measuring only twenty-two meters in diameter (Wetzel 1970:plate 48). Yet the tomb of Ḥasan Sūr is an enormous three-storied octagonal tomb measuring approximately thirty-four meters in both diameter and height. Thus, these Sūrī tombs are endowed with an inflated but convincing sense of grandeur; by extension, the status of the interred thus assumes the same grandeur.

Not only are the tombs of Hasan Sūr and Ibrāhīm Sūr magnified versions of the traditional types intended for royalty and well-placed *amīrs*. Other devices are used to endow these structures with a poignant religious aura. The exterior façade of Ibrāhīm Sūr's tomb is profusely embellished with medallions containing pious formulae. While similar medallions are frequently found on tombs, they are rarely seen in such

18. Nath (1978:79) is aware that Sher Shāh expressly built a royal tomb type for Ḥasan Sūr but misunderstands Sher Shāh's motivations in erecting the tomb of Ibrāhīm Sūr, whom Nath mistakenly believes is a high-placed Lodī noble. Nath does not deal with the implications raised by Sher Shāh's patronage of Sūrī tombs at any greater length.

profusion.[19] Usually they are limited to the top of a battlement; however, at Ibrāhīm Sūr's tomb, medallions with such phrases as "*Allāh*" and "*al-mulk al-Allāhī*" ("the kingdom is God's") are not only found on the battlement; many of these are also visible at eye level. Furthermore, an inscription situated at the top of the east façade states that this structure, in addition to being a tomb, was intended to double as a school (*madrasa*), thus giving the tomb a continuing religious function (Asher 1985:276).[20] In addition, this tomb is adjacent to that of a local saint, Shāh Wilāyat, an object of frequent pilgrimage (Yazdani 1907:639). Such proximity to the shrine of a holy *pīr* serves to heighten Ibrāhīm Sūr's status. Likewise, a Persian inscription on the tomb of Ḥasan Sūr at Sasaram states that Sher Shāh built it at the request of a Shaikh Abū Sarwānī (Kuraishi 1931).

Hence, the tomb was built not simply at the command of a sultan but at the behest of a religious sage, thus elevating the sanctity of the structure and, by extension, the status of the interred. Sher Shāh thus appears to have bestowed religious respectability upon his forebears, albeit posthumously. The result of doing so is identical to the result of erecting monumental tombs over the graves of low-ranking predecessors. It lends credibility to the Sūrī line and elevates its alleged status. In a sense, these tombs serve as visual forms of legitimation for the Sūrī name, in much the same fashion as the Sāmānid and Ghaznavid dynasties, among others, produced fictitious genealogies to prove their royal worthiness (Bosworth 1963:39–40).

In addition to being symbols of legitimacy, the Sūrī tombs served other propagandistic purposes. Narnaul, where Ibrāhīm Sūr's tomb is located, was an important pilgrimage center. Atop Narnaul's highest hill was a well sacred to Hindus that enjoyed such repute that Abū al-Fazl considered it Narnaul's most distinguishing feature (Abū al-Fazl 1978:192). Muslim devotees were drawn to the shrine of a much revered saint, Shāh Wilāyat. Not coincidentally, Ibrāhīm Sūr's tomb is situated immediately adjacent to that of the saint and, sitting high on a plinth, it towers over the saint's small, austere shrine and thus commands the landscape. Moreover, Narnaul was an important Sūrī mint town (Wright 1974:384–85) and lay on a major trade route. Narnaul was strategically situated midway between Delhi, the Sūrī imperial capital, and the territories newly acquired by Rāja Māldev of Marwar; Rāja

19. An example is the tomb of Imām Ẓāmin dated to 1537/38 near the Qutb Minar in Delhi (Cole 1872:plate 23).
20. I was the first to note and decipher this inscription.

Māldev's proximity remained a constant threat to Sūrī authority until 1544, when all Marwar was finally annexed by Sher Shāh (Qanungo 1965:395ff). Sasaram, the site of Sher Shāh's tomb, today lies on the Grand Trunk Road, the modern highway that essentially follows the road built by Sher Shāh from Sonargaon in Bengal to the Indus ('Abbās Khān 1964:170). Hence, the lavish tombs built by Sher Shāh were appropriately situated. Having himself risen to power from the provinces, Sher Shāh kept a wary vigil over events in the hinterlands. Accordingly, he placed imposing architectural monuments at strategic points, and on important routes outside the capital, to serve as constant reminders of the center's power.

Sher Shāh may have had yet another reason for building the tomb in Narnaul over the remains of his low-ranking grandfather. In his own day, Sher Shāh was often considered a provincial *amīr* whose administrative experience was limited to the remote Eastern provinces. To demonstrate, however, that his heritage was more pan-Indian than local, he built a tomb at the site of his grandfather's *jāgīr*, far removed from the Eastern provinces, emphasizing his suitability to be sultan of all Hindustan.

The mausolea built under Sher Shāh's patronage all evoke a sense of grandeur, but they do so in two very different ways. The austere, massive Sasaram tombs are but larger and more elaborate versions of the octagonal type developed earlier in the Sayyid and Lodī periods; the more decorative yet lighter-appearing Narnaul tomb, embellished with elaborately carved multicolored stone, prefigures Akbarī architecture. This presents a peculiar problem, for it is axiomatic in the history of art that only one style of architecture prevails under the patronage of a single ruler. The implications of this axiom are fundamental to an understanding of art historical methods based on stylistic analysis. Simply stated, the date of any structure can be determined by its style, and this axiom, when applied to premodern structures, does, by and large, withstand scholarly scrutiny. Using this axiom, most scholars such as Brown and Burton-Page have explained Sher Shāh's patronage of two disparate styles by assigning the tombs to two different periods in Sher Shāh's life: the Sasaram tombs are customarily considered products of Sher Shāh's pre-Sultan days, when he was the uncrowned ruler of Bihar (ca. 1530–38); the Narnaul tomb is rarely discussed, but when noted it is described as an imperial product dating ca. 1540–45 (Brown 1968:84–86; Burton-Page 1974:18; Burton-Page 1971:449). However, both epigraphical evidence and historical evidence counter this argument and indicate instead that all three tombs were constructed concurrently.[21]

Sher Shāh was apparently not a patron especially concerned with overall style or even details of decoration. That, in large measure, must explain the two different styles of the Sasaram tombs on the one hand and the Narnaul tomb on the other. Rather, the design was left to the discretion of the architects: 'Alawal Khān, considered on the basis of local tradition to be the architect of Sher Shāh's own tomb (Kuraishi 1931:192), and Abū Bakr Kundī of the Niyāzī tribe, whose name is prominently identified on the mausoleum's exterior epigraphy as the architect of the Narnaul tomb (Nicholls 1906:33–34). Indeed, Abū Bakr Kundī's name appears on this tomb three times, that is, twice more than Sher Shāh's own name, a likely indication that the architect's will assumed greater significance in shaping the monument than did that of the patron. Sher Shāh, instead, was concerned with the overall impact that his architecture made upon the viewer, but not in most cases with how the aesthetic appearance or minor details were rendered.[22] The particular style in which a building was rendered mattered little to Sher Shāh—as long as each was of the appropriate shape, and each structure was among the biggest and most elaborate of its type to date. By mere dint of its overall appearance, each tomb was to elevate the status of the Sūrī name.

Sher Shāh's son, Islām Shāh (r. 1545–54), apparently recognized the impact of the tombs that his father had raised. Although he ruled from Delhi for nine years, almost twice as long as Sher Shāh was on the Delhi throne, Islām Shāh also commenced his tomb at Sasaram, not at his capital. This mausoleum, too, was to have been octagonal and situated in the middle of an enormous artificial lake; had it been completed, it would have been even larger than Sher Shāh's own tomb (Nath 1978:95, plate 105). In short, Islām Shāh sought to be buried with his now

21. Nath (1978:82, 91–92) recognizes that both the Narnaul and Sasaram tombs date to the same period but does not address the problem of two separate styles.

22. Elsewhere I have suggested that Sher Shāh played an active role in designing some of the most prominent features of his own tomb, the lake setting, its three-storied octagonal shape, and the massive dome originally painted white. Each of these elements was influenced by specific structures with which Sher Shāh came into contact in his military exploits (Asher 1977:278, 287–88, 295–96). As Sher Shāh appears to have had considerable interest in the final appearance of his own mausoleum, there is reason to believe that he directed the architect to include these specific features. However, in light of Sher Shāh's lack of personal feeling for his grandfather, it is probable that he cared little about anything but this tomb's size and shape. Thus, the architect, Abū Bakr Kundī, felt free to engrave his name three times upon the façade of Ibrāhīm Sūr's tomb.

elevated and illustrious predecessors. With the placement of his tomb in Sasaram, this town became a sort of dynastic burial ground. Islām Shāh sought to gain prestige by associating his tomb with that of his father. Sher Shāh had been unable to do this; instead he began by building mausolea for his predecessors where none previously existed, and in this way enhanced his legacy.

Conclusion

One question still remains: were Sher Shāh's attempts to enhance his legacy and thus his worthiness of the monarchy successful? The answer is yes, for today illustrations or descriptions of the tombs of Ḥasan Sūr and Ibrāhīm Sūr are invariably captioned the mausolea of Ḥasan K͟hān and Ibrāhīm K͟hān or even, Ibrāhīm Shāh;[23] so, too, read the signs posted by the Archaeological Survey of India on the exterior façades. Thus, four hundred years later, Sher Shāh's insignificant forebears have been elevated by reputed scholars to noble positions with titles they never bore. The very appearance of these mausolea insists that only the high-ranking are buried inside; only the text of little-read histories and inscriptions reveals otherwise. The architectural legacy created by Sher Shāh did indeed successfully resolve the tension created by the expectation that kings, however just, must present the credentials of *sharīf* lineage. Expenditure on lavish mausolea, which at first would seem self-serving and contrary to the practice of an ideal sultan, in fact enabled the monarch to appear endowed with the prerequisites of an ideal sultan.

References

'Abbās K͟hān [Sarwānī]
1964 *Tārīk͟h-i Sher Shāhī*. Vol. 2. S. M. Imamuddin, trans. Dacca: University of Dacca.
'Abd Allāh
1969 *Tārīk͟h-i Dā'ūdī*. Abdur Rashid, ed. Aligarh: Aligarh Muslim University.
Abū al-Faẓl
1972 *Akbar Nāma*. Vol. 1. H. Beveridge, trans. Delhi: Rare Books (reprint edition).
1978 *A'īn-i Akbarī*. Vol. 2. Jadunath Sarkar, ed.; H. S. Jarrett, trans. New Delhi: Oriental Books (3rd reprint).

23. For example, see Nath (1978:79, 82, plates 97–99); Brown (1968:plate 60, fig. 2); Nicholls (1906:32). Nicholls calls Ibrāhīm Sūr "Ibrahim Shah," thus giving him even greater status than a K͟hān.

Aḥmad, Niẓām al-Dīn
1936 *Ṭabaqāt-i Akbarī*. Vol. 2. B. De, trans. Calcutta: Asiatic Society of Bengal.

Ahmad, Qeyamuddin
1973 *Corpus of Arabic and Persian Inscriptions of Bihar*. Patna: K. P. Jayaswal Research Institute.

Ansari, Ghaus
1960 *Muslim Caste in Uttar Pradesh*. Lucknow: Ethnographic & Folk Culture Society, Uttar Pradesh.

Asher, Catherine B.
1977 "The Mausoleum of Sher Shāh Sūrī." *Artibus Asiae* 39:273–98.
1981 "The Qal'a-i Kuhna Mosque: A Visual Symbol of Royal Aspirations." In *Chhavi II*. Anand Krishna, ed. Banaras: Bharat Kala Bhavan.
1985 "The Tomb of Ibrāhīm Sūr: Epigraphs and Implications." In *Indian Epigraphy: Its Bearing on the History of Art*. Frederich M. Asher and G. S. Gai, eds. New Delhi: Oxford and IBH Publishing Co.

Athar Ali, M.
1978 "Towards an Interpretation of the Mughal Empire." *Journal of the Royal Asiatic Society of Great Britain and Ireland* 1:38–49.

Bābur, Ẓahir al-Dīn Muḥammad
1970 *Bābur Nāma*. A. S. Beveridge, trans. Delhi: Oriental Rare Books (reprint edition).

Badāyūnī
1973 *Muntakhab al-Tawārīkh*. Vol. 1. George S. A. Ranking, trans. Patna: Academic Asiatica (reprint edition).

Bosworth, Clifford
1963 *The Ghaznavids, Their Empire in Afghanistan and Iran, 994–1040*. Edinburgh: University Press.

Brown, Percy
1968 *Indian Architecture: Islamic Period*. Bombay: D. B. Taraporevala Sons & Co. (5th edition revised).

Buchanan-Hamilton, Francis
1925 *Journal of Francis Buchanan (Afterwards Hamilton) Kept during the Survey of the Districts of Patna and Gaya in 1811–12*. V. H. Jackson, ed. Patna: Superintendent, Government Printing, Bihar & Orissa.

Burton-Page, John
1971 "Architecture," under *Hind* in *Encyclopaedia of Islam*. Vol. 3. Leiden: E. J. Brill (new edition), pp. 440–52.
1974 "Indo-Islamic Architecture: A Commentary on Some False Assumptions." *Art and Archaeology Research Papers* 6:14–21.

Cole, H. H.
1872 *The Architecture of Ancient Delhi, Especially the Buildings around the Kutb Minar*. London: The Arundel Society.

Cousins, Henry
1976 *Bijapur and Its Architectural Remains. Archaeological Survey of India*, New Imperial Series. Vol. 37. Varanasi: Bhartiya Publishing House (reprint edition).

Farid, G. S.
1976 "A New 942 Coin of Sher Shah and His Accession." *Islamic Culture* 50:115–21.

Goetz, Hermann
1938 "Sher Shah's Mausoleum at Sasaram." *Ars Islamica* 5, 1:97–99.
Growse, F. S.
1883 *Mathurā: A District Memoir*. Allahabad: Northwestern Provinces and Oudh Government Press (3rd edition, revised).
Habib, Muhammad, and Khan, Umar Salim
1961 *The Political Theory of the Delhi Sultanate Including a Translation of Ziauddin Barani's "Fatawa-i Jahandari," circa 1358–59 A.D.* Allahabad: Kitab Mahal.
Hayauddin
1954 "Rohtas." *Pakistan Quarterly* 4, 1:44–47.
Hoag, John D.
1976 *Islamic Architecture*. New York: Henry N. Abrams.
Jahāngīr, Nūr al-Dīn
1968 *Tūzuk-i Jahāngīrī*. Alexander Rogers, trans. Delhi: Munshiram Manoharlal (reprint edition).
Jāīsī, M. Muḥammad
1944 *Padmāvatī*. A. G. Shirreff, trans. Calcutta: Royal Asiatic Society of Bengal.
Jauhar
1970 "Tazkiratu-l Wāki'āt." In *History of India as Told by Its Own Historians*. Vol. 5. H. M. Elliot and John Dowson, eds. and trans. New Delhi: Kumar Brothers (reprint edition).
Kai Kā'ūs
1951 *Qābūs Nāma*. Ruben Levy, trans. New York: E. P. Dutton.
Khwānd Amīr, Ghiyāṣ al-Dīn
1940 *Qānūn-i Humāyūnī*. M. Hidayat, ed. Baini Prasad, trans. Calcutta: Royal Asiatic Society of Bengal.
Kuraishi, M. H.
1931 *List of Ancient Monuments Protected under Act VII of 1904 in the Province of Bihar and Orissa. Archaeological Survey of India*, New Imperial Series. Vol. 51. Calcutta: Government of India, Central Publication Board.
Misra, S. C.
1969 "Sikka and Khutba: A Sher Shahi Experiment." *Medieval India, A Miscellany* 1:39–47.
Naṣīr al-Dīn Ṭūsī
1964 *The Nasirean Ethics*. G. M. Wickens, trans. London: George Allen & Unwin.
Nath, R.
1974 "Chauburj: The Tomb of Babur at Agra." *Islamic Culture* 48:149–58.
1978 *History of Sultanate Architecture*. New Delhi: Abhinav Publications.
Nicholls, W. H.
1906 "Ibrahim Shah's Tomb." In *Annual Progress Report of the Northern Circle of the Archaeological Survey of India, 1905–06*. Lahore: Economic Press.
Ni'mat Allāh
1873 "Tārīkh-i Khān Jahān Lodī." In *History of India as Told by Its Own Historians*. Vol. 5. London: Trubner & Co.
1960 *Tārīkh-i Khān Jahānī wa Makhzan-i Afghānī*. Vol. 1. S. M. Imamuddin, ed. Dacca: Asiatic Society of Pakistan.

Niẓām al-Mulk
1960 *Siyāsat Nāma*. Trans. by Hubert Darke as *The Book of Government or Rules for Kings*. London: Routledge & Kegan Paul.

Qanungo, Kalikaranjan
1921 *Sher Shah*. Calcutta: Kar, Majumder & Co.
1965 *Sher Shah and His Times*. Bombay: Orient Longmans.

Rosenthal, Erwin I. J.
1968 *Political Thought in Medieval Islam*. Cambridge: Cambridge University Press (3rd edition, revised).

Sa'dī
1964 *Gulistān*. Edward Rehatsek, trans. London: George Allen & Unwin.

Sharma, Y. D.
1964 *Delhi and Its Neighbourhood*. New Delhi: Archaeological Survey of India.

Siddiqi, Iqtidar Husain
1966 *Afghan Despotism in India, 1451–1555*. New Delhi: Indian Institute of Islamic Studies.
1971 *History of Sher Shah Sur*. Aligarh: P. C. Dwadash Shreni & Co.
1969 *Some Aspects of Afghan Despotism in India*. Aligarh: Three Men Publication.

Wetzel, Friedrich
1970 *Islamische Grabbauten in Indien aus der Zeit der Soldatenkaiser, 1320–1540*. Osnabrück: Otto Zeller (reprint edition).

Wright, H. Nelson
1974 *The Coinage and Metrology of the Sulṭāns of Delhi*. New Delhi: Oriental Books (reprint edition).

Yazdani, G.
1907 "Narnaul and Its Buildings, Continued." *Journal of the Asiatic Society of Bengal*, n.s. 3:639–44.

5

Eloquence and Authority in Urdu: Poetry, Oratory, and Film

DAVID LELYVELD

Mirza Asadullah K͟hān G͟hālib (1797–1869) claimed for himself a special qualification among Indian poets of Persian and Urdu: his poetic preceptor, or *ustād*, had been a native speaker of Persian from Iran, one of the true "people of the language," the *ahl-i zubān*. According to his disciple and biographer Alṭāf Ḥusain Ḥālī, G͟hālib "turned up his nose" at the linguistic competence of Indian authorities on Persian grammar and diction, such as Dilva'i Singh Q̣ātil: "I do not accept the pronouncement [*qaul*] of Dilva'i Singh, the khatri of Faridabad, and I do not consider anyone worthy of reliance [*istinād*] aside from the *ahl-i zubān*." But G͟hālib's claims were not limited to his dubious exposure to an actual Irani; they were founded on the mastery of a large but finite body of literary texts: "the pronouncements of the *ahl-i zubān* are presented in the *sanad* of their *kalām*," that is, in the backing or certification of their literary work (Ḥālī 1963:29). "Unless I see an expression or a compound in the works of the great classical or good modern poets such as Sā'ib, Kalīm, Asīr or Ḥazīn," he said on another occasion, "I do not use it in prose or verse" (quoted in Bausani 1959:106–7).

Aside from issues of grammatical correctness, idiomatic accuracy, and lexical availability, G͟hālib was addressing himself to the relationship between poetic inspiration and linguistic virtuosity in the subtle and complex poetics and rhetoric of Arabic and Persian. A formidable heritage, at once immensely rich and immensely restrictive, stood between a would-be speaker and the full power of verbal expression. Nor, as Ghālib's comments about Qātil indicated, was long and laborious study sufficient to achieve this mastery. Precise and exacting as the literary language was, it was founded on the living spoken language of a model community, past or present; it was a distillation and codification of that language, not an abstract model of logical perfection.

In the intellectual tradition of Islam to which Ghālib was heir, the initial value or, at least, justification for the sciences of grammar, rhetoric, and poetics was their use in enabling Muslims, removed in time and place from the Prophet and the Revelation, to understand the Qur'ān. "We have revealed the Qur'ān in Arabic so that you may understand" (sura 12, verse 2). It was a mark of God's grace that the final revelation existed in an available spoken language, the language of Muḥammad's listeners in Mecca and Medina. But if the language of the Qur'ān could be understood, its literary qualities could not be imitated; there is a virtuosity of language that could only be God's (sura 10, verses 38–39). The spread of Islam to non-Arabs and the transformation of Arabic as spoken by new populations in new settings required that even initial comprehensibility be assisted by the work of inspired scholars, whose knowledge (*'ilm*) was founded in their understanding of the Qur'ān. Study had to compensate for the loss of natural understanding. There is in all this an ambivalence about language: nostalgia for the lost accessibility of a mother tongue and insistence on painstaking erudition as compensation for this loss. In the fourteenth century, for example, Ibn Khaldūn praised the natural eloquence of the Bedouins insofar as they had been untouched by citified corruptions, and at the same time conceded superior scholarship to non-Arabs, who must work all the harder to overcome the handicap of their origins (Ibn Khaldūn 1967:428–58).

Applied first to the Arabic of the Qur'ān, these ideas about the language of ordinary speech and the language of literature were extrapolated to the fields of poetry and administrative documents and extended from Arabic to other languages, most notably Persian. If the primary basis of language was in speech, writing, too, had a formidable authority as something more than conventional signs for sounds. Letters engraved and embodied cosmic forms, as in numerology (*sīmiyā*); but even in less esoteric ways, in decorative arts or in composing chronograms, for example, letters were manipulated for their own sake, apart from speech. And in many activities in which speech might be prior, the nature of the written language formed what Ibn Khaldūn called the mold or loom, as in the calculation of poetic meter (Ibn Khaldūn 1967:428–58; Pybus 1924).[1] To an Indian of Ghālib's time, the Persian literature to which he deferred was available in written texts. One could give them oral realization by memorizing them and quoting them on appropriate occasions, but it was rare that one had the assistance of some member of the *ahl-i zubān* to help decipher an obscure or cryptic piece of writing.

Starting in the eighteenth century the concept of Urdu as "literate speech" (Bloomfield 1964:391–96) was founded on well-developed attitudes toward Persian. But in the nineteenth century Urdu became increasingly a language for a broad range of public occasions, addressed to a wide and diffuse public audience. Having gained recognition as a language of courtly and religious poetry only in the declining days of Mughal cultural dominance, Urdu was swept into new uses associated with new genres and technologies of communication that were introduced into India under British colonial auspices. Access to the literary language became bound up with access to new social and political roles, and in the process there arose highly articulated controversies about the definition of the language. Ultimately, by the latter half of the nineteenth century, some of these controversies created conditions for a clear bifurcation of literary languages, Hindi and Urdu. But even within the agreed confines of Urdu as a public language there were sharp contrasts of linguistic attitude. In the development of Urdu as a language suitable for public purposes there arose a conflict between the concept of appropriate language as ordinary speech (*rōz-marra bōlchāl*) and the requirements of a refined, literate, pure (*khāliṣ*) Urdu; the former readily available to speaker and audience in a wide and far-flung language community, the latter accessible only to those formally educated in a literary tradition.

One may sketch the historical development of Urdu as a language and as community with the help of a temporal series of some of its more prominent uses since the eighteenth century: first as a language of highly demanding and exclusive lyrical poetry; then, in the nineteenth century, as one suitable for orations and public meetings; and finally in the last fifty years, as a language for popular mass communications. What is significant about this series is its discontinuity, the place of literary Urdu in substantially different contexts from one era to another.

1. I am indebted to Bruce R. Pray for this reference.

The examples offered here may serve to raise the question of the relation of language to moral authority as a matter of historical transformation: who has been authorized to make utterances; what kinds of speech have been appropriate to the exercise of social leadership (Foucault 1976)?

Poetry: From Persian to Urdu

Persian, more than Arabic, was India's link to the wide international Islamic community during the centuries of Muslim political dominance culminating in the Mughal Empire. In 1582 Persian was recognized as the uniform language of administration in the empire, and this seems to have gone hand in hand with an increasingly complex bureaucracy and a greater volume of official paper. But Persian had been important in India both in literature and administration long before that, at least since the early thirteenth century. Only a small part of this prominence could be attributed to the status of Iranis in India, people with Persian as their mother tongue, although there were periods, such as the reigns of Akbar and Jahāngīr, when Iranis were particularly welcome and influential. More often, however, there was within the Muslim ruling class something of a religious and cultural stigma associated with Iranis—religious because they were usually Shīʿa, cultural because they were more often associated with the pen than with the sword. Their literacy did not command the deference due to the Sunni *ʿulamā* as religious authorities. If Iranis were recognized as particularly competent with regard to Persian, this may have secured them patronage and appointments as poets, teachers, and record keepers in the service of others. But India had its own standards of competence in Persian, and they were not confined to Persians.

Persian was taught to the non-Irani literati in India through the example of literary texts, which were memorized and then read before students learned to write, as was the Qur'ān in Arabic. These texts could be learned with little or no comprehension; nevertheless the sounds, meters, and letters of the text would loom large as emblems of a ruling culture. Most students read Saʿdī, but the literary models might be Indians as well, especially as one moved on to learning language appropriate to administrative purposes and social correspondence. Abū al-Faẓl, Chandrabhan Brahman, Madhoram, were read; all were "Hindustanis," and two were Hindus. G̱ẖālib's remarks notwithstanding, the appeal to an authoritative speech community was not considered necessary by most people learning and using Persian; the language was available in an exemplary literary archive. Works of lexicography, grammar, rhetoric, and poetics surrounded this literary corpus, and their authors, like Khān-i Ārzū and Qātil, were widely respected despite the complaints of some. The literary language was sufficient unto itself. And it was this language, or language based on these models, that dominated political communication until the early nineteenth century (Adam 1868:101–5; Chopra 1955:172–73; Khaṭak 1944:36–48).[2]

The texts that recent generations have identified as the earliest examples of an Urdu literary heritage—they usually identify themselves as being in "Hindi"—did not claim the status of literate speech, even though they were set down in writing. "Hindi" was used as an earthy vernacular, mixed in with Persian (as in Amīr Khusrau) for the sake of literary novelty or, more substantially, as the means for reaching a wider popular audience for whom Persian was either inaccessible or less effective and inspiring. "There is nothing the matter with speaking Hindi," wrote Shāh Burhān ud-dīn Janam in sixteenth-century Bijapur, "open your eyes to the meaning in the treasure" (quoted in Eaton 1978:143). Using this kind of language for literary and religious purposes called for some special apology. One might say that making religious truth available to a wide popular audience was in its way reminiscent of the spirit of sura 12, verse 2; Dakhni was used for the Dakhnis in the same way that Arabic was for the Arabs, though of course the former was not the direct word of God. But most of the major writers of this "vernacular" literature, starting with Khwāja Gesudarāz Bandanawāz in fourteenth–fifteenth-century Gulbarga, were accomplished masters of Persian and Arabic and reserved these languages for their more complex and profound work in theology and mysticism. Dakhni was appropriate to simple devotionalism and the basic tenets of the faith, not to the hidden meanings behind them (Eaton 1978:141–44).

The *zubān-i urdū-i mu'allā*, language of the exalted camp, that blossomed forth in eighteenth-century Delhi as a language of courtly love, and, less often, as religious poetry, also existed side by side with Persian. It was often difficult to disentangle the two, as in some of the "mixed" *rekhta* poetry and verses that could be either Urdu or Persian except for the clue of an inflection or a copula. Although a good deal of the earlier Dakhni literature had been written in the genres of Arabic and Persian, notably by Muḥammad Qulī Qutb Shāh, this Delhi poetry fit far more rigorously into the formal Persian matrix of meter, rhyme, diction, and

2. I am indebted to Sajida Alvi for this last reference.

imagery. The first indigenous metalinguistic proscriptions for the language, by Sirāj ud-dīn Khān-i Arzū, were aimed at holding Urdu as closely as possible to the standards of Mughal Persian rhetoric and poetics (Sadiq 1964:70–71).

The use of Urdu in this kind of poetry was an assertion of personal virtuosity and originality within the highly restrictive conventions already established for Persian. Writers could find new possibilities in the spoken language of the court, and the language of everyday life could draw with increasing satisfaction on possibilities developed by the poets. Still, to establish what was correct speech one had to refer back to Persian and sometimes Arabic. Sauda, who confessed to a lack of confidence in his command of Persian, was still able to satirize the language of those outside courtly circles—a Hindu moneylender, for example—for errors of pronunciation and diction based on ignorance of Persian (Sauda 1971:319–22; Garcin de Tassy 1871:76–77).

Eighteenth-century Urdu poets were associated with the Mughal nobility or were nobles themselves, though some of them threw off the vanity of courtly life in favor of mystical poverty. Poetry was, in large measure, a display of craftsmanship, though it might also reveal intimate feelings or religious insights. The poems were initially recited aloud in small gatherings of fellow poets, in a court setting, or perhaps in a *khānaqāh*, the abode of a mystical teacher. Sometimes a manuscript edition would be copied out, each copy different, to be offered as a presentation in a society bound together by symbolic exchanges. In this way, orally or in manuscript, some poets—starting with Vali Deccani in the early part of the century—received economic rewards as patronage from the mighty to whom their presentations were made. Poetry was an offering of personal service to specific persons, or to God.

The poetic career of Mirza Asadullah Khān Ghālib (1797–1869) coincides with a marked transition in the position of the Urdu text as a social object. For most of his lifetime there was a Mughal ruler in Delhi and a Nawab of Awadh; there continued to be a Nizam of Hyderabad and a Nawab of Rampur and numerous other Mughal successors to carry on the system of patronage for literary service. But alongside these continuities there arose with the British a new social space for Urdu utterance, artistic or otherwise, and eventually new concepts of Urdu as a language and how it might be used.

Although Ghālib read newspapers and had much of his work published, he insisted in his poetry on a rigidly conservative standard of correctness in language and form within the *ghazal* tradition. It was a severely restrictive matrix for a restless, creative imagination, but Ghālib asserted his originality in a heroic virtuosity of language and wit in the face of these limitations. His intention was to take on the genre in all its conventionality and force through it his special voice and insight. Bruce Pray has shown that in the hands of the great *ghazal* writers there were rich possibilities for alliteration, assonance, and internal rhyme that could be set in a kind of counterpoint to the line-by-line repetition of one of the stock Perso-Arabic meters. Similarly, the grammar of the sentence could operate in tension with the prosody (Pray 1979:143–67).[3] But it would take a highly educated ear to compose or appreciate such subtleties, even unconsciously. Ghālib's more obvious assertions of originality were in ideas and images, which nonetheless did not depart from the standard themes of the poetic tradition.

Ghālib's deference to the most exacting standards of Persian poetry may be taken as a protest against a changing, upstart world; it was also a challenge to his contemporaries in a competition of wit under the severest handicaps: "this is an open invitation to subtle-minded friends."[4]

Rules in classical literature, like etiquette in a courtly milieu, restrict communication to a defined body of initiates. Such formal requirements make style itself an allusion to the past, which can be reinforced by thematic and imagistic references. The literary tradition as a whole serves as a metaphor of order, continuity, and control. But in Ghālib's time such an allusion conveyed a heavy irony, coming from an Indian of Turani military background in a world in which Persian courtly culture no longer represented political and economic dominance. A poet had to find patrons and an audience in an age when the Persianized milieu was rarely replenished by immigrants from a cosmopolitan Islamic civilization. Ghālib often "deliberately cultivated a difficult style to rise above the rank and file of poets," says Muhammad Sadiq, "and when people failed to respond to his style, he was angry at them for not doing him justice" (Sadiq 1964:180). But Ghālib was writing the way he believed a poet should write, as an act of defiance against his environment, "as if in a cage a captive bird still gathered twigs for its nest."[5]

For Ghālib, virtuosity with language is the basis of his whole poetic enterprise; the act of creation itself, mind as prior to object, is the theme

3. One might add that the contrast between Persian and Hindi phonemes and constructions (*iẓāfat* [the joining of two nouns in a genitive construction] vs. post-position, for example) can serve a similar dramatic effect.

4. "Salā'ē 'ām hai yārān-i nuktahdān kē liyē."

5. "Miṣāl yeh mirī kōshish kī hai, ki murgh-i asīr/karē qafas meṅ farāham khas āshīyān kē liyē."

that underlies his most striking work. Love, mysticism, irony, bravado, religious humility, hedonism—these are all conventional poses into which he pours his skill as a poetic craftsman. The fact that G͟hālib is treating a subject makes that subject important: "the recital of her spriteliness, and what is more in *my* description. . . ."[6] It is the poet's power with words that sets the world in motion, but the act of poetic perception and creation continues to hold the world at bay.

Oratory and Public Leadership

The history of oratory in Islamic civilization is obscure, partly because of its transitory character. For the pre-Islamic Arabs the orator (*k͟hāṭib*) was, like the poet (*shā'ir*), an important public role, and some of this tradition was adapted by Islam in the institution of the *k͟huṭba* set in the context of congregational prayers. Treatises on rhetoric address themselves to public speaking, and there are instances of preaching (*w'āẓ*), disputation (*munāẓarat*), and extended quotations in the chronicles. Religious teachers like Gesudarāz are said to have preached the message of Islam in Urdu, but the form and setting of such speeches have not been adequately recorded. In India, it seems, the *k͟huṭba* was a set-piece recitation in Arabic, but the institution of preaching was rare (Schaade 1960; Wensinck 1979; on Gesudarāz, see Schimmel 1975:133).

In the nineteenth century, speaking in extended discursive utterances before freely assembled public audiences became a significant means of establishing social loyalties and ideological commitment. The most prominent and perhaps earliest examples of Urdu oratory in the early part of the century are associated with the Ṭarīqa-i Muḥammadiyya under the leadership of Sayyid Aḥmad Barelvī and Shāh Muḥammad Ismā'il, who toured north India extensively in the two decades before they died in battle fighting a "holy war" (*jihād*) against the Sikhs in 1831. Sayyid Aḥmad Barelvī stood forth as the *pīr* of a new line (*silsila*) that combined the major Sufi lines, all in the interest of overriding what he considered corruptions of the religious beliefs and practices of Muslims since the time of the Prophet. His disciple, Muḥammad Ismā'il, a grandson of Shāh Walīullāh, became famous as a writer and orator on behalf of the cause of a purified Islam. Like the Dakhni Sufis of earlier times, the leaders of the movement attempted to put forth the tenets of Islam "very clearly in the Hindi language so that everyone should

6. "Ẕikr us parivaish kā aur phīr bayān apnā."

benefit." Again the use of a simple spoken language called for apologies: "It is hoped that the learned will not object to imperfections with the Hindi language" (quoted in Pearson 1979:139). Like others in the line of Shāh Walīullāh, the enterprise involved translation from the Qur'ān and, eventually, use of the printing press.

The opening up of Indian territory under East India Company rule to Protestant missionaries after 1813 had already led to public preaching in the marketplace, counter-preaching by Muslims, and formal disputations (Pearson 1979:139; Aḥmad K͟hān 1958:44). A different form of public meeting, also on a European model, developed at the same time in Calcutta, where it was associated with organizations like the Brāhmo Samāj and the Hindu School Book Society. Such organizations had formal deliberative procedures, with a presiding officer, a speaker's platform, and an etiquette of audience responses.

Sayyid Aḥmad K͟hān (1817–98) was witness and heir to these developments, as he was to the traditions of lyrical poetry of G͟hālib and the learned dialectics of Shāh Walīullāh. The first recorded public address by Sayyid Aḥmad was an Urdu prayer (*munājāt*) read before some fifteen thousand people who overflowed a Moradabad mosque in July 1859 to offer thanks for the end of the "Mutiny" and to praise Queen Victoria, "our Queen, the Empress of the World" (Ḥālī 1965:101–2; Aḥmad K͟hān n.d.:157–60). In 1863 Sayyid Aḥmad journeyed to Calcutta and addressed a gathering at the home of Maulawi 'Abdul Laṯīf, founder of the Anjūman-i Islām, an organization modeled on British and Bengali prototypes. Sayyid Aḥmad's address on that occasion was in Persian and was more a formal essay than an oration, frequently quoting Persian couplets to carry its message: Muslims should be prepared to learn European languages and sciences (Aḥmad K͟hān 1963:285–96). The following year in Ghazipur was the real beginning of Sayyid Aḥmad's career as a public speaker, marking the occasions of the founding of the Ghazipur school (*madrasa*) and the Scientific Society, but here too the speeches seem to have been essays read aloud. What is significant here is the full adoption of the public meeting format: a series of speakers on a platform, the audience in chairs.

In later years, in auditoriums, tents, railway stations, and at banquets, Sayyid Aḥmad was to travel throughout north India, establishing his role as a great public leader through the device of the public oration. These speeches, generally reported in newspapers and published in pamphlets, became increasingly a genre unto themselves, called *Ispīchas o laikcharz* (Speeches and lectures). His trip to Britain in 1869–70 exposed him to new settings and styles, which he brought back with him to India. He could now participate extemporaneously in lengthy deliberative procedures, speaking forcefully and colorfully. His formal speeches became more intimate and often emotional, punctuated with "Ai dōstō!" "Ai bhāīyō!" or, in Persian, "Baradarān-i man!"—"O, friends!" "O brothers!" "My brothers!" The language became looser, with long, easygoing sentence constructions and frequent use of Persian and Arabic words inflected as Hindi. There continued to be some poetic quotations, but more often Sayyid Aḥmad avoided calling attention to linguistic and literary self-display. The language was intentionally plain, with few images, rhetorical figures, or difficult words. It was a language deliberately intended for a wide, popular audience; the impression given was that these were things that one could say oneself. The mark of authority was the speaker's simplicity and apparent sincerity.

Starting in 1886, the gatherings of the Muhammadan Educational Conference at the end of each year brought hundreds of people together for several days of speeches, lectures, resolutions, and poems. The poems, notably by Alṭāf Ḥusain Ḥālī, claimed to be written in everyday speech (*rōz-marra bōlchāl*) and extended the subject matter of poetry to themes of current interest like education and politics (Ḥālī 1953:95, 106, 115; Lelyveld 1978:300–302). Some of the speakers, Nawāb Muḥsin ul-Mulk and "Deputy" Naẕīr Aḥmad, for example, mixed the plain style of Sayyid Aḥmad K͟hān with more ambitious displays of learned quotations in Persian and Arabic and rhetorical complexity, but these were always embedded in straightforward, if lengthy, discourses. The very fact that there was an array of speakers and that the deliberations culminated in passing resolutions, enacted the themes of participation and solidarity which were the overall purposes of the gathering. Access to such an occasion was a matter of traveling to the place of meeting and paying a subscription. Afterward one could purchase a printed copy of the proceedings.

But for all this seeming availability of access to public speech, one may wonder as one reads the texts how far they really were from the standards of "literate speech." They possessed neither the conciseness of poetry nor the complexity of literary Persian prose (*inshā*) but had, at least, the comfortable informality of the learned and fluent—a style established several decades earlier with the publication of G͟hālib's "conversational" letters. It is true that in the twentieth century public leaders have been allowed to hold forth in a less literate language (Gandhi, Nehru, Jinnah, and Bhutto are examples), but generally they had established their linguistic competence in English, in place of Persian. In contrast to English public-speaking patterns, it is the convention in contemporary Urdu speaking to start with a soft, hesitant voice, searching for words, a mark of humility and intimacy, a kind of *alāp*, or musical prelude, before the tempo of eloquence takes over and sweeps all before it. The quiet, conversational beginning is a kind of entrapment; it prevents the listener from asking by what authority does this person speak. Such a question would be inhospitable and ungrateful.

Film Speech: Who Is Talking?

In the 1930s two new media of communication, radio and the talkie film, introduced new sorts of public speech to India. In both cases some single version of Hindi-Urdu-Hindustani was assumed to be the all-India language (aside from English), and the question arose which version was legitimate for reaching an audience potentially far larger and more widespread than any ever before assembled. For All-India Radio, founded on the model of the BBC, linguistic decisions were made by political and bureaucratic processes: influencing the language of radio was a matter of influencing government policy and controlling the channels of recruitment. In fact, during the pre-independence period the "Hindustani" of the radio was largely determined by its director-general, Aḥmad Shāh Bu<u>kh</u>ārī Paṭras, according to standards of literary Urdu, of which he was a master (Bu<u>kh</u>ārī 1966).

In film, however, despite all sorts of government regulation regarding other matters, linguistic decisions were a matter of market calculation by fairly large-scale industrial enterprises organized on the Hollywood pattern. Although the centers of film production were outside areas identified with Hindi-Urdu, it was assumed that Hindi/Urdu/Hindustani, variously defined, was the only possible language for the entire country, not so much because of the size of the Hindi-Urdu region itself, however loosely conceived, but because this was the only language that could be disseminated outside its home region. The only alternative, occasionally attempted, was English, but English was not widely enough known and was hard to identify with most Indian subjects (Barnouw and Krishnaswamy 1980:59–64).

Cinema, like drama, is in the Aristotelian sense an art of imitation; one is meant to believe that what one is witnessing is something other than itself. The audience is watching and listening to a conversation, for example, not seeing moving lights and shadows across a bedsheet and hearing sounds reverberate in a box. There is some precedent for this in reading, including reading make-believe conversations (as in the satires of Sauda), but in cinema there is an even more powerful illusion of closeness. We know that this is a manufactured product which is shown again and again, even simultaneously in different places, and that we are not, as it seems, experiencing a unique event. Cinema is pieced together from scraps of film and sound recording, disparate moments of photographing, recording, and editing carried out by different people. The person who seems to be there talking is just part of the process, an instrument of someone else's text, direction, and, in the case of playback singing, voice. Yet the language acquires a special power, a language of people and situations, times and places one would generally have little opportunity to experience. What a given cinema chooses to portray can help define for a community the kinds of people, situations, and languages that exist in the world, the limits of what is available (Altman 1980:67–79).

But what is "available" in cinema is a matter of complex financial arrangements, organization of production, distribution of tasks, and marketing of the product. In India it has been assumed that to make a film at all required a large investment and the search for a mass audience. Especially for Hindi-Urdu films, as opposed to those in "regional" languages, a large part of such an audience had a particularly limited experience and comprehension of the language. A process of simplification, neutralization, and lack of specificity served to limit the range of events that could be imitated.

Yet in some cases the limitation of the language, the narrowing of the available code, could be reminiscent of the standards of the literary language, not as an imitation at all but as an ideal standard of perfection, available to the learned. Occasionally there have been films with such pretensions, in which an exhibition of erudition and virtuosity in language could be appreciated by a fairly large audience even if the details (for example, the meaning of the words) were incomprehensible. In many film songs, as in popular public poetry recitations, the aura of Persianized Urdu is of more importance than the merely denotative meaning. One such genre of film, from time to time quite popular, has been the so-called "Muslim Social," a term that covers both historical subjects and contemporary ones. These have been presented in a clearly identifiable literary Urdu, and they have tended to emphasize lengthy speechmaking as well as the singing of *ghazal*s.

Some of the earliest sound films were transcriptions of the Urdu theater in the tradition of Aghā Hashr Kashmīrī and influenced in a way by Shakespeare (Shaikh Zubair). The dialogue was full of rhyme and other rhetorical and poetic devices. Within a few years, however, this high-flown language was superseded by attempts to reproduce the simplest possible everyday Hindustani. Many actors still required a *munshī* (language tutor), one of the services provided by the dialogue and lyric writers (*ahl-i zubān*) from north Indian centers of Urdu culture, often recruited to adapt the text of a Bengali or Marathi screenplay (Chaudhuri 1956:131, 139).

Pukār ("The Outcry") (1939), directed by Sohrab Modi with dialogue by Kamal Amrohi, was an attempt to make a film in exemplary literary Urdu. Set in the court of Jahāngīr, the film portrays elaborate ceremony, unfamiliar Persian titles and expressions, great dramatic orations, and rapid repartee. The songs are *ghazals*, sung very slowly in static staging. *E'lān* ("The Declaration") (1947), directed by Mahboob with dialogue and song lyrics by Zia Sarhady, was set in a modern urban Muslim environment; the characters recited couplets and used mildly marked Persian and Arabic constructions. The film, on the eve of Partition, was a clear statement of Muslim separateness, even if a number of the leading stars were Hindu. It was not intended for a non-Muslim audience. The film portrays contemporary Muslims in everyday domestic situations talking like members of the Mughal court. The use at that time of such courtly Urdu represented cultural aspiration and self-assertion, even if it probably was beyond the reach of a good part of the audience. *Rōz-marra bōlchāl* (everyday speech) was thus portrayed as *khāliṣ* (pure) Urdu. *Pukār* had made a point of putting some of its most high-flown Urdu in the mouths of Rajput characters. In the context of the other films of the era, *E'lān*, a plea for Muslim education, identified literate speech entirely with Muslims. The Muslim community had become the *ahl-i zubān*.[7]

The Denial of Diglossia

The development of Urdu since the eighteenth century as a literary language and the diffusion of the literate speech of the Delhi court to a wide population as a standardized speech form stands in contrast to the sharp and recognized distinction between the language of writing and

7. I am indebted to Mr. P. K. Nair of the Indian National Film Archives for allowing me to study these films while in Pune on a research grant from the American Institute of Indian Studies in 1979.

the language of speech so familiar in other Indian and Islamic contexts, past and present (Ferguson 1964:429–39). Since the middle of the nineteenth century, authority has increasingly purported to rest on persuasion, and the ideal of ordinary speech presents itself as a means to make discussion, persuasion, and wide participation possible. The roots of Urdu in a vernacular distinct from literary Persian justified its claim to be in some sense a popular language. Raising the status of Urdu to a language of prestige associated with the courtly Persian of the Mughals satisfied the desire to make it suitable for all occasions. Whether that prestige could actually be diffused through a large population was another matter, involving the limits of educational opportunity and the competition of other literary standards rooted in other literary traditions, in particular English and Sanskritized Hindi. The concept of literate speech as the only legitimate vernacular, in fact, has served to maintain the distance between the educated (if not learned) and those not qualified to speak for lack of knowledge. Speaking in public or, now, creating public speech for mass distribution has become increasingly bound up with the direct exercise of political leadership. Access to the legitimate language of public speech is an important part of access to authority, and the existence of competing styles of that speech helps mark off channels of allegiance.

The public for literate Urdu, it was once hoped by some, would be India as a whole. Both "Hindi," in the pre-nineteenth-century sense of vernacular speech of India, and "Urdu," the spoken language of the Mughal court, cut across religious boundaries. By the time of Partition, Urdu, marked as Muslim, could be claimed as the appropriate language for what had come to be defined as "the Muslim community." In post-Partition India, the status of Urdu has been a major concern of those demanding protection for Muslim minority rights. In Pakistan, on the other hand, Urdu has no special "Muslim" status as against other languages of the country, and the geographic roots of its *ahl-i zubān* fall outside the national borders. In such shifting social and political constellations, mastery of literate Urdu has often been the mark of isolation as much as of public leadership.

References

Adam, William
1868 *Report of Vernacular Education in Bengal and Behar*. J. Long, ed. Calcutta: Home Secretariat Press.

Aḥmad Khān, Sayyid
1958 *Asbāb-i Baghhāwat-i Hind.* Aligarh: University Publishers, Muslim University.
1963 "Targhīb-i Ta'alīm Angrezi." In *Maqālāt-i Sir Sayyid.* Vol. 12. Muḥammad Ismā'īl Panīpati, ed. Pp. 285–96.
n.d. "Sir Sayyid's Prayer for Peace at Moradabad." In *Sir Sayyid Ahmad Khan's History of the Bijnore Rebellion.* Hafeez Malik and Morris Dembo, trans. East Lansing: Asian Studies Center, Michigan State University, pp. 157–60.
Altman, Rick
1980 "Moving Lips: Cinema as Ventriloquism." *Yale French Studies* 60:67–79.
Barnouw, Erik, and S. Krishnaswamy
1980 *Indian Film.* New York: Oxford University Press.
Bausani, A.
1959 "The Position of Ġalib (1796–1869) in the History of Urdu and Indo-Persian Poetry." *Der Islam* 34:99–127.
Bloomfield, Leonard
1964 "Literate and Illiterate Speech." In *Language in Culture and Society.* Dell Hymes, ed. New York: Harper & Row, pp. 391–96.
Bukhārī, Zulfiqār 'Alī
1966 *Sarguzasht.* Karachi: Ma'arif.
Chaudhuri, R. S.
1956 "Teething Troubles of the Talkie." In *Indian Talkie, 1931–56.* Bombay: Film Federation of India.
Chopra, Pran Nath
1955 *Some Aspects of Society and Culture during the Mughal Age (1526–1707).* Agra: Shiva Lal Agarwala.
Eaton, Richard
1978 *Sufis of Bijapur.* Princeton: Princeton University Press.
Ferguson, Charles A.
1964 "Diglossia." In *Language in Culture and Society.* Dell Hymes, ed. New York: Harper & Row, pp. 429–39.
Foucault, Michel
1976 "The Discourse on Language." In *The Archaeology of Knowledge and the Discourse on Language.* New York: Harper Colophon Books.
Garcin de Tassy, J. H.
1871 *Histoire de la Littérature Hindouie et Hindoustanie.* Vol. 3. Paris: Adolphe Labitte (2nd edition).
Ḥālī, Alṭāf Ḥusain
1953 *Muqaddimah-i Sh'er o Shā'irī.* Delhi: 'Ilmī Kitāb Khāna.
1963 *Yādgār-i Ghālib.* Lahore: Majlis-i Taraqqī-i Adab.
1965 *Ḥayāt-i Javīd.* Lahore: Majlis-i Taraqqī-i Adab.
Ibn Khaldūn
1967 *The Muqaddimah.* Franz Rosenthal, trans. Abridged by N. J. Darwood. London: Routledge & Kegan Paul in association with Secker & Warburg.
Khaṭak, Sarfarāz Khān
1944 *Shaikh Muḥammad 'Alī Ḥazīn: His Life, Times, and Works.* Lahore: Sh. Muhammad Ashraf.

Lelyveld, David
1978 *Aligarh's First Generation.* Princeton: Princeton University Press.

Pearson, Harlan O.
1979 "Islamic Reform and Revival in the Nineteenth Century: the 'Tariqah-i Muhammadiyya.' " Ph.D. dissertation, Duke University.

Pray, Bruce R.
1979 "A Re-examination of Structure and Continuity in the Urdu Ghazal." In *Studies in the Urdu Ghazal and Prose Fiction.* M. U. Memon, ed. Madison: South Asian Studies, University of Wisconsin.

Pybus, G. D.
1924 *A Textbook of Urdu Prosody and Rhetoric.* Lahore: Rama Krishna & Sons.

Sadiq, Muhammad
1964 *A History of Urdu Literature.* London: Oxford University Press.

Sauda, Mirza Muhammad Rafi'
1971 "Masnavī hasthtum dar hajv Fidvī." In *Kulliyāt-i Sauda.* Vol. 1. Amrit Lal Ishrat, ed. Allahabad: Ram Narayan-Beni Madhav.

Schaade, A.
1960 "Balāghā." Revised by G. E. von Grunebaum. In *The Encyclopaedia of Islam.* Vol. 1. Leiden: E. J. Brill (new edition), pp. 981–83.

Schimmel, Annemarie
1975 *Classical Urdu Literature from the Beginning to Iqbal.* Wiesbaden: Harrasowitz.

Wensinck, A. J.
1979 "Khutba." In *The Encyclopaedia of Islam.* Vol. 5. Leiden: E. J. Brill, pp. 74–75.

6

Conflict and Contradictions in Bengali Islam: Problems of Change and Adjustment

RAFIUDDIN AHMED

Religious revivalism has emerged as one of the dominant themes of Indo-Muslim historiography in recent times. The upsurge in religious spirit that found expression in the rise of a number of remarkable religious reform movements in Indian Islam in the nineteenth century (see Ahmad Khan 1965; Q. Ahmad 1966; Kaviraj 1982) is often considered crucial to the growth of Muslim self-consciousness in the Subcontinent. This paper examines the process by which the movement for religious revivalism progressed among the Muslims of rural Bengal.[1] It was a process which drew together a variety of groups not always in agreement, including fundamentalist preachers in the countryside, reformist *'ulamā*, and—eventually—even secular nationalists from the cities. It was also a process which helped to create a new tract literature (known as Musalmani *pūthi*), written in a mixed language (Musalmani Bangla) in order to express its reform message with minimum reference to local Bengali culture. At the same time, a new format for debate—the public meeting, or *baḥaṣ̤*—was developed. With these innovations came a new pattern of self-consciously Islamic culture, a new pattern that had to relate, however uneasily, to pre-existing local culture. Tension between reformism and Bengali culture provides the basic theme of our discussion.

Bengal, particularly the low-lying districts of eastern and southeastern

1. Bengal in this study refers to the Bengali-speaking districts comprising the present Bangladesh and the state of West Bengal in India.

Bengal where Islam found most of its adherents, has been a peasant society for the whole of her recorded history; agriculture, including the attendant occupations—e.g., fishing, woodcutting, boating, etc.—has provided the foundations of the region's distinctive culture. The rice cultivator, the woodcutter, the boatman, the fisherman, and all others living in this part of the Gangetic delta found themselves pitted against a nature rich but unpredictable and unkind. Their desire to tame the cruelties of nature distinctly affected and shaped their visions of religion and culture. Folk beliefs reflected these values and hence could not be instantly eliminated by the introduction of Islam. As in many other Muslim societies (see Geertz 1971; Trimingham 1949), Islam in Bengal thus has taken many forms and has assimilated values and symbols not always in conformity with Qur'ānic ideals and precepts. The cultural idioms of Islam underwent rapid transformations here, giving birth to a set of popular beliefs and practices which in essence represented the popular culture of rural Bengal rooted in the pre-Islamic past.

Historical studies of blame for these transformations in the practice of Islam in the Subcontinent have contributed to the frequent ignoring of the basic fact that there existed in India in premodern times not one but several regional Islamic cultures; instead, the focus has been placed on the classical civilization that flourished under Muslim rulers in the upper Gangetic valley. Despite assumptions of historians and reformers alike, it is equally questionable if a "pristine, pure, Islamic order" ever existed in India. On the contrary, it may even be said that Islamization of the average Indian Muslim only *began* in the nineteenth century with the rise of the revivalist movements. Bengali Islam stands as a case pre-eminent.

Throughout history, the *'ulamā* have consistently, if not always successfully, focused attention on the urgent need of the community to conform to the orthodox way of life as they interpreted it, insisting upon a literal application of the Qur'ān and *sunnat*, and rejecting all compromises with local custom. Although pressure for Islamization mounted progressively in the nineteenth century, this did not succeed in establishing a universal, well-integrated system of ritual and belief. Indeed, this has not happened anywhere in the Islamic world: reform and Islamization do not inevitably result in the spread of orthodox beliefs and practices at the cost of the traditional ones. It is with this problem, as it was played out in rural Bengal, that we are chiefly concerned.

This essay discusses the rural context in Bengal in which several religious reform movements occurred. Central to these movements was the participants' assumption that the political, social, and economic disaster that had overtaken the Muslims was the outcome of their religious degeneration (A. Mallick 1961:26; Mujeeb 1967:22–23; Q. Ahmad 1966:4ff). Revivalist efforts were thus directed toward rediscovering the past, asserting the present, and assuring the future of the Indian Muslims. Yet historical Islam in the Subcontinent does not lend support to such assumptions. Unquestionably, revivalism and reform contributed in a large measure to the growth of a new pattern of Islamic culture, but the reformist theory of disaster and degeneration is debatable. This essay suggests an interpretation of the impact and significance of reform and revivalism that is different from the interpretation of participants themselves.

Thus the present study leads to an understanding of the problems of cultural adjustment in twentieth-century Bengali Islam. It begins by examining the social and cultural bases of Islam in Bengal in the premodern period, and then compares changes occurring in more recent times, when the impact of the West was keenly felt. It necessarily pays special attention to the historical background of developments in the nineteenth and early twentieth centuries, and to the pattern of change and adjustment taking place in rural society. Finally, it attempts a brief review of the consequences of these crosscurrents on Bengali Muslim society as a whole. The implications for contemporary Bangladesh will be inescapable.

In the course of this analysis we draw heavily on a source often passed over by scholars, a source known as *pūthi* literature. "*Pūthi*" or "*pūnthi*" in Bengali may literally mean a "book" or a "manuscript" (see A. Sharif 1968:112–13), but the term has generally come to denote a particular literature in that language composed in verse. From the middle of the sixteenth century this new trend of poetical compositions grew up in Bengal in a mixed Bengali, incorporating dozens of Persian and Hindustani terms, authored by men who lived close to the poorer sections of the society. The early compositions were by both Hindu and Muslim authors, and they dealt with a variety of subjects, including religious questions. Again, many of these were mere tales of pre-Muslim Persia and of early Islam and were not necessarily Islamic in character (Anisuzzaman 1964:15–16; Chatterji 1926:211). By the mid-nineteenth century, however, the *pūthi* became a concern of the semiliterate Muslims, while the modern educated among them took to the modern chaste language evolved by the *puṇḍit*s of Fort William. The Islamic reform movements of the period, in their drive to educate the masses in the basic principles of their faith, relied heavily on this literature and became instrumental in infusing a new life into it; it became a vehicle for transmitting to the Bengali-speaking rural masses both stories relating to the Islamic cultural heritage and otherwise inaccessible manuals of religious instruction. At the same time, the traditionalist *mullā*s and *pīr*s, who had reacted sharply to reformist propaganda against many of their age-old customs and practices, particularly those associated with the cult of the *pīr* and the privileges of the *mullā*, found it convenient to take recourse to the same kind of literature in presenting their ideas to the public. Although both the reformists and the traditionalists had strong reservations about the use of Bengali for religious purposes, they had no option in this case. There were others who wrote purely for entertainment and concentrated on folk tales and fictitious stories relating to early Islam.

We are particularly concerned here with the first two categories of literature, representing the reformist and the traditionalist formulations. The *pūthi* at times became a vehicle for polemics against each other, but the authors of both the viewpoints before long focused on what they saw as the basic problems of the society and concentrated more and more on the religious education of the masses, giving full attention in their *pūthi*s to existing vices: the evils of local culture and the deviations of the masses from God's way. They stressed the urgent need for making Muslims into "good Muslims." These *pūthi*s, in effect, became a part of the movement for reform and Islamization in the later nineteenth century. Thus, the fundamentalist concept of a rigid, monotheistic Islam found explicit expression in this literature. Although the traditionalist viewpoints differed from those of the reformists, the former clinging to their justification of the cult of *pīr*s, et cetera, the emphasis on Islamization was similar in the compositions of both groups of preachers during the period. The distinction between a Muslim and a Hindu, between "Islamic culture" and "local culture," was thus usually stressed, and the public was constantly reminded of their separate identity as Muslims. This was in marked contrast to the *pūthi*s of the medieval period, which were generally marked by a spirit of accommodation and compromise with the local culture.

Although often intended for the edification of the masses, the Musalmani *pūthi*s offer much more than mere discussions of religious issues. Indeed, they reflect the rural scene with rare authenticity. The authors, either *pīr*s or their disciples, reformist preachers or *mullā*s, were, in most cases, part of the rural hierarchy themselves and, in many instances, depended on the support—financial and otherwise—of their wellwishers in getting these works published by the cheap printing presses of Calcutta and the *mufuṣṣal* (division) towns. Popular enthusiasm for *pūthi* can be gauged from the lists of donors and wellwishers, appended to many such works, who helped in their publication (Hesab al-Dīn 1876:36; Abd al-Karim 1903:appendix; Rahman 1872:1). The number of *pūthi*s published in the later nineteenth century is countless, and their pages reflect the uneasy state of the society, as well as the urge among the Muslims for an Islamic identity—and the inevitable conflict which it occasioned with local traditions.

Muslims of Bengal

We begin with a very basic question: who are the Bengali Muslims? It is not enough to say that anyone living in Bengal and calling himself a Muslim is a Bengali Muslim. Indeed, much of the problem in conceptualizing South Asian Islam stems from such definitions, as they tend to categorize Muslims as a monolithic cultural unit. To do so not only ignores the local variations of Islamic culture and the dynamics of inherited attitudes of the Muslims in different regions but has also led to a misrepresentation of the historical traditions of various regional cultures and social groups. A proper understanding of Bengali Muslim culture thus requires that we try to understand the social character of the Muslim population in the area, as we assess the trends in social and cultural ethos of the various groups who together formed the community.

It is a curious fact of history that Bengal, long regarded as the backwoods of Indian Islam, contained within its borders the largest concentration of Muslims in South Asia. Although figures for the premodern period are not available, it does not seem likely that the phenomenal numbers enumerated in the first nineteenth-century census were caused by a sudden growth in the Muslim population. In all probability, it was by a gradual process of conversion and immigration that the number of Muslims rose in Bengal until it reached the 1872 figure of more than seventeen million, or nearly one-third of all Indian Muslims (*Census of Bengal* 1872:xxxii–xxxiii). In some of the most populous districts in eastern, southeastern, and northern Bengal—roughly the area of present-day Bangladesh—they comprised upwards of 70 percent of the total population (*Census of India* 1901, vol. 6, pt. 1:156). A plausible explanation for the presence of such a massive

Muslim population, in an area far removed from the centers of Imperial power, is the possibility of large-scale conversions of indigenous tribes who probably had never been fully Hinduized, either professing a localized form of Buddhism or adhering to the animistic rituals and beliefs of their ancestors. A vigorous and highly successful propaganda campaign in the days of the pre-Mughal sultans (1338–1539) may have been largely responsible for the conversion of the local inhabitants. Under the protection of the Muslim rulers, but not necessarily with their support or approval, the Muslim missionaries, more often the pantheistic Sufis, went about the countryside preaching the gospel of Islam, and they were eminently successful.[2]

But while the number of people labeled "Muslim" increased dramatically, their spiritual orientation did not demonstrate the same degree of change. As Tarafdar puts it, "By virtue of their being converted to Islam, they were called Muslims; but in reality, they did not differ much from their Hindu brethren" (Tarafdar 1965:318). The great majority of them lived in rural areas. Even in the nineteenth century the Bengali Muslims remained principally country-dwellers: not more than 3 or 4 percent of them in Bengal proper lived in towns. In some of the eastern districts, the rural population was composed almost entirely of Muslims, with the exception of some "helot classes and a kind of dominant class of high caste Hindus" (*Report on the Administration of Bengal 1871–72* 1873:103; also Seal 1971:301).

It was thus no mere coincidence that the vast majority of the Bengali Muslims supported themselves economically by "husbandry and by the provision of economic goods and services for others" (*Census of Bengal* 1881, vol. 3:768–813, table 27). They lived under the same conditions as did the Hindus of the same social classes and shared views on life which no scripture could alter. Their connections with the religion which they adopted were both distant and ideological, but their links to the local conditions into which they were born and brought up were always direct, helping to shape their ideas and attitudes. The local syncretic beliefs and practices, predating the advent of Islam in the region, thus formed part of the popular culture in Bengali Islam from the very beginning.

The average member of the Muslim community of Bengal thus did not form part of the "ruling nation," nor did he participate in the cultural traditions brought in by Muslim immigrants. In Bengal proper,

2. For an illuminating discussion of conversions, see A. Momin Chowdhury (1983); also Titus (1930:40–49, 51–53).

the proportion of immigrants to local converts was definitely insignificant, and not many of them, Hunter's rhetoric notwithstanding,[3] belonged to the upper strata of the society. The racial purity of most was in any case lost by centuries of intermarriage and concubinage.

Those who claimed foreign ancestry and belonged to the cultural traditions of the Mughals formed a distinct social entity. From the early Muslim period, the immigrants—who included Turks, Persians, north Indians, Afghans, and a few Arabs—considered themselves different from, and in status superior to, the converted Muslims. They harbored strong prejudices against the "natives" and maintained a conscious distance from the latter. The social and cultural influences coming from outside Bengal remained restricted mostly to the town-dwelling *ashraf* (well-born), leaving the *ātrāp* (the lowly born) in the same situation that they had been in prior to their conversion. Perhaps one reason prompting many to change faith was the desire for an elevated status, but such elevation often proved impossible to achieve. Khondkar Fuzli Rubbee, a *sharīf* (well-born) stalwart, dismissing the idea that conversion helped in social mobility, wrote in the late nineteenth century that the "social position of a Muslim convert exactly corresponds to the station he held previous to his conversion" (Rubbee 1968:26). As a matter of fact, most such converts to Islam continued to live in their ancestral villages, in the midst of those very people whose faith they had previously shared, doing the same kind of job they had done formerly. Thus, although technically they had changed allegiance to a new faith, this change little affected their normal way of life.

Even in the nineteenth century, the cultural ethos of the upper classes and the masses remained quite distinct. In dress, manners, and social appellations, they differed widely from each other. While the basis of culture of the former was Perso-Arab in inspiration, the latter was born as a Bengali. While the former had names and modes of address similar to those current in the north Indian seats of Mughal culture, the latter—particularly those at the poorer levels of society—had a tendency to retain local names and appellations, such as Mondol, Pramanik, Sarker, which the orthodox Islamists considered un-Islamic.

The cultural dichotomy in Bengali Islam was thus part of its own heritage. Islam could not do much to cement the bond between these two layers of the society, nor did it succeed in giving form and substance in Bengal to an integrated Islamic community. Maulawi Abdul Wali,

3. W. W. Hunter spoke of the "remains of a once powerful and grasping Musalman aristocracy" in Bengal in eloquent terms (Hunter 1872:155).

himself a *sharīf*, gave an interesting picture of the situation in 1904, remarking:

> If any ancient culture and civilization are to be sought among the Musalmans, they should certainly be sought among the members of this class [the *ashraf*]. The other classes may become very prosperous, but such higher qualities as uprightness, independence, honesty and implicit reliance on God [Islam] can hardly be expected from them, and must be sought among the members of the genuine Arab families. . . . no Ashraf Muhammadan of India cares what the majority of the Muslims are called. To them they are wine venders, weavers, etc., with all their pretensions. Some of the writers go so far as to say that they are not truly Musalmans, but for political and other reasons it is well that they should be called Muslims. (Wali 1904:98–103)

Thus it was not material conditions alone that created conflict in Bengali Muslim society: a contradiction between the core values respectively of the *ashraf* culture and the *ātrāp* way of life were real. There was apparently little or no communication between the inheritors of the two cultures although, at the same time, we hardly notice any sign of tension between them. Most *ātrāp* Muslims, including the village *mullā*, who for all practical purposes belonged to the *ātrāp* category but would deny that, looked upon the *ashraf* as their social superiors and never questioned their claims to represent the "true" Islamic heritage. However, a number of reformist *pūthi*s of the later nineteenth century expressed strong resentment against the "un-Islamic conduct" of the *ashraf* and challenged the latter's claims to social superiority (Samir al-Din 1868:87; also Latīf n.d.:3). Despite such challenges and resentments, the *ashraf* continued to enjoy superior social status, and the gap between the aristocrat and the plebeian continued to remain as wide as before until about the middle of the present century.

Language and Bengali Islam

The cultural problem in Bengali Islam was reinforced by the absence of a language for communication between the two major cultural groups described above. The language of the average Bengali Muslim was Bengali, shaped by associations with that indigenous culture abhorred by the *ashraf*. Arabic, Persian, and lately Urdu, were proper Islamic languages: this was a view shared by the *'ulamā* and the village *mullā*, even though the latter had little knowledge of these languages (Ahmed 1981:29).

Conflict over the status of Bengali dates back to the medieval period. The *'ulamā* were openly hostile to the idea of using Bengali, or any other local language, for religious purposes. Even the village *mullā*, whose mother tongue was Bengali, was opposed to its use. The basic question was not whether the Bengali Muslims spoke Bengali, but rather what *should* properly be their language. Thus Nawāb 'Abd al-Latīf (1828–93), known as a pioneering modernizer among Bengal's Muslims, expressed a keen desire to "create" a special kind of Bengali, "a mean between the highly Sanskritized Bengali of the Hindu *pathsalas*, on the one hand, and the Musalmani Bengali *patois* on the other," for the Muslim masses of Bengal (Ahmed 1981:125–26). As Bengali was tainted by its association with the local culture, some even advocated its total replacement by Urdu. Sayyid Amir 'Ali (1849–1928), a London-trained lawyer, categorically demanded this in 1882 (Ahmed 1981:125–26). But this was not merely an opinion of those who were not in touch with the ordinary people; even the rural Muslims of some status thought and believed that their mother tongue was not really Bengali. They found pleasure and pride in discarding their links to the local culture. Even when they wrote in Bengali, as they had very little choice in the matter, they would invariably begin with a long apology lamenting their local birth. Poet 'Abd al-Hakim (1620–90), one of those who dared to advocate the cause of Bengali and wrote exclusively in Bengali, expressed his bitter disappointment at this attitude of the *mullās* and others when he wrote in his celebrated *pūthi*:

> Whatever language a people speak in a country, the Lord understands it. He understands all languages, whether it is *Hinduani* [*sic*] [Hindustani?], or the language of Bengal or any other . . . Those who hate Bengali despite being born in Bengal cast doubt on their birth. (*Nūr Nāmah*, quoted in Huq 1965:205–6).

'Abd al-Nabi, another sixteenth-century poet, also felt the necessity of writing in Bengali although he was not so forthright about it as 'Abd al-Hakim was. Apologetically, he opted to write his *pūthi* in his mother tongue: "I am afraid in my heart lest God should be annoyed with me for having rendered Islamic scriptures into Bengali. But I put aside my fear and firmly resolve to write for the good of common people" (*Vijay-Hāmzā*, quoted in Huq 1965:214–15). Other liturgical writings of the period bear traces of a similar tension. Thus Sayyid Sultān (1550–1648), Nasr-Allāh Khondkar (1560–1620), Shaikh Muttālib (1595–1660), and others who chose to write instructive *pūthi*s in Bengali incurred the wrath of the *mullā*s and were branded as heretics. Sayyid Sultān wrote, "They call me a turn-coat. And say I have rendered into a Hindu language the Islamic scriptures" (*Shab-i Miraj*, quoted in Huq 1965:161). However, such criticisms did not dampen his enthusiasm for writing in Bengali. His confidence emanated from a belief in the infallibility of his mission, and he felt "the Almighty knows that I mean it all for the best, Him alone I am to answer" (Huq 1965:122). Elaborating further he wrote:

> Know then, that I am your well wisher
> I have given the message of *Iman* and Islam
> And described the creation of the three worlds
> Of the Angels and devils,
> Of Adam and Eve,
> And the advent of the Prophets,
> These were unknown to the people of Bengal;
> They learnt them from the *pānchāli* of *Nabi Vaṁsa*.
> (*Shab-i Miraj*, quoted in Huq 1957:116)

Although not much is known about the social background and economic status of these men who defied the *mullās*' ban on Bengali, their writings indicate why they did so. Apparently a class of "liberal" *'ulamā* of the Sufi tradition, they thought it important to transmit the message of Islam to the ordinary believer in his own language. But why this urgency? These people, whom I have called the liberal *'ulamā* for lack of a better term, discovered to their dismay that the average Bengali Muslim in the countryside, long after his conversion to Islam, did not know the basic principles of Islam. Sayyid Sultān, who was a *pīr* himself, explained that the rural Muslims of Bengal did not bother much about Allāh or *rasūl*. The *Mahābhārat*, the Hindu religious scripture, was still read in every house, Hindu and Muslim, and the local deities were propitiated by members of both communities (Huq 1965:142). The lower orders of the Muslim society were more like Hindu caste groups and observed rituals common to the Hindus of the same social classes. Nasr-Allāh Khondkar records the presence of restrictions on interdining: "Some say it is not allowed to eat in the house of an oil-presser, or a barber, or [of those] who sell fish or catch fish" ("Sharī'at-nāma," quoted in A. Sharif 1977:152). The caste rules may not have been enforced with the same degree of rigidity among Muslims as they were for Hindus, but the existing system represented social distinctions similar in nature to those of the Hindu caste system. Even the Brahmin priest had a place of honor in the Muslim family; he was often consulted on important occasions. Nasr-Allāh Khondkar records that "whatever the Brahmin priest says the ignorant [Muslims] obey without hesitation" ("Sharī'at-nāma," quoted in A. Sharif 1977:154).

Such practices do not appear to have been isolated experiences of particular groups of people but were fairly widespread throughout Bengal:

In Bengal, before the recent crusade against idolatry [writes an observer of the Muslim social scene in the early twentieth century] it was the practice of low class Musalmans to join in the Durgā pujā and other Hindu festivals. They are very careful about omens and auspicious days, and dates for weddings and other rites are fixed after consulting Hindu pandits. Hindu deities, like *Śitalā*, who controls small pox, and *Rakshyā Kāli*, who protects her votaries from cholera are worshipped during epidemics." (J. Sharif 1972:8; Samir al-Din 1879:72)

Thus contradiction between doctrinal principles and popular beliefs and practices in Bengali Islam was very real. As Tarafdar puts it, "Islam in its simple and austere aspect does not appear to have characterized the life of the people. . . . a careful study of the literature of the time shows that there prevailed a sort of folk Islam having hardly any connection with the dogmas of religion" (Tarafdar 1965:163–64).

Pre-Nineteenth-Century Concessions to Local Culture

In this situation, where religious principles contrasted sharply with social values and realities, perhaps the best that men like Sayyid Sultān and others, who were keen on educating the people in the basic principles of Islam, could do was to achieve some measure of alignment between the two. The real challenge to the purity of belief and practice in Bengali Islam, as we have seen, was the people's ignorance of the requirements of their faith. The need, then, was to transmit the recognized ideals of Islam to the average person. The orthodox reservations about Bengali had created a difficult situation in this regard. Muhammad Khān (1580–1650) explained in his *pūthi* that the "people of Hindustan do not understand the religious scriptures [written in Arabic]; they thus indulge in sinful activities without realising it" (*Maqtul Husain*, quoted in Huq 1965:190). His master Sayyid Sultān had already emphasized the point in his work *Shab-i Miraj*, referred to above. The average Bengali Muslim had no access to the religious scriptures of Islam; even the *mullā*, despite his pathological dislike for Bengali and local culture, was quite ignorant of the languages in which these were written, namely, Arabic and Persian. The latter's own knowledge of the Islamic dogma was mainly derived from the incomplete education he received in the village *maktab*s and *madrasa*s, the Islamic schools. As such, he could not be expected to take the lead in any program of religious reform requiring adjustments with the existing beliefs and practices in the society. Sayyid Sultān is the classic example of those who dared to make a breakthrough. He defied the ban on Bengali and went about his business undaunted. He did not even stop there. When he understood that his efforts alone would not be enough for the gigantic task, he encouraged others to follow his footsteps. He particularly advised his principal disciple, Muhammad Khān, to carry forward the mission, and the latter willingly obliged. Muhammad Khān wrote in his *pūthi*:

> He could not complete his work on the Prophet's death,
> And at last asked me to do so.
> In obedience to his command,
> I have composed these *padāvalis* about the four As'hab.
>
> (*Kiyāmat Nāmah*, quoted in Huq 1957:113)

Muhammad Khān's efforts were not confined to writing about God and his prophets; he extended this to present a basic history of Islam to the public. His magnum opus, *Maqtul Husain*, thus narrated the events leading to the tragedy of Karbala.

But Sayyid Sultān and Muhammad Khān were no longer alone in the field. Others joined them soon and produced volumes of *pūthi*s for the edification of the masses. Among them were Shaikh Parān (1550?–1615?), Hājī Muhammad (1550?–1620?), Nasr-Allāh Khondkar (1560?–1625?) Shaikh Muttālib (seventeenth century), and a host of others. All of them were inspired by the same ideal of instructing the masses of believers which had earlier inspired Sayyid Sultān. As Nasr-Allāh Khondkar emphasized in his *pūthi*:

> Listen to the sayings of *Shariat Nāmāh*,
> Anyone who is a true Muslim will surely obey these;
> If a Muslim does not observe Islamic laws,
> He no longer remains a Muslim.
>
> (*Shariat Nāmāh*, quoted in Huq 1957:131)

The most difficult problem faced by the author-preachers in educating the people was in making Islamic symbols and ideals "acceptable" to the masses. They had to formulate religious questions in such a fashion as to make these look similar to existing local concepts while at the same time giving the truth about Islam. Their mission was to preach *tauḥīd* (the unity of God), but they preferred to use the familiar local model of *avatār*, the Hindu belief in incarnation. In other words, liberal preachers of the medieval period, men like Sayyid Sultān and Muhammad Khān, thought it necessary to make some concessions to local needs in an effort to bring home the message of Islam to the ordinary people, who were rather unfamiliar with its symbols and forms. They recognized that popular persistence in the study of Hindu religious scriptures was due basically to the absence of Muslim works in Bengali, but realized that writing in Bengali was not enough.

Bengali alone would not bring Islam closer to the heart of the people; the cultural idioms and symbols must be familiar to them as well. The search for such a medium of cultural communication for a people more familiar with local Hindu gods and goddesses than with their own heroes and prophets led many preachers to the tacit use of traditional local concepts and symbols. Prophets honored in the Islamic tradition were thus compared with, and likened to, the Hindu deities and manifestations (*avatārs*), and Hindu gods were glorified in the same fashion as were Muslim heroes. The truth of the mission of Prophet Muḥammad was thus described by Sultān in one of his *pūthi*, *Nabi Vamsa*, in terms that would appear sacrilegious to many. He analyzed the sources of the four Vedas of the Hindus, calling them revealed books, and asserted that the advent of Muḥammad was forewarned in these holy books (*Nabi Vamsa*, quoted in A. Sharif 1977:229). Again, the name of Prophet Muḥammad appears with Brahma, Vishnu, Maheshwār, Rāma, Krishna, Nara Singha, Vāmana, and others, in a list of prophets (*Nabi Vamsa*, quoted in Huq 1965:149). Surely this was not quite Islamic.

These "concessions" and "adjustments" were not acceptable to the conservative section of the *'ulamā*, who were determined to present their view of monotheistic-fundamentalist Islam to the masses in its austere doctrinal garb. This is evident from the testimony of the *pūthi* literature of the period, which contains sufficient hints on how the liberal authors of didactic works were chastised by the orthodox *'ulamā*, who opposed the use of Bengali and, particularly, the use of local symbols and idioms. They considered any such "concessions" as deviations from the concept of unity in Islam and opposed them steadfastly. The consequent bitterness and tension in the society were unavoidable (see Huq 1957:116, 121, 122ff). They were thus strong in their condemnation of all un-Islamic activities, and deprecated any attempt at "localization" of the scripture. They emphasized the observance of Islamic rituals like *namāz*, *roza*, *ḥajj*, *zakāt*, and living a pious life compatible with the injunctions of Islam. In their own personal lives, the "conservatives," who included the *'ulamā*, the *qāẓīs*, village *mullās* and *pīrs*, among others, tried to remain as "Islamic" as possible, maintaining their cultural identity as Muslims (A. Karim 1959:159–62). Writing on this impact of Islam in medieval Bengal, Tarafdar observes:

Literary and epigraphic sources indicate that offering prayers regularly, keeping the Ramadan fast tenaciously, reading the Koran together with other religious scriptures, paying the poor rate and going on pilgrimage to Mecca were common practices. The vernacular literature of the time depicts the mulla and the qadi as extremely orthodox in their religious beliefs and ways of life (Tarafdar 1965:163–64).

Such a picture of orthodox society, as found in a section of the vernacular literature of the medieval period, notably *Kavi-kankan Chandi* by Mukunda-Rām, *Manashā-Vijaya* by Vipra-dās, and *Chaitanya-Bhāgavat* by Vrindāban-dās, and as hinted in the *pūthi* literature of the sixteenth and seventeenth centuries, however, represented only a partial picture. Those who are mentioned as "extremely orthodox" were not the representatives of the average society. They were, however, socially dominant by virtue of their wealth and status, and exerted a continuous pressure toward discrediting local accretions.

But efforts of the orthodox *mullā* had only limited success, partly due to the geographical-historical factors discussed earlier in this essay, and partly due to their limited contact with ordinary people. At the level of popular religion, Sufi and syncretic traditions continued to hold sway. As Islam spread farther, Muslim society came to include still more divergent social groups and castes with their own ways of life, rituals, and practices. Even the immigrants, proud of their ethnic heritage and belonging to distinct cultural traditions, brought with them the characteristic features of their ethnic and non-Islamic backgrounds.

Islam in Bengal thus had to deal with such a varied and complex cultural situation that the question was not whether to reject all syncretic compromises, although on the surface it so appeared at times; the real problem was to define the degree of compromise that was acceptable. Fundamentalist rejection of local accretions created tension in the society, and also helped ultimately in the "idealization" of Islam, but on the basic cultural issues the fundamentalists' mission remained far from complete. There was, in this, more than a mere conflict of religious attitudes involved. The social dichotomy in Bengali Muslim society, as evident in the *ashraf-ātrāp* pattern, created a deep and unavoidable gap in the process of transmission of religious knowledge from the upper to the lower level. Until late in the nineteenth century the masses had hardly any idea about the virtues of their own religion; they had no way of knowing them. Undoubtedly, beliefs and practices in *ashraf* society did not always necessarily conform to Islamic dogma (see A. Karim 1959:passim). But *ashraf* practices had the required Islamic veneer. The living circumstances of the *ashraf* and the *ātrāp* were different, too. The *ashraf*, a predominantly urban-dwelling class, had a life style and cultural orientation very different from those of the masses who lived in the swamps of the delta and were constantly fighting for survival. The problem thus was not merely confined to making available to the masses manuals for formal religious observances in their own language. They needed more than what a vague presentation of the *sharī'at* could offer them. Their difficult life in this nature-ravaged area made them associate religion, and their God, with the supernatural and miraculous powers of nature in its varied expressions. The *'ulamā* and the Sufis, each in their own way, did try to spread the message of *sharī'at*. But these were highly individualistic efforts and had no real backing from the state. Such isolated and individualistic efforts could, under the circumstances, have only a limited success. This will be further evident in the following discussion of Islamic movements in Bengal.

Nineteenth-Century Islamic Movements

The nineteenth-century reform movements in Bengali Islam represented a break with the overwhelming tendency toward "compromise" and "concession" of the earlier period. To these movements may be traced the first concerted effort by the conservative *'ulamā* to break the hold of what was regarded as idolatrous heresy. Historically, reform and revivalism in the nineteenth century owed their origins to the impact of Western colonialism. The foundations of a new economy shattered the old social structure and gave rise to new conditions and classes, affecting particularly the dominant Muslim upper classes (Hunter 1872: chapter 4; Hardy 1972:34–50). The psychological effect of these changes was enormous and stirred the imagination of even the "have-nots." Perhaps this explains why countless penniless and landless Bengali Muslim peasants responded to the call of holy war (*jihād*) fought in the North West Frontier under the banner of the revivalists early in the century (Hunter 1872:1; Ahmad Khan 1971:52, 54, 56, 276).

The impact of Western colonialism created a unique politico-cultural situation affecting all classes of people. Inevitably this prompted powerful indigenous reactions, with religion playing a dominant role in the resulting conflict. The forms of Muslim reaction to the situation were varied and wide-ranging, but broadly the tendency was in favor of an "oppositional" and "identity-preserving" (to quote the useful terminology of Clifford Geertz) movement bringing people closer to their own religious scriptures and traditions. As Geertz puts it, "Before, men had been Muslims as a matter of circumstance: now they were increasingly Muslims as a matter of policy" (1971:65).

The religious response of the Muslims found expression in two clearly identifiable forms. The first of these was the reformist-revivalist (or fundamentalist) reaction, led by the *'ulamā* with the dual aims of religiously restoring the Muslim community to what it was perceived to have been in the time of the Prophet and of politically protecting the worldly interests of the community. The second reaction came mostly from urban intelligentsia who, with similar ends in view, sought to "reinterpret" Islam and identify problems of the Muslim community in the light of knowledge derived from the West. There was also a third group, represented by a section of the traditionalist *'ulamā*, who were opposed to the fundamentalists on theological grounds but did recognize the validity of a reform program. They generally supported the urban group. It should be stressed, however, that the fundamentalists sensed the problem long before it was taken up by the intelligentsia and the traditionalists.

The reformist-revivalist response in Bengal was initiated primarily by two movements: the Farā'izī movement founded by Ḥājī Sharī'at Allāh (1781–1844) of Faridpur in eastern Bengal, and the Ṭarīqa-i Muḥammadiyya movement of Shāh Sayyid Aḥmad (1786–1831) of Rae Bareli. They both belonged to the tradition of the Walīullāhī movement of Delhi and may have had some connections with the Wahhābī tradition of Arabia, although no direct link to the latter can be traced. The tenets of their reformism were a renewed emphasis on *tauḥīd* (the unity of God); adherence to the right of the individual to interpret the Qur'ān and the *ḥadīs̱* (*ijtihād*); opposition to all forms of polytheistic associations, including reverence to the *pīr*; and an earnest endeavor to remove all traces of animistic and Hindu beliefs and practices from Muslim society.

Activities of the two movements may be divided broadly into two distinct phases. From the beginning of the nineteenth century to the Mutiny of 1857 (although the last date perhaps may be pushed further, to 1870–71, when the so-called Wahhābī trials formally ended), the reformers were active revolutionaries. This was the period when the *jihād*, under the leadership of Shāh Sayyid Aḥmad, was raging on the Frontier. Significantly, although the war was fought on the Frontier, large contingents of recruits came from areas in Bengal, where the movement had local agents in the villages for the collection of funds and recruitment of fighters. The Farā'izī movement assumed an equally militant role during this period under the leadership of Dudu Miyān (1819–62), who succeeded his father in 1840. He transformed the movement into a political platform resisting *zamīndārī*—in most cases

Hindu—oppression and fighting the excesses of European indigo planters (Wise 1894:51; Ahmad Khan 1971:276, 288, 289).

By the 1860s and 1870s the militancy of the two movements had gradually ebbed. The failure of the *jihād* and the collapse of the Mutiny led reformers to revise their strategy and concentrate on internal reforms. The new spirit was reflected *inter alia* in the numerous *fatāwā* issued by a section of the *'ulamā*; these demonstrated their hostility to all anti-British agitation by the fundamentalists.[4] Islamization of the Muslims was the key note of their thrust. The aim was to rid Islam of all that was considered spurious accretion, including much that was revered by the traditionalists as part of the Islamic way of life. This at times reached a point where the reformists rejected as unacceptable such institutions as *mīlād* (birth day observances), *'urs* (death day observances), and *fātiḥa* (prayers for the dead) that for centuries provided strength to Islam in South Asia. Even reverence to *pīr*s, as deeply ingrained in the socio-religious system of the Muslims of the region as it was, was condemned by the reformers' uncompromising attitude toward all elements not in conformity (in their opinion) with the Qur'ān and *sunnat*.

Unlike most elite *'ulamā*, the reformists chose as their sphere of activity not the intellectual elite or the urban population but the rural masses in general. They built networks of centers for the propagation of the religious ideals of Islam, using village mosques as their basic units. Preachers spread over much of the countryside, teaching ordinary Muslims basic Islamic law and observances and, above all, inculcating in them the perception of themselves as "Muslims" religiously and ideologically. Arnold notes that the revival of missionary activity in Bengal during this period led to large-scale conversions.[5] Whether this represents an exaggerated picture is difficult to ascertain, but the intensity of missionary work is evident and well-acknowledged.

The dominant theme of the new drive to return Muslim society to the proper practice of Islam was reflected in scores of Musalmani *pūthi*s—manuals of religious instruction—published during the period. Like the medieval tracts, these were written in Bengali, but in a very special kind of Bengali. The wholesale incorporation of Arabic and Persian terms

4. See, for instance, the *fatwā* issued by Maulana Karamat Ali of Jaunpur, *Abstract Proceedings of the Mahomedan Literary Society of Calcutta* (1871:6); see also Hunter (1872:217–19) for a few other *fatāwā*.

5. "Estimated at ten, fifty, one hundred and six hundred thousand" (Arnold 1965:285; Titus 1930:49).

("Islamic" terms, in their authors' parlance) gave a particular character, and a distinct name—Musalmani Bangla—to this new literary language. Unlike the medieval preachers, these nineteenth-century authors were unwilling to make any concession to local needs or to adopt any model familiar to the ordinary people. They would not accept "*īshwar*" for "Allāh," or "*avatār*" for "*nabī*" and "*rasūl*." Explaining why they chose to write in Bengali, one author stated: "That we were born in Bengal [cannot be denied]. Most people do not understand Arabic and Persian. As such, I write this [religious] book in Bengali" (M. Muhammad 1876:71). But he considered the Islamization of the language essential because, in his opinion, "many of the religious terms found in the *kitāb* [holy book] should never be translated into Bengali" (M. Muhammad 1876:19).

The contents of the literature showed the same uncompromising attitude and a total dislike for all local and syncretic associations. The authors did not venture to find similes for religious expressions in the existing symbols and ideas of the people, openly condemning even minor "deviations." While the bulk of these works concerned themselves with very basic principles and observances of Islam, a contempt for local culture is conveyed in most of them. Their definition of the true Islamic way of life required cultural similarity with the traditions of the Middle East. As a calculated move to establish an imaginary link with the Islamic lands, they advocated the use of Arabic or Persian terms for names and appellations. In the process they hoped to sunder the links with the culture of the Bengali Muslims' land of birth.

The fundamentalist challenge to traditional beliefs and practices did not go unanswered, however. This fundamentalism questioned some of the valued institutions of the existing system, threatening particularly the long-held supremacy of the priestly class—the *pīr*s and *mullā*s. As religious guardians, or *guru*s (*hujur* is the Muslim term), the *mullā*s commanded unswerving respect and obedience from the rural people and presided over all social and religious ceremonies in the villages. They plied a lucrative trade in charms, amulets, incantations, divination, astrology, and various other occult aids. The success with which they defended practices associated with *pīr*s against the reformist attack clearly demonstrated their power and influence in the society.

The defense of *pīr*s, and many other traditional institutions and practices, however, did not depend solely on the power of the *mullā*; the inherent strength of these institutions also contributed to their survival. The figure of the *pīr*, for instance, though generally recognized as possessing non-Islamic elements, hardly suffered from the hostile propaganda. The *pīrs*, living and dead, retained a special place in the hearts of millions for their supposedly miraculous powers. The people looked to the *pīrs* for immediate help and protection in times of illness and misfortune, regarding them as intermediaries between God and man. As stated in a *pūthi*,

> If you are faithful to a pious *pīr*, he will guide you through the right path. . . . Without such help from a *murshid* you cannot expect to find the way.
>
> One who does not have a *pīr* falls in the trap of a *shaiṭān* [devil]. There is no way out without the help of the *murshid*. (Mallik 1876:36)
>
> You will find God through His *murshid*. [But] the Wahhābīs are asking you not to pay him any respect. (Mallik 1876:19)

Counter-propaganda was thus launched by the older *pīrs* and *mullās* to defend the institution. They published a number of *pūthis* in its support, explaining its social and religious significance. It is doubtful if the reformists succeeded in making any real headway against the entrenched position of the *pīrs* and *mullās*. But propaganda and counter-propaganda continued; both sides were openly abusive, accusing each other of heretical deviations. A traditionalist *pūthi* thus described the reformist preachers:

> They are the disciples of the devil, you must know. . . . They can eat food prepared by Hindus with a proper justification. . . . In which *ḥadīs̤* did the Prophet give such advice? They have gone to dogs by following such actions. My brother, you must know that these people are the Wahhābīs. (Mallik 1876:12; also Naim al-Din 1904:28ff, 180)

The reformist attack was equally strong:

> Even a child of this order [the Ṭarīqa-i Muḥammadiyya] knows the meaning of *kalma*. [But] the veterans of the irreligious *pīrs* do not know the meaning. . . . In the houses of these irreligious *pīrs*, there is only magic and charm [and nothing more]. (Aziz 1876:125)

The issues that proved most controversial, such as *mazhab* (sect), *pīr*, *mīlād*, *fātiḥa*, *'urs*, *muḥarram* (observance of the death of Ḥusain—ostensibly a Shī'a practice), and associated practices, were openly debated in public meetings, or *baḥas̤*. Such meetings represented an entirely new pattern of religious activity in Bengal. Countless *baḥas̤* were held between the contending parties and were attended by people from all walks of life. Subscriptions were collected from house to house by supporters of each group for staging the meetings. A condition of battle readiness existed during the period, with both parties using their muscle men to terrorize their opponents and extract a verdict in their favor. But the debates never succeeded in giving a verdict, often ending in pandemonium. Unable to settle any issue, they instead kindled the passions of ordinary people on both sides, creating conditions of conflict and tension. As a consequence, most villages in which the reformists had any significant following found themselves divided into rival camps, each governed by rules and laws of its own creed. On the positive side, the principal achievement of these debates was to create an enthusiasm in the countryside about religious matters, inspiring the Muslims there to discuss and learn more.

Nevertheless, though their sensitivities to issues of religion and identity were raised, the basic Bengali character of life in the countryside could not be permanently altered or erased. The villagers continued with their older ways: a whole range of observances and ceremonies, recognized by fundamentalists as borrowings from Hinduism, persisted. The Islamic veneer which was imparted to many local systems and practices did not represent any clear-cut change in the attitude of the people. Even the *mullā* consciously wrapped an Islamic garb around certain practices which he himself had earlier denounced as un-Islamic. Typical of this was the *mullā*'s business in amulets and incantations. When these practices could no longer be defended as Islamic, he imported "Islamic" incantations to give them an Islamic character, and this was generally accepted by the *mullā* as compatible with Islamic injunctions (Khodadad 1871:3). The massive assault on local traditions in the nineteenth century sharpened the focus of the Bengali Muslims on "Perso-Arab culture" as Islamic culture, distinct from local, Hindu culture, as never before. The propagation of the *sharī'at*, with emphasis on absolute monotheism, gradually led the masses away from beliefs and practices which were openly "Hindu." But their understanding of Islamic doctrines was so vague and incomplete that they often continued to adhere to almost the same local traditions, rejected by the fundamentalists, perhaps with an Islamic veneer. The "Islamic amulet" and the continued existence of a host of other beliefs and practices attest to this situation. That the purificatory campaign did not find an easy acceptance is evident from the pages of the *pūthi*s. Even the preachers' notion of the *sharī'at* suffered from a degree of ignorance. There was no problem with the essential principles, *kalma*, *namāz*, *roza*, *ḥajj*, *zakāt*, and so forth; these are clearly defined and elaborated in most didactic *pūthi*s. But on other theological and cultural issues, like the question of *mazhab* in Islam, rights and privileges of men and women, *mīlād*, *muḥarram*, et cetera, they showed a clear lack of comprehension of the *sharī'at* (see Samir al-Din 1872:passim.). There was also a considerable backlash from the traditionalist *mullās* and *pīrs* on certain practices rejected by the reformists (Aziz 1876:162–63).

Islamization, in the overall context of Bengali Islam, could thus lead only to a limited imposition of the fundamentalists' conception of the *sharī'at*. Some of the rituals and practices, such as ceremonies relating to birth and death, marriage, and beliefs in the miraculous powers of the *pīr* and associated practices, held a strong attraction for ordinary Bengali Muslims, and the most they could do was to discard the outer labels to make them look "Islamic." A close observer of the Muslim social scene in eastern Bengal, now Bangladesh, in the present century thus discovered that "popular rituals and beliefs . . . exercise no less influence on man's life and are not less important than 'official Islam' itself. Some of the rituals and beliefs," he further noted, "verge on primitive animism while in more advanced sections they merge with developed form of monotheism of the Islamic type" (Karim 1955:29). Significantly, he was talking about the rituals and practices prevalent among the Muslims of the district of Noakhali, "where the influence of reforming priests has been most persistent" and which was fully exposed to the reforming zeal of the Islamicists in the early decades of the present century. As we shall see, this desire to be "Islamic" in practice, while remaining Bengali in culture, would have far-reaching consequences, leading in time to the creation of Bangladesh.

Separatism for the Elite

The struggle between the champions of the older order and the fundamentalist viewpoint in the later nineteenth and early twentieth centuries, despite all the tension and bitterness generated by it, had the immediate effect of heightening the public's awareness of its identity as Muslims. As described above, this had far-reaching effects among the people in the countryside. A similar battle raged among the religiously educated as well.

The alignment of mass and elite concerns was significant for the countryside because constant emphasis on the religious identity of the Muslims, a part of the strategy of both groups, helped in the socialization of Bengalis to the concept of exclusive symbols and ultimately in the cultural self-definition of the Bengali Muslims as Muslims. In this development, the small group of Western-educated intellectuals, representing the emergent middle classes and a section of the declining aristocracy, played a pivotal role. These included a number of enlightened *maulawīs*, men like Maulana Karamat Ali of Jaunpur and Munshī Meher 'Allāh (1861–1907) of Jessore. Their relationship with the reformists had never been friendly (with the exception of Karāmat 'Alī, who had been a disciple of Shāh Sayyid Aḥmad in his early life), but they were clearly inspired by the ideals and ideology preached by the reformists.

The efforts of the modernist intellectuals were directed toward reviving an interest in the study of Islam by reinterpreting it in the light of Western knowledge. Though never acknowledging it, they took their cue from the fundamentalists, defending Islam and formulating a general cultural policy for the Muslims of South Asia. They tried to find a means to reconcile the validity of imported Western ideas with a revived Islam. Thus Sayyid Amīr 'Alī (1849–1928), who was one of the few Western-trained Muslim intellectuals writing exclusively on Islam, sought to show in *The Spirit of Islam* (1891) that science, rationalism, liberalism, and democracy were not only compatible with Islam but were contained in the fundamental teachings of the Prophet (W. C. Smith 1963:46–53; also D. E. Smith 1966:34–35). He repeatedly stressed the separate cultural identity of Muslims, spoke in favor of what was essentially an Urdu-based urban culture, and lent support to a system of Western education that incorporated elements of the Islamic system. He argued before the Education Commission in 1882 that "Urdu should be to the Mahomedans what Bengali is to the Hindus of Bengal" (Education Commission 1884:222). His other contemporary, Nawāb 'Abd al-Latīf (1828–93), similarly spoke in favor of a Muslim culture with Urdu as the basic medium. He advocated an "Islamic form of Bengali" for ordinary Muslims and Urdu for the higher classes (Education Commission 1884:213).

The arguments put forward by Amīr 'Alī and 'Abd al-Latīf were in tune with the aspirations of the dominant upper-class Muslims of north India who saw in an Urdu-based culture the hopes of retaining the glories of Muslim civilization in India, and of maintaining their own social dominance and status. The movement in favor of Urdu culture, championed by the *ashraf* and the *'ulamā*, and enjoying the support of a section of the Muslim intellectuals who valued the traditions associated with it, was continued through the first half of the twentieth century.

This pro-Urdu cultural movement, however, did not touch the hearts of the masses. Men like Amīr 'Alī, 'Abd al-Latīf, and others of their class were far removed socially and culturally from the average person: the middle classes were their principal concern, and it was only the latter who benefited from their activities and writings. But the social scene was so dominated by the pro-Urdu leaders that a new generation of Bengali-speaking Muslim intellectuals could not make their presence felt until the second decade of the present century.

This new group included Mīr Musharraf Hussain (1848–1912), Muhammad Naim al-Din (1832–1916), Reaz al-Din Māshādi (1859–1919), Reaz al-Din Ahmed (1862–1933), Nausher Alī Khān Yusufzai (1864–1924), Delowar Hossain Ahmed (1840–1913), Yaqin al-Din Ahmed (1852–1914), Kāzi 'Abd al-Wadud (1894–1963), and a few others. They set about writing in modern Bengali on things Islamic and took a more rational view of the situation obtaining in the Muslim society of Bengal. Yet only when the balance clearly shifted in their favor, helped by political factors and the weight of numbers, did their message emerge. Though this message took shape over a very long period, the spirit of rationalism in their early writings laid the basis for a new development in Bengali Islam, that of secular nationalism. Despite this innovation, their audience was still largely limited to the urban areas and their emphasis on the historical role of Islam did not appeal much to the common people.

The exclusivist emphasis on religious identity became, then, the dominant trend in the society for both *ashraf* and *ātrāp*; cultural separatism had taken firm root through the efforts of the *'ulamā*, the fundamentalist preachers, and others. The alignment of rural and urban perceptions coalesced along this issue of cultural separatism. Competition and confrontation with the dominant upper-caste Hindus for shares in the privileges of the state further sharpened communal antagonism and stimulated separatist thinking. Although this affected directly only a small number in the urban areas, the message was filtered to the rural areas through the efforts of men like Karāmat 'Alī and Munshī Meher 'Allāh. Such men had close links with the urban intelligentsia and also commanded great respect from the rural people (Ahmed 1981:48, 99, 100). Their propaganda helped transmit urban politico-cultural symbols to the rural areas. In this initiative, the Calcutta Madrasa played a role.

Unlike Deoband, the Calcutta Madrasa was a state college set up by the government in 1781 for the education of the higher classes of Muslims. It combined the study of the Qur'ān, *ḥadīs̤*, and *fiqh*, with law, logic, and philosophy; English and other modern subjects were later introduced into its curriculum. Basically a Sunni institution, the *madrasa* did not propagate any particular ideology, nor did it enjoy the exclusive support of any religious school. It attracted pupils from as far away as Chittagong, Noakhali, Sylhet, Barisal, and other outlying areas, most of whom belonged to lower-middle-class families in the villages. Scores of graduates passed from this college every year and went to work as missionaries of Islam, teachers in schools and *madrasa*s, and authors of religious tracts—many of them contributing to the store of *pūthi* literature. They took part in public debates against their opponents—the reformist preachers and Christian missionaries—and preached against the Hindus. Although the graduates of Calcutta Madrasa never apportioned to themselves the responsibility of offering spiritual guidance to the entire community, they had a role in the activation of religious sentiments at the mass level, and in the propagation of the ideology of Islam. As products of a semimodern Islamic college where elements of the Western sciences and English language were taught along with Islamic subjects, they could not altogether escape from the modernizing influences of European civilization. In a very limited sense they acted as unwilling agents of Western ideas in Bengal. At the same time they reinforced the impact of the *'ulamā*, fundamentalist preachers, and urban intelligentsia. Along with the *pūthi* literature and the open-air discussions of the *baḥaṣ*, they helped to disseminate ideas about Islamic reformism and community identity throughout the countryside. In their wake the dilemma between local culture and Islam was brought into even sharper relief.

Conclusion

We have now looked at several phases in the religious experiences of the Muslim peoples of Bengal, in the medieval period as well as modern times. The overall picture that emerges is that "scripturalism" (Geertz 1971) has not met all religious needs of the people. Islam as a system of belief and a culture should not be perceived as something divorced from the material existence and experience of human beings. "It is," according to Lapidus, "precisely a way of conceiving, of articulating, the ordinary issues of worldly experience—whether in moral, family, economic or political matters" (1980:101). It could hardly be expected that the Muslims of Bengal would forget about the realities of their own surroundings and concern themselves entirely with a system which had only a distant relationship with their situation. However powerful as an ideology, Islam in Bengal has not been able to escape the influences of local culture: the Bengali Muslims have remained Bengalis.

Islamic movements in the sixteenth and seventeenth centuries and the fundamentalist movements in the nineteenth century, therefore, did not succeed in changing the basic pattern of religious culture for Bengali Muslims. We have seen how the sale of amulets was given the veneer of proper religion by the use of "Islamic" incantations. Such Islamic amulets are on open sale even today, and the most respected of *pīr*s in the countryside gladly offer water they have blessed to their disciples for such purposes as the cure of illness.

Nevertheless, Muslims did not continue to observe uncritically all Bengali cultural practices. The psychological dilemma of ordinary Muslims—caused by opposing allegiances, first, to local culture and, second, to Islam—was most fully expressed in their attempts to find suitable origins for their ancestors in the distant lands of Arabia. Their efforts surpassed all previous records: by 1901 such claims had increased so dramatically that well over 19 million (out of a total of slightly more than 21.5 million) Muslims had discovered some connections for themselves with the Middle East (*Census of India* 1901, vol. 6a, pt. 2:288, table 13)! Claims to foreign ancestry were followed by a quick renunciation of local names and personal titles: as noted above, the issue of "Islamic" names had been close to the hearts of the reformers. Renunciation of Bengali names became increasingly evident in the pages of the *pūthi*s. Hindu terms and appellations, like *sri* (for mister) and *īshwar* (for God), were discarded, and Islamic terms like *janāb* or *maulawī* (for mister) and Allāh or *khudā* (for God) were substituted.[6]

Thus efforts to adopt certain "Islamic" practices existed simultaneously with a defiant retention of a "Bengali" way of life. These attempts at Islamization of personal names and titles, claims to nonlocal ancestry and the imparting of an Islamic veneer to local practices, when considered along with the persistent adherence to local customs and practices, reflect a cultural phenomenon common to many peasant societies. This coexistence also goes far to explain why the same region could support movements first for Pakistan, and then for Bangladesh.

Reformism had a great effect on the "ideologization" of Islam. By their repeated efforts to bring ordinary Muslims within the fold of what was thought to be a pure and unalloyed Islamic way of life, reformists

6. K. Muhammad (1868), Husain (1876), M. Muhammad (1876), and other works of the period bear testimony to the changing pattern.

encouraged people to look upon themselves as Muslims. Gradual changes were introduced into aspects of external appearance such as dress. The number of mosques increased in the villages and so did the number of devotees. A feeling of "national consciousness" now linked them with Muslims in other provinces of India. The ultimate result of this ideological linkage was the creation of Pakistan.

Although the birth of Bangladesh in 1971 was a negation of this religious ideology, Islam remains a powerful force in Bangladesh and seems at the moment to be gaining ground. The basic contradiction in Bengali thought and culture persists. The search for a creative interpretation of their religious ideas has not paved a definite path which Bengali Muslims may follow. Ambivalence about fundamentalism, traditionalism, local culture, and modern secularism is obvious. The danger of this situation lies in the fact that opposing principles, if left to themselves, can only produce confusion and disorder. The impunity with which the political *mullās* and those in authority are taking recourse to Islamic slogans in present-day Bangladesh brings us once again face to face with a situation similar to the crisis of confidence experienced by Muslim society in Bengal in the early twentieth century.[7]

References

Abstract Proceedings of the Mahomedan Literary Society of Calcutta
1871 Calcutta.

Ahmad, Aziz
1967 *Islamic Modernism in India and Pakistan, 1857–1964.* London: Oxford University Press.

Ahmad, Qeyamuddin
1966 *Wahabi Movement in India.* Calcutta: Firma K. L. Mukhopadhyay.

Ahmad Khan, Muin-ud-Din
1965 *History of the Fara'idi Movement in Bengal, 1818–1906.* Karachi: Pakistan Historical Society.

Ahmad Khan, Muin-ud-Din, ed.
1971 *Selections from Bengal Government Records on Wahhabi Trials, 1863–1870.* Dacca: Asiatic Society of Pakistan.

Ahmed, Rafiuddin
1981 *The Bengal Muslims, 1871–1906: A Quest for Identity.* Delhi: Oxford University Press.

Ahmed, Rafiuddin, ed.
1983 *Islam in Bangladesh: Society, Culture and Politics.* Dacca: Bangladesh Itihas Samiti.

7. An excellent analysis of the current trends in Bangladeshi Islam may be found in Maniruzzaman (1983).

Anisuzzaman

1964 *Muslim Manos o Bānglā Sāhitya*. Dacca: Lekhak Sangha Prakashani.

Arnold, T. W.

1965 *The Preaching of Islam*. Lahore: Sh. Muhammad Ashraf (reprint of 1913 edition).

Aziz, 'Abd al-

1876 *Tariqa-i Muhammadiyya*. (*Pūthi*.) Calcutta: Islamiya Library.

Census of Bengal

1872 Calcutta: Bengal Secretariat Press.

1881 Calcutta: Bengal Secretariat Press.

Census of India

1901 Vol. 6, pt. 1: The Lower Provinces of Bengal and Their Feudatories. Calcutta: Bengal Secretariat Press.

Chatterji, Suniti Kumar

1926 *The Origin and Development of the Bengali Language*. Pt. 1. Calcutta: Calcutta University Press.

Chowdhury, A. Momin

1983 "Conversion to Islam in Bengal: An Exploration." In *Islam in Bangladesh: Society, Culture and Politics*. R. Ahmed, ed. Dacca: Bangladesh Itihas Samiti.

Education Commission

1884 *Report by the Bengal Provincial Committee*. Calcutta: Government Printing.

Geertz, Clifford

1971 *Islam Observed: Religious Development in Morocco and Indonesia*. Chicago and London: University of Chicago Press.

Hardy, Peter

1972 *The Muslims of British India*. Cambridge: Cambridge University Press.

Hesab al-Dīn, Ahmad

1876 *Khulasat al-Nasihat*. (*Pūthi*.) Dacca: The author.

Hunter, W. W.

1872 *The Indian Musalmans*. London: Trubner & Co. (2nd edition).

Huq, Muhammad Enamul

1957 *Muslim Bengali Literature*. Karachi: Pakistan Publications.

1965 *Muslim Bāngla Sāhitya*. Dacca: Pakistan Publications (2nd edition).

Husain, 'Abul

1876 *Ketab Haqiqat al-Anbia*. (*Pūthi*.) Calcutta: Islamiya Library.

Karim, A

1959 *Social History of the Muslims of Bengal (Down to A.D. 1538)*. Dacca: Asiatic Society of Pakistan.

Karim, A. K. Nazmul

1955 "Some Aspects of Popular Beliefs among Muslims of Bengal." *The Eastern Anthropologist* 9, 1:29–40.

Karim, 'Abd al-

1903 *Irshad-i Khaliqiya*. (*Pūthi*). Calcutta: Islamiya Library.

Kaviraj, Narashari

1982 *Wahabi and Farazi Rebels of Bengal*. New Delhi: People's Publishing House.

Khodadad

1871 *Muksudnāma*. (*Pūthi*.) Mirzapur: The author.

Lapidus, Ira M.
1980 "Islam in the Historical Experience of the Muslim Peoples." In *Islamic Studies: A Tradition and Its Problems*. Malcolm Kerr, ed. Malibu: Undena Publications, pp. 89–102.

Latīf, 'Abd al-
n.d. *Dharma Prākās*. (*Pūthi*.) Purnee: Azizia Library.

Mallick, Azizur Rahman
1961 *British Policy and the Muslims in Bengal, 1757–1856*. Dacca: Asiatic Society of Pakistan.

Mallik, Muhammad
1876 *Akhtār al-Reñfāt*. (*Pūthi*.) Dacca: The author.

Maniruzzaman, Talukder
1983 "Bangladesh Politics: Islamic and Secular Trends." In *Islam in Bangladesh: Society, Culture and Politics*. R. Ahmed, ed. Dacca: Bangladesh Itihas Samiti.

Muhammad, Jān
1892 *Nāmājnāma*. (*Pūthi*.) Dacca. The author.

Muhammad, Khatir
1868 *Akhbar al-Wajud* (*Pūthi*.) Calcutta: The author.

Muhammad, Munshī Māl-i
1876 *Kitāb Sahi Ahkām-i Jumā* (*Pūthi*.) Dacca: The author.

Mujeeb, M.
1967 *The Indian Muslims*. London: George Allen & Unwin.

Naim al-Din, Muhammad
1904 *Adella-i Hanifiya*. (*Pūthi*.) Karatia: The author.

Rahman, Fakir 'Abd al-
1872 *Hedāyet al-Musāllin* (*Pūthi*.) Calcutta: Islamiya Library.

Report on the Administration of Bengal, 1871–72
1873 Calcutta: Government Press.

Rubbee, Khondkar Fuzli
1968 *The Origin of the Musalmans of Bengal*. Reprinted as an appendix to the *Journal of the East Pakistan History Association*, March 1968 (Dacca) (first published 1895).

Samir al-Din, Munshī
1868 *Bedār al-Ghāfi-lin* (*Pūthi*.) Calcutta: The author.

Seal, Anil
1971 *The Emergence of Indian Nationalism: Competition and Collaboration in the Later Nineteenth Century*. Cambridge: Cambridge University Press.

Sharif, Ahmad
1968 *Bichita Chintā*. Dacca: Chowdhury Publishing House.
1977 *Madhya Yuger Sāhitye Samāj o Sanskritir Rup*. Dacca: Muktadhara.

Sharif, Jafar
1972 *Islam in India: The Customs of the Musalmans of India*. William Crooke, ed.; G. A. Herklots, trans. Delhi: Oriental Books Reprint Corporation (first published 1921).

Smith, Donald Eugene, ed.
1966 *South Asian Politics and Religion*. Princeton: Princeton University Press.

Smith, Wilfred Cantwell
1963 *Modern Islam in India*. Lahore: Sh. Muhammad Ashraf.
Tarafdar, Mumtazur Rahman
1965 *Husain Shahi Bengal, 1494–1538 A.D.: A Socio-Political Study*. Dacca: Asiatic Society of Pakistan.
Titus, Murray T.
1930 *Indian Islam*. London: Oxford University Press.
Trimingham, J. Spencer
1949 *Islam in the Sudan*. London: Oxford University Press.
Wali, Maulawi A.
1904 "Ethnographical Notes on the Muhammadan Castes of Bengal." *Journal of the Anthropological Society of Bombay* 7:98–103.
Wise, James
1894 "The Muhammedans of Eastern Bengal." *The Journal of the Asiatic Society of Bengal* 63, 1:51.

7

Ambiguous Public Arenas and Coherent Personal Practice: Kanpur Muslims 1913–1931

SANDRIA B. FREITAG

The "small, plain building" of the Macchli Bazaar mosque[1] was an implausible object for the sudden notoriety it acquired in the middle of 1913. From an inconsequential mosque for peddlers in a congested part of Kanpur, it became likened to the "hundreds of mosques . . . destroyed in Macedonia" and "the tombs of Imam Raza . . . desecrated in Meshed."[2] Indeed, as a result first of the "Cawnpore Mosque Affair" of 1913 and then of the fierce communal riots of 1931, the mosque of Macchli Bazaar evolved from an inconsequential building into an evocative symbol. This paper examines the use of such symbols in 1913 and 1931 to highlight an important shift in the way many Muslims in north India perceived themselves and their world.[3]

Viewed through the analytic constructs of this volume (Ewing, introduction), we see that these symbols were used in the early twentieth century to preserve the ambiguous public place of Muslims in north Indian society. By the 1920s and 1930s, however, symbols of identity forced individuals—even ordinary people—to make choices. During this transition in the impact of symbolic rhetoric, certain standard

1. Lieutenant-Governor James S. Meston's description. "Minute by the Lt. Gov. on the Cawnpore Mosque and Riot," dated 21 August 1913 [hereafter, "Meston"]. India Office Records [hereafter IOR] L/P & J/6, vol. 1256, file 3374 for 1913, p. 11. (Also located in IOR European Manuscripts collection no. f136/15.)

2. *Muslim Gazette*, 2 June 1912. *Selections from the Vernacular Newspapers . . . for the Year 1913* [hereafter *SVN 1913*].

3. See chapters 5 and 6 in Freitag (1980) for full discussions of these two events.

features of Islamic life were isolated—such as prayer, the mosque, the Qur'ān, the *sharī'at*—and then used as a "shorthand" vocabulary to represent all that it meant to be a Muslim. After the 1920s, individuals who chose to support these symbols were aware in a new way that their choices constituted political acts. The self-consciousness engendered by these political acts made it impossible to sustain the levels of ambiguity that had previously integrated public life in north India.

The transition, in which 1913 and 1931 figure as high points, grew out of the changed circumstances of British India. In the north Indian province of U.P. (Uttar Pradesh) at least, Muslims were faced with a new situation, created first by the decline of the Islamic state and imposition of colonial rule, and then by the impetus of Islamic reformist movements and the development under the British of self-governing institutions. Conflict was an integral part of this new situation; it emerged in internal disputes (among Muslims) and in external ones (between Muslims and other groups, including "Hindus" and the British government). Paradoxically, such conflict was frequently expressed through symbols and assumptions drawn from a shared language.

Practice, Ambiguity, and Shared Symbols: Divisions among Muslims

To sketch briefly the relevant characteristics of nineteenth-century Muslim society in U.P., Muslims in the Kanpur area made up about 14 percent of the population; they could be divided into two main clusters—the *ashraf* and the lower "caste" Muslim groups. The *ashraf* constituted the Muslim elite. Enjoying superior status based on being "well-born," these constituent groups shared an Indo-Persianate culture fostered by the Mughal court (based in Delhi for the previous two centuries) and exported to the *qaṣba* urban centers that developed throughout northern India during the seventeenth and eighteenth centuries. Despite the nineteenth-century decline in the fortunes of those espousing *sharīf* status, this culture continued to thrive in *qaṣba* centers, emphasizing education, literary and other artistic accomplishments, the holding of administrative positions in Muslim states, study of Islamic law, and Muslim reformist activities (see Metcalf 1982). Although long shared by non-Muslims as well, this elite way of life was perceived by the Muslims who embraced it as "Islamic." This identification would prove a significant bridge to the concerns held by Muslims of lower status.

Alongside this *ashraf* elite was a cluster of lower-class groups (*ajlāf*), designated by their traditional occupations as butchers, weavers, and so forth. These groups were characterized by strong corporate identities (measured by the presence of effective group *panchāyat*s, or caste councils) and were capable of enforcing appropriate codes of behavior and, often, mobilizing for collective action (Ahmad 1976:319–46). Although not always punctilious in observing *sharī'at* injunctions, these groups had begun placing great emphasis on maintenance of certain Islamic activities, particularly those occurring in public spaces, such as the parading of *ta'ziya* (representations of the shrines of Ḥasan and Ḥusain, sons of 'Alī) during *muḥarram*,[4] sacrifice of cattle on *'īd*, or prevention of music-playing in front of mosques. Indeed, the foremost group—*julāha*s (weavers)—was consistently characterized in late nineteenth- and early twentieth-century documents as "bigoted" or "fanatic," volatile in their defense of Islamic practices.

Despite the class gulf, there were a number of occasions and contexts in which Muslims would cooperate.[5] Significantly, these occasions were pre-eminently those occurring in public spaces or arenas—on the city's streets and lanes, or within its mosques and *'īd-gah*s (enclosed public grounds used for sacrifices and other *'īd* observances). Moreover, though perceptions of the significant issues within Indo-Islamic culture were not identical across the class divide, they did overlap. Perceptions came to be expressed by a shared vocabulary emphasizing symbols such as the mosque, prayer, and the Qur'ān, and were frequently expressed through the emerging Urdu literature (both poetry and newly shaped newspaper journalism). That these symbols could be shared, even by those with widely differing notions of how they should be used, provided an effective way to imply the existence of a single identity for groups who might disagree on substantive issues.

A crucial issue was how the practice of Islam should be linked to this implicit assumption of community. Before the nineteenth century, emphasis had been placed on a Muslim ruler who employed men learned in Islamic law in service to the state as judges (*qāẓī*s) and legal scholars (*muftī*s); he patronized religious education, supervised religious charities, and in general provided a symbolic focus for Muslims. Such

4. *Ta'ziya*s are replicas of tombs that are paraded during the mourning observance of *muḥarram*. Ostensibly a Shī'a observance, *muḥarram* was widely popular among many urban Muslims, particularly in the nineteenth century.

5. See Freitag 1980 for a more detailed discussion of this localized activity and the styles of leadership associated with it.

an approach provided the public setting in which the free exercise of Islam could occur, and so long as that was provided, it was less necessary to pay close attention to *sharī'at*, to particular personal practices. When it later proved impossible to provide an Islamic state (first because no substitute Muslim ruler could be found for the declining Mughal aristocracy, and then because India became part of the British imperial system), attention shifted to other patterns. While these alternative patterns existed side by side in the nineteenth-century colonial state, they nevertheless differed in their emphasis on the public or personal observances of Islam.

In the first alternative pattern, many activities continued in public arenas—such as public ceremonials, religious charities, and other collective activities perceived to be "Islamic." Because leadership in this context retained much of the form it had had under an Islamic ruler, the ambiguous relationship between public life and Islamic identity could be maintained. A second pattern was provided by the political structure of the British Raj—which relied (much as had the preceding state) on intermediaries; to the extent that these Muslims continued to be publicly prominent, this also permitted an ambiguous construction of political life that implied the preservation of an "Islamic" way.

These assumptions were challenged, however, by a third pattern—that of a reformation of personal religious practice. In this pattern, a structure drawing on Qur'ān and *ḥadīs̤* (sayings, actions of the Prophet) provided an explicit and coherent model of personal behavior to substitute for the ambiguity previously possible in an Islamic state. This third pattern demanded a new attention to the details of living and provided an enhanced role for the *'ulamā*, one which focused on guiding ordinary Muslims in their everyday lives. Not all Muslims were drawn to this new emphasis on personal practice, but the numbers exposed to the reformist arguments expanded rapidly in the late nineteenth century. The internal debates that emerged over details of personal practice (see Fusfeld, this volume), though often a source of conflict, were important in heightening the self-consciousness with which Muslims perceived themselves and the practice of Islam (see Rafiuddin Ahmed, this volume).

By the early twentieth century, the dynamic of debate had been extended beyond the details of personal practice. Leaders utilized such modern innovations as printing presses and newspapers to publicize and propagate their points of view. They adopted new forms of organization and structures for education, in the process training additional *'ulamā* and other educated Muslims in their respective values. They also used existing mechanisms, such as Friday prayers and the issuance of *fatāwā* (pronouncements on the Law applied to everyday problems), to make clear their respective viewpoints. From traditional networks of kinship, *barādarī* (patrilineal "brotherhoods"), and Sufism, and through the spiritual and emotional connections that developed in training schools for *'ulamā*, a sense of shared community emerged among the elite.

From the interaction of these three patterns, a new self-image emerged for many north Indian Muslims. Central to this self-image was a perception that they were a persecuted minority, suffering setbacks because they were a community in decline. Such a perception was in sharp contrast to the original vision of Islam informing the sacred literature of Qur'ān and *ḥadīs̤*, in which there was an assumption that Islam's early worldly success was a reflection of divine approval. This sense of persecution proved crucial to the selection of community issues to champion—such as threats to symbols like the mosque, and access for Muslims to resources and patronage (which they presumed had previously been available). It justified the efforts to "recapture" those personal practices seen as responsible for the success of Muslims in the period of the Prophet.

The impact of these reformist *'ulamā* on the personal practice of religion made increasingly difficult the ambiguous references to an Islamic framework based on the elite role of intermediaries. The tension between this public but ambiguous framework and the increasing emphasis on reformed personal practice provides a focal point for understanding twentieth-century events in Kanpur that is different from that used previously by scholars. Indeed, it can be argued that the inability to fuse public and personal aspects of Islam led not only to an increased use of collective violence in midcentury but, ultimately, to Partition.

The Cawnpore Mosque Affair of 1913

Perhaps ironically, one of the first important attempts to fuse the personal and public expressions of Islam emerged in a north Indian city hitherto untouched by this emerging sensitivity to Muslim community identity. Kanpur stands in dramatic contrast to the older cities of north India, for it was a creation of the British, who had been in need of an inland industrial center. In the words of one inhabitant, "Cawnpore is neither a cultural nor a historical place. It is an industrial town with shifting population . . . without much regard for their neighbours."[6] Its recent creation meant that it did not have either an established commercial elite or a landed elite to affect twentieth-century political and social configurations as did the older centers. As a consequence, those in powerful political positions owed their influence to factional alignments to a much greater degree than in other parts of U.P. These factions were based on personal relationships which shifted frequently and which were virtually never related to ideological, class, or religious issues (Brass 1965).

The result for collective action was that the basic and most important divisions of society—those of class and religious community—were not expressed through the factional alignments in the political structure. Increasingly in the twentieth century, these divisions sought outlets, instead, in violent action. Kanpur is noteworthy, then, as the site in 1900 of a coalition of millworkers—leather-working *chamār*s joined by those in the cotton, woolen, and jute mills—who first met and then rioted against plague-control measures imposed by civil authorities. Moreover, the riots in both 1913 and 1931 marked innovative uses of violence to express an Islamic language of community identity. In the late 1930s, too, an especially effective and virulent labor movement emerged in Kanpur, only to be sapped eventually by its connections to the factionalized political structure.

All of these characteristics made Kanpur a unique place for the staging of an event which would dramatically attempt to fuse the public and personal exercise of Indian Islam. In this process the interests of the members of a small neighborhood mosque coalesced around symbols significant to Muslims outside their neighborhood, their city, even their province.

The small, plain mosque of the Bazaar had been built before the Mutiny and was, by 1913, located in one of the most congested parts of Kanpur.[7] The peddlers whose shops surrounded the mosque were its principal worshipers. They chose informally from among themselves the manager of their mosque; the last decision, made in 1906, had designated two such managers. Not long afterward, a municipal improvements scheme planned a new road through the mosque site. In large part because the route endangered two temples and three mosques,

6. IOR L/P & J/7/75 for 1931, "Evidence on the Cawnpore Riot of 1931" [hereafter, "Evidence"].
7. Narrative based on Meston. The account is corroborated (except as noted) by stories in the vernacular press in 1912 and 1913 (see *SVN* volumes for those years).

the plans were amended in 1909 so that only a bathing place (*dālān*), which had been added sometime after the mosque was built, had to be relocated. A final amendment in the plan was made to avoid harming a nearby temple. All inhabitants were left undisturbed until 1913, when other work on the road was completed. In February of that year the European chairman of the Municipal Board made a last visit to the mosque. He was accompanied by several Muslims, all of whom walked, without incident, through the *dālān* with their shoes on, an event which soon assumed great significance.

Though a deputation had earlier pleaded with the District Magistrate that the bathing place be left intact, and the Chairman had outmaneuvered the Indian members to pass a resolution in favor of the route, the Magistrate ignored this evidence and dubbed the issue a "factitious grievance." The administration thought itself on firm ground, for "trustworthy and good Muhammedans" had unanimously assured the Lieutenant-Governor that the bathing place need not form an integral part of the mosque, and provided him with examples of exceptions. The fact that it was permissible to walk with shoes on through the *dālān* suggested that the area was viewed as "less sacred."

Nevertheless by mid-May the protests from within as well as outside Kanpur were becoming more widespread. Lieutenant-Governor Meston firmly defended the plan to both the Raja of Mahmudabad and Mohamed Ali; his correspondence with the latter was published in Ali's *Comrade*. The washing place was removed swiftly and without fanfare on the first of July; "as soon as news reached the mills, large crowds of julahas [weavers] left their work and went to the spot . . . and [then] went off to see their moulvis." At a meeting of three thousand Muslims it was decided to telegraph the Viceroy and, while awaiting his reply, to seek legal redress. The legal issues arose because the official notices had never been properly served to the mosque managers, who had refused to act as legal representatives for the mosque.

This refusal to act as legal representatives, and the recourse of the crowd to (unnamed) learned men (*maulawīs*), suggest that *bisāti* (peddler) leaders were unwilling to operate in this larger public arena. Other Muslims, however, soon moved in, to act in ways the original managers would not. At a small meeting attended by some 125 Muslims from all quarters of the city, a body of eleven new managers was chosen for the mosque. Though the two original managers were included among this number, it is clear that this new body was a radical departure from traditional practice. It is also clear that, despite Meston's protests, it was more than a political ploy by out-of-towners. The new method of selection for the managing committee suggested to every Muslim of Kanpur that he had a potential stake in any mosque, regardless of location.

The move meant, too, that when the demand arose, traditional positions of leadership could be infused with new purpose—for the new body of managers began immediately to act as the corporate representatives of the mosque. They first addressed the Municipal Board Chairman, to find out who were the Muslims who had worn shoes through the bathing place.[8] And when Meston issued a press communique to "counteract misrepresentations" printed in the newspapers, the eleven published a rejoinder. They then called two public meetings to discuss Muslim reaction to the demolition.

The second meeting, which took place at the *'īd-gah* on August 3, was elaborately planned. Placards urged "all Mohammedan gentlemen whose hearts [were] upset and agitated by the martyrdom of part of the mosque" to "postpone their urgent duties and take part in the assemblage." Muslim neighborhoods were canvassed door-to-door. Mourning symbolism was invoked: "large groups of Muslims from every quarter of the city were seen proceeding towards the 'id-gah barefooted and carrying black flags. . . . some of the groups used to halt at intervals during their march. . . . and at every halt a man recited an elegy on the demolished portion" (*Muslim Gazette* 7/6/13, in *SVN 1913*). Early speeches evoked shared cultural values by reciting Persian poetry; aggrieved Muslim sensibilities were expressed as the rhetoric became increasingly heated. Yet when the crowd of ten to twelve thousand left the *'īd-gah*, it did not seem bent on violence. It headed for the mosque, where efforts were made to symbolically rebuild the washing place by piling the bricks back up. When the police chief tried to break this up, the crowd began showering police (and then the nearby temple) with debris from surrounding, demolished houses. After some ineffectual efforts at crowd control, armed police fired into the crowd and eventually dispersed the rioters.

Thus a number of important symbols and examples of Islamic symbolic rhetoric were brought to bear on the issue. The invocation of a shared literary heritage, the concept of martyrdom, and the replication of mourning practices were now applied to a mosque—the pre-eminent

8. Though this information was refused to them, they must have discovered at least some of the culprits. One told Meston that "he dared hardly stir out of his house on account of the fury of his co-religionists" (Meston 1913:13).

structure representing Muslim sacred space. The institution of mosque management was reshaped to fulfill new purposes. Face-to-face contact (through neighborhood canvassing to publicize the protest meeting) was used to reinforce and personalize the sense of shared community among Muslims. The result was an unprecedented scale of protest against the government's actions.

For some time before this, Muslim opinion had been coalescing against the government. Heavy coverage in the press stated the case plainly. The *dālān* had been demolished because "Muslims are loyal and they obey all the just as well as the unjust orders of the authorities," another in a long line of laments filling the newspapers over the reunification of Bengal. Moreover, "when hundreds of mosques have been destroyed in Macedonia, when the tomb of Imam Raza has been desecrated in Meshed, it is no wonder that a mosque is being demolished in India," a reflection of the anguish felt by Indian Muslims for the international condition of Islam (*Muslim Gazette* 6/2/13, in *SVN 1913*). Newspaper editors and prominent Muslims from other areas of India came to Kanpur to see the site for themselves and passionately to urge local Muslims to express their concern. "Every day," admitted Meston, "brought news of meetings and telegrams in different parts of India."

The form taken by these protests suggests the style of public language that was evolving. The treatment of Islam in Kanpur, Bengal, and elsewhere in the world was perceived as a measure of its decline. Once powerful in the world, it seemed helpless to stave off these assorted blows; the fate of the mosque in Macchli Bazaar was symptomatic of the "martyrdom" of Muslims in general. The invocation of this idiom, involving mourning, martyrdom, and defeat, would powerfully shape the demand for action—and the symbols around which such action would revolve—in the ensuing decades. The K͟hilāfat movement (Minault 1982) is perhaps the most obvious example, but in Kanpur itself, other issues involving Muslims ranged from participation in the Tanz̤īm (community defense) movement to limitations on employment and access to patronage; all of these came to be expressed through a martyrdom motif. We might note that, as martyrdom and its symbols coalesced as the basis for a shared Muslim identity, it became increasingly difficult for "Muslims" to maintain ambiguous but integrative public roles—to both participate in factional politics and simultaneously represent "Muslim" interests. But this was a product of the 1920s and 1930s. In 1913, ambiguity still served to protect leaders who had to operate in two very different public arenas.

A revealing indication of the wide range of Muslims affected by the Kanpur affair was the juxtaposition, on the one hand, of the roster of rioting mill hands and other lower-class Muslims and, on the other, of the delegation to Meston led by the Raja of Mahmudabad. All fourteen of the signatories to a memorial presented by the Raja were from outside Kanpur (generally Delhi- or Lucknow-based) and had been active in province- or India-wide Muslim causes ranging from the anti-Nagri campaigns, the Turkish Relief, and South African committees, to the Muslim Defence Association, the Muslim League, and the Board of Trustees for Aligarh University. They included lawyers and judges; landholders and *pīrs*; Legislative Council and municipal board members; Sunnis and Shī'as; "young" and "old" party members.[9] Both factions of several strong rivalries were represented. They were certainly living proof of their memorial's first contention that "the feelings of our community on this question as a whole are neither individual, local nor manufactured." Indeed, by this time they could speak as well for the rioting Pathan and *julāha* weavers when they insisted "these feelings are genuine, real and founded upon the bedrock of religious faith."

It was the government's misfortune to have been caught unsuspecting in the changing perceptions of community. It seems clear, for instance, that while local practice had tolerated the wearing of shoes in the *dālān*, once this became common knowledge it proved an embarrassment to the Muslim community in general—and for this reason the new managers made it their first act to try to find the culprits. While inexplicable to British administrators of the day, this "witch hunt" demonstrates clearly the impact of reformed personal practice on a previously ambiguous public context for Islam. Similarly, an agreement to relocate part of the mosque might have been possible to arrange quietly, locally; but once the cause received some publicity, in an atmosphere already heavily laden with despair over the position of Islam, this became impossible. (Indeed, there is a special irony in this. Though the government had previously pointed to cooperation by Lucknow Muslims in a similar case, Meston now had to admit that, as a result of the Kanpur agitation, managers of the Lucknow mosque had suddenly told the government that they could not move a similar washing place.)

9. List of signatories for "Address by Muhammadan delegation and Lt. Governor's Reply" (n.d.), Appendix 11 to Meston (1913:4). Biographical information on signatories from Robinson (1974).

Still insisting that the Kanpur Muslims were innocent dupes, the Lieutenant-Governor issued a general pardon and closed the city to newspapermen. The government quietly helped the managers close up the hole in the wall so that the mosque could be used for *ramaẓān* prayers, and the issue slowly died down. Press coverage continued; a fund was established to help with the legal expenses and to assist survivors of the men killed in the riot. Though the government held firm in its refusal to rebuild the *dālān* (except on a different side of the mosque), it finally had to stage a dramatic appeasement of Muslim feeling, arranging for the Viceroy to come to the city to release 106 prisoners awaiting trial. Though it exacted a formal apology from Kanpur's Muslims in return, it was clear that public opinion had carried the day (Hardy 1972:185).

More than the power of Muslim public opinion was at issue, however. The exhortations at the mass meeting preceding the riot make it clear that a sense of urgency attended the new concern for protecting the public aspects of Islam. This expansion of the vision of community carried the possibility of transcending the localized, competing demands for allegiance which Muslims faced. It reflects significantly on the nature of the two patterns of alternative ambiguous public expressions of "Muslimness" that this, the most successful effort, was aimed not against Hindus but against the government. In the vocabulary used that day, its success could be measured by the amount of "zeal" exhibited by Muslims. Exhorters of the crowd had lamented that in the past Muslims had passively accepted their treatment at the hands of the government. No more. "There are 47,000 Muslims in the city [of Kanpur] and only women are left in our houses; cannot our zeal now be called real? . . . Can Government have any objection to recognizing our zeal now?"

The triumphant tone was well taken, for the "Cawnpore Mosque" agitation had set a new pattern for the future. It was a pattern which transcended not only local, or provincial-level, concerns, it transcended even the Indian context. A more sustained effort for a larger cause—the K͟hilāfat movement—would be required before a broad spectrum and substantial number of Muslims could be pulled into the communal arena. But the vision of a declining community had coalesced in the minds of Muslims throughout India. In the process, this new concern for the public aspects of Islam made it increasingly difficult to maintain a public ambiguity.

From Ambiguity to Coherent Definitions of Community

As we have seen, much of the structure in Muslim community life was provided through leadership exercised in a variety of settings; to the extent that the elite functioned as intermediaries, an ambiguous public recognition of an "Islamic" way of life was achieved. Thus the most significant changes in the early twentieth century were those affecting the processes by which urban leadership was legitimized. The expansion of the franchise, and reliance on the psychological pressure of mass protest, meant that much of the recognition of leadership status began to come from popular support. At the same time, the debate around Islamic symbols and the personal practice of religion polarized that very expression of popular support.

The form of politics, fostered by evolving government institutions, contributed powerfully to the tension of the 1930s. The careful balancing of assorted interests in an urban center, created by British appointments to municipal committees and other bodies of local administration, was largely maintained even when a majority of these positions became elective. To achieve results in these bodies Indian leaders formed factional alliances. Of necessity, these factions bore little relationship to the ideological constructs of religion or class. The appeal of these latter concepts did not lessen for leaders in the 1920s and 1930s, but they could not use them as their sole inspiration for actions when they operated at a practical level in the political arena.

Underlying tensions emerged especially when those leaders successful in the factional politics of the day tried to demonstrate their legitimacy through popular appeals and by organizing mass agitational activities. Since the language they seemingly shared with ordinary Muslims was ideological, it was natural that they should look to common symbols. They could not have done otherwise. By the early 1920s a series of political and economic changes had increased dramatically the number of Indians participating in agitational politics, compelling those who would be leaders to make more broadly based appeals. Dissatisfaction among the professional and government servant groups resulting from economic reversals after the War; the Congress reorganization which led for the first time to widespread popular recruitment in neighborhoods; the expansion of political arenas under the Montague-Chelmsford reforms; the Khilāfat movement—all of these experiences helped to pull ordinary Indians into national-level politics. These changes proved especially significant because they were accompanied by the large-scale replacement of so-called "natural leaders" by professional men.[10]

The use of ideological appeals had been especially encouraged in the late 1920s by movements aimed at conversion (the Arya Samāj's Shuddhi and Muslim retaliatory Tablīgh) and community defense (Hindu Sangāthan and Muslim Tanẕīm). Tablīgh was an effort to thwart Hindu appeals to particular groups of converts (such as the Malkana Rājpūts of Agra). Muslim reformists aimed at removing a number of Hindu practices retained by these groups after conversion, and at protecting the groups' Muslimness from the proselytizing advances of the Arya Samāj. Perhaps the most significant result of these movements was their translation of personal practice into public political acts. As a form of political mobilization joined to religious ideology, they profoundly altered north Indian collective activities.

Pra-bhāt pherīs, for instance, were introduced in Kanpur in 1929–30 by the local Congress Committee. Hindu in style, and designed to appeal to youthful supporters, they were a "sort of morning prayer in which young men and students [made] a round in [the] city . . . singing national songs on the way" ("Evidence" 1931:92). These processions were "small parties of people, about 10 or 12, [who] used to go to the Ganges for their morning bath and in returning they used to form themselves into groups, one leading singing and the others following. . . . They were singing Congress songs" ("Evidence" 1931:258). Adorned with flags and nationalist rhetoric, such *pra-bhāt pherīs* were soon incorporated into the Congress's special "Sunday Programmes" as well, thus providing the youthful activists with special recognition throughout the city (Pandey 1978:81).

These localized processions joined other distinctly populist Hindu activities that were meant to be anti-British at the same time. All of these attempted both to propagandize the nationalist message and to effect social and religious reform among ordinary people. Thus part of the Congress program was to picket toddy shops, whose clientele was estimated to be about 60 percent lower-class Hindus and 40 percent Muslim ("Evidence" 1931:92). The Municipal Board, moreover, seems to have used its funds to start physical fitness groups (*akhāṛās*) to teach

10. For a discussion of the British conception of "natural leader," see Freitag 1980, chapter 2. The involvement of a new and different kind of leader meant that the old-style patron-client networks—which so often in the past had been used to mobilize large numbers—were supplanted, or at least had to be supplemented, by ideological appeals. For details, see chapters 5, 6, and 7 of my forthcoming monograph.

"the art of warfare"; Muslims felt that only Hindus were permitted to attend these municipally sponsored *akhāṛās*.[11] In each of these experiments the organizers deliberately evoked the same sense of identity, the use of a "shorthand" symbolic vocabulary, even as they incorporated certain quasi-religious practices for emulation.

Among Kanpuri Muslims the Tanẕīm movement enjoyed a resurgence in direct response to the organization of the *pra-bhāt pherīs*. Neighborhood groups were used to improve the religious and social practices of Muslim lower classes, of whom the mills had attracted a substantial number to the city. One witness saw "some youngsters coming both morning and evening and persuading people to offer prayers and observe Ramzan etc. In honor of the death of Maulana Mohamed Ali these youngsters used to recite 'mersias' " ("Evidence" 1931:76). Another said that "the slogans shouted by the processionists were 'say your prayers regularly' and during the last Divali 'do not gamble' " ("Evidence" 1931:116). Tanẕīm fostered feelings of group identity and solidarity by giving processionists green flags and banners and as much of a special uniform as they could afford; in this activity, Tanẕīm followed the pattern established by the *pra-bhāt pherīs*. The values being inculcated emerge in the verses sung by one such Tanẕīm procession (translated by a witness):

> Wake up now, sleeping Muslims: get ready to support Islam. Time is coming for you to sacrifice yourself (when time comes). Losing your life (getting beheaded) become the Leader (sardar) of your community.
>
> Even the sceptics (denyers) [*sic*] acknowledge your sensitiveness and courage. It is a mere trifle for you to get ready for fighting.
>
> Those who ridicule your Shariat and worship, such unpious persons should be consigned to flames.
>
> We shall wake up the world; we shall shake the world when, united, we shall raise the monotheistic cry. With the light (splendour) of Monotheism, we shall light a fire and shall obliterate, O Infidelity, thy existence out of the world.
>
> We shall place our throats on swords, on spear heads. Where religion is involved, we shall get beheaded.[12]

Though the verses support Hindu testimony that many of the actions of the Tanẕīm committees were aimed against them, it is also clear that the perception of Islam as endangered, and of Muslims as an abused minority, was central to the movement. A remedy was seemingly offered for the martyrdom imagery now so familiar to U.P. Muslims. Seen in

11. "Evidence" 1931, testimony of Khaliluddin, p. 105.
12. "Evidence" 1931, p. 249, statement of L. Diwan Chand, who translated the verses.

this light, the efforts by some branches of the movement to teach the "use of lathi, ballam and sword, pharik gadka and wrestling" may be construed as defensive rather than offensive.[13] In any case, their message was violent.

This violent redress by the martyred Muslim community of north India marked an important departure from the previous ambiguity of public life. In the process of redefining their relationship to north Indian society, these Muslim activists—both *ashraf* and, increasingly, the ordinary people of urban *maḥalla*s (neighborhoods)—formulated a coherent pattern of what it meant to be a Muslim.[14] This coherent pattern combined reformist observance of personal practices with popular support of political causes identified as "Islamic." The combination precluded ambiguous integration; instead, divisions between communities rigidified.

These perceptions of martyrdom led to a reinterpretation of past events. Even events that had had no communal overtones at the time they occurred took on communal significance in retrospect. In turn, these reinterpretations led to re-enactment of such events in a new, communal guise. For example, in Kanpur the targets for the first attacks in the riot of 1931 were places which loomed large retrospectively from 1913 and from a riot in 1927. Though the Macchli Bazaar temple, for instance, had previously commanded little attention, by 1931 there was a tradition (fostered by the administration as well as popular opinion) which viewed it as the antagonist in what was now often described as the Hindu-Muslim riot of 1913.[15] Similarly, Hindu Kanpuris viewed a particular Muslim cap merchant as aggressively competitive, dating his activities from the 1927 riot. His shop, not surprisingly, was one of the first attacked in 1931.[16]

As the definition of what it meant to be a Muslim was systematized in a new way affected by reformed personal practice, and as past events and current treatments were coherently reinterpreted, aspects of urban life in north India were evaluated anew. Under this scrutiny, the faction-based political life of Kanpur became especially problematic. Refracted through the self-conscious lens of martyrdom, factional fights were transformed into a phenomenon we now recognize as communalism.

13. "Evidence" 1931, pp. 300–391, "Statement of Azizuddin . . ." in court of Additional Sessions Judge. Court case included in the collection of "Evidence."

14. For details of *maḥalla*-level Tanẓīm activities, see chapter 5 of Freitag 1980.

15. *British Parliamentary Papers* 1931:12.

16. "Evidence" 1931, p. 422, written statement of Syed Zakir Ali.

Communalism and the Kanpur Riot of 1931

As befitted the nature of Kanpuri civic life, it was primarily the commercial interests who ran the municipality, and much of their control stemmed from their participation as municipal commissioners and members of the District Board, the Cawnpore Improvement Trust, and the Provincial Legislative Council.[17] They had also joined Congress. But in this, most were not responding to an ideological appeal. Rather, they joined and controlled Congress as a way of extending their established power in Kanpur and of precluding the use of the Congress organizational network by any newcomers or challengers (Brass 1965). Through the Kanpur Congress organization these same leaders then ran a variety of programs, not all of which were fostered by the provincial or all-India Congress committees. These included not only neighborhood-level Congress committees, but the *pra-bhāt pherīs* described above, and the Shuddhi and Sangāthan movements as well.[18]

However, the evidence seems to suggest strongly that those in positions of power were not acting in a distinctly communal manner. Instead, they moved to control each new arena of public participation as it emerged; in the process they successfully shut out all those without pre-existing power bases in the city. Since those shut out were consistently, though not entirely, Muslims, this process was perceived as communally inspired. This frantic scramble for control was prompted by the deep but distinctly personal pattern of factionalism among those with influence.[19] That competition for control centered on personal animosities, rather than on ideological or class differences, meant that the increasing ideological concerns of Kanpuri Muslims were neither reflected in, nor provided an outlet through, the political structures of the city. Instead, factionalism fostered fragmentation.

Even the political activism of such organizations as Tanẓīm and Sangāthan was fragmented in the neighborhoods. Only such fragmentation would have permitted the factional rivals on the District and Municipal Boards, and in the Congress, to ignore the issue of communalism. Those Muslims who found places in the loci of power were

17. See "Evidence" for the variety of positions held by those testifying.

18. "Evidence" 1931, testimony of Sabu Narain Nigam on 22 April 1931, pp. 89–93; testimony of L. Diwan Chand, p. 254.

19. See Brass (1965) for a detailed discussion of this factionalism, which dictated power alignments in Kanpur for at least forty years. Both of the faction leaders discussed by Brass were politically active in 1931: see discussions of Municipal Board activities, etc., in "Evidence" 1931.

there not as "Muslim" voices, but as members of one or the other faction. Indeed, few were so included. This might have had less significance, had there not been an escalating commercial competition between successful Muslims and Hindus with municipal connections. Perceptions of this competition were shaped by the Muslim preoccupation with martyrdom.

Most Muslim merchants dealt in foreign goods, and thus had little sympathy with the Civil Disobedience movement launched in 1930. Consequent resentment of Congress picketing was especially strong among the cloth merchants who had, in the previous two years, moved to large shops located prominently on one of the main roads. At the same time, other Muslim merchants were being forced out of certain professions and locations by successful "Hindu" entrepreneurs. The first celebrated issue among Kanpuri Muslims was the forced ejection of a group of Muslim dyers from their traditional market area.[20] Prolonged litigation was used against wealthy and influential timber merchants, and then against vegetable and fruit sellers. Internal evidence[21] suggests that, again, these actions were not directed against Muslims per se, but that the men in question, like others in the city, fell prey to those who could manipulate municipal connections to their own economic advantage.

In a similar way, the patronage distributed by Municipal Commissioners found its way to few Muslims, as they were seldom in a position to be useful to the competing factions on the Board. Figures were presented, for instance, showing that between 1926 and 1929 only six Muslims were hired when fifty-three municipal clerical positions were filled ("Evidence" 1931:592). The statements given to the Commission make it clear that all Muslims testifying were aware of these slights and perceived them as a sign that Muslims were both powerless and systematically discriminated against. Though few witnesses put together as integrated an interpretation as the advocate Syed Zakir Ali—who linked together "an organized legal attack on the mosques in Cawnpore district" with the calculated harassment and impoverishment of Muslim merchants and the psychological pressure exerted on all by the "non-violent" persuasion of Congress ("Evidence" 1931:422–36)—all Muslim witnesses saw their exclusion from power as deliberate and

20. See, for instance, testimony by Syed Zakir Ali, 4 May. "Evidence" 1931, p. 427.

21. See machinations amongst Municipal Board members, "Evidence" 1931, pp. 303–13: "Proceedings of the 37th Meeting of the Cawnpore Municipal Board, March 5, 1930."

communally based. It is small wonder, then, that those who had been excluded from access to power finally responded with a violent resistance to the "martyrdom" of their community. This should not have come as a surprise; the connection between the martyrdom motif, community defense, and violent action had been forged as many Muslims moved from ambiguity to coherence, from integration in the public life of U.P. to separation and a coherent communal activism.

When this communal activism came face-to-face with the Hindu populist style of Congress mobilizers, the results were violent.[22] In 1931 a strike was called by Congress to protest the execution of the bomb-throwing revolutionary Bhagat Singh in Lahore. This was but the most recent in a long list of strikes called (primarily by Congress, though important occasions for Muslims had been observed as well). Few Muslims willingly observed the Congress-initiated protests, as Congress by this time, particularly in Kanpur, had become identified with the majority "Hindu" community. To achieve strict observance of the strike meant youthful Congress volunteers had to coerce Muslim (as well as British and some Hindu) cooperation. When frustrated, these volunteers smashed windows of shops, especially Muslim ones, along Halsey Road. Soon after, a similar attack was made by a crowd on a Muslim shop in Meston Road, the other major artery of Kanpur. The crowd moved down the road to attack the peddlers' now-famous Macchli Bazaar mosque and a bookstore located within its confines. Shortly thereafter, the nearby temple was attacked in retaliation. Violence continued this way for several days, moving from commercial to residential areas. Crowds used "hit-and-run" tactics, attacking people hiding in houses and then looting and / or setting fire to the houses afterward. Though evidence shows that neither of the most turbulent elements of Kanpur—the millworkers and the large *bad-ma'āsh* (gangster) population—initiated the riot, its scale increased dramatically when they became involved.

22. This riot is extraordinarily well-documented. A government-appointed Commission of Inquiry was ordered on 13 April 1931, and more than six hundred pages of richly detailed evidence were collected. It is available in IOR L/P & J/7/775 for 1931 ["Evidence"]. The official report published by the Commission (which does not, in fact, adequately reflect the insights provided by the evidence) was printed as "Report of the Commission of Inquiry and Resolution of the Government of U.P." Command Paper no. 3891, *British Parliamentary Papers* 1930–31, vol. 12, pp. 3–66. Congress conducted its own investigation and then issued a massive report which attempted to put this riot in a general historical context. This has been recently edited and published (see Barrier n.d.). Because Congress did not give the names or identity of any of its witnesses, I have instead used the testimony to the Commission to express the general complaints which the Congress committee also encountered.

Official incompetence was clearly responsible for the duration of the riot and perhaps to some degree for the level of violence as well. Severely understaffed, confused about tactics, the few policemen stood in the streets and watched attacks made on shops and homes. The beleaguered District Magistrate, a man of unsympathetic temperament, disdained the assistance of prominent Indian civic leaders. The degree of ignorance about conditions admitted by these officials was striking; not until the third day did they tour the city to see what had happened.

In that interval at least three hundred people were killed,[23] untold houses were burnt and looted, and a substantial number of temples and mosques were desecrated or destroyed. Its unprecedented scale made the event a dramatic watershed in the history of north Indian communal relations. No doubt much of this scale can be attributed to a criminal level of official ineptitude, but the underlying factors which turned an ostensible civil disobedience action into a large-scale communal riot cannot be explained so simply.

It is not coincidental that both the civil disobedience *hartāl* (strike) and the communal riot were collective activities conducted in the public arena. Where, at the turn of the century, such public activities could ambiguously imply an "Islamic" framework for many U.P. Muslims, this had become impossible by the 1930s. Instead, the reformist influence on personal practice had joined with a new emphasis on popular legitimation of leaders to shape a demand for a coherent, systematically delineated community of "Muslims."

The transition is an important one. Too often, scholars have assumed that leadership continued to operate in the intermediary-based style of the earlier period; as a result, "secular" politicians have been characterized as calculating manipulators of popular religious values (e.g., Pandey 1978). We must focus instead on the change in meaning that was being imputed to the symbolic rhetoric, by *ashraf* and *ajlāf* alike. Nor can these decades be described simply as a quest for political rule by Muslims. The realm affected by changed perceptions and charged symbolism was much larger than that traditionally represented by state rule. The alteration in public perceptions of the political implications inherent in personal religious acts is a truly profound one. It is no explanation to characterize the dichotomy of this period as being between Congress secularism and Muslim communalism, as was done in a recent volume (Hasan's own essay in Hasan 1981). On the contrary,

23. That was the official death count. Even the Government report admits that probably two thousand more people were killed (*British Parliamentary Papers* 1930–31:4).

the very real transition that we traced here by looking at Tanẓīm and its opposite (a distinctly Ḥindu populist style fostered by *pra-bhāt pherī*s and *akhāṛā*s under Congress aegis) casts the search in entirely new terms. This evidence turns our attention, instead, to changes in the way people behaved and symbolized their concerns in public arenas.

Not only did it become impossible to perpetuate an ambiguous public framework that implied a safe home for those observing Islam in this charged atmosphere. It became virtually impossible for individuals, even ordinary people, to act without self-consciousness. When almost every act takes on political as well as religious significance, the public context of such acts becomes crucial.

Against this added self-consciousness, the faction-focused and fragmented style of government created an impossible tension. In part this was the result of having to operate in a colonial context. As David Gilmartin has shown (in this volume), it was a matter of deliberate British policy that the state operated without reference to religion. In such a system, political effectiveness was judged not by a leader's ability to integrate an ideology with day-to-day political machinations, but by his ability to move from one public context to another. With few outlets in the factionalized politics of the day, Muslim community concerns were forced into another arena, an arena of fixed quantities of recognition and power allotted to each community. Any self-conscious action taken by one community of necessity affected the standing of the other.

And yet it was impossible for Indians to replace British administrators without innovation in the public context. The Hindu populism that came to characterize Congress-style self-government could not accommodate the public ambiguity on which U.P. Muslims had previously relied. Coupled with the new coherence and self-consciousness among many classes of Muslims, this fact led to an increasing reliance on violence—a combination which haunted the Subcontinent through the chaos and turbulence of Partition, and which continues in the specter of communal riots today.

References

PRIMARY SOURCES

Files from several India Office Records (IOR) series, including "Public and Judicial [L/P & J/]"; U.P. "General Administration Proceedings"; European Manuscripts collection; and U.P. Selections from the Vernacular Newspapers.

SECONDARY SOURCES

Ahmad, Imtiaz

1976 "Caste and Kinship in a Muslim Village of Eastern Uttar Pradesh." In *Family, Kinship and Marriage among Muslims in India.* Imtiaz Ahmad, ed. Delhi: Manohar Book Service.

Barrier, N. Gerald

n.d. *Roots of Communal Politics.* Columbia, Mo.: South Asia Books.

Bayly, C. A.

1975 *Local Roots of Indian Politics: Allahabad, 1880–1920.* Oxford: Oxford University Press.

Brass, Paul R.

1965 *Factional Politics in an Indian State.* Berkeley: University of California Press.

British Parliamentary Papers

1930–31 "Report of the Commission of Inquiry and Resolution of the Government of U.P." Command Paper no. 3891, vol. 12, pp. 3–66.

Freitag, Sandria B.

1980 "Religious Rites and Riots: From Community Identity to Communalism in North India, 1870–1940." Ph.D. dissertation, University of California, Berkeley.

forthcoming *Communalism Emerges: Public Arenas and Religious Activism in North India, 1870–1940.*

Hardy, Peter

1972 *The Muslims of British India.* Cambridge: Cambridge University Press.

Hasan, Mushirul, ed.

1981 *Communal and Pan-Islamic Trends in Colonial India.* Delhi: Manohar.

Metcalf, Barbara Daly

1978 "Conflict among Muslims: New Sects, New Strategies, Old Paradigms." Paper presented to the American Historical Association, December.

1982 *Islamic Revival in British India: Deoband, 1860–1900.* Princeton: Princeton University Press.

Metcalf, Barbara Daly, ed.

1984 *Moral Conduct and Authority: The Place of Adab in South Asian Islam.* Berkeley: University of California Press.

Minault, Gail

1982 *The Khilafat Movement.* New York: Columbia University Press.

Mujeeb, M.

1967 *The Indian Muslims.* London: George Allen & Unwin.

Pandey, Gyanendra

1978 *The Ascendancy of the Congress in Uttar Pradesh, 1926–34.* Delhi: Oxford University Press.

Robinson, Francis C. R.

1974 *Separatism among Indian Muslims.* Cambridge: Cambridge University Press.

8

Sardār, Hakom, Pīr: Leadership Patterns among the Pakistani Baluch

STEPHEN L. PASTNER

The primary emphases in most discussions of South Asian Muslim *adab*—the moral bases of behavior—have been either textual, historical, or centered on the beliefs and behavior of *ashrafī* (well-born) elites. That is, a "Great Tradition" bias has prevailed. The relative neglect of the behavioral and ideological components of *adab* among more unlettered, hinterland, or tribal Muslims is the result of many factors, a major one being—in the case of Pakistan at least—reluctance on the part of authorities to encourage research among such peoples, who may belong to ethnic groups seen as irredentist or otherwise dissident.

The Baluch, along with the tribal area Pukhtuns (Pathans), are perceived in just such a light. But despite some rather substantial barriers to research among them, a fair amount of work on the Baluch has been carried out in the last two decades, including the fieldwork Carroll Pastner and I conducted among nomads and oasis farmers in Makran (Southwest Baluchistan) and maritime Baluch on the Sind and Las Bela coasts.[1] This work among diverse groups, along with the writings of others, provides a representative picture of the relationship

1. In 1968–69, five months of fieldwork in Makran were funded by predoctoral grants and fellowships from the National Institute of Mental Health and from the Sigma Xi Society. In 1976–77, eight months of research on coastal Baluch society were supported by the American Institute of Pakistan Studies. Follow-up summer fieldwork on the Sind coast was carried out by the author alone in 1979, under a faculty fellowship from the University of Vermont, and in 1982 under a grant from the American Institute of Pakistan Studies.

between Baluch jural ideology—the indigenous notions of how social life *should* be conducted—and the ways in which social organization is actually constituted. This discussion will concentrate on male-oriented ideology and behavior, most specifically those aspects of Baluch *adab* (or as they would term it, *riwāj*, or normative custom) relating to matters political and economic in contexts both secular and religious.

The Baluch

The Baluch, an Iranian-speaking people, are centered on an approximately 210,000-square-mile arid tract—Baluchistan—which occupies the western third of Pakistan, the southeastern section of Iran, and the southwestern part of Afghanistan. Substantial Baluch populations are also found in Punjab and Sind. Population estimates for the Baluch are all no more than guesswork, ranging from "official" Pakistani figures of around 2.5 million in that country (probably too low and an outgrowth of various regimes' desires to downplay Baluchi "ethnic power" movements) to the 30 million postulated by some secessionist leaders. A more realistic figure is about 5 million, 60 percent of whom reside in Pakistan.

Those who call themselves Baluch and speak Baluchi as a mother tongue are of heterogeneous origin: various tribal and lineage groups trace descent to ancestors as diverse as Syrian Arabs, Rajputs, Kurds, and Pathans. Certainly the dominant form of Baluch political organization, based as it is on powerful patron-client bonds, is an agglutinative one which for centuries has encouraged incorporation of outsiders into the retinues of aspiring leaders (see Barth 1969).

Despite the fact that they live in some of the bleakest terrain on the planet, the Baluch have a certain diversity in their ecological and economic adaptations and socio-political organization. In easternmost and westernmost Baluchistan (the Sulaiman mountains of Pakistan and the Iranian Sarhad plateau, respectively), a way of life predominantly based on sheep/goat pastoral nomadism is followed by the Baluch. This is organized, jurally at least, along tribal, segmentary lineage principles. Such tribes as the Marris (Pehrson 1966), Bugtis (Matheson 1967), and Yarahmadzai (Salzman 1971) are dominated by *sardārs* (chiefs) who stand at the apex of patrilineal genealogical pyramids embracing rulers and ruled.

In date-growing oases of southern Baluchistan (Pastner and Pastner 1977) a more castelike feudal order prevails. At the top are lineages known generically as *hakom*, which traditionally squabbled amongst themselves for the right to exploit a broad middle rung of free-born Baluch agriculturalists, and hinterland nomads. At the bottom of the hierarchy are a large underclass known as *hizmatkar*. Many are of markedly negroid appearance, testifying to an ancestry rooted in the African slave trade; many Baluch mercenaries were active in slaving, serving in the retinues of the Gulf Arab *amīrs* who dominated the trade.

Along the Arabian sea coast as far east as Karachi are maritime Baluch settlements of varying size. Fishing, from lateen-sailed boats, and smuggling are the mainstays of these Baluch, many of whom belong to a Mahdist sect known as Zikri because of its emphasis on Sufi meditation practices.[2] Regarded as infidels (*kāfirs*) by the Sunni Baluch majority, since the mid-eighteenth century the Zikris have been a much-maligned and harassed minority whose allegiance is less to *hakom*-style chiefs (on the model of interior groups) and more toward village chiefs or *waderas* and Zikri *pīrs*.[3] The mantle of spiritual power (*barakat*) and the legends surrounding their *pīrs* provide Zikris with a measure of self-esteem lacking through more secular paths of status elevation.[4]

There are, then, several different patterns discernible among Baluch populations. Despite this evident variation in local and regional political and economic organization, certain common themes can be discerned in the ways the Baluch conceptualize and enact behaviors relating to leadership and normative values.

Baluch Leadership and Politico-economic Values

In our research among the Baluch I came across the term *adab* only once, when it was used by a fisherman to designate a desirable quality

2. Zikriism among the Baluch originated in the late fifteenth or early sixteenth century. It is suggested by scholars (e.g., Hughes-Buller in the *Baluchistan District Gazetteer*) that its founder was either Sayyid Mahmud Jaunpuri or one of his disciples. But most Baluch attribute the founding of the sect to a mythical figure—"Khoda Dad"—who was born not of man and woman, and who taught the Baluch the technique of the *ẕikr* and the belief in the *mahdī* (future deliverer) "a long time ago." Zikris and Sunnis differ on a number of doctrinal and ritual points. Although Zikriism was once widespread among the Baluch, after Nasir K͟hān of Kalat mounted a *jihād* against them, Zikris fled to remote desert areas in Makran or on the coast of Baluchistan and Sind, escaping persecution from hinterland Sunni Baluch.
3. These are the charismatic religious leaders defined as "saints" by Barth writing of the Pathans (1959).
4. See Pastner (1978a and 1978b) for more on maritime Baluch adaptations and Zikri doctrine and history.

in a prospective wife. In this context it meant "gentility." Much more prominent, when informants discussed the moral principles dominant in social life, were concerns relating directly to economics and power politics. Similarly, the *ādāb* characteristically propounded for the *ashrafī* gentility or for Sufi ascetics were far less central to Baluch *riwāj* (custom) than values similar to those of the Pukhtunwali code of tribal Pathans (Ahmed 1980) or the "Three Z's" (*zar, zamīn, zan*: "gold, land, and women") of Punjabi martial castes.

Idioms commonly used by Baluch men to describe the ideal qualities of both political leaders and common men include readiness (*tiyyar*; Urdu: *taiyarī*) to protect the honor (*'izzat*) of one's family or followers, by force if necessary; shrewdness combined with toughness of character (*zabr-dost*; Urdu: *zabar-dastī*); personal strength (*takat*; Urdu: *ṭāqat*); and strength measured in terms of kin or political retainers (*zohr*).

Notable adages relating to power and its prerogatives include: "Strong water can flow uphill" ("Zuraki ap jhala sha borza ro:t"): that is, the powerful can violate even nature's laws; and, "If your fortress is strong and your supporters numerous, for you there shall be neither danger nor trouble" ("ko:t o kalat sohn abant, ho posht ho bras baz abant, khatr o taklif hich nabant").

An exemplary man is often portrayed as a "guardian" or "watchman" (*pannagi*) of his dependents, be they kin or political subordinates. He must defend his own honor or that of his in-group (the latter being defined relative to the scale of opposition, in accordance with classic segmentary politico-kinship principles). But if a man's personal moral duty (*ḥaqq*) includes the willingness to use violence against *outsiders* in this defense, he should also be prepared to employ reasoned arbitration to settle conflicts *within* the in-group.

This relationship between violence and moderation as guiding forces of social life grows out of a basic Baluch view of human nature, characterized by a dualism shared by many Islamic peoples. The Baluch see themselves as basically a "hot" tempered people, the term for temperament (*tāṣīr*; Arabic: "effect") being applied to a range of personality-related phenomena, from foods to entire ethnic groups. "Hot" temperament (*garm tāṣīr*) is said to be characteristic of such aggressive, martial peoples as Pathans and Punjabis, in contrast to more docile and "cold" (*sard tāṣīr*) peoples like Sindhis, Bengalis, and Englishmen (Kurin 1982).

A major component of "hotness" is sexual volatility. Certain foods promote this; as one informant said, " 'hot' foods produce blood and blood produces semen [*mardī*]." Gender, too, promotes this, women being seen as even "hotter" than men. This sensual basis for Baluch aggressiveness is believed to be rooted in the baser aspects of the soul (Baluchi *nasp*; Arabic and Urdu *nafs*). Schimmel (1975:112–13), in a review of Sufi sources, notes that *nafs* has been variously likened to a restless and gluttonous male, an unruly camel, a pig, and a wanton woman. Certainly the Baluch are explicit in their notion that *nasp* is a trait more pronounced in women than in men, women being associated with greater emotional instability.[5]

Valued though this potentially disruptive influence of the individual's *nasp*-generated hotness may be in certain contexts (e.g., confrontations with enemies), the Baluch balance it by professing esteem for rationality (*'aql*). A praiseworthy man must be able to juggle these two conflicting elements of human nature. Along with aggressiveness should go generosity and conciliation. "If your tongue is sweet, the world shall be yours" ("Agar gap shirin, mulk girin") is one mandate of an aspiring Baluch leader. Extreme values of wealth and generosity ideally should coexist with the clearheadedness and strength necessary to attract and retain supporters. For example, among the Baluch nomads with whom we worked, camp headmen (*komash*) were said to be men of "property and [good] speech" (*mal o gop*), the former to fulfill their official role as hosts to visitors in the camp, the latter to arbitrate disputes between campmates (*hamsayag*; Urdu: *ham-sāya*, "those who share the shade") (see Pastner 1971).

For nonleaders, too, generosity and kindness are highly valued in Baluch *riwāj*. Donations to those in need (*bijjar*), offerings (*chunda*; Urdu: *chandā*) to shrines in hopes of gaining blessing (*sawab*), and contributions on behalf of someone who must pay blood compensation in a feud are a few of the myriad occasions for "free" gifts. Stinginess (*kunjus*) is frowned upon in Baluch society.

The realities of Baluch political and economic life accord with the

5. Women are said to have seventy-seven kinds of *nasp* to men's seventy. A story is cited in this connection: "One day, Hazrat Adam quarreled with Bibi Hawa [Eve]. Adam went to God and asked to be granted children independent of Hawa. So God brought forth the beings who would become slaves and kings. They are the sons of Adam. Hawa likewise asked God to have children separate from Adam. So God created *jinn* and *lak* [demons], the true children of women." Interpretation: The "sons of man" are either agents (kings) or objects (slaves) of "control." The children of Hawa, however, are the capricious, uncontrollable forces directly antithetical to rationality and social order. From such a perspective, the complex of customs relating to *parda* flow naturally, women being seen as requiring protection from their own worst instincts.

above ideals only to a point. Certainly the Baluch have a well-deserved historical reputation as tough and aggressive fighting men. Firdausi's tenth-century *Shāhnāma* first describes the ferocity of "Kuch and Baluch." This is a theme that continued through the days of the British Raj—whose frontier policies favored bribing the Baluch rather than fighting them—and into the contemporary Pakistani era, when as recently as 1977 the central government found itself embroiled in a shooting war with secessionist Baluch guerrillas.

But a number of points of departure exist between the "ideal" and the "real." To begin with, Baluch leaders often gained and maintained their power more by grossly self-serving collusion with powerful external authorities than by exercising righteous militancy on behalf of their followers against outsiders. The feudal hierarchy of Makran, for example, was dominated by elite lineages who intermarried with the family of the superordinate Khans of Kalat, the heads of a powerful confederacy founded by the Ahmadzai Brahuis in the early eighteenth century. Makrani *hakom* groups, such as the Gitchkis, curried favor with the Khans and later with the British as a means of being left alone to exploit the subordinate strata through a variety of oppressive taxes. As long as they acted as "wardens of the march" for external powers (such as the British, who were obsessed with Russian ambitions toward South Asia), this state of affairs was allowed to continue.

In more recent times Pehrson cites the Marri tribal leader who remarked: "I kiss the political agent's boots and get a thousand to kiss mine" (1966:26). Among the coastal Zikri Baluch, village headmen are much involved in patronage politics (*chamcha*, "spoon"; i.e., "you feed me and I'll feed you"), often lining their own pockets with bribes from city-based party bosses in return for votes bullied out of villagers.

Such headmen hold their position through a combination of force of character, the clout of a large group of kin, and hereditary right. They generally emerge from the lineage of the village founder, specific leaders being chosen in *jirga*s, the village councils of adult men. The "hotness" of temperament that propelled them to power is indeed seen as a "plus" in dealing with often-hostile outsiders, such as the Sunni Baluch and Sindhis who surround the Zikri villages. However, the other ideal facet of character, their conciliatory abilities supposedly rooted in *'aql*, is often less evident, particularly in situations where the headman has a direct interest in an intravillage dispute. In such cases it is typical for headmen of other villages or for *pīr*s to intervene and settle a dispute that the local *wadera* was supposed to handle in the first place.

During research among the coastal Zikri Baluch, I collected seventy-three cases of disputes and their settlements which illustrate both fulfillments of, and lapses from, the ideals of leadership. A typical example of the former occurred when Sunni Baluch living in a village (located inland from the fishing community we were studying) refused the Zikris permission to bury their dead in the Sunni graveyard. An armed band of Zikris led by the headman's son, and urged on by the elderly headman himself, marched on the Sunnis, forcing them to back down.

But on another occasion, when the headman was expected to act in a conciliatory way to head off a dispute, he only fueled it because of his personal stake in the matter. On this occasion a group of women had gathered to draw water from a tank truck operated by the fishing cooperative to which the villagers belonged. The wife of the headman shoved another woman aside and an argument ensued. The headman appeared on the scene, and, rather than calming things down, he struck his wife's adversary. This catapulted the conflict to a potentially serious level. This was not only a major breach of *riwāj* (women—other than one's own wife—are supposed to be immune from violence, along with religious leaders, mendicants, and guests), but it was also a direct challenge to the honor of the victim's husband, who would have been well within his rights to react violently in defense of his wife. What did happen is quite illustrative of the nature of actual Baluch political behavior. The husband of the attacked woman was in fact outraged at the headman's act, but he realized he could not match the headman in terms of village-level supporters. Instead he made it into the concern of his brother-in-law, a wealthy Karachi fish broker. As the brother of the victim the townsman also had "guardianship" responsibilities for her. He therefore threatened to use his patronage ties with influential power brokers in Karachi to chastise the headman. The matter was finally resolved when a *jirga* of other headmen forced the local chief to pay a fine (*dand*) and to apologize to the woman.

The individual Baluch, then, has a keen sense of his place in a hierarchical pecking order. Normative rules stressing the need for unequivocal defense of personal honor coexist with real behaviors that often vacillate between marked "machismo" and obsequiousness. This pattern is expressed in the adages: "If you don't know who farted, blame the powerless" ("Ke tir data? Gharib a data!", literally, "Who gave a fart? The poor man!"); and "Beat the old woman, Malu, because she is the property of God" (i.e., there is no human being who will protect her: "Bejant Malua ke Malu male khodae").

Certain of the Zikri fishermen we studied achieved an interesting reconciliation between the ideal self-image combining power and control, and a reality of relative political powerlessness. They often referred to themselves as *gharīb*—a word of subtle shadings. Among interior Baluch groups, for example, the term means one who is impoverished, a social outsider or stranger and an all-around wretched specimen. But the fishermen employed the word to convey a self-image of modesty, straightforwardness, and honorable unpretentiousness—in a word, what urban Pakistani elites mean when they use the English "simple" (a term usually uttered in a sympathetic but condescending tone of voice, as when speaking of the rural poor among whom one has just had a weekend picnic!). This difference in usage of *gharīb* is probably attributable to the fact that Baluch of the interior can compare themselves only to other Baluch who share the same value system and against whom one is either more or less powerful. The fishermen, however, are in daily contact with relatively sophisticated and wealthy, but culturally alien, Karachites whose prosperity is seen as a sign of decadence, based on no such honorable code of morality as the *riwāj* of the Baluch.

In the area of economic life, too, reality is often at variance with ideals. Baluch fishermen, for example, professed strong values of cooperation and sharing among kin and neighbors. However, when boats were beached each day and those same neighbors and kin clustered around to lay claim to a share of the catch, successful fishermen would try (albeit unsuccessfully) to fob them off with all sorts of disclaimers ("Oh, I didn't catch much, just a few rotten catfish!"), despite the fact that fat mackerel and croakers would momentarily be held up for bids from fish buyers from Karachi.

When free giving does occur it is often done ostentatiously. At marriages and circumcisions guests give gifts of money (*dela*), the amounts of which are publicly proclaimed by a crier (*wank wallah*) in a display not unlike that of the potlatches of the American Indian tribes of the north Pacific coast. On one occasion a headman, whose gift was inadvertently overlooked by the *wank wallah*, was so outraged that he stormed out of a wedding feast, returning with an armed following to attack the hosts. A confrontation was avoided only through the intercession of some *mullā*s and other headmen.

In short, despite a tremendous amount of lip service given to normative values of honor, harmony, and generosity within an in-group, and the need for mutual protection amongst *wat ma wat* ("those united among themselves" by marriage, clientage, or friendship), actual Baluch political and economic behaviors are marked by a high degree of impulsiveness, shifting political alliances, and obsequiousness toward those with greater power. Self-interest is high at all levels of society. The perceived dual and unstable nature of humanity is, for the Baluch as for many Muslims, a self-fulfilling prophecy, leading to what Gulick (1976) has called a mentality of "peril and refuge." Emphasis is on protection of one's personal honor, and of the honor of one's dependents. The importance placed on the concept of "guardianship" grows from these roots, as do many other aspects of society. Kin-endogamy, for example, is related to this; it exists in virtually all Middle Eastern traditional societies as a jural ideal and in many as a statistical reality (e.g., among maritime Baluch over 60 percent of marriages were between actual bilateral first cousins). That is, one should cleave to those most like oneself, since others are not to be trusted. To the Baluch, *riwāj* is the principle which should obviate the fundamental contradictions in human nature. But when *nasp* and *'aql* collide, in fact, the former is at least as likely to prevail as the latter.

Baluch Leadership and Religious Values

Thus far I have dealt with secular concepts of right behavior as they relate to political and economic life. But the Baluch also have well-defined normative images of "sacred" as well as profane exemplary conduct. I will focus now on a particular category of Baluch religious adepts, the *pīr*s, or "saints," especially those of the Zikri Baluch. Like other Muslims, the Baluch recognize a variety of religious personnel, from theologically trained *'ulamā* through often idiosyncratic and illiterate *miyān*s and *malang*s. Because of their greater amount of *barakat*, however, the *pīr*s are the apogee of the Baluch ideal of the "holy man" and therefore an appropriate counterpoint to the jural images of secular right-behavior.

Baluch *pīr*s are not expected to engage in such total renunciation of the world as that often found in the history of Judeo-Christian mysticism (e.g., the ancient Hebrew Essenes, Trappist monks, etc.). Instead, the Baluch *pīr*, like his secular counterpart, should use his power in and for the world. Ideally, in the case of the *pīr*, this means acting as spiritual exemplar (*murshid*) to a body of lay followers (*murīd*s), who are encouraged to "repent" of evil and carnality (*tobo kanag*; Urdu: *tauba karnā*; from the Arabic *tauba*, "repentance"). But whereas, in the quest for the exemplary life, laymen are supposed to achieve a balance between "hotness" and "cool" reason—between *nasp* and *'aql*—the *pīr* is supposed to eradicate or "kill" his *nasp* altogether (*nasp kashag*) so as not to act from passion or from base personal motives. This is accomplished through meditation (*azrat*; Urdu: *'uzlat*), prayer, and self-denial such as extended fasting (*chillag*; Urdu: *chillā*—literally "forty days"). *Pīrs* are supposed to use their powers altruistically, warding off illness and misfortune from their *murīds* and acting as arbiters in disputes which cannot be settled by more hot-headed secular leaders.

This personal, spiritual virtuosity in achieving acknowledged "sainthood" is balanced by an element of ascription: saints are usually drawn from *pīr-zāda* (the son of a *pīr*) or *sayyid* lineages.[6] Individuals of great piety and spiritual power who lack such "family connections" usually become *miyāns* or extra-*'ulamā* religious adepts of somewhat lesser status than *pīrs*.

When a renowned *pīr* dies, his burial place can become a shrine, while ground that he has consecrated with his power may become a *tik-khana* ("house of wellness", i.e., curing [Urdu: *ṭhīk* = "well, right"; *k͟hāna* = house]), associated with geophagy by pilgrims and various other contagious or sympathetic magical practices. For example, the Baluch *sarakut* ritual—analogous to the *'aqīqa* rite of other South Asian Muslims—involves invoking the blessing of a saint on a young child whose hair is then shorn and hung next to the shrine with accompanying sacrifices of goats or sheep.

The real behaviors and roles of Baluch *pīrs* can be evaluated against this normative image. Forty-eight stories I collected about *pīrs* and their exploits provide the corpus of data from which certain generalizations can be made. Many of these cases, to be sure, reveal the *pīr* in his role as altruist—curing illness, finding lost objects, ending droughts, locating fish for hungry villagers, and, in the case of Zikri *pīrs*, providing a vicarious sense of self-esteem to people denied more mundane avenues of status elevation.

But fully one-half of the cases have as their dominant theme the use of *barakat* by *pīrs* in competitive contexts. Fourteen cases describe *pīrs* engaged in holy-power contests (*chikasag*) with rival holy men; six deal with *pīrs* using their *barakat* against secular enemies; while two each deal with contests of men versus women, and humans versus *jinn*. Several examples of the saint as competitor can be cited:

6. For an explanation of how the schismatic Zikris define saintly pedigrees see Pastner 1978a.

Case 1. Barakat used against a lay rival: A turn-of-the-century Zikri *pīr* had a beautiful female servant. The ruler (*jam*) of Las Bela (a former princely state, now an administrative district in Baluchistan), upon hearing of her beauty, ordered the saint to send him the woman. The saint refused, and the ruler sent a troop to force the holy man to give her up. The saint got word of the approaching force and went into the hills to the west of the ruler's capital at the town of Bela. He fired off his pistol, and so great was his power that the bullet wounded the ruler in his distant capital.

Case 2. A power contest between Zikri and Sunni *pīrs*: A Sindhi Sunni *pīr* threatened to steal the *barakat* of a famous Zikri *pīr* (a common theme), and force him to embrace Sunni Islam. The Zikri accepted the challenge, mounted his camel, and traveled to the Hab (the river marking the border of Sind and Baluchistan), where the Sindhi was waiting. As soon as the Zikri came into view the Sindhi's limbs grew rigid and he became mute, unable to return the *salām* (greeting) of the Zikri. The grandfather of a prominent Zikri in our village was witness to the event. At the time, he was himself a Sunni, but on seeing the power of the Zikri he converted.

Case 3. Test of power between Zikris (also involving revenge on a Sunni): Not long ago a Zikri *pīr* traveled to Koh-i Murad, the mountain in southern Baluchistan said to be the site where their *mahdī* once sat and the primary goal of the Zikri pilgrim (*ḥājī*). When he arrived, he learned that the golden offerings (*chunda*) to the shrine had been stolen. Chiding the other holy men present for not having sufficient *barakat* to recover the gold, he announced that his power would cause a snake to attack the guilty party. That night a Sunni Baluch in the oasis of Turbat near the holy mountain was bitten by a cobra. He surrendered the gold and begged the Zikri to cure him. The saint replied that he was destined to die for his crime—and so he did.

Case 4. A *pīr* helps a client (sort of!): A leader of the Baluch guerrillas, who for some years had been waging a war of secession against Pakistan, came to a Zikri *pīr* for an amulet that would protect him against Pakistani troops. The guerrilla was a Sunni, but the reputation of the saint was such that the fighting man decided to forget sectarian matters. To the guerrilla the *pīr* gave a turban he said was so imbued with *barakat* that it would turn the army bullets to water. One night as the guerrilla leader slept in his camp, a Pakistani commando force attacked, blowing the guerrilla to bits. The turban, however, came through without a scratch!

From a behavioral standpoint it is irrelevant whether or not *pīrs* really do exercise such powers; for it is clear their *murīds* believe that they do. When the story of the guerrilla and the turban was recited to me, the fishermen with whom I was sitting exclaimed "*wah wah*!" and "*shabāsh*!" (bravo) even though the outcome of the story was, to me at least, somewhat ambiguous.

The support of his *murīds* can be parlayed by the Baluch *pīr* into tangible political and economic rewards. *Pīrs* spend much time traveling to the homes of their far-flung supporters, being lavishly feted and offered gifts and money. Sometimes *pīrs* will exercise their power in the political arena via the *chamcha* system, in ways quite similar to secular leaders. For instance, during the ill-fated 1977 general election, a well-known Zikri *pīr* delivered a large bloc of votes to the incumbent Pakistan People's Party in return for a plum bureaucratic job for one of his relatives.

I would go so far as to suggest that, despite professions of the ideals of asceticism and altruism—following the Sufi model—Baluch *pīrs* are granted the mantle of sainthood only after they have validated their *barakat* in the competitive arena. Thus, at the turn of the century, one well-known saint of proper lineage who had performed several *chillag* did not gain a following of *murīds* (the sine qua non of "*pīr*-hood") until he had used his power to halt a train on which he had been refused a seat. The competitive persona of the Baluch *pīr* can be seen in one old photograph which sits like an icon in many Baluch houses. The *pīr* sits not bedecked with the woolen cloak of the Sufis, or holding the bowl and staff of a mendicant, but rather with a bullet-filled bandolier.

Leadership Patterns Symbolized

In pointing out the parallels between Baluch secular and sacred power-related ideologies and behaviors, I have tried to stay close to matters manifest in the words and actions of the Baluch. At this point I would like to suggest briefly a similarity between *sardār*, *hakom*, and *pīr* which I believe exists on a more symbolic plane. The symbolic motif I refer to centers on the importance of headgear—that is, turbans—to high status in both sacred and temporal contexts. "Tying the turban" (*pag bandag*; Urdu: *pagṛī bandhnā*) is the investiture ceremony of secular Baluch leaders, while turbans are conspicuous items bedecking the biers of dead saints in mausolea (*mazār*), or resting atop crude stone shrines in the desert.

Leach (1973) has suggested that in many societies the human body is seen as a phallic symbol, with the elaborate headgear of rulers or clerics (e.g., a bishop's miter) emphasizing the "potency" of the individual wearing it. Baluch epistemology parallels this notion quite closely, though with its own peculiarities. Head hair and beards are seen both as symbols of virility (i.e., emanating from *nasp*) and as being attached to the seat of *'aql*, or rationality. There are, then, ambiguities attached to the head and its hair effusions not found in relation to other parts of the body (which may be viewed as unequivocally base).[7]

7. For example, axillary hair (*bogal*) and pubic hair (*rom*) are cause for shame and are shaved regularly by both sexes.

I suggest that the problem of the head and its hair is resolved by the often-dramatic turban styles affected, at least on public occasions, by powerful men (e.g., the erect-tailed Mashadi style). The turban at once contains the negative aspects of *nasp* (lust, greed, etc.), while at the same time rendering more explicit and dramatic the positive side of *nasp* (e.g., aggressive righteousness), as well as *'aql*. In this connection it is relevant to note the elaborate turbans often worn by watchmen and doormen of public buildings. Like secular and sacred leaders these people also represent the responsibility, control, and guardianship (albeit in attenuated form) central to notions of power and authority.

Conclusion: Evaluating the Moral Bases of Islamic Behavior

During Israel's 1982 seige of Beirut a well-known Baluch *sardār* made a much-publicized demand that Pakistan undertake *jihād* on behalf of its beleaguered Palestine Liberation Organization brethren. To those who knew this man his exhortation was seen as a transparently political ploy. Oxford-educated and urbane, the *sardār* was not an individual known for any particular piety beyond his commitment to power and that personal and tribal honor typical of the Baluch chiefly ideal. This sudden attack of Islamic zeal was therefore widely interpreted by my informants as a calculated attempt to embarrass Pakistan's "Islamic" regime for purely self-serving reasons: the Zia-ul Haq administration, seen as forcing *sharī'at* on the often-unwilling Pakistani citizenry, was clearly waffling in its support of the Palestinians—ostensibly to curry favor with the United States, whose money and arms were Zia's primary props. The *sardār*, in very explicit terms, called for Zia to "put his money where his mouth was" and to sever ties with the United States in order to advance the cause of Islamic solidarity with the PLO. The *sardār*—and everyone else—knew that Zia could not and would not heed this call if he were to survive politically (and perhaps physically). By failing to act on the *sardār*'s challenge, Zia's credibility as a champion of Islam would be further eroded, and the climate for his own overthrow improved. From such a climate the *sardār* hoped ultimately to profit. He had recently settled a long-standing feud with an important Baluch nationalist leader from a rival tribe and reasonably hoped to rise to greater power should the Zia government collapse.

The cynicism with which my informants regarded the purity of the *sardār*'s piety in no way detracted from their admiration of him as the embodiment of the toughness and craftiness of an ideal Baluch leader. Thus the case illustrates the inextricable interweaving of Islamic ideology and power politics among the Baluch and, I would suggest, in many other Islamic settings. Although the normative values of Islam urge Muslims to exhibit the *communitas* of shared faith, both those who preach this faith (whether they are *mullās*, *pīrs*, *āyatullāhs*, or more secular defenders of the faith like Zia or the *sardār*) and those who listen to them often come from social backgrounds steeped in the motifs of kin and ethnic rivalry, feud, revenge, and self-interest. This is especially true in the tribal areas of the Muslim world, where normative Islam, with its emphasis on the brotherhood of all the faithful, seems to be the antithesis of real society.

In such settings—notwithstanding the impact of Islam on the day-to-day lives of many sincere and pious individuals—the most salient collective function of the faith seems to be as a mortar, temporarily applied to chinks in the political edifice during crisis situations, when other means of unification have failed in the face of a fissile and segmentary social life.

From the Atlas mountains to Baluchistan's deserts this theme recurs again and again. Among the Berbers, for example, we find that the social role of Sufi marabouts is most pronounced precisely in the weakest spots of the temporal social order: they are often called upon to act as mediators in intertribal feuds; they locate their lodges along buffer zones between tribes; and they provide a locus for armistices in potentially explosive market towns where rival tribesmen must meet in trade (see Gellner 1969; Benet 1957). Similarly, the late nineteenth-century Sudanese Mahdī functioned as a catalyst uniting rival groups in times of a crisis brought on by British expansionism in Africa, while among the Pathans of Swat another holy man—the Akhund—served an identical purpose at almost the same time. Secular leaders like Zia-ul Haq or our *sardār* have also found it useful to wave the banner of Islam in order to better manage a divided polity in times of crisis.

But from the Mahdī to the Āyatullāh Khomeini and Zia, such leaders, while promising the ascendancy of a new and pure Islamic social order, invariably find that once the specific threats that push them forward are gone, their power base becomes more and more shaky. They must, then, increasingly play a game of naked power politics that maintains a connection to normative Islamic values more through rhetoric than through observance. Such cases, and that of the Baluch discussed here, suggest that any attempt to understand the bases of behavior in Islamic societies must necessarily look beyond "text" to "context" and must balance portrayals of ideal world views—whether they are propounded as *adab*, *riwāj*, or *islāmīya*—with detailed observation of how life is actually lived.

The methodological problem of separating "ideal" from "real," rhetoric from substance, and self-image from objectivity is complicated further by the fact that among many Muslims the notion of dissimulation (*taqīya*) makes a positive virtue out of duplicity if it is used to confound those who are potentially harmful, or to advance one's own aims. Thus, both informants' statements and textual exegeses must be regarded by an outside observer with a measure of healthy skepticism.

The anthropological approach, with its emphasis on long-term participant-observation, is, therefore, a necessary adjunct to the perspectives of the Islamicist and historian who rely more on data that are normative or that cannot be cross-checked against direct observation. That the present volume has been assembled to address such issues directly is a hopeful sign that new and fruitful directions in the study of South Asian Muslim society will emerge.

References

Ahmed, Akbar S.

1980 *Pukhtun Economy and Society*. London: Routledge & Kegan Paul.

Barth, Fredrik

1959 *Political Leadership among Swat Pathans*. London: Athlone Press.

1969 "Pathan Identity and Its Maintenance." In *Ethnic Groups and Boundaries*. F. Barth, ed. Boston: Little, Brown.

Benet, Francisco

1957 "Explosive Markets: The Berber Highlands." In *Trade and Markets in the Early Empires*. K. Polanyi, C. Arensberg, and H. Pearson, eds. New York: The Free Press.

Gellner, Ernest

1969 *Saints of the Atlas*. Chicago: University of Chicago Press.

Gulick, John

1976 *The Middle East: An Anthropological Perspective*. Pacific Palisades, Calif.: Goodyear.

Kurin, Richard

1982 "Hot and Cold: Towards an Indigenous Model of Group Identity and Strategy in Pakistani Society." In *Anthropology in Pakistan: Recent Sociocultural and Archeological Perspectives*. S. Pastner and L. Flam, eds. Ithaca: Cornell South Asia Monograph Series no. 8.

Leach, Edmund R.

1973 "Levels of Communication and Problems of Taboo in the Appreciation of Primitive Art." In *Primitive Art and Society*. A. Forge, ed. London: Oxford University Press.

Matheson, Sylvia
1967 *Tigers of Baluchistan*. London. Arthur Barker.
Pastner, Stephen
1971 "Ideological Aspects of Nomad-Sedentary Contact: A Case from Southern Baluchistan." *Anthropological Quarterly* 44:173–84.
1978a "Pirs and Power among the Pakistani Baluch." *Journal of Asian and African Studies* 13:3, 4:231–43.
1978b "Baluch Fishermen in Pakistan." *Asian Affairs* 9, 2:161–66.
1982 "Feuding with the Spirit among the Zikri Baluch." In *From the Atlas to the Indus*. Akbar Ahmed and D. M. Hart, eds. London: Routledge & Kegan Paul.
Pastner, Stephen, and Carroll McC. Pastner
1972 "Agriculture, Kinship and Politics in Southern Baluchistan." *Man* 7, 1:128–36.
1977 "Adaptations to State Level Politics by the Southern Baluch." In *Pakistan: The Long View*. R. Braibanti, L. Ziring, and H. Wriggens, eds. Durham: Duke University Press.
Pehrson, Robert
1966 *The Social Organization of the Marri Baluch*. New York: Wenner-Gren Foundation.
Salzman, Philip C.
1971 "Adaptation and Political Organization in Iranian Baluchistan." *Ethnology* 10, 4:433–44.
Schimmel, Annemarie
1975 *Mystical Dimensions of Islam*. Chapel Hill: University of North Carolina Press.

9

The Mullā of Waziristan: Leadership and Islam in a Pakistani District

AKBAR S. AHMED

Although Said's *Orientalism* (1978) captured a powerful mood among Third World scholars, it may be time for us to move beyond this position toward a dispassionate examination of our own societies. Self-knowledge may assist us in improving them. This paper is, accordingly, an exercise in social anthropology: it is neither philosophic nor historical in content. I will discuss Muslim society as it is, not as it should be. In particular, through a case study I will attempt to identify the distinctive character of recent social movements in the Muslim world, as well as elucidate the causal principles creating tension and conflict between the forces of tradition and modernity in contemporary Muslim society.[1]

In recent years, Islamic social movements have occurred in widely differing regions—from Kano in Nigeria to Wana in Pakistan. The attack on the mosque at Mecca, the very heart of the Islamic world, indicates the intensity and seriousness of the contemporary Muslim mood. Recent events in Iran provide dramatic evidence of the revolutionary capacity of Islamic movements. Many other such upheavals, smaller-scale and less dramatic, may have gone unreported, and more can be expected to take place. The unrest remains largely unstudied, and its complexity, due in part to the diversity of the contexts within

1. I thank Monique Djokic for suggesting revisions in the first draft of this paper. A version which emphasizes my "district paradigm" analytical model in examining this material has been published in *Middle East Journal* (1982b). Themes in the two papers are explored at greater length in Ahmed 1983.

which it appears, defies easy analysis. Yet understanding contemporary Islamic movements and their long-term impact on social structure and organization is fundamental for Muslims and for those dealing with Muslim societies.

Leadership Roles and Internal Ferment among Muslims

During the colonial phase of modern Islamic history, Islamic social movements were explicitly anti-Western and anticolonial, but this is not the case today. Contemporary movements, instead, are aimed primarily *within* society and thus may not be understood through a simple anti-Western framework. The shadowy figures of religious leaders—the *mullā*, *maulawī*, *shaikh*, or *āyatullāh*—perceptible beneath the ferment, challenge more generally the ideological tenets of the modern age. In these movements the emphasis is placed on the central role of God and so marks a reversion to orthodox ideology. Revulsion is expressed against materialism as a philosophy and as a code for conduct. The target is not the king or president as a symbol of the state, but the modern state apparatus itself. These movements, though emerging from a state of general economic betterment rather than deprivation, are nonetheless revolutionary in form and content; transformation of the social and political structures, not merely a change of government, is desired. Death and destruction follow in their wake; it is not only the kings of Islam who sleep uneasily.

Anthropological methods may provide useful tools for the analysis of the dynamics and processes of contemporary Islamic movements. In studying power, authority, and religious status—the central issues of Muslim society—it may be heuristically useful to look beneath the surface of the large configuration of Muslim society, and away from its main centers of power, when examining social structure and process. Here we focus not on the typical anthropological village, but on that critical intermediary level, the district or agency, the study of which remains neglected.[2]

2. The district was the basic and key unit of administration in British India (Woodruff 1965). It was subdivided into subdivisions and *thanas*, and it, in turn, was part of a division, which was part of a province. In the tribal areas, the agency corresponded to the district in the administrative universe. Although I have called this intermediary level "district" to help conceptualize the unit of analysis, district (or agency) boundaries do not always correspond with ethnic ones, a fact which continues to create political problems. In some cases new ethnicity has developed as a result of a new district, for example Hazarwal in Hazara District (see Ahmed 1982a). Most districts and agencies

Three broad but distinct spheres of leadership, interacting at various junctures, may be identified at this level of Pakistani society: traditional leaders (usually elders); official representatives of the established state authority; and religious functionaries. The last group is the least well defined, due to the ambiguity of its locus of power and the elasticity of its social role. Each group is symbolically represented in the society by its base of operations: the house(s) of the chief or elders, the district headquarters (flying the government flag), and the central mosque.

Personnel from these three spheres of leadership vie for power, status, and legitimacy in the society. The competition is exacerbated by the fact that all the major participants are Muslims; there are no simple Muslim versus non-Muslim categories to fall back on, as in the recent colonial past. Moreover, the participants of each category do not remain aloof from one another; some form of alliance and collaboration between competing leaders is characteristic of district history. If the religious leader hopes to expand his role in the society, therefore, he must confront and challenge the domains of control held by the traditional leader and official representative. Political competition among these leaders inevitably leads to competing claims for the authority to speak for society. The question of who is recognized as legitimately speaking for society thus becomes a central concern for the analyst as well.

I will examine the process by which the contemporary Islamic movement manifests itself in local-level politics through an extended case study of traditional agnatic rivalry in a tribal agency in Pakistan.[3] The central focus will be on the Mullā[4] of Waziristan as he attempted to expand his field of political influence at the district level by manipulating to his advantage the structural tensions which exist among the various

---

remain profoundly rural in character and somewhat isolated from national developments. There is a vast literature on district life, much of it written by British district officers themselves (for a fresh contribution, see Hunt and Harrison 1980). The academic neglect of the topic may be partly due to methodological considerations, for the district does not correspond either to the larger subject matter—state, nation, or region—traditionally studied by political scientists, sociologists, and historians, or to the village society studied by anthropologists.

3. I shall employ the term "agnatic rivalry" for conflict between males descended in the patrilineage from a common ancestor.

4. "*Mullā*" is the generic name for a religious functionary; according to the *Oxford English Dictionary*, one "learned in theology and sacred law." I refer to the Waziristan Mullā with a capital "M" to distinguish him from other such functionaries in the text. Waziristan, when used generally, refers to the area of North and South Waziristan Agencies. The name derives from the Wazīr tribe. *Wazīr* in Arabic and Urdu means "minister."

tribal, religious, and administrative groups coexisting within the district.[5] Through the ethnographic case study, it will be possible to discover meaning and structure beneath the diversity of contemporary Muslim society.

A *Mullā*'s Bid for Power: The Waziristan Case

The case at hand is based on South Waziristan Agency, Pakistan. Beginning in the late 1960s, a *mullā* among the Wazīrs utilized Islam to forge a particular tribal ideology into a political movement against the other major tribal group, the Mahsuds, while accusing the administration of supporting the latter. A migrant from neighboring Bannu District, he built in Wana a beautiful mosque, unique in the Tribal Areas, as well as a surrounding complex of schools and dormitories. With his emergence as a political leader in the agency, the mosque came to symbolize the Mullā and his policies. The objectives of the Wazīr Mullā were explicit: a redefinition of social boundaries and a transformation of social structure and organization. His method alternated between a secular political model and a religious-charismatic model. This shifting use of leadership role models gave him a large area in which to maneuver, and partly explains his social and political success.

The agency population affected by the Mullā numbers about three hundred thousand according to the last official census in 1972. It is divided into two major Pukhtun tribes, the Mahsuds and the Wazīrs. The tribes, being segmentary, egalitarian, acephalous, and living in low-production zones, are somewhat similar to other Muslim tribes in North Africa and the Middle East (Ahmed and Hart 1984). There are about two hundred fifty thousand Mahsuds and about fifty thousand Wazīrs. The agency also has smaller nomadic groups (Ahmed 1981b). The ability of these tribes as fighters is well-recognized: "the Wazīrs and Mahsuds, operating in their own country, can be classed among the finest fighters in the world," wrote the British Indian Army General Staff (1921:5).[6] Their participation in the "Great Game" between

5. My own experience as political agent—in South Waziristan Agency from 1978 to 1980—allows me to comment on the ethnographic narrative from within the structure.
6. Recent colonial history is important to Waziristan. Countless British soldiers have died here in savage encounters. In the 1930s there were more troops in Waziristan than on the rest of the Indian Subcontinent. In 1937 an entire British brigade was wiped out in the Shahur Tangi. To John Masters, who fought in Waziristan, the tribes were "physically the hardest people on earth" (1956:161). Some famous British imperial names are associated with Waziristan, among them Curzon, Durand, Kitchener, and

imperial Russia and imperial Britain further added to the historical importance of the Waziristan tribes (Ahmed 1979).

South Waziristan shares borders with Afghanistan on the west and Baluchistan, across the Gomal River, on the south. It is distinguished for the most part by desolate valleys and barren mountains. With an area of 3,936 square miles, it is the largest and southernmost of the North-West Frontier Province's seven Federally Administered Tribal Areas. A political agent heads the administration and represents the government. His powers are vast, and the tribes call him "king of Waziristan" (*de Waziristan bādshāh*).

In Pakistan the district structure and personnel, with its official head the district commissioner (or, in the agency, the political agent), remain a legacy of British rule. The continuing importance of the district and its personnel after independence, in spite of its clear association with the colonial past, heightens tension in the society. Although "native," the administrative personnel are often regarded by the social groups under their jurisdiction as distant and unsympathetic. The current power and importance of district officials are further exaggerated with the suspension of normal political activities (a common phenomenon during periods of martial law).

This story really begins with the migration of one Maulawī Khān to the Agency. An appointment as *mullā* in their small mud mosque was offered by the Mughal Khel (a cousin lineage to the Bizan Khel) to Maulawī Khān. Wana was then a small settlement. "There are only about 120 houses altogether of these tribes living in Wana, where they will be found chiefly at Moghul Khel village just outside the camp" (Johnson 1934a:8). A son, his first, had been born to Maulawī Khān in 1931 in his Bizan Khel village, and named Nūr Muḥammad; shortly thereafter Maulawī moved his entire family to Wana. Maulawī Khān sent his son Nūr Muḥammad to Multan in the Punjab for religious schooling at the Dār al-'Ulūm as a religious scholar (*ṭālib*). The school

T. E. Lawrence (whose note to the South Waziristan Scouts is on display in the Scouts Mess at Wana). Tradition, in name and custom, is preserved. The main western gate of the army camp at Wana, the summer agency headquarters and main settlement, is still called the Durand Gate, and the main picket is Gibraltar. Bugles still play at sunset as the Pakistani flag is lowered, and the entire camp comes to a halt for those few minutes. Farewells to officers are conducted with traditional ritual in the Scouts Mess, with the band dressed in kilts, providing bagpipe music. The romantic aspect of the colonial encounter which created a "mystification" in British eyes is perhaps most evocative in Waziristan (Ahmed 1978; Bruce 1929; Curtis 1946; General Staff 1921, 1932, 1936; Howell 1925; Johnson 1934a, 1934b; Johnston 1903).

was organized and supervised by Maulānā Muftī Maḥmūd. After completing his education Nūr returned to Wana. He inherited his father's position upon his death.

The new Mullā, as Nūr Muḥammad became known, distributed talismans (*ta'wīẕ*) to cure the ill and provided counsel for the grieved. Men and women brought their problems to him for solution. He was soon reputed to possess healing powers; his talismans were symbols of this power. Payments were made to him in gratitude for such favors; thus dyadic links were cemented and economic favors were exchanged for spiritual patronage. The Wazīrs had found a spiritual leader they could trust. He was becoming a symbol of revived Wazīr pride and identity. For them he was building an emotionally contagious atmosphere suggesting spiritual powers around his person.

This was in part because, apart from the religious functions he had assumed, the Mullā imposed a general Wazīr peace in the area. Those quarreling among themselves were fined and punished by the Mullā. His peace patched up such old cousin enmities as the one between Jalat and Bangul. He also began to arbitrate actively between groups in conflict. Clearly he was appropriating the role of the traditional elders in a *jirga* (council of elders) and, at the same time, that of the political administration in this regard.

Various larger developments in Pakistan helped provide a suitable frame for the Mullā's emergence. The late 1960s and early 1970s were characterized by new sources of wealth, both internal (Ahmed 1977) and external, such as remittances from employment in the Arab States (Ahmed 1980, 1981a). For the first time, a tribesman with initiative could make considerable money. Some of the Wazīrs' money was diverted to the Mullā; they perceived him as their champion, and he needed funds for his organization. As demonstrated below, the Mullā's religious organization was thus tied to complex economic networks. He also invested some of the money in items that confer prestige among Pukhtuns: Japanese cars, buses, guns, and lavish feasts for visiting politicians.

Two important economic developments in the Agency coincided with the construction of the new mosque at Wana. First a market (*adda*) developed between the mosque and the main road. This was a gradual process: in the late 1950s and early 1960s encroachments resulted in a cluster of small mud shops. The Scouts, a paramilitary organization, protested since this violated rules prohibiting civilian construction near their posts and campus. Numerous letters were exchanged and meetings were held between the Commandant of the Scouts, the political agent, and his superior the commissioner, but the market continued to grow. Because it was on the property of the Mughal Khel Wazīrs, it came to be known as Adda Mughal Khel. Eventually there were four hundred shops, each not larger than a small room or two. The market became a thriving center of commerce for the Agency.

At the same time, a major dam, the Gomal Dam Project, was started by the government in Wazīr territory. Wazīrs provided labor and were given building contracts. Both developments—market and dam—generated local money.

The integration of mosque and market was guided by the Mullā, who thus channeled some of the new Wazīr wealth into appropriate Islamic concerns. The mosque's connection with the market remained explicit; it was popularly called Adda Mughal Khel mosque, that is, the mosque of Mughal Khel market. Costing between seven and eight hundred thousand rupees (about U.S. $70–80,000), the magnificent mosque was soon completed. The minarets and dome were resplendent with tiles and glass of many hues. The interior reflected depth and space. A stream, filled with colored fish, passed through the mosque. No monument so splendid had ever before been seen in that or any other agency. The Mullā also built a religious school (*madrasa*) adjacent to the mosque and dormitories for visiting scholars (*ṭ̤ālib*), most of them sons of Wazīr elders. Elders from other agencies came to marvel at the mosque and to compliment its builder. A set of rooms was built for the Mullā on the second floor of the mosque, overlooking its courtyard. As a mark of deference, people now referred to him as "Maulawī Ṣāḥib" rather than by his name. The Mullā basked in this acclaim and concentrated his energy on expanding an organization around the mosque.

To this religious-styled leadership role the Mullā added a popular political style. In 1971, after the war with India that resulted in the breakup of East Pakistan, Z. A. Bhutto, rallying a dispirited nation, emerged as the political leader of Pakistan; the Mullā watched and learned. Both were relatively young leaders with considerable political skill and organizational ability who relied on their charisma and oratory to secure and stir their followers. Both spoke in the language of hyperbole and poetic populism. To critics, their demeanor bordered on arrogance, and they seemed obviously opportunistic. They brooked no opposition. The politics of the 1970s in Pakistan were cast in the mold of Bhutto, and these politics had their impact on Waziristan.

In the early 1970s the Mullā, considering the time ripe, made a bid for the control of the minds of the Wazīrs. As one strategy, he forbade the use of radios in the Adda as un-Islamic. Having banned them, he then listened to the radio commentary and news avidly. Selecting information, he would "predict" national events at the Friday congregation in the mosque. His announcement of the National Pay Commission was one such example. The Mullā informed his following that he was praying for an increase in pay for the poorly paid Wazīr tribal levies (*khassadars*) and Scouts, who received about Rs. 200–250/month. An increase in official salaries was being debated nationally during 1972 and 1973, and an announcement on the matter was imminent. The debate was reported in the mass media, but, forbidden to listen to the radio and generally illiterate, the Wazīrs were unaware of the national debate. When the government announced an increase in salaries, they saw it as proof of the Mullā's powers to predict and influence events. The *khassadars* were particularly impressed and committed a monthly contribution of Rs. 4 each to the mosque fund.

Other devices reinforced his prescient image. In his door he installed a wide-angle viewer sent by a follower from the Arab Gulf States. He could thus "foresee" and predict who his visitor was, what he looked like, or what he was wearing. His capacity for seeing through doors was taken as further evidence of his powers. Wazīrs believed he possessed "the magic eye" ("*de jado starga*"). Even educated people believed that the viewer was a magical device.

Shortly afterward, the Mullā imposed various taxes on almost every aspect of commercial activity at the Adda, ostensibly to support the mosque. Each shop paid a monthly contribution of Rs. 10, and smaller charges were imposed for other items. The *khassadars*, to display their loyalty, further increased their monthly contribution to Rs. 5. Fines brought in more money. A shop owner violating the radio ban could be beaten and fined Rs. 500 by the Mullā's armed supporters (the *chalweshti*). Mīr Askar, the Khojal Khel elder who was defiant throughout, was regularly fined and manhandled by the *chalweshti*. Wazīr *māliks* receiving a Timber Permit were expected to donate half of its market price to the Mullā. Estimates of the income from these sources varied from twenty to thirty thousand rupees daily. The Mullā kept half the sum and distributed the other half to his followers and the *chalweshti* who organized the collection of taxes and fines. Though almost a kind of echo of official activity, these fines and taxes were not audited, nor were the figures made public.

The Mullā had been biding his time before challenging the traditional leaders of Wazīr society: the *māliks* and the *pīrs* (religious leaders). When he felt strong enough he came into the open and poured forth scorn and venom upon them. Traditional and somewhat ineffective leaders such as the Mughal Khel elder, Mālik Pasti, or the established religious figures such as the Pīr of Wana, were under considerable pressure from the tribe. They held their peace "to save their self-respect." An occasional bomb blast (at Mālik Pasti's home) or ambush (of Khojal Khel elders) made the point of the Mullā's authority on recalcitrant elders.[7]

The political administration read the Mullā's attack on their traditional allies, the *māliks*, as a prelude to a challenge of established authority.[8] In this it may have been correct, for, dismissing traditional leaders as "government toadies" who worked only for their own selfish interests, the Mullā built up an alternative leadership. Around himself he gathered a group of twelve men (*dolass kassi*), mainly from the Zilli Khel, which assumed the status of his cabinet and conducted affairs on his behalf. The cabinet included emergent and eloquent *kashar* (younger elements) like Ba K͟hān of Zilli Khel. The *chalweshti* was streamlined to ensure immediate implementation of his directives. Those who opposed his wishes were incarcerated for short periods in a jail established for this purpose.

However, many traditional elders (particularly those of the Zilli Khel, such as Jalat) supported him wholeheartedly, as they saw in him a viable form and focus of opposition to traditional opponents such as the Mahsud. The Mullā had become the very embodiment of Wazīr aspirations, particularly against the Mahsuds and the political administration, which was seen as a tool of the Mahsuds. Thus traditional leaders had been outflanked by the Mullā's approach to the hearts of the Wazīr. In bypassing traditional leadership and exposing it as impotent and corrupt, the Mullā had created a powerful base among the populace, or common people (the *tīman*). The *tīman*, which included

7. The Mullā's antipathy to Malik Pasti is perhaps explained by memory of his father's employment as *mullā* with Pasti's father.

8. From the Political Agent's Office (1977:4) comes the following: "His first target was the institution of Maliki. He started condemning the Maliks openly and at times he abused them on the pulpit. The idea was to weaken the institutional arrangements so that he could bulldoze his way by shattering all the norms and forms of administration. The Maliks started feeling uneasy but owing to his deepening influence on the tribe they found themselves absolutely helpless. They had no other option but to join his umbrella where they felt they could shelter themselves against the wrath of the *teeman* [populace, common people] who would go into a state of frenzy at the slightest provocation by Maulvi."

women and children, manifested their confidence in him through expressions of personal loyalty.

Three economic issues expressed Wazīr aspirations and formed the main platform of the Mullā: first, he emphasized the Wazīr nature of the market at Wana; second, he challenged Mahsud rights to the timber funds from Wazīr forests that were distributed among the Agency's tribes in the form of Timber Permits; third, he demanded an alternative route for the Wazīrs, bypassing the Mahsud area, to the Settled Districts along the Gomal River. Each demand had clear social and political implications. The Mullā would not lead the Wazīrs to the promised land but would bring the promised land to the Wazīrs.

At the same time, the Mullā imitated and developed some of the formalistic aspects of bureaucracy associated with the political agent. Armed guards escorted him wherever he went; meetings (*mulagats*) with him were arranged by formal, often written, requests through his supporters. He issued chits to his followers ordering admission to official schools or medical dispensaries; he wrote asking officials to give interviews "to the bearer of this note." His requests were honored and his whims humored. These were visible symbols of his growing importance in and to the society. By appropriating some of the form and content of the political agent's function, he was setting himself on a collision course with that office.

From being a traditional *mullā* serving the tribe, he had now emerged as a leader representing and speaking for the tribe. The transformation from sub- to superordinate position in society was as visible as it was portentous; however, the passage from one category to the other was smooth and was not marked by any dramatic event. The Mullā was impressed and somewhat awed by his own growing popularity: "there was such a multitude of people which reminded people who had performed *ḥajj* of Arafa [where the Holy Prophet preached]" (Nūr Muḥammad n.d.:21–22). He perceived a sense of destiny pervading his actions. Addressing himself, he noted: "God Almighty has given you status and influence matched by few men in history" (Nūr Muḥammad n.d.:21–22). He referred to himself in the plural form of royalty. Indeed, the theme of royalty was not far from his mind: "When they insisted you address the gathering they introduced you as *the uncrowned king* [*bādshāh*] *of Wana*" (Nūr Muḥammad n.d.:21–22). The title was underlined thrice by the Mullā.

The Mullā's campaign to discomfit the political agent and force his transfer also continued unabated. A course of action was charted out by the Mullā which was repeated at Wazīr *jirgas*: "no one should see the Political Agent however the Ahmedzai Wazīr may keep their relations good with the APA Wana. If the Government is not going to transfer the present Political Agent, then the Ahmedzai have no objection to it but no Ahmedzai will see him. Defaulters will be liable to pay penalty of Rs. 20,000."[9] Acts symbolizing humiliation of the administration became commonplace in Wana: a dog was placed on a cot and carried by a large procession. The dog, representing the political agent, was then administered a sound thrashing. The symbolic representation of relations between the administration and the Wazīrs was to be repeated in the next months. For instance, those who continued to see the agent were punished: "After the speech of Mulla Nur Muhammad, Khudaimir Matak Khel (member of *dolass kassi*) announced that Malik Hakim is fined for seeing the political agent, South Waziristan, some days back. The amount of fine is not known and will be told to them after three days."[10]

The political agent, faced in early 1973 with the multiple dimensions of the growing Wazīr-Mahsud problem, decided on firm action by taking two steps: first, he abolished the Timber Committee (which dealt with the disposal of the Agency timber and permits for timber) and sold the permits from his office. In the context of the hysteria being built up in the Agency, the action did not please or suit either the Mahsuds or the Wazīrs. Although the Wazīrs continued to buy the permit and resell it at an inflated price, they resented the dissolution of the Committee. The Mahsuds, on their part, insisted the permits be sold in the open market and not at fixed prices. Second, he ordered the arrest of the Mullā's cabinet and the *chalweshti*. If they refused to surrender, the Adda was to be blown up. Such an act would have cost the Wazīr the loss of millions of rupees; the shops did a thriving business and were full of goods, and most owners also kept safes with their money on these premises. The order was kept secret until it could be implemented on the following day. As the political agent's relations with the commandant of the Scouts were strained (a fact advertised and exploited by the Mullā), the action was ordered to take place while the commandant was away. Unfortunately for the political agent, however, the commandant arrived in Wana late at night and, evidently, upon learning of the plans passed the information on to the Mullā (Nūr Muḥammad n.d.:102).

9. Situation Intelligence Report of Wana Tehsil, dated 30 May 1973.
10. Situation Intelligence Report of Wana Tehsil, dated 30 May 1973.

Calling an emergency meeting of his key men in the late hours of the night, the Mullā observed that in the past "whenever the Scouts came to arrest our people they ran and hid in fields and mountains" (Nūr Muḥammad n.d.:102). Tomorrow, he commanded, "no one will offer themselves for arrest and if necessary they will fight" (Nūr Muḥammad n.d.:102). Thus the lines were drawn for a struggle of power between the Mullā and the representative of the government. In the initial skirmish, confusion brought on by the antipathy between the Scout commandant and political agent allowed the Mullā to publicly defy and humiliate the political authorities.[11]

As the battle between the Mullā and the political agent deteriorated into scattered but persistent confrontation, the Mullā underscored his role of religious leadership by expressing the campaign against the Mahsuds in a religious idiom. His most effective strategy was the articulation of his views in sermons in the mosque. In these he declared *jihād* against the Mahsuds. Having raised Wazīr emotions to a high pitch he condemned the Mahsuds as *kāfir*s (unbelievers). The Mahsuds, he argued, had dominated and exploited Wazīrs against the spirit of Islam. They were no better than Hindus. The time had arrived for the Wazīrs to rid themselves of the Mahsuds. The imminent *jihād* would be between good and evil, between Muslim and Hindu. God was on the Wazīr side. If, he declared in his fiery sermons, a Wazīr killed a Mahsud, it would be the equivalent of killing a Hindu *kāfir*. If, on the other hand, a Wazīr was killed by a Mahsud, he would become a martyr (*shahīd*) and win paradise, as he had been killed by a *kāfir*. Wazīrs were inflamed by such rhetoric. By deploying religious arguments in what was fundamentally a tribal conflict, the Mullā was bringing about an internal fusion in society between the spiritual and the social.

Simultaneously, the Mullā opened the issue, hitherto closed, of an alternate route for the Wazīr from Wana along the Gomal River to the settled districts. This, too, was a strategy aimed against the Mahsuds: the conception of a separate road was tied to that of a separate Agency. A separate Agency would deprive the Mahsuds of the entire timber funds; it would also reduce the importance and size of the Agency. Above all, for the Mahsuds, it would allow their agnatic rivals to escape from the Agency arena and establish their own identity.

The Mahsuds, not being able to dismiss the Mullā as an "unbeliever," stepped up their attack on his character. Their charges—debauchery,

11. For details of this political confrontation, see Ahmed 1982b.

homosexuality, the practice of black magic—indirectly reflected upon Wazīr morality. In the process, the Mahsuds impugned the Mullā's "Pukhtun-ness" and accused the Wazīr of being without shame, therefore of deviating from the social code of *pukhtunwali*. Thus mystification of Pukhtun-ness was a strategy employed by the Mahsud to counter the accusation by the Mullā of being *kāfir*, or outside the Islamic fold: an ethnic counterattack was made in reaction to a religious attack. Feelings on both sides ran high. The battle hysteria divided the Wazīrs and Mahsuds sharply, and the two camps began to prepare for armed confrontation.

In late 1975 the Mullā reiterated the connection perceived between the Mahsuds and the government by focusing on a new front: to strike out at the government, he ordered the Wazīrs to block the main Agency road. Despite a fierce and bloody battle with the Scouts, the Wazīrs again blocked the road a few days later; but this time, when the Scouts arrived, the Wazīrs had melted into the night, and the road was deserted.

Then an abortive attempt to involve Wazīrs from outside the Agency was made. The involvement of Wazīrs from the Northern Waziristan Agency or Afghanistan would have extended the theater of conflict beyond the Agency borders and created serious complications for the government. Already Kabul was watching developments in Waziristan with interest; ideal material was at hand for its claim that Pukhtuns in the North-West Frontier Province wished to secede.

The Mullā now ordered general civil disobedience. Wazīrs blocked the main roads, shot at the Scouts, and, at the climax of the movement, imposed a physical boycott on the Wana camp. Major clashes between Wazīrs, Mahsuds, and the administration took place, involving the death of tribesmen and soldiers. The Agency was in flames. In such a situation with international ramifications, the administration had to act. In May 1976, after obtaining clearance from the highest authority, armed tanks moved into the Agency and the air force was alerted. The Scouts destroyed the Wana markets of the Wazīrs, "captured" the mosque, and arrested first the Mullā's "cabinet" and eventually the Mullā himself. He and his key men were tried, found guilty, and sent to jail in Hazara, across the Indus.

The action, possibly the most serious of its kind in the history of the Tribal Areas, became the center of controversy. The Wazīrs were left in disarray, the Mahsuds jubilant, and the administration self-righteous. And well they might be: Afghan propaganda characterized the conflict as a simple Pukhtun struggle for autonomy against a Punjabi-dominated central government. Not since the merger in 1969 of the Frontier States (Swat, Chitral, Dir, and Amb) had such a live issue presented itself to Kabul. Kabul propaganda underlined the ethnic nature of the Mullā's struggle and pointed out that some of the key men in the drama (the central interior minister, the chief secretary of the province, and the political agent) were non-Pukhtun and hence, they argued, unsympathetic to Pukhtuns.

To the Mullā's followers, however, the issue had more than ethnic overtones. The blatant tilting of the administration toward the Mahsuds, the arrest of the Mullā, and the "capture" of the mosque were tantamount to heresy. They argued that the house of God had been desecrated and his faithful servant, the Mullā, arrested. They explained their continuing boycott of the mosque as an Islamic response to a captured house of worship. Religion carries with it a sense of intrinsic social obligation; it not only induces intellectual conformity but demands emotional commitment. The Mullā's *jihād* had this effect.

How does one explain the Mullā's success in gaining the political following of the Wazīrs? Islamic values were certainly involved. It became fashionable to ask Wazīrs, "Are you first Muslims [implying the laws of Islam] or Wazīrs [implying those of the Mullā]?" Either way, the answer posed dilemmas for the Wazīrs since to answer "Muslim" would negate Wazīr ethnicity as manifested through the movement and the Mullā. Furthermore, the Mullā violated the Islamic teaching of unity and equality among Muslims. Although *mullās* had traditionally upheld Islamic ideology among the tribes, the Wazīr Mullā both divided Muslims and created a highly centralized organization around himself with a well-defined hierarchy.

Moreover, in supporting the Mullā's practices, the Wazīrs assented to aberrations in Pukhtun social values, thus exposing themselves to social and moral criticism. For example, the Mullā's willingness to meet with women bearing personal requests provided the enemies of the Wazīr the opportunity to assail Pukhtun morality. By encouraging their children and women to pay him homage, the Wazīrs violated a cardinal principle of *pukhtunwali* and left themselves open to charges of shamelessness. Moreover, the Mullā's emergence as a political force in peacetime further contradicted the intensely democratic and egalitarian nature of ideal Pukhtun society.

Why, therefore, did the Wazīrs nonetheless support the Mullā's political aspirations and practices? Certainly some of the central issues were economic in nature. There may have been the hope of a separate Agency, with all its political and social implications. The Mullā's wealth no doubt helped him patronize the elders and the poor. Fear, too, may have played a part, for the Mullā's men were effective in keeping shops open and collecting fines and taxes. Thus a number of different reasons may be given for why the Wazīrs felt the need for a savior to deliver them from their enemies.

Above all, the ground was fertile for the emergence of a leader who could organize cultural and religious forces on behalf of his followers. Most important, the Mullā was successful in redefining the socio-political order. In part he accomplished this through an adept exploitation of the structural ambiguities which characterize, in a period of social transformation, relationships both within and across the religious, tribal, and administrative forms of social organization which coexist at the district level. In particular, the undefined nature—within Islamic doctrine—of the Mullā's religious (and therefore his social) role forced the Mullā to define and create his own leadership pattern within a particular social context. Furthermore, the common expression of tribal, religious, and administrative social relations through the conceptual framework of Islam allowed the Mullā access to spheres of influence which were distinct from the political leadership of the tribal elders and political agent. The willingness of the Wazīrs to assist the Mullā in his appropriation of political power, however, must be understood within the context of the transformation of tribal social organization. That is, the imposition of an administrative structure (the drawing of agency borders) without regard to tribal boundaries had previously served to obstruct the traditional segmentary alignments characteristic of agnatic rivalry. Instead, the configuration of political forces provided alternative strategies of alliance, while encompassing and constraining the dynamics of agnatic rivalry.

Islam and Local Level Leadership

Three overlapping categories may be distinguished among religious personnel providing leadership in Muslim society. The first two are defined by their functions, the third by genealogical links with holy ancestors. The first, the *'ulamā* (sg: *'ālim*, from *'ilm*, "knowledge of the Qur'ān, *ḥadīṣ*, etc.")—defined by religious and legal learning—includes *muftī*, *qāẓī*, *maulānā*, and *maulawī*; the second—defined by esoteric, sometimes unorthodox practice, includes groups such as the Sufis; and the third—defined by genealogy and thus claiming superior social status—consists of the *ashraf* or *sayyid*s (descended from the Prophet) and the *miyān*s (descended from holy men). The *'ulamā* represent the orthodox, bureaucratic, formal, and legalistic traditions in Islam. They interact with the state even at the highest level and advise the kings, captains, and commanders of Islam. In contrast, the mystical orders largely restrict themselves to rural areas, shunning worldly pursuits and avoiding formal interaction with the administration. They command the hearts as well as the minds of their followers. The holy lineages and their members command a vague and generalized respect, especially if they live up to the behavioral ideal, which is pacific, dignified, and neutral with regard to warring groups.

What is of interest here is the difficulty of placing the *mullā* easily in any one category. The difficulty is not simply taxonomic, but is related to the ambiguity and elasticity of his social role. Not quite the learned *muftī* (sure of his orthodox Islamic knowledge) or the Sufi (sure of his Islamic faith), the *mullā* is forced to define and create his own role. He may, indeed, borrow from all three categories, elevating himself to *maulawī* in one place (as in this case) and *miyān* in another (Ahmed 1980:167). It would be misleading, however, to use the gloss "saint" for *mullā* as some anthropologists have done (Bailey 1972; Barth 1972). *Mullā*s aspiring to spiritual status, such as the Wazīr *mullā*, may employ transparent tricks and devices to convince people of their special powers. The *sayyid* or *miyān*, assured of his position, does not need to do this. In general, then, the *mullā* occupies a junior position in the religious hierarchy and is defined as "a lesser member of the religious classes" (Algar 1969:264). Except in extraordinary circumstances, the *mullā* restricts himself largely to the village level of social and political life. He appears to thrive in crises. Although the *mullā*'s role is one of the most interesting and important in village and rural society, it is also one of the least studied; the serious writing of the *'ulamā* and the imaginative practices of the Sufis appear to attract the most scholarship.

The Mullā of Waziristan was a Wazīr, that is, a Pukhtun, from Bannu. He was not a *sayyid* or a *miyān*. The distinction is important in the Pukhtun universe. The claims to superiority of *sayyid* and *miyān* are backed by marriage rules and idealized behavior patterns. Pukhtuns, notoriously endogamous and reluctant to give their women to non-Pukhtuns, are prepared to waive the prejudice for *sayyid*s (Ahmed 1980; Barth 1972). They are settled between Pukhtun clans, a placement which is symbolic of their role as mediators between warring groups.

The Mullā, as is often the case, was a poor Pukhtun of a junior or depressed lineage. The transformation of a *mullā* from religious to political spokesman within the society was thus almost inevitable once the Mullā had attracted a following. No lineage structure constrained him; as the son of a migrant member of a junior lineage, he remained outside the local lineage charter yet part of the larger Wazīr tribe. From a *mullā* supervising religious functions, he became a leader promising specific political goals. How did the Mullā define and integrate his newly assumed political function within the existing social framework?

Among Pukhtuns the *mullā* remains subordinate to the lineage elders and usually does not feature in the genealogical charter. As I have shown elsewhere (Ahmed 1980), Pukhtun elders saw political activity as their preserve and restricted the role of the *miyān* or *mullā* to religious functions. The important function of the *mullā* is to organize and supervise rites of passage based on Islamic tradition. Social leadership, on the other hand, is firmly lodged in the lineage charter. A *mullā* must explore other areas if he is to enhance his role and authority in society.

He may rise to power in extraordinary times, rallying Muslims against invading non-Muslims (Ahmed 1976). In the Tribal Areas, *mullā*s have led widespread revolts against the British with singular courage and conviction (e.g., in 1897). Their bold stand provides a contrast to those quiescent elements in society who preferred to sit on the fence in the struggle against the British, such as traditional leaders and bureaucrats. The struggle, to the *mullā*s, was a *jihād*, to be conducted irrespective of success.

The role of the *mullā*, however, is negligible when the invading army is Muslim; a *jihād* cannot be invoked against Muslim brothers in the faith. When the Pukhtun tribes fought the Mughal armies (representing a Muslim dynasty) they were led by traditional tribal leaders. The Mullā of Waziristan thus provides an interesting example of a *mullā* who mobilized an entire tribe by creating a religious battle hysteria against kin groups belonging to the same sect and local administrative unit in peacetime. For the majority of Muslims in the Agency, the weakness of the Mullā lay in his redefinition of the *jihād*.[12]

12. "*Jihād*" has been used in the contemporary world in dramatically nontraditional ways. For instance, in April 1981 an Indonesian Muslim group calling itself Komando Jihad ("Holy War Command") hijacked a DC-9 belonging to Garuda Indonesian Airways. Indonesian commandos foiled the attempt at the Bangkok airport, killing all five hijackers. Although the idiom of *jihād* was employed, the case remains obscure. "*Jihād*" is also used for other daily, even secular activity; there is at least one daily newspaper called *jihād* in Pakistan.

Scholars of Islam have held different opinions on the exact nature of the *jihād*, a discussion that dates to the time of the Prophet. However, its importance for the believer is not in doubt. The Qur'ān is explicit about the central role of the *jihād*.[13] Sufis quote the Prophet as distinguishing two forms of *jihād*: the lesser *jihād* or holy war and the greater *jihād*, the struggle against one's own passions; the importance of the moral life is thus emphasized (Hodgson 1974, vol. 2: 228).[14] For our purposes, *jihād* may be defined as a "holy struggle in the way of Allāh."

There is thus no theological support for a *jihād* against fellow Muslims. However, the *jihād* becomes operative when *takfīr* (declaring someone an unbeliever or non-Muslim) is involved. The Qur'ān and the Prophet define a Muslim as a person reciting the *kalma* (the declaration of faith in the uniqueness of God and the prophethood of Muḥammad). The Mahsuds fitted neither the unbeliever nor the heretic category. To condemn them as *kāfirs* was in itself an act of considerable audacity. The Mullā's *jihād* clearly rested on a weak theological but a strong sociological base.

The facility with which the Wazīrs adopted the religious medium of the *jihād* to protest their social grievances attests to the centrality of Islam in the self-conception of these tribes. In a sociological and cultural sense they may be defined as Islamic. The tribesman equates his Pukhtun lineage with Islam; to him the two are inextricably bound together. Concepts such as *jihād* are therefore potent and meaningful to him. Although he is aware of certain deviations from Islamic theological tradition, especially regarding women's rights, he is never in doubt about his Muslimness. To the tribesman Islam provides the political and socio-religious formations within which his Pukhtun-ness operates. The two are in harmony and he regards them as a unified logical construct: whether embarking on a religious war or stealing cattle, the Pukhtun invokes his God. Focusing on the process by which Pukhtun

13. Sura 2, "*al-baqarah*," verse 190, reads "Fight in the way of Allāh against those who fight against you, but begin not hostilities. Lo! Allāh loveth not aggressors." The next verse actually employs the term *kāfir* with reference to the preceding verse. The *jihād* is an all-encompassing struggle, a total commitment. "Go forth," Muslims are exhorted, "and strive with your wealth and your lives in the way of Allāh!" (sura 9, verse 41).

14. Modern Sufi scholars, too, emphasize "personal striving" in defining *jihād* (Algar 1969:263), as do contemporary Islamic scholars: "one must also admit that the means of *jihād* can vary—in fact, armed *jihād* is only one form" (Rahman 1980:63). The *jihād*, then, is "systematic endeavor" (Maudūdī 1948) against oppression (*fitna*) and injustice (*fasād*), to "establish the Islamic socio-moral order" (Rahman 1979:37). Recent Western scholarship discusses the *jihād* mainly as an instrument against the European colonial venture (Dale 1981; Peters 1979).

custom and tradition are brought into accordance with Islamic tradition is the most useful way of analyzing this issue, for recognition of the overlapping of the two partly explains the success of the Mullā.

Once Islam was equated with kinship, and the Islamic idiom was employed, his success in leading and consolidating the Wazīrs was ensured. The instruments for maintaining and reinforcing the Wazīr ethnic boundary were drawn from an Islamic idiom; the mosque was the base of the Mullā's operations and the key symbol of Wazīr identity.

Conclusion: Agnatic Rivalry and Local Leadership Patterns

Although the conflict between the Wazīrs and Mahsuds was conducted according to religious principles, the source of the conflict rested in tribal principles of agnatic rivalry. Consciousness of agnatic divisions is high in Waziristan society and is locally so perceived. Political action is articulated on the basis of the relationships defined in and by the genealogical charter. The agnatic rivalry between Wazīrs and Mahsuds may be interpreted as a fundamental articulation of segmentary opposition. Mahsud inheritance of poorer lands, which presupposes junior lineages in the tribal charter, reinforced solidarity and sharpened strategy. Indeed, it may be stated that the genesis of the Waziristan problem is lodged in the genealogical charter. The escalation of the conflict between the Wazīrs and their agnatic rivals, however, did not proceed according to the pattern described by segmentation theory.[15]

Figure 9.1 depicts, in encapsulated form, the Wazīr-Mahsud genealogy. In the ideal, segmentary theory suggests that the Ahmedzai would be assisted by their Wazīr kin when in conflict with the Mahsud. The Mahsud clans, in turn, would unite against the Ahmedzai (the

15. The first important elaboration of segmentation theory was Evans-Pritchard's study of the Nuer. The theory became, and remains, particularly popular in examining Islamic tribal groups. Ernest Gellner's study of the Berbers of the Atlas is, for instance, a highly regarded example (1969). In a sense, segmentation theory has thus returned to its natural place of origin, in the segmentary genealogical charters of Islamic tribal groups, whence it originated a century earlier in the writings of Victorian scholar-travelers such as W. Robertson Smith. Recently there has been considerable and mounting criticism of segmentation theory, particularly in America. The criticism is led by Clifford and Hildred Geertz and such younger American anthropologists as Dale Eickelman and Lawrence Rosen (Geertz, Geertz, and Rosen 1979; Eickelman 1976). The following, in capsule form, are some of the major criticisms: segments are neither balanced nor equal; on the contrary, there is disparity in political resources, and this is exacerbated with the emergence of lineages claiming seniority. Furthermore, in times of political crisis, groups do not combine according to segmentary patterns. In spite of these criticisms, satisfactory alternative explanations have not been put forward.

Figure 9.1
The Wazīr-Mahsud Lineage

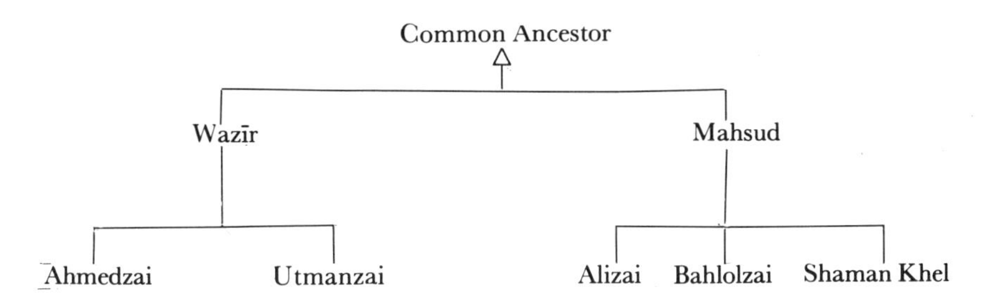

unity of the three Mahsud clans—the Dre Mahsud—remained unshaken by internal politics and was a formidable factor in defeating the Wazīr). Although the Wazīr conceptualizes himself as part of a large tribal configuration, a universe which includes his lineage kin in North Waziristan Agency and across the border in Afghanistan, in times of need he is realistically restricted to the administrative unit of the Agency. In spite of appeals for assistance, no kin arrived to participate in the struggle against the Mahsuds. Administrative boundaries served to obstruct the traditional dynamics of segmentary conflict and alliance.[16] If we impose a map of the South Waziristan Agency onto figure 9.1, the importance of administrative boundaries in affecting tribal life may be clarified (see figure 9.2). In the ideal case, as segmentation theory suggests, the Ahmedzai Wazīrs would be assisted by their Wazīr kin when in conflict with the Mahsuds. But the Wazīrs find themselves divided and restricted by agency borders.

Thus the Waziristan case study illustrates how new political realities have forced the creation of new social boundaries that take precedence over traditional alignments. Like other tribes in the region, the Ahmedzai Wazīrs have confronted the fact of British-created borders for three generations. On either side of the Durand Line, differing

16. At the turn of the century, the British created administrative districts and agencies as well as the new international boundary of the Durand Line, often without regard for tribal boundaries. Major tribes such as the Wazīrs were divided in two by the international border; others were untidily distributed between district and agency. The Ahmedzai Wazīrs were separated from their Utmanzai Wazīr cousins, confined to the North Waziristan Agency, and placed with their traditional rivals, the Mahsuds, in South Waziristan Agency. The Wazīrs live in both Afghanistan and North Waziristan Agency. Not only are the Utmanzai Wazīrs separated by administrative boundaries from their Ahmedzai cousins, but the Ahmedzai themselves are divided by the international boundary.

Figure 9.2
The Wazīr-Mahsud Genealogy Superimposed on a Map of the South Waziristan Agency

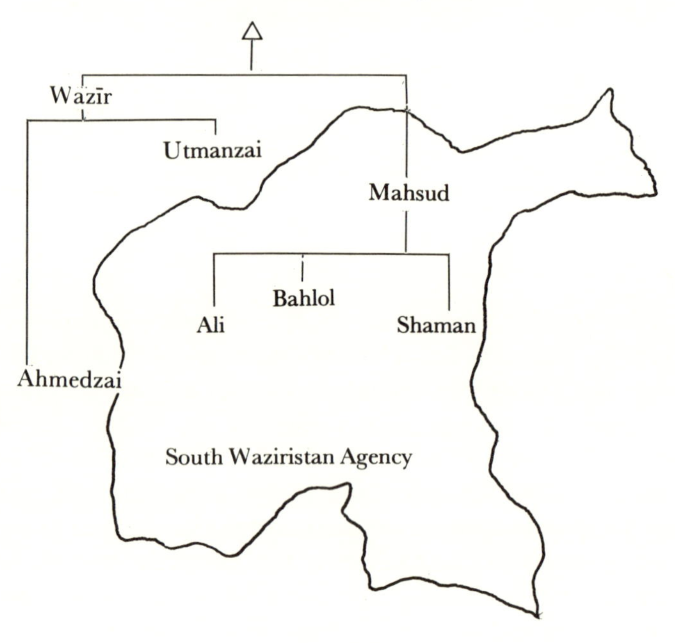

political, educational, and economic factors have widened the gap between Wazīr and Wazīr. New political alliances must therefore be sought.

In this context, new significance attaches to the roles of religious and administrative leaders.[17] The Wazīrs, then, sought the political support of the Mullā in their conflict with the Mahsuds (who, in turn, were backed by the district administration). The Mullā and political agent likewise manipulated tribal rivalries in order to advance their respective positions. Each of the political leaders vying for power at the district level—the tribal elder, the religious leader, and the representative state authority—can advance his political aspirations only through alliance and collaboration with one of his opponents. The example of the Mullā of Waziristan suggests that the local-level religious leader, in particular, finds new opportunities for political leadership in the structural

17. For a fuller discussion of the analytical implications of my district paradigm when applied to this issue, see Ahmed (1982b).

dynamics distinctive of district-level politics. The Wana case testifies to the relevance of the Islamic idiom in this district context.

References

Ahmed, Akbar S.

1976 *Millennium and Charisma among Pathans*. London: Routledge & Kegan Paul.

1977 *Social and Economic Change in the Tribal Areas*. Karachi: Oxford University Press.

1978 "The Colonial Encounter on the NWFP: Myth and Mystification." *Journal of the Anthropological Society* (Oxford) 9:3.

1979 "Tribes and States in Central and South Asia." *Asian Affairs* 11, 2:152–68 (o.s. vol. 67).

1980 *Pukhtun Economy and Society*. London: Routledge & Kegan Paul.

1981a "The Arab Connection: Emergent Models of Social Structure and Organization among Pakistani Tribesmen." *Asian Affairs* 12:2.

1981b "Nomadism as Ideological Expression: The Case of the Gomal Nomads." *Nomadic Peoples* (IUAES) 9:3–15.

1982a "Hazarawal: Formation and Structure of District Ethnicity in Pakistan." Paper presented to the American Ethnological Society. Published in *The Prospects for Plural Societies*, D. M. Lewis, ed. Washington, D.C. (1984).

1982b "Order and Conflict in Muslim Society: A Case Study from Pakistan." *The Middle East Journal* 36, 2:182–204.

1983 *Religion and Politics in Muslim Society: Order and Conflict in Pakistan*. Cambridge: Cambrige University Press.

Ahmed, Akbar S., and D. M. Hart, eds.

1984 *From the Atlas to the Indus*. London: Routledge & Kegan Paul.

Algar, Hamid

1969 *Religion and State in Iran, 1785–1906: The Role of the Ulama in the Qajar Period*. Berkeley: University of California Press.

Bailey, F. G.

1972 "Conceptual Systems of the Study of Politics." In *Rural Politics and Social Change in the Middle East*. R. Antoun and I. Harik, eds. Bloomington: Indiana University Press.

Barth, Fredrik

1972 *Political Leadership among Swat Pathans*. London: Athlone Press (2nd edition).

1981 *Selected Essays of Fredrik Barth*. Vol. 2. London: Routledge & Kegan Paul.

Bruce, C.E.

1929 "The Tribes of Waziristan." Confidential. London: His Majesty's Stationery Office for the India Office.

Curtis, G. S. C.

1946 "Monograph on Mahsud Tribes." Confidential. Government of NWFP.

Dale, Stephen F.

1981 *Islamic Society on the South Asian Frontier: The Mappilas of Malabar, 1498–1922*. Oxford: Oxford University Press.

Eickelman, Dale F.
1976 *Moroccan Islam: Tradition and Society in a Pilgrimage Center.* Austin: University of Texas Press.

Geertz, Clifford, Hildred Geertz, and Larry Rosen
1979 *Meaning and Order in Moroccan Society: Three Essays in Cultural Analysis.* Cambridge: Cambridge University Press.

Gellner, Ernest
1969 *Saints of the Atlas.* London: Weidenfeld & Nicolson.

General Staff
1921 "Operations in Waziristan, 1919–1920." Confidential. Compiled by the General Staff, Army Headquarters, India. Calcutta: Superintendent Government Printing.
1932 "Summary of Events in North-West Frontier Tribal Territory: January 1, 1931, to December 31, 1931." Confidential. Simla: Government of India Press.
1936 "Military Report on Waziristan, 1935." Confidential. Calcutta: Government of India Press (5th edition).

Hodgson, Marshall G. S.
1974 *The Venture of Islam.* 3 vols. Chicago: University of Chicago Press.

Howell, E. B.
1925 "Waziristan Border Administration Report for 1924–25." Confidential. Delhi: Government of India.

Hunt, Roland, and John Harrison
1980 *The District Officer in India, 1930–47.* London: Scholar Press.

Johnson, H. H.
1934a "Notes on Wana." Confidential. Delhi: Government of India.
1934b "Mahsud Notes." Confidential. Delhi: Government of India.

Johnston, F. W.
1903 "Notes on Wana." Confidential. Delhi: Government of India.

Masters, John
1956 *Bugles and a Tiger: A Volume of Autobiography.* New York: Viking Press.

Maududi, S. Abul A'la
1948 *Al-jihād fil-Islām.* Lahore.

Nūr Muḥammad, Mullā
n.d. "Personal Diaries" (Urdu). Unpublished.

Peters, Rudolph
1979 *Islam and Colonialism: The Doctrine of Jihad in Modern History.* The Hague: Mouton.

Political Agent's Office
1977 From Political Agent's files, South Waziristan Agency.

Rahman, Fazlur
1979 *Islam.* Chicago: University of Chicago Press.
1980 *Major Themes of the Quran.* Chicago: Biblioteca Islamica.

Said, Edward W.
1978 *Orientalism.* London: Routledge & Kegan Paul.

Woodruff, Philip [pseud. for Philip Mason]
1965 *The Men Who Ruled India.* 2 vols. London: Jonathan Cape.

PART THREE

Negotiating Community Boundaries and Codes of Personal Behavior

10

The Boundaries of Islam and Infidelity

WARREN FUSFELD

Continuity with the past is an aspect of Islam which permeates many concepts of the religion itself, and many of the institutions within Muslim societies. Its opposite, innovation or deviation (*bid'at*), is equivalent to heresy. When events occur which lead Muslims to question their position in society, the relationship of society to God, and the true path of Islam, the issue of continuity becomes extremely forceful. It is linked to the conception of that which is Islam as opposed to that which is not. It looms large in debates over what path and vision of Islam is best for the Muslim community.

In India prior to the nineteenth century, as in many areas of the Islamic world, Sufism was virtually coextensive with Islam. The organized Sufi orders placed great emphasis on continuity, even defining themselves in terms of linkages which stretched back to the very origins of Islam. It is thus not surprising that when debates over the true character of Islam and the boundaries of the Muslim community arose in India, Sufis took an active role. This paper presents a description of the efforts made by one nineteenth-century Sufi leader, Shāh Aḥmad Sa'īd, to define the boundaries of the Muslim community through reference to his conception of the Naqshbandī Mujaddadī Sufi order which he represented.

The collected teachings of Shāh Aḥmad Sa'īd emphasize the limits of propriety set for good Muslims and define the characteristics of infidelity of other self-proclaimed Muslims. Such concerns, though relying on the

Naqshbandī Mujaddadī teachings, are not seen in the teachings of the *shaikh*s who directly preceded Shāh Aḥmad Sa'īd. Yet this change took place within a tradition which is defined as unchanging. It indicates the importance of looking beyond ideology in order to understand the complex interaction between ideas and the context in which they are formulated.

The Life of Shāh Aḥmad Sa'īd

Shāh Aḥmad Sa'īd (1802–60), a descendant of Shaikh Aḥmad Sirhindī, was the third successor of the *khānaqāh* located at the tomb of the eighteenth-century saint and poet Mīrzā Maẓhar, in the Chitli Qabr

Figure 10.1
The Genealogical Position of Shāh Aḥmad Sa'īd

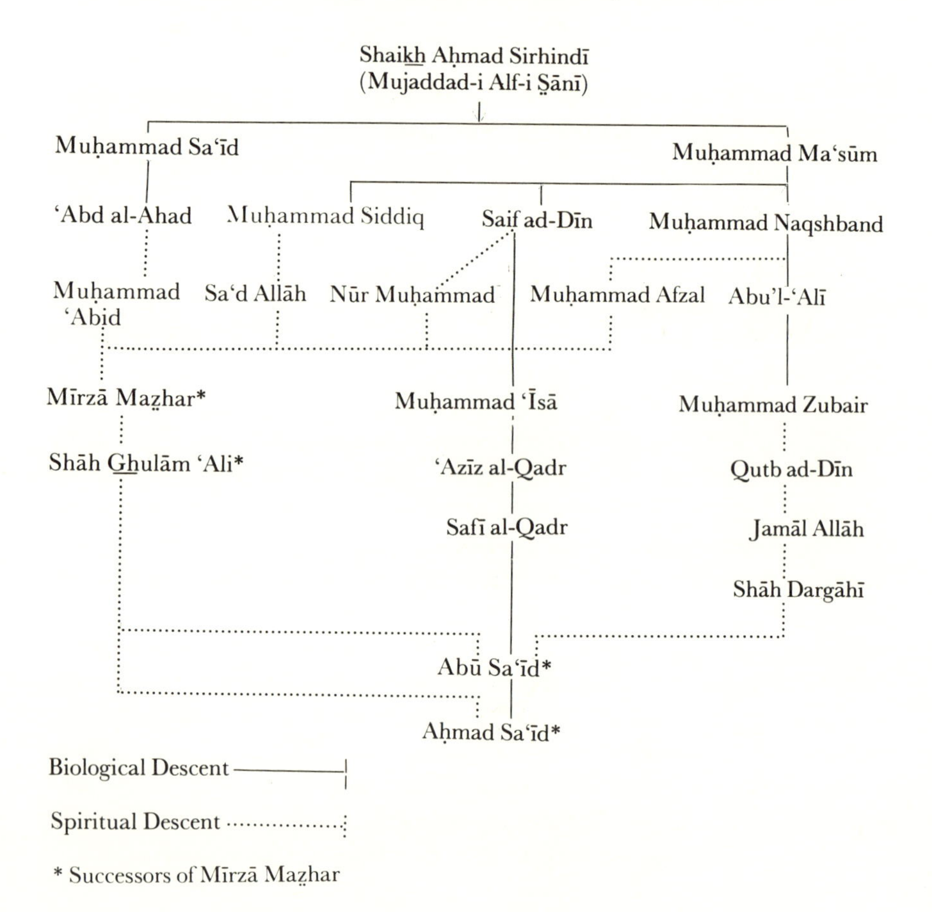

neighborhood of Delhi. The genealogical chart showing Aḥmad Saʿīd in the context of the descendants of Shaikh Aḥmad Sirhindī indicates that Aḥmad Saʿīd succeeded to his position combining several lines of spiritual and biological descent. Born in Rampur in 1802, he had no connection with Mīrzā Maẓhar other than a common link to Shaikh Aḥmad Sirhindī, known as the "Renewer of the Second Millennium" (*mujaddad-i alf-i ṡānī*, or simply *mujaddad*). His original exposure to the Sufi traditions of his family was at the circle (*ḥalqa*) of Shāh Dargāhī of Rampur. But his formal initiation into the Mujaddadī order did not occur until the age of ten, when he traveled to Delhi with his father, where they both met Shāh Ghulām ʿAlī, first successor of Mīrzā Maẓhar. At the age of seventeen he was given deputyship (*khilāfat*) by Shāh Ghulām ʿAlī.

Aḥmad Saʿīd's father was designated by Shāh Ghulām ʿAlī as his successor. After this establishment of a descendant of Sirhindī as head of the order, succession remained in the family, passing from father to son until the present. Thus, on the death of his father, Aḥmad Saʿīd sat in his place, remaining an active Sufi *shaikh* and member of the Delhi elite until 1857. Forced out of the city at the time of its capture by the British, he managed to travel safely, using road passes obtained from a friendly Afghan officer serving with the British. He went first to the Punjab, then to the *khānaqāh* of his disciple Dost Muḥammad Qandahāri in Dera Ismaʿil Khan, and then by sea first to Bombay and thence to Arabia, where he settled. He died in Medina in 1860.[1]

The Context

Early nineteenth-century Delhi was a focal point of active intellectual ferment among the elite of the Muslim community. While the scope of political activity became increasingly limited throughout the first half of the nineteenth century, the city of Delhi was preserved by the British, who had established themselves in Delhi in 1803, as a thriving Muslim environment (Fusfeld 1981). Both by their original intent, and as a result of the legal situation of supposed subordination of the British to the Mughal sovereign, the Muslims of Delhi enjoyed the status which official Muslim rule and law afforded their community. Yet they were also aware of the virtual destruction of independent Muslim power and political opportunity. While this decline of political well-being was very

1. Short biographies of Shāh Aḥmad Saʿīd appear in Sayyid Aḥmad Khān (1965:472–73); "Sair al-Kāmilīn" (1881:40–45).

much a continuation of eighteenth-century developments, the loss of political autonomy became all the more clear at the same time that Delhi itself became physically more secure. This set up an environment in which Muslim intellectual endeavors benefited from the protection of the Pax Britannica just as the Muslim elite of Delhi faced the clearest limitations they had yet confronted on their power to control their own world.

In the context of the active intellectual life of the Muslim elite of Delhi and the political problems which those Muslims felt they confronted, the reformist position which had been taken in the eighteenth century by Shāh Walīullāh developed, through the efforts of his three sons and many of their followers, into a variety of arguments both for reform and for reorganization of Muslim religious and social life. Seeking to eliminate the cause of Muslim decline through elimination of aspects of Muslim society and activity, nineteenth-century reformers took the ideas of Shāh Walīullāh to ever more extreme forms. The reformist effort to define and limit proper behavior and thought raised the issue of the boundaries of the Muslim community. Once such an issue was raised, especially when done in the name of a well-respected Muslim thinker such as Shāh Walīullāh (whose legacy was claimed by virtually all nineteenth-century reformers), the debate as to proper behavior and the boundaries of the Muslim community had to be confronted by all.

Among the elements of Indo-Muslim society under criticism from the nineteenth-century reformers were many of the practices associated with Sufism, and in some cases Sufism itself. More traditional Muslims considered such reformers Wahhābīs, followers of the eighteenth-century Ḥanbalī Arab reformer who sought to eliminate all elements of tomb and saint worship that supposedly persisted in the practices of Sufi orders. The intellectual current from which the nineteenth-century Indian reform movements drew inspiration, however similar in its elements, had a separate, Indian source. The critique made of Sufi excesses, transmitted through Shāh Walīullāh, was itself largely a product of earlier reformist inspiration seen in the works of the founder of the Mujaddadī family, Shaikh Aḥmad Sirhindī. Sirhindī was himself a Sufi *shaikh*, a *khalīfa* of the Naqshbandī Khwāja Bāqī Bi'llāh. His reformist critique should not therefore be understood as having been aimed at Sufism itself. His critique accepted Sufism as legitimate and was concerned with those practices of Sufis and others which were beyond the realm of what was permitted in Islamic law, or beyond the desirable practices (*sunnat*) of Muḥammad. But the development by the nineteenth century of elements of this critique into a critique of Sufism as a whole forced a reconsideration of legitimate practice. This criticism could not be ignored by those who felt themselves to be direct inheritors of Sirhindī's mystic teaching, and yet simultaneously under criticism by others who, at least indirectly, claimed their own legitimacy through continuity with that very same tradition.

We can see in the teachings of the Naqshbandī Mujaddadī *shaikh* Shāh Aḥmad Sa'īd a deliberate attempt to deal with such criticisms. This produced a style of religiosity greatly different from that of his predecessors. He took on a new argumentativeness, issued legal decisions (*fatāwā*) dealing with these issues, and generally attempted to act, not exclusively as a mystic *shaikh*, but also as a defender of true Islam, venturing into the areas of study which the reformists themselves took to be central to Islam. Thus, while defending Islamic mysticism he had to move outside the realm of mysticism onto the ground of the reformist scholars, dealing with them in their own terms, something which his own *shaikh*s had never done.

The Muslim Community and the Boundaries of Islam

The society that mattered for Shāh Aḥmad Sa'īd was the Muslim community. It was primarily within it that his role was defined. Disputes within that community linked him to the wider historical development of the society in which he lived. While reference was made to the foreigners (*amīrān-i farang*) in relation to the events of 1857 leading up to his migration to Arabia (Maẓhar 1281H:196), his reaction to those events was exclusively in terms of the development of his desire for pilgrimage to the cities of Arabia (Sa'īd n.d. a:145, 147). There was no reference whatever to Hindu society or even to individual Hindus in the writings directly concerned with Shāh Aḥmad Sa'īd's life, nor did he mention them in his own writings.[2]

In contrast to the lack of reference to non-Muslims is the great number of references to other Muslims, either other Sufis or other "sects" (*firqa*). The belief system of the Naqshbandī Mujaddadī Sufis incorporated an institutionalized reform which started with or was attributed to Shaikh Aḥmad Sirhindī. As noted above, this aspect of

2. The sole reference to Hindus is in the description of a miracle performed by Sirhindī in which his followers are protected from Hindu revenge after they had broken some idols, but even in this statement there is only the most superficial mention of them (Maẓhar 1281H:13).

Naqshbandī Mujaddadī belief provided a background from which later reformist patterns were developed. Shāh Aḥmad Sa'īd drew on elements of this reformist vision of Islam both in challenging the non-Mujaddadī groups whom he opposed and in confirming those Mujaddadīs who had, in his view, gone astray, through emphasizing and pushing to extremes the reformist elements in their tradition.

It is not surprising that *shaikh*s of the Mujaddadī family criticized other Sufis, given the reformist element present in Sirhindī's writings. But in Sirhindī's writings, this criticism coexisted with acceptance and general respect for the various popularly accepted Sufi orders. The deliberate reliance of the successors at the Delhi *khānaqāh* on unsolicited donations rather than on endowments made attraction of disciples a stimulus to fulfilling their mission of spreading the true path and assisting seekers in reaching their goal. Their appeal was furthered by the incorporation in the Mujaddadī system of all the orders, particularly the popular Qādirī and Chishtī traditions. Criticism was directed not at the orders but at their contemporary representatives.

The most vital element of reform in the general Mujaddadī inheritance was the emphasis on the coincidence of law (*sharī'at*) and the Sufi path. The clear exhortation to follow the *sunnat* and the law served as a criticism of Sufi groups who disregarded the law or saw it as subordinate to the Sufi path. It also exposed to criticism those Sufis who deliberately used dubious methods to place themselves in spiritually intoxicated states. The Mujaddadī pattern of stages of spiritual progress accepted the various Sufi orders as stages on the mystic path, although the Mujaddad rejected critical aspects of their teachings. As the earlier stages, legitimate but linked with offensive behavior, are replaced by higher stages, the offense is eliminated and the traveler comes to a higher understanding of reality. Particularly, this involves the two experiences of unity (*tauḥīd*) which succeed one another in the Mujaddadī path. Briefly stated, the experience of "unity of existence" (*tauḥīd-i wujūdī*) occurs when one sees only the existence of God, and consequently is unable to perceive, when looking at creation, anything other than that perception of God. This is superseded by a higher level of perception in which all of creation is seen as coming from God, but is not identified with Him. In this second stage, one understands the perceptual nature of the earlier experience, hence the name of this stage, "unity of perception" (*tauḥīd-i shuhūdī*). The first stage is associated with spiritual intoxication and statements of an incorrect nature, such as "all is He" and "I am God." The second stage restores one to sobriety and allows one to see the error of the earlier stage. The logic of this provided for the incorporation of Sufi orders which advocate *tauḥīd-i wujūdī* as their view of reality, while at the same time giving a claim of superior understanding to those who progress beyond that.

The treatment of this pattern of stages can vary in the degree of emphasis either on the inclusion of the other orders or on the superiority and exclusiveness of the higher stages of the Mujaddadī path. Respect for the great saints of other orders was no impediment to criticism of contemporaries:

> Ḥaẓrat Ghauṡ as-Saqilain [ʿAbdu'l-Qādir Jīlānī] was retired in the Burj-i ʿAjami for eleven years. He satisfied himself on the branches of trees until he arrived at the rank of *ghauṡīyat* [one who assists]. And Bābā Farīd hung himself upside down in a well for eight years, and passed the entire night in remembrance and thought of God. . . . And Ḥaẓrat Ḥusain Manṣūr Ḥallāj prayed all day and night, until he became submerged in the ocean of unity. Not like the Sufis of this age who eat whatever they want and wear whatever they choose, and say "all is He." (Maẓhar 1281H:121)

Shāh Aḥmad Saʿīd emphasized the possibility of reconciling the wisdom of unity with the law by interpreting unity in the light of the law. But he criticized as ignorant those who took the belief in unity to be the source or basis of the law, making the law of secondary importance. He accused his contemporaries of such ignorance while he added a disclaimer avoiding accusations against the respected founders of the various Sufi orders, who were in spiritually intoxicated states that legitimately provided an excuse for statements which otherwise could be objectionable. He went on to exclude *tauḥīd-i wujūdī* from the teachings which he espoused, noting that in the Naqshbandī tradition that stage is unnecessary. "It is a blunder that some of the proponents of *tauḥīd-i wujūdī* make, depicting that as an essential stage of the path, and even giving it weight in matters of the law, that we are protected from" (Saʿīd n.d. a:27). Shāh Aḥmad Saʿīd further displayed his criticism of contemporary Sufis by citing the distinctions which had been made by Sirhindī himself, who refused to criticize the great Sufis of the past who spoke of unity while cursing those intoxicated with *tauḥīd* through deliberate and dubious techniques (Saʿīd n.d. b:201). Criticism was aimed not at the great figures but at the contemporary Sufis who forced themselves into trances and deliberately misled others into believing that they possessed the ultimate truth. In support of the superiority of his own teachings he said that "one knows this much, that additional to this mystic knowledge is another mystic knowledge, and beyond this state, another state is established. Those who are imprisoned in this stage [of *tauḥīd-i wujūdī*] are forbidden from many perfections and are forbidden from countless stages" (Sa'īd n.d. b:10). These lines from Sirhindī's letters were cited by Aḥmad Sa'īd in defense of practices of his own family that had been questioned as innovations. He sought in the argument to distinguish his own family from those Sufis who may be truly blameworthy. The practices were said to be the practices of Sirhindī and of the great Naqshbandīs who "followed the *sunnat* day and night. . . . And none of their habits were without knowledge like other Sufis" (Sa'īd n.d. b:190).

Shāh Aḥmad Sa'īd's desire to distinguish himself from other Sufis appeared in matters other than those related to interpretation of *tauḥīd*, though this was one of the most important distinctions. At a much more general level he felt himself distinguished from them with regard to Sufi practices of questionable legality. In response to accusations that his disciple, Dost Muḥammad, brought on trances voluntarily, Aḥmad Sa'īd defended him and the Mujaddadī family by pointing out that, unlike Chishtī Sufis, they refrained from practices such as listening to music with instruments. Further, by pointing to the legitimacy of involuntary states of ecstasy and trances which occur because of the strong power of the Mujaddadī *shaikhs* he was able to emphasize the power of the Mujaddadīs at the same time that he defended them against accusations of unorthodoxy (Sa'īd n.d. a:91, 102–8). He thus preserved the legitimacy of activities which he declared to be hypocritical in others yet which, by their spontaneity among the Mujaddadīs, were attractive and demonstrative of the greatness which is found in his family.

The other side of the coin, and another stimulus for the complex arguments by which Aḥmad Sa'īd distinguished himself from other Sufis, was the attack which reformist "sects" leveled against practices associated with Sufism and the shrines of saints. This reformist tradition had itself emerged to some extent from divergent branches of the Naqshbandī Mujaddadī family, with the eighteenth-century figure of Shāh Walīullāh prominently in the background.[3] Aḥmad Sa'īd responded to reformist criticism by defending the orthodoxy of his own tradition and pointing out the error of those arguing for a radicalized

3. Mīrzā Maẓhar, the founder of the Maẓhari line, was often in contact with Shāh Walīullāh, and there were acknowledged common lines of spiritual affiliation. The article "Al-Dihlawi, Wali Allah" in *The Encyclopaedia of Islam* (Hosain 1924:971), points out his training in the Naqshbandī order and his succession to his father's position as spiritual guide.

version of the Mujaddadī tradition. Aḥmad Sa'īd's concern with this defense of his tradition was important enough to be noted even in the short biographical notice of Shāh Aḥmad Sa'īd in the "Sair al-Kāmilīn" ("The Journey of the Perfect Ones") (1881). In this matter Shāh Aḥmad Sa'īd himself was quoted: "however much the writing of legal decisions is not my task, in these latter days, ignorant persons have established themselves as *'ulamā* and are spreading ignorance. . . . I have taken this task on myself, especially in opposition to the Wahhābī sect" ("Sair al-Kāmilīn" 1881:44; Maẓhar 1281H:131, 157).

The defense against the "Wahhābīs," a term which must be understood here to mean any opponents of Sufi practices associated with tombs and saints, operated on several levels. He criticized those opponents for failing to understand the nature of that which they opposed.

> Often those who don't understand object to the *shaikh*s and the great ones who have said things in intoxication . . . in which there was room for error, and they denigrate them. In answer to these foolish ones, one word is sufficient, "Don't compare the deeds of the Pure Ones to oneself." Everything which comes from the beloved of God is beautiful, as that which grows from the special pure ones and from their company, though appearing reprehensible is clean and pure. (Sa'īd n.d. a:60)

Shāh Aḥmad also pointed to the essential superiority of the Sufis over the *'ulamā* who have criticized them.

> You should look at books concerning the problem you seek answered, not books on other things. For example, on a problem of *fiqh* the answer will be found in books and there is no need of anything else. The externalist *'ulamā* have one task, while the internal *'ulamā* [i.e., the Sufis] have a separate system of thought. The denial of the inner secret-seeing *'ulamā* by the external-seeing *'ulamā* has been going on since ancient days, and because of their defective understanding they are excused. From their denial one should not move from one's place. (Sa'īd n.d. a:100)

From this perspective, the inability of the externalist *'ulamā* to understand the problems of Sufism and their lack of experience of the stages of Sufism disqualified them as critics and prevented them from understanding the validity of experiences. This resulted in statements appearing to be in error to those of superficial understanding.

The attack against the practices of the Mujaddadī *shaikh*s was of even more critical importance to Shāh Aḥmad Sa'īd than the general attack on Sufism. In that attack he took aspects of Sirhindī's own teaching, in an effort to show that commonly accepted Mujaddadī practices were counter both to the *sunnat* of Muḥammad and to the statements of

Sirhindī. To make his argument he used his training both in *ḥadīs̤* and as a Sufi *shaikh*.[4] This is seen most clearly in several tracts produced by Aḥmad Sa'īd dealing with customary displays of respect for the Prophet (Sa'īd 1920) and in the practice of picturing the image of the *shaikh* in the mind as a method for spiritual progress (Sa'īd n.d. b). Another tract was devoted entirely to a detailed refutation of a work by a contemporary figure who was a scholar of *ḥadīs̤* (*muḥaddis̤*) in the tradition of the Walīullāh family (Sa'īd 1386H).

Shāh Aḥmad Sa'īd's defense of traditional displays of respect for the Prophet was a response to criticism of those practices as unacceptable innovations. He noted that he wrote in opposition to the "sect of *muḥaddis̤*" (*firqa-i muḥadis̤s̤a*) who "forbid the remembrance of the birth, rising, miracles and death of Muḥammad. Some call it detestable in legal decisions which they have issued, and some say that it is bad innovation" (Sa'īd 1920:50). Whether this is a reference to *muḥaddis̤* of the Walīullāh school, or a specific derogatory reference to the Ahl-i Hadīs̤, the character of the text and the response are clear.

The argument itself is oriented toward praise of the powers of the Prophet, specifically as an intermediary between man and God, a role which is important for legitimizing the portrayal of the great Sufis as characters similar to and in complete imitation of the Prophet. The bitter character of Aḥmad Sa'īd's sentiment toward the "sect of *muḥaddis̤*" is made clear after a discussion of the Prophet's revelation from God that he would be allowed to intercede to save his own followers from the torment of the grave. He related that "this was told on his [Muḥammad's] return, to Abū Bakr, and then others, and all the Muslims agreed while the infidels denied it."

The infidelity of those who denied this ability of the Prophet raises the issue of the boundary of Islam. By implication, those contemporaries of Aḥmad Sa'īd who denied such powers in the Prophet were also excluded from the community of Muslims.

The defense of picturing the image of the *shaikh* is also a self-conscious reply to attacks on Mujaddadī practices. Aḥmad Sa'īd is quoted as saying:

> in this time of dispute and heresies, the mention of the problem of *rābiṭa* [devoting oneself to a *shaikh*], which is the practice of the Sufis, arose. And some of the people of the time believing it to be among the innovations, in accord with their own understanding have written a thing and sent it to this

4. Maẓhar (1281H:131) notes that he was expert in *tafsīr*, *ḥadīs̤*, and in the truths of Sirhindī's teachings.

faqīr. Helpless, in answer to that I wrote a few lines despite a lack of free time so that the orthodox Muslims and especially the faithful Ḥanafī *'ulamā* and the pure Sufis, to which group Ḥaẓrat Imām Rabbani [Sirhindī] belonged, would know that he followed the *sunnat* day and night and in remembering and occupation and habits and devotions, none of his habits were without knowledge like the other Sufis. (Sa'īd n.d. b:190)

The statements of Sirhindī himself became critical in the discussion, since he was cited by the critic of this practice as saying that all innovation is bad. Thus, according to the critic, the practice was bad because it was an innovation, and was to be condemned even in the Mujaddadī tradition. Aḥmad Sa'īd's response pointed out the existence of the practice in the writings of Sirhindī, as well as in writings concerning the practice of many important *shaikhs*. He further argued that the two seemingly opposing aspects of Sirhindī's teachings are reconciled by understanding the true meaning of his words.

Thus, the words and deeds of these great ones come for us as a necessity and a proof. It is not necessary for us to prove the *sunnīyat* [validity as *sunnat*] of their actions and words. Thus all the Sufis among the people of innovation have called Ḥaẓrat Mujaddad-i Alf-i S̤ānī a denier of Sufis and their thinking. And he has also said that all innovation is deviation, and deviation is for Hell. . . . [But] the collected and gathered words of Ḥaẓrat Ishan [Sirhindī] are so beneficial that dissent between him and those who accept the validity of good innovation is but a work, and in truth, there is no innovation. And those matters which the *'ulamā* have placed in the category of good innovation, he has placed within the *sunnat*. (Sa'īd n.d. b:190–91)

The practices which were being criticized as innovations, and therefore bad, were in fact good innovations, new practices which support or are within the principles of the *sunnat*. These actions were considered by Sirhindī to be, by analogy, a part of the *sunnat*, and therefore immune from his own condemnation of all innovations. Sirhindī's own words could thus not legitimately be used to condemn his own practices. Rather, Sirhindī's words and deeds are properly seen as having a status of unquestionable validity, according to Aḥmad Sa'īd.

In his *Taḥaqīq al-Ḥaqq al-Mubīn* (1386H) Aḥmad Sa'īd responded to a work called *Masā'il-i Arba'īn* (*Forty Problems*), which consisted for the most part of answers to a set of problems put by the contemporary ruler of Bhikampur to Shāh Muḥammad Ishaq Dihlawī (d. 1854), the grandson of Shāh 'Abdu'l-'Azīz, son of Shāh Walīullāh, and a well-known figure in the Delhi community.[5] According to Aḥmad Sa'īd's

5. See his biography in Sayyid Aḥmad Khān 1965:554–56.

introduction, people had asked him about the *Masā'il-i Arba'īn*, and accordingly he felt that he should write "a few lines" in order that "the truth may be distinguished from error, and the correct from the incorrect" (Sa'id 1386H:5). Shāh Aḥmad Sa'īd saw Muḥammad Ishaq's statements as an unreasoned criticism of contemporary customs. Muḥammad Ishaq's failure to understand the intention behind the customs, according to Aḥmad Sa'īd, lay behind his errors of interpretation. Thus, typically, he cites first the statement of Muḥammad Ishaq, and then gives his critique.

> He said: all the customs which are current among the people of the age, such as spreading out the carpet on the third day, and setting up the tent, and spreading perfume, and things like these, are all shocking innovations, and are not legal. I say: the argument is without reason, and the basis of [the legality of] acts is in the intentions. If it is for the veneration of those reciting the Qur'ān . . . it is good that they should sit on clean carpets for recitation, and for remembering God, and it would become the cause of acceptability [of the act]. And if someone does not have a large house and he erects a tent for these people, what is the fault? . . . and the use of perfume is itself a *sunnat*. (Sa'īd 1386H:15)

Shah Aḥmad Sa'īd clearly perceived Muḥammad Ishaq's work as a radical attack on the basic practices of the Mujaddadī Sufis. Aḥmad Sa'īd's arguments against Muḥammad Ishaq were based on the study of *ḥadīṡ* (both Aḥmad Sa'īd and Muḥammad Ishaq had studied with the same teachers) and also on Mujaddadī Sufi concepts. Statements by Muḥammad Ishaq were criticized on technical grounds, such as pointing out his use of the term "permissible" (*jā'iz*) for division of food after obtaining a boon when "it was simply wrong, he should say it is *sunnat*" (Sa'īd 1386H:9). Similarly, the use of henna on the hands and feet of children was termed "forbidden" by Muḥammad Ishaq, while Aḥmad Sa'īd claims it was, in fact, "detestable" (Sa'īd 1386H:9). Here there was no disagreement on the basic issue of whether one should or should not do a particular thing, but rather Aḥmad Sa'īd sought to show his superiority in the field of *ḥadīṡ* and discredit Muḥammad Ishaq on his own terms. He pursued the argument further, arguing that many of the customs which had been criticized by Muḥammad Ishaq were in fact acceptable. Where Muḥammad Ishaq had criticized a custom because of its practice by the Hindus, Shāh Aḥmad Sa'īd argued that the fact of their doing a thing could not be an argument, in itself, against its validity (Sa'īd 1386H:11–12). Muḥammad Ishaq's proclamation of all acts not within the *sharī'at* as being either detestable or forbidden provoked Shāh Ahmad Sa'īd's agitated response:

I sigh! It is amazing that [Muḥammad Ishaq] in spite of knowledge of writings, brings together opposing and contradictory statements, and gives interpretations opposed to the *'ulamā*. . . . Thus if he had said in his statement the word "principle" instead of "vision" [i.e., had he said within the principle of the law, rather than literally seen within it] it would have been fine. (Sa'īd 1386H:14)

Activities and customs acceptable within the principles of the law, or which promote the tenets of Islam, were considered by Aḥmad Sa'īd as permitted. This view allowed most of the essential practices of Sufism to be preserved. These were justified, not because they were the practices of the Prophet, but because they preserved the inner meaning of the teachings and practices of the Prophet. In this sense they were worthy of being considered part of the *sunnat* itself.

The attack on Muḥammad Ishaq went beyond a demonstration of his inferiority as a scholar of *ḥadīs̤*. Aḥmad Sa'īd claimed that Muḥammad Ishaq had violated the statements of his own teachers (Sa'īd 1386H:33), and had attempted to venture beyond the realm of that which he could legitimately claim as knowledge (Sa'īd 1386H:26). Aḥmad Sa'īd argued that since the Sufi *shaikh*s had inherited the complete legacy of Muḥammad, both its inner and outer reality, they represented a more correct exemplification of the *sunnat* than that which was available to the externalist *'ulamā* through their studies. While Muḥammad Ishaq was shown to be an inferior scholar, it was here made clear that even the most expert in that field would still have an incomplete basis for understanding these issues.

The final offense committed by Muḥammad Ishaq in his critique was his discussion of Muḥammad as a man with no special powers different from the powers of other men. The depiction of Muḥammad as an ordinary man was, by implication, an attack on the mediational role claimed by Sufis themselves, and was totally unacceptable to Shāh Aḥmad Sa'īd. He cited, in response, a line of the Qur'ān which states that the infidels will say of the prophets that they are men like others. He thereby pointed to the final inadmissibility of Muḥammad Ishaq's ideas, placing him in the realm of infidelity and not Islam (Sa'īd 1386H:50). Pushing the attack yet further, Shāh Aḥmad Sa'īd went on to detail the many superior and special abilities of the Prophet, concluding that "the person who thinks himself equal to that, his mind has become deranged, and his thought wrong. He is like the fly that sat down on a piece of straw floating in the urine of an ass and believed, 'I have sat on a boat in the ocean and am traveling' " (Sa'īd 1386H:56).

Conclusion

While the issue of proper behavior (*adab*) had always been of concern to all Sufi *shaikh*s with an interest in maintaining followers and keeping discipline and control over them, this concern manifested itself for the most part in the context of traditional expectations of the *shaikh*, on the one hand, and of deference to be shown by disciples on the other. Implicitly accepted as part of this was an unquestioned system of mystic thought and traditional activities associated with the organized institutions of Sufism. Criticism of other Sufis within such a context was in no way a criticism of the system, but rather a criticism of hypocrisy or of insufficient advancement along the pathway which the Naqshbandī Mujaddadī *shaikh*s believed to be correct. Judgments concerning other mystics were made with the implicit understanding that all, whether Naqshbandī or not, were nevertheless following a single path. Non-Naqshbandīs, through failure to perceive this, often believed they had reached deep and profound mystic goals, though they still remained in one of the lower stages of spiritual advance.

As long as there was general acceptance of Sufism as a legitimate, and even as the most important, part of true Islam, there was no need to relate to other Muslims outside the framework of mystic thought which was the inheritance of Shaikh Aḥmad Sirhindī, and the basis for Aḥmad Sa'īd's—and his predecessors'—understanding of Islam and the world. But the development of a reformist sentiment, growing out of a school of thought increasingly alienated from the realm of mysticism, necessitated a response which itself moved out of the mystic framework.

Shāh Aḥmad Sa'īd defended his role as a *shaikh*, and the traditions of Sufism which he had inherited, not in the language of dreams and mystic visions, but rather in the manner of a scholar of *ḥadīs*. He augmented the role of *shaikh* by taking on the additional tasks associated with the *'ulamā*, using legal argumentation and issuing legal decisions. But beyond the use of these forms of argument, he brought some degree of the reformist content into his teachings. As the reformists sought to define the boundaries of the Muslim community, so too Aḥmad Sa'īd confronted that issue. When the reformists depicted the Sufism of Aḥmad Sa'īd as beyond the pale of legitimate Islam he responded with all the intellectual tools at hand, both those within the Sufi tradition and those used by the reformists themselves. Just as his critics had tried to place Aḥmad Sa'īd outside the community of Islam, he took on the task of drawing the boundaries as he believed them to exist. He located himself and his mystic tradition directly within the bounds of *sharī'at* and *ḥadīs̤*, and he placed his critics firmly outside. To understand his arguments it is necessary to see the whole context in which he argued and to recognize that in the dialectic of argument both sides are changed.

References

Fusfeld, Warren
1981 "Communal Conflict in Delhi: 1803–1903." *Indian Economic and Social History Review* 19, 2:181–200.

Hosain, M. Hidayat
1924 "Al-Dihlawi, Wali Allah." *Encyclopaedia of Islam*. Vol. 2. Leiden: E. J. Brill, p. 971.

Maz̤har, Muḥammad
1281H *Manaqib-i Aḥmadiyya*. Delhi: Akmal ul-Matabi'.

Sa'īd, Shāh Aḥmad
n.d. a "Maktūbāt-i Ḥaẓrat Shāh Aḥmad Sa'īd Mujaddadī Dihlawī." Manuscript.
n.d. b "Risāla al-Fawa'id az-Zabita fi Isbat ar-Rābiṭa." Manuscript.
1920 *Sa'īd al-Bayān fi Muwallid Sayyid al-Uns wa'l-Jan*. Meerut: Shams al-Matabi'.
1386H *Taḥqīq al-Ḥaqq al-Mubīn fi Ajwibat Masā'il Arba'īn*. Hyderbad, Sindh: Hakim Mahmud az-Zaman.

"Sair al-Kāmilīn"
1881 Anonymous manuscript.

Sayyid Aḥmad K̲h̲ān
1965 *As̤ar as-Sanadid*. Delhi: Central Book Depot.

11

The Culture of Ethnicity in Pakistan

RICHARD KURIN

Urdu-speaking refugees from India (*muhājirīn*) and their descendants constitute perhaps 8 percent of Pakistan's population (Nyrop 1971:58). Residing mainly in the cities of Karachi, Lahore, and Hyderabad (Johnson 1979:15–16), this group was quite influential in the Pakistan movement, and has expressed its self-consciousness dramatically several times during the country's subsequent development (e.g., Sayeed 1967:214–25). Historically tending to be an urban population, and continuing by and large to assert their genealogical ties to exogenous origins in western Asia, members of this group have particular notions of the moral, proper, and honorable life—perhaps, as several suggested, encapsulated in the national slogan of Pakistan: "īmān, ittěḥād, naẓm" ("faith, unity, and discipline").

Punjabis, if defined on a linguistic basis, constitute approximately 65 percent of the country's population (Nyrop 1971:58). Historically identified with a particular and well-delineated geographical area, Punjabis are predominantly a rural population. While the Punjab sports the great cities of Lahore and Multan, and scores of marketing towns and trading centers, 75 percent of its population continues to reside in villages, on farms, and in hamlets (Government of Pakistan 1973). Influential in the building of Pakistan, in the army, in the bureaucracy and, by sheer weight of numbers, in the electorate, Punjabis have had a self-conscious, expressed identity possibly stretching back to the eighth century (Gankovsky 1971:106). Native (*desī*)

Punjabis, continuing to recognize their pre-Islamic origins in reference to their identities as Jāts, Rājpūts, Arains, Gūjars, and so forth, also have their notions of the exemplary life—possibly revealed, as several villagers intimated, in a popular aphorism borrowed from the Persian—"Zan, zar, zamīn" ("women, wealth, and land").

Both Pakistan's Punjabi- and Urdu-speaking populations are predominantly Muslim, and in this share many basic terms, definitions, and ideas about the nature of persons, groups, humanity, and the way in which life is lived. Within this context of a shared cultural system, however, Punjabis and Urdu speakers do, as in choosing a slogan or aphorism, clearly enunciate their differences. While both communities have been closely juxtaposed for several centuries, the formation of Pakistan accentuated their relationship demographically, sociopolitically, and culturally, drawing these differences into vivid relief.

As Paul Brass (1979) notes in his analysis of South Asian Muslim ethnicity, common symbols may be used to distinguish people who, in fact, share similar cultural understandings. Values may be attributed to such symbols in order to promote separate identities and attribute relative worth to different groups. This chapter describes one common symbol pool manipulated by Punjabis and Urdu speakers to construct images of their own (and alter's) identity. It also compares and contrasts images of the proper life and the exemplary person expressed by members of these two communities, and discusses the way in which different values attributed to the symbols constituting these images articulate with Islamic socio-philosophical discourse and the ideology of Pakistani nationalism.[1]

This chapter proceeds from the finding that deliberations concerning the moral value of social actions and conceptualizations of the proper life are neither enunciated only by elites or specialists nor necessarily restricted to expressions in religious texts, theological pronouncements, or reports of spiritual experiences. The statement of these ideas is certainly explicitly and conveniently available through *'ulamā*, *pīrs*, scholars, literary figures, and rulers, all of whom may be highly committed to their formulations and records thereof. But it is here demonstrated that the common man and woman (*'ām ādmī*) also have

1. Field research for this chapter was conducted under grants from the Social Science Research Council and the Department of Education Fulbright-Hays Program. The views expressed here are those of the author and are not necessarily shared by these organizations. The author is grateful to Dale Eickelman, Vincent Crapanzano, McKim Marriott, Ralph Nicholas, C. M. Naim, and Barbara Metcalf for their comments and suggestions.

something to say regarding the moral worth of social action and ideas of the proper life, and that these are often expressed in rather mundane contexts—implicit in informal discussions and debates about ethnic, linguistic, regional, and political identity. This is not to argue that the principles and concepts of Islam are removed from commonplace usage. To the contrary, it is to say that while the nonspecialist may not know or make explicit bases of legitimacy, references to textual sources, theological distinctions, and technical terminology, concepts associated with Islam may be used to give meaning and value to a wide range of events and experiences which on the surface do not seem to have much to do with "religion" (*dīn, maẕhab, sharī'at*) per se.

The ethnographic analysis in this chapter is based largely upon interviews conducted with Urdu-speaking *muhājirīn* in Karachi and with Punjabis from Chakpur, a village in Okara District.[2] In each setting, fieldwork was conducted with a core of about twenty families over a nine-month period. Information obtained from members of these families is supplemented by interviews, censuses, and surveys involving hundreds of others from each of the two communities. The two core groups, while not probability samples of their respective populations, were nonetheless chosen because they were characteristic of their larger communities and also exhibited significant internal variations. To characterize the Urdu-speaking group, they generally lived on the west side of Karachi; had family members engaged in business, clerical, and white-collar service; were generally educated through high school; claimed to be the descendants of *sayyid*s or other noble (*ashraf*) groups; and had come to Karachi between 1947 and 1952 from Uttar Pradesh, Delhi, Bombay, or coastal Gujarat.

In contrast, the Punjabis were all from Chakpur, a village of approximately fifteen hundred people living in a former canal colony settled by the British in the 1930s. Engaged largely in agriculture and its support occupations, members of this group had little or no formal educational training; claimed to be descendants of Hindu Rājpūts who had converted to Islam upon conquest and proselytization several centuries ago; and had been long-time rural residents of the district (or surrounding districts) before the village settlement.

As members of these two communities attribute different values to their images of what they, as persons, are (and are not), what they should be (and should not be), and how they should live (and should

2. Chakpur is a pseudonym. See Kurin (1981) for an extended description.

not live), it is necessary to provide an analytic framework for the discussion of those differences. Here, following an ethno-sociological orientation to the study of South Asian conceptual systems (Marriott and Inden 1974, 1977; Marriott 1976; Inden and Nicholas 1977), this framework strives to be an indigenous one, constructed from those assumptions and concepts that members of *both* communities seem to share.

A Shared Culture of the Person

Chakpuris and Karachites commonly speak of the person (*shakhṣ*) in terms of how spirit (*rūḥ*) is related to the body (*jism*) and its corresponding psychobiological energy and powers (*nafs*). The contact point of spirit and body is the heart (*dil*), and the union of the two allows for the development and functioning of a distinctly human intellectual-moral faculty (*ʿaql*).

The terms "*rūḥ*" "*ʿaql*" and "*nafs*," apparently drawn from Hebraic, Arabic, and Persian sources,[3] are used in many ways, sometimes by both informants and scholars in semantically marked, unmarked, and residual senses. *Nafs* in its unmarked and most general sense, is usually glossed as "lower soul" but could perhaps be better translated as psychobiological energy, since in the Pakistani context it is conceived of as a force which issues directly from the body and is, in life, coincident with it. *Nafs*, in this sense, is often spoken of as referring to general life energy—the innate heat associated with the blood (*khūn*) and life (*jān*) itself. It is this energy which, pulsing through the body, is channeled or displaced through different organs and faculties, serving as a "power plant," so to speak, for both physiological and psychological processes. In its marked sense, *nafs* refers to a specifically *uncontrolled* energy—physical power, desire, animal passion, and carnal appetite. In Punjabi *nafs* may refer to the genitals, specifically the male genitalia. In a residual sense, however, *nafs* may refer to *ʿaql*, the powers of the mind or intellect, as, for example, when speaking of *nafs-i natīqa* (the rational faculty), or *rūḥ nafs-ānī* (the psychic essence).

3. "*Rūḥ*" in Urdu and Punjabi (s.f.) is derived from the Persian and Arabic (s.f.) meaning "cooled by the wind" (Platts 1968:604), whence the Hebrew term "*ruakh*." "*Nafs*" in Urdu and Punjabi (s.m.) is derived from the Persian, and from the Arabic (s.f.) meaning "desire greatly" (Platts 1968:1144) and is a cognate of the Hebrew term "*naphesh*" (Hughes n.d.:604). The term "*ʿaql*" in Urdu and Punjabi (s.f.) is derived from the Arabic, and means "reason" or "rationality."

Similarly, "*rūḥ*" is also used in several different ways. In one sense *rūḥ* can be understood to be noncorporeal spirit which issues not from the body or any particular combination of elements, but rather from a transcendent and purely moral intellect—Allāh. In quite another sense, however, *rūḥ* may be conceived of as a spiritous substance, a fine ethereal vapor (*bukhārat laṭīfa*), light (*nūr*), or breath (*nafas*) which is capable of combining with corporeal elements.

" '*Aql*" is an intriguing concept requiring interpretation. Without *'aql*, so informants argue, there can be no use of language, nor moral conscience. It is *'aql* which enables men to think, to discriminate, to decide, and hence to exert control over their nature. Human *'aql* is distinct from the *'aql* of both angels and animals in that it combines aspects of both *nafs* and *rūḥ*. Human *'aql* partakes of a dual nature, and it is because of this that man may be said to be the noblest of creation (*ashraf-i mukhlūqāt*). On one hand, *'aql* is a ratiocinative energy (*nafs*) which arises from the constituents of the body and draws on innate heat for its source of power (*quwwat*). On the other hand, it has a spiritual (*rūḥānī*) aspect, for as intellect *'aql* is dependent upon images, principles, rules, and concepts of value that transcend the corporeality of psycho-biological substance and energy. As one informant from Karachi suggested, the person is composed of both *rūḥ* and *nafs*: "The *rūḥ* has two parts, one is pure [*pāk*], the other is impure [*nā-pāk*], and the *nafs* also has two parts, one pure and the other impure. *'Aql* is that which joins the two [i.e., the impure *rūḥ* with the pure *nafs*]."[4]

Using this notion, *'aql* itself serves Karachites and Chakpuris as both a metonym and a metaphor for humanity (*ādmīyat*, literally "mankind," but also "reason, judgment, civility"). It is *'aql* which both combines and mediates otherwise mutually exclusive orders of existence, and makes man (at least in this world) the distinctive being he is.[5]

Angels, in contrast to humans, are thought of as being composed only of spirit (*rūḥ*) and do not have physical bodies (*jism* or *nafs*). They have the ability to speak, and are therefore said to posses *'aql*. Yet their *'aql* is

4. This statement, offered by an aged Karachi grandmother with no formal education, provides the basis for the model of personhood suggested here. While possibly not the only verbal model, it both encompasses and makes intelligible statements from other informants of both communities.

5. This combinatory and mediative aspect begins at birth and is reversed in death. Death marks a *wāpasī* or return to a pre-life situation, both for the individual and for the species, as body and spirit joined in life become separated once again. *'Aql* ceases to be of importance as humans assume either a spiritous existence in heaven or a base existence in hell (Kurin 1984).

incomplete when contrasted to that of man, since it does not have a corporeal component. Being composed solely of spirit, itself defined as moral, angels are necessarily bound to obey Allāh. Angels cannot then be immoral, and it can be argued that in relation to man, they are super-moral. Significantly, angels are universally described as having a cool (*ṭhanḍa*) disposition (*mizāj*) both in terms of their constitution (as *rūḥ*) and the character of their actions (as angelic, rule-bound, moral, intellectual, nonphysical, generally asthenic).

Animals, on the other hand, while possessed of *nafs* and *jism*, have a deficiency in terms of spirit. Animals possess one constituent of human *ʿaql*, that of sensation (which is rooted in the *nafs*), but not another, that of intuition, which makes image-making (imagination) possible. Devoid of this spiritual quality, animals can only be immoral, or, perhaps more arguably, amoral. As opposed to angels, animals are generally accorded hot (*garm*) dispositions, both in terms of their constitution (the elements of *jism*, the powers of *nafs*) and in terms of their actions (animalistic, blindly satisfying their physical wants and desires, nonmoral, nonintellectual, generally sthenic).

Given this general view, the human person can be seen as being both an angel and an animal as well as a combination of the two. Insofar as he engages in both animalistic actions and spiritualistic actions, he exists in a somewhat uniquely balanced or moderate state. This moderate state, however, is seen as dynamic, as involving the ever-constant need to balance the power or raw energy of life (*nafs*), the *jalālī* (terrible, powerful, active, hot, sthenic) aspects of one's nature with the beauty and order of life (*rūḥ*), the *jamālī* (sedate, beautiful, passive, cool, asthenic) aspects of one's nature. It is this dynamism, the shifting balance or imbalance between the necessity of order and the intractibility of physical existence, that sets the stage for human action in the world, as Punjabis, Urdu speakers, and many other Muslims view the challenge of living.[6]

6. This model, a composite of informant accounts, is general enough to allow for variation, yet specific enough to account for the meanings of concepts manipulated by Karachites and Chakpuris. It is similar to those models of the person found in the Qur'ān (Ali 1974:22–26n); commentaries by Muslim scholars such as G͟hazālī (n.d.), al-Hujwiri (1976:196–209), Razi (1969: part 1), Shāh Walīullāh (Hermansen 1984), Iqbal (Dar 1971:97–181), and Ibn Sina (Qarshi 1974: part 1); by scholars of Islamic metaphysics and personality such as Schimmel (1975:112–16), Lapidus (1984), and Corbin (1977:90–105, 222–36); ethnographers of Muslim societies such as Levy (1962:211–41), Siegal (1969), Geertz (1960:310–28) and Ewing (1984); and Muslim social thinkers in contemporary societies, e.g., Maududi (1972) in Pakistan and Ali Shariati (Yadegari 1980) in Iran.

It is perhaps this challenge, and its inevitability that Iqbal had in mind when he wrote in *Darb-i Kalim*:

> To me, beauty and charm consist in this,
> That the heavens bow before power.
> If there is no *jalāl*, *jamāl* is superficial.
> If the song is not fiery, it is mere breath.
> (Dar 1971)

Foremost in this challenge is the determination by groups and individuals of what types of persons they are, what type of persons they should be, and where the balance in man's dual nature is to be struck.

Images of the Person in Karachi and Chakpur

In his aforementioned discussion of South Asian Muslim ethnicity, Brass (1979) describes the tendency for groups in conflict to distinguish themselves through the use of multiple symbols. He also notes that efforts are often made by such groups to make congruent the messages such symbols seek to express. In this section, three such symbols—habitation (*abād, rahaish, muqām* [Urdu]); mother tongue (*mādarī zubān* [Urdu], *mādrī bolī* [Punjabi]); and genealogical origin (*nasl, qaum*)—used by Chakpuris and Karachites are investigated with regard to how they describe and differentiate types of persons in the two communities and how they are thought to convey messages that are congruent.[7]

These three symbols are by no means the only ones used by informants to speak about and contrast their identities. Considered individually, however, habitation (city/village), mother tongue (Urdu/Punjabi), and genealogical origin (exogenous nobility/indigenous convert) have been particularly salient, given the history and ethnography of the two communities. They are also spoken of by informants as having particularly meaningful congruencies. City dweller, Urdu speaker, and exogenous noble tend to be associated as a set, as do villager, Punjabi speaker, and native. And the differences expressed between comparable elements of each set tend to reiterate the same general message, so that

7. Unless clear from the context, Urdu terms are indicated by "[Urdu]" and Punjabi terms by "[Punjabi]." In order to limit repetition of transcriptions where terms from both languages differ only in regular phonetic ways (e.g., as in the alternative use of Punjabi tonals and Urdu aspirated stops), only the Urdu form will be transcribed.

differences between city and village may be seen as parallel to those between Urdu and Punjabi and between noble and native.[8]

Urbanites and Villagers as Persons

For both Karachites and Chakpuris, the city and the village are different types of places, exerting specific effects upon their inhabitants, and thus providing for different ways of living. Karachites regard themselves, and are regarded by Chakpuris, as city dwellers (*shahrī*), while Chakpuris consider themselves, and would be considered by Karachites, to be villagers (*piṇḍu* [Punjabi]; *gāoṅwāle, dihātī* [Urdu]). There are dramatic differences between Karachi and Chakpur in terms of size, level of development, and technological and social characteristics. The documentation of objective rural and urban characteristics, however, does not in itself reveal how such differences may be regarded as salient with respect to the persons that dwell in or are identified with such environments. What is revealing is the way in which members of the two communities conceive of urbanites and villagers as being somewhat different types of persons.

In discussing views of urbanites and villagers with informants from each community, two related contrasts emerged again and again, often with the same informant, and often during the same interview. In one contrast, the villager is represented as a *janglī*, literally a person living in the wild, a savage, a man close to nature; and the city dweller as a *bābū log*, or noble, literally a respected elder, but also a sophisticate, a child (as "master"), and even a clerk. In the second contrast, somewhat akin to the American one between the "country bumpkin" and the "city slicker," the villager is described as *sīdhā-sādhā*, a straight and simple-minded innocent, and the urbanite as *chālāk*, a clever and cunning plotter. These two views, taken both separately and together, invoke a

8. The demographic basis of this congruency is well established. The 1921 census of Punjab and Delhi (Government of India 1923) allows for the calculation of such associations. Of the Punjab's Muslim population, 10 percent spoke Urdu and 90 percent Punjabi. Only 6 percent of the Muslim Punjabi population were identified with *ashraf qaums*. Of Delhi's Muslim population, 76 percent were *ashraf*, and all save one or two percent claimed Urdu as their mother tongue. The congruency of these identifications is mitigated by such circumstances as the migration of rural Punjabis to urban centers like Karachi (Streefland 1979), the existence of a highly literate and urbane Punjabi aristocracy, and the impoverishment of some of Karachi's Urdu-speaking refugee population over the past thirty years.

common language of the person, as elucidated above, to express perceived differences between people of the city and people of the village. It is important to stress that both sets of contrasts are made by Karachites and Chakpuris, sometimes in self-elevating and sometimes in self-effacing ways.

The first contrast, that between the *janglī* and *bābū*, is quite complex, separable into either meliorative or pejorative views of villagers and city dwellers. In one view, it is the villager who is demeaned; in the other it is the urbanite. Both views are described separately and then considered together.

In the first view of the *bābū/janglī* contrast, it is the villager who is the savage and the urbanite who is the noble. Implicit in this image is the idea that the villager is someone just out of the *jangal*—the wild forest or harsh desert—a place unfit for human habitation (*abādī*). Villages, having less populace, and surrounded by relatively large expanses of open land, are seen as less habitable and wilder places to live. The villager as *janglī* is viewed, by both Chakpuris and Karachites, as being illiterate (*anpaṛh*), and without manners (*be-adab*), certainly part of mankind (*admīyāt*) but less certainly part of humanity (*insānīyat*). He is, as more than one Chakpuri put it, "without a *qānūn* [law, rules, principles], barely better off than the animals around him." As a "savage," the villager can neither read, nor write, nor speak correctly. He is attributed little ability to understand complex thoughts. Possessed of deficient linguistic and intellectual skills, as evidenced by the lack of educational facilities, and instruments for artistic or scholarly expression, villagers are seen to have limited or defective *'aql*. Hence, instead of controlling their lower natures through the exercise of mental and spiritual powers, villagers are thought to be dominated by the exercise of *nafs*. Villagers, as savages, are hot persons, victims of their emotional and physical energies.

Given this framework, rural society is said to be a passionate and physical one, as villagers, without the benefit of rationalistic and spiritualistic constraints, will do all they can to satisfy their animal desires. The satisfaction of sexual wants, say informants, plays a major role in village life. Hence men will kidnap and rape other people's women, women will seek affairs with other people's husbands, and nobody will be beyond the temptation of taking a tumble in the wheat fields if given the opportunity to do so.

This attributed display of *nafs* will also be translated into acts of violence, so that such crimes as murder, assault, and armed robbery will be relatively common. Even friendly competition, as interpreted by informants, is likely to be manifested in very physical forms, such as wrestling and *kabaḍḍī* (tag-tackle). Since the fulfillment of externally oriented—physical and emotional as opposed to mental and spiritual—desires will be paramount in rural society, and given the lack of cooling personal characteristics such as patience, it is argued that villagers exhibit high levels of frustration. Thus, in this view "savage" society is expected to be anarchistic and fissiparous. Hence cooperation is infrequent, limiting the growth of public institutions or the establishment of public works projects.

In this view, the villager is sometimes equated to a youth (*jawān*) who is led by his bodily desires instead of by rationally formulated goals. Lacking in *'aql*, the villager is dominated by *nafs*. City and village informants seize on a host of "objective" criteria to support this view. To paraphrase stereotypic responses, villagers spend much of their time in the fields with animals. Animals even live in their homes. Villagers eat without the aid of manufactured implements, bathe in streams or irrigation ditches, and perform their toilet in the fields. They are usually dirty. Their homes are primitively constructed. They wear immodest clothing which barely conceals their nakedness. They barter with each other and steal when given the opportunity. They lack the intellectual prowess to build roads, schools, housing, hospitals, and the like. They have no compunction about lying, have little moral fiber, are rude, barbarous, and unsympathetic. In sum, all they know is farming, fighting, and fornication.

In contrast to the image of the "vulgar villager" is that of the "noble city dweller." Urbanites, in the meliorative view of the *bābū/janglī* contrast, are literate, sophisticated, and eminently civilized—the embodiment of humanity. As informants state, it is the urbanite who reads, writes books, creates poems, and designs and builds schools, factories, hospitals, and machines. Urbanites, so it is said, are inventive and smart, having developed their *'aql* to a great extent. Their physical wants and emotions are subjected to the control of reason, and so the personal and social life of the city person is said to be relatively cool. As city dwellers can suppress their sexual impulses, their anger, and their capability for violence, crime and conflict in city life are expectedly reduced. City society is governed by rational goals and higher moral ideals which make for unification and cooperation. Hence great institutions are evidenced in the city.

The city person, as *bābū*, is equated with the status of an elder. Calm and dispassionate, he is supposedly ruled by rationally formulated goals and spiritual principles, not by the demands of his *jism/nafs*. He manufactures items, using his *'aql* to differentiate himself from animals. He bathes and performs his toilet indoors, lives in houses with conveniences produced by the serious application of intellect to the problems of the world. Urbanites wear clothing, such as *sherwānī, shalwār qamīz*, and sari, which is intricately designed and crafted. The city person uses money and trusts his fellow man to make good on his word in transactions. When conflicts arise, he resorts to the police, the courts, or the press for their resolution. The city person is honest, moral, well mannered, and sympathetic. He does not exorcise the demands of his lower nature, but rather controls them. He enjoys sports such as squash, cricket, and field hockey which require careful discipline and are low in bodily contact and overt violence. He is careful to restrict his contact with members of the opposite sex, observing *parda* in buses, shops, schools, and on the street. If the city man seeks an extramarital outlet for his sexuality, he opts not for a raw affair in the fields, but rather for a "courtesan" who showers him with flowers, rosewater, and poetry in order to cool and cultivate his passion.

In this first view, then, it is the city person who is moderate, who balances the need for control with the demands of psychobiology, and the villager who is "too" hot, losing the battle of life to his own animality.

In the second view of the *janglī/bābū* contrast, the definition of urbanite and rustic remains largely the same: the city person is dominated by an *'aql* which controls *nafs*, and the villager by a *nafs* uncontrolled by *'aql*. However, in this view it is the villager, as the person closer to nature, who is moderate, and the urbanite, as the person removed from nature, who is "too" cold.

In this view of the *janglī/bābū* contrast, it is the villager who gives proper respect to the *nafs* (*'izzat-i nafs*), recognizing that *nafs* constitutes an integral part of man's nature. From this perspective, the physical and emotional aspects of man's nature cannot be denied. People and societies that attempt to do so are *naqlī* (artificial). The villager, in the meliorative view, lives close to crops, animals, the earth, and the elements. He is constantly in touch with and intimately aware of the precariousness of man's position. He is "closer" as several informants say, "to life itself," living in a natural manner.

It is the villager who senses and acts upon the reality of life, knowing about the basics of survival. As a group of farmers declared, "poetry and literature are beautiful things in life—but we cannot dip our bread into them." According to this view villagers are necessarily concerned with the basic (*aṣlī*) desires and their satisfaction. Recognition of the role of *nafs* in the definition of these desires as well as in the means of obtaining them is of primary importance. Life, in short, must be asserted. The villager is not afraid to say what he wants and undertake the requisite actions to fulfill his desires. Viewing village life, and life in general, as occurring in a harsh world dominated by the more animalistic drives of human nature, intellectual and spiritualistic pursuits are seen as luxuries, additions, which, while admirable, are nevertheless superfluous to the daily business of living.

In this view, the villager is still the youth dominated by *nafs* rather than *'aql*. Different from the first view, however, is the shape of the world and the place which humans occupy within it. Here the villager is the person who perfects his lower nature, not the person who fails to achieve the capabilities of his higher nature. The villager as *janglī*, in this context, eats the pure (*k͟hāliṣ*) produce available from his farm, drinks the unadulterated milk of his cow, and breathes the fresh air of the countryside. He is, above all, the healthy and strong youth. From dawn to dusk and with ceaseless energy, he labors in his fields, she works her household. The speech of the villager is unpretentious and direct. Villagers know where they stand with one another. Faith is a simple and honest matter, involving less speculative metaphysics and ethics, and more concern over the survival of crops, animals, and members of the family.

In contrast to the view of the self-assertive villager actively living life is that of the city person as the *bābū*, or clerk. In this regard, the urbanite is afraid to live life, to, as one informant put it, "even urinate in the fields." City people, it is said, know little of the ways of nature, of animals and crops. They do not even know where their food and clothing come from. They, by self-delusion, attempt to negate the role of *nafs* in the life of the person. They are afraid of their desires and passions. Emotionally they are cool and hard. As such, they cannot, as a farmer said, "feel passion." "They cannot know what it is to love." Afraid of each other, meek and timid, endowed with feeble bodies, city folk are expected to build walls around themselves, thus isolating themselves from outsiders, as well as each other.[9]

9. Mehta (1979) presents a personal account of these images and counterimages. Mehta's Mamaji was from Lahore and his Daddyji from rural Punjab. Although they were Hindu, their assessments of each other's characteristics as city person and village person bear close resemblance to the views discussed here.

As elders, in this view, city folk are deficient in *nafs/jism*. They lack the courage and assertiveness of youth. Instead of being simple and direct, they hide behind their flowery idiom. Instead of seeking their lover with vigor, they write poetry and fantasize from a distance. Unduly reserved, formal, and devoted to etiquette, urbanites are seen as artificial human beings.

To summarize, the *bābū/janglī* contrast begins with certain assumptions about urbanites and villagers. The former are seen as cooler than the latter, with *'aql* rather than *nafs* playing the dominant role in both society and psyche. Depending upon how such features of city persons and village persons are valued, informants paint vivid contrasts between their different ways of being human (see table 11.1).

Table 11.1

Bābū/Janglī Contrasts of Village and City People

	Villager as *janglī*	City dweller as *bābū*
Basic Features	equated with youth hot disposition *nafs* dominates *'aql*	equated with elder cool disposition *'aql* dominates *nafs*
Viewpoint I	pejorative *janglī* as savage too hot illiterate, violent, ill-mannered, criminal, uncooperative, stupid, sex-crazed, animalistic	meliorative *bābū* as noble moderately cool literate, controlled, mannered, peaceful, civic-minded, intelligent, temperate, humanistic
Viewpoint II	meliorative *janglī* as natural moderately hot healthy, strong, assertive, direct, brave, well-adjusted, realistic	pejorative *bābū* as artificial too cold sickly, weak, afraid, timid, cowardly, maladjusted, deluded

The second contrast is that between the villager as *sīdhā-sādhā*, the innocent or simpleton, and the urbanite as *chālāk*, the schemer. While sharing some features with the first contrast, it is nonetheless sufficiently distinct to warrant separate consideration.

In this contrast, the villager is often equated with the child. He is innocent (*m'aṣūm*) and unassuming. He is the drinker of milk, or *lassī*, par excellence. His desires and thoughts are supposed to be very simple and relatively easy to fulfill. In short, the villager is the happy, carefree peasant. Hospitable, receptive, respectful, and loving, the villager lives a very basic life, very close to what nature prescribes. The villager naively heeds authority figures such as village leaders, elders, parents, and urbanites who must tell him what to do. Also equated somewhat with angels, villagers, in this view, are not quite mature enough to take care of themselves.

In this contrast, the villager as *sīdhā-sādhā* has neither the animal passions to take notice of, nor the human ability to control them. He is naive and amoral. Informants cite numerous "facts" to support this position. Villagers are supposedly satisfied with simple foods. Their houses, tools, and clothing are simple. Villagers are honest—they do not know how to cheat. Villagers must always seek guidance when catastrophe strikes, et cetera. In short, in this image, the villager has neither developed his *'aql*, nor has his *nafs* reached the peak of its development.

Contrasted with the villager as simpleton is the city man who lives in a complex world of temptation. The city man is clever, as he plots to control the many objects in his purview. According to informants, the urbanite as *chālāk* greedily attempts to gain objects of desire through the use of his intellect. He is selfish, not out of innocence but rather by design. He seeks enjoyment not out of the simple exigencies of life, but from the challenge of controlling the exotic and forbidden. He is a manipulator par excellence. The city person may be equated, in this contrast, with middle age, for he is the person, who, as informants suggest, uses his *'aql* in the service of his *nafs*. That is, with the "fires of desire" still hot within him, he engages his intellect for the purpose of fulfilling those desires of his "lower" nature. Hence, the urbanite is the drinker of alcohol, the viewer of pornographic movies, the moneylender, the ruthless entrepreneur, the adulterator of consumer goods, and the politician who knows, but does not follow, the rules. In this view, the city man, unlike his rural counterpart, is knowledgeable and immoral (see table 11.2).

Taken together, the *janglī/bābū* and *sīdhā-sādhā/chālāk* contrasts are capable of expressing fairly wide-ranging views of city persons and village persons. Although they allow for, and indeed may be permeated with, rather harsh value judgments about these respective populations, there are certain features, as expressed by Karachites and Chakpuris,

Table 11.2

Sīdhā-Sādhā/Chālāk Contrasts of Village and City People

Villager as *sīdhā-sādhā*	City dweller as *chālāk*
equated with childhood	equated with middle age
moderately hot disposition (cooled heat)	moderately cool disposition (heated coolness)
neither strong *'aql* nor *nafs*	both strong *'aql* and *nafs*
naive, unassuming, simple, respectful, accepting, amoral	savvy, manipulative, complex, disrespectful, controlling, immoral

which seem constant. Whether judged in a positive or negative way, the villager is associated with childhood and youth (the first half of the life cycle), and the urbanite with middle and old age (the second half of the life cycle). While informants recognize similar constituents of the person, village life is seen as placing greater emphasis upon the body and its psychobiological energy (*jism/nafs*), and city life on the intellect (*'aql*). The villager is thought to accentuate the physical (*jismānī*) and emotional (*jazbātī*) aspects of his nature—both as the major constraints in life, and as the means to happiness. The city person, on the other hand, is said to stress the intellectual (*zěhnī*) and spiritual (*rūḥānī*) aspects of his nature—again as they involve the central dynamic of life.

It is the villager who supposedly strives for the perfection of *jism/nafs*, attempting to create a balance between the imperatives it defines as human nature, and the excesses, as found in animals, of which this "lower" nature is capable. It is the city person who strives for perfection of *'aql*, attempting to strike a balance, first between the conflicting ends that may be pursued (those of *rūḥ*, those of *nafs*), and second, between the ability to control and the presence of a component of the person that, in life, is uncontrollable. It is in this exegetical context, when considering the general features of persons as of the city or of the village, that village society and personality are represented as hot, and urban society and personality as cool. Implicit in the contrasts explored above is the notion that the challenge of living can be faced in terms of several basic strategies—live the hot life of the rustic, the cool life of the urbanite, a life at the extremes that is either too hot or too cold, or a balanced life somewhere in between.

Urdu and Punjabi as the Languages of Communities

The relationship between city folk and villagers, involving as it does the contrast between the cool and hot, between *'aql* and *nafs*, between the *bābū* and *janglī*, the *chālāk* and *sīdhā-sādhā*, and the elderly and youthful, is consistent with that posited between the languages spoken by Karachi *muhājirīn* and Chakpuris. The Karachi refugee population is preeminently identified with Urdu, and the Chakpuri population with Punjabi. Language, as a sign of *'aql*, as indicated above, may be seen as a metaphor for mankind—with different languages indicating different types of persons and different strategies of being.

Punjabi, having developed from the western Prakrit and been influenced by surrounding languages (e.g., Sindhi, Rajasthani, Kashmiri, Hindi), is indigenous to the land of the five rivers. The unity of the region's languages seems to have been recognized possibly as early as the twelfth century and certainly by the seventeenth, when the ethnolinguistic term "*punjābī*" begins to appear in the literature (Gankovsky 1971:110). Spoken by three different religious communities, that is, Muslim, Sikh, and Hindu, Punjabi remains relatively nonstandardized in both spoken and written forms. Despite a vital oral tradition perpetuated by bards and minstrels who traverse the region reciting folk tales and singing the ballads of Punjab, the saying that "the language changes every fifteen miles" still seems to be a popular description of its variation. Occurring as major components of subregional movements, attempts to distinguish such dialects as Seraiki and Bahawalpuri from Punjabi have played heavily upon this lack of standardization (Richter 1980). The Punjabi literary tradition, which did not materialize until the eighteenth century, was vitalized by Sikhism and remains active and influential in India. In Pakistan, the Punjabi literary tradition is a limited one, as the paucity of books, magazines, and newspapers published in Punjabi indicates.

In contrast to Punjabi, Urdu owes its origin to exogenous elements. The details of the birth of Urdu are the subject of some scholarly controversy and debate. Urdu is said to have developed as a means of allowing in-migrating Muslims (i.e., the army camp, or horde—hence "*urdū*") from central and western Asia to communicate with the indigenous Hindus of the Delhi region. The language is supposed to have been formed from a grafting of Persian, some Arabic, and some Turkish vocabulary onto either medieval Punjabi or Khari Boli, a form of Hindi (Sirani 1928; Bailey 1938; A. Ahmad 1964). The literary nature of Urdu was stimulated by Persian, the language of the Mughal court in northern India. However, it was as the court language of the South, in a form called Dakhni, that Urdu was to receive the strongest impetus for its promulgation.

Although Urdu was perhaps disparaged by Persian-speaking elites in medieval north India (Lelyveld, this volume) it nonetheless came to be identified with the exogenous conquering and proselytizing Muslim population. Many of those who submitted to the court or converted to Islam also adopted Urdu as their language.

Perhaps as a result of its spread through the cities and centers of South Asia through the administration of dynasties and the teaching of Sufis, Urdu is not associated with a particular bounded region or territory. It has neither a folklore nor an elaborate oral tradition. A literary language, it spans Muslim South Asia, in many cases serving as a substitute for alternative regional literary traditions. Urdu has been subjected to explicit and even rigorous standardization through the publication of dictionaries, grammars, and commentaries, and the institutionalization of boards and committees to monitor literary works.

As a result of reform movements of the nineteenth century (Metcalf 1982a) and nationalistic movements of the twentieth (Brass 1979), Urdu came to be identified as a symbol of Muslim identity in South Asia. Although Urdu was not the language spoken as the mother tongue by the majority of Muslims or the mother tongue of any sizable population in the territory that was to become Pakistan, it did stand in contrast to Hindi (for those who differentiated both from Hindustani). Hence Urdu defined an aspect of Muslim identity which could be used by Muslims to distinguish themselves from their Hindu neighbors. In becoming a symbol of Pakistani nationhood, Urdu was brought into conflict with other, regional languages—particularly Bengali and Sindhi, but also Punjabi, Pushto, and Baluchi. In this context, the question of what Urdu stands for, as opposed to regional languages, such as Punjabi, becomes quite salient (e.g., Rafiuddin Ahmed, this volume).

Formally, Urdu and Punjabi are not very different. Their grammatical structures are fundamentally the same. Sampling of lexical items reveals a high coincidence of vocabulary. Phonetically, save for the Punjabi tonal and Urdu voiced aspirate variation, they are basically the same. Yet, taking cognizance of their historical development, they have come to symbolize two often opposed life styles.

Punjabi is a language rich in the idiom of rural life. Even the religious poetry of Sufis abounds in the use of metaphors drawn from the technology of crop production and processing (Krishna 1977). The "earthiness" of Punjabi is held in high esteem by villagers. Chakpuris refer to the genuine Punjabi as "*ṭheṭh*." *Ṭheṭh* Punjabi is regarded as the quintessential Punjabi precisely because it is so basically the language of the village and the fields—uncorrupted by urbane syntax, terminology, and delivery. *Ṭheṭh* Punjabi is regarded as the language of the folk. It is not a "high" (*lammī chorī*) language, nor is it often written. It may be recited, as in folk tales, or sung in ballads. But primarily it is Punjabi in its spoken form—informal, unpretentious, and highly animated. For someone to claim he can "really" speak Punjabi, and be admired for it, he must be able to use and understand the *ṭheṭh* form.

Urdu, on the other hand, has been and still is a language spoken in primarily urban areas. It has been called the *darbārī zubān*, or the language of the court or government. While Urdu was initially regarded with some disdain by Muslim ruling elites and the *'ulamā*, it has come to be popularly accepted as a relatively sophisticated language: the language of poets, intellectuals, and administrators. The ability to use "refined" Urdu is recognized by Karachites as a notable achievement. The person who can speak and use *ṣāf* or *k͟hāliṣ* Urdu, the pure or refined language, is one who uses standard grammar, poetic metaphors, and constructions, vocabulary and idioms borrowed from Persian and Arabic. Refined Urdu is regarded as formal and sophisticated. And he who "really" knows Urdu must be able to speak, read, and write the *k͟hāliṣ* form of the language, and be adept in such sophisticated arenas as poetry recitals (*mushā'ara*).

The ability to use language is clearly a characteristic of *'aql*. Punjabis and Urdu speakers train their tongues to speak in different ways, indicating differences in the ways in which that ability may be used and the ends it may seek. Both Punjabi and Urdu have their pure forms. Punjabi is valued by Chakpuris for its simplicity, its folk and oral traditions, and its purity—defined as its *ṭheṭh* form. Punjabi seeks within itself and its own indigenous origins for its perfection. Urdu, however, looks outward to the incorporation of exogenous elements from whence it originated. It borrows freely from Persian and Arabic, two languages accorded special status in the thinking of South Asian Muslims—Arabic, because it is the language of the Prophet, and the spiritual revelation of the Qur'ān; and Persian, because it is looked upon as a language of culture, poetry, and intellectual sophistication. For Urdu, purity is defined as refinement, carefully and rigorously achieved.

Urdu, with its literary, courtly, and administrative traditions, its association with cities, and, since the late nineteenth century, its use by aristocratic and religious elites, is regarded as a cool language. It is Urdu that may be associated with the cultivation and control of *'aql* as a strategy for expressing oneself in the world. Punjabi, with its nonliterate, agricultural tradition, associated with rural village life, farmers and peasants, is regarded as a hot language. It is Punjabi that may be associated with the immanence and immediacy of *nafs*, to which man's *'aql* must accord a proper and realistic place.[10]

Nobles and Natives as Persons

The identification of city life with nobility and of village life with savagery, and of Urdu as the language of civility and Punjabi as the language of the field, makes for an image consistent with that attributed to the respective genealogical origins of Karachi's *muhājir* population and the people of Chakpur.

Karachi's refugee population is composed almost wholly of urban peoples from Uttar Pradesh, Delhi, Bombay, and Punjab-Haryana. As Muslims from the urban areas of northern and western India, they for the most part identify themselves with *ashraf qaum*s or *nasl*s, that is, exogenous Muslim peoples, who, coming from western Asia, had initially introduced and fostered Islamic civilization in the Subcontinent. Upon Partition, the *ashraf* who left India primarily settled in the cities of Pakistan—centers of administration, commerce and industry, and scholarship. Most settled in Karachi, enlarging the city by three times its pre-Partition size and turning it into an Urdu-speaking city (Hashmi 1964).

The vast majority of the Chakpuri population is made up of Nunaris and Bhattis. Both claim to be Rājpūt *qaum*s, recognizing both their Hindu origins and their conversion to Islam by medieval *pīr*s (Kurin 1980). They regard themselves as *desī*, or native, and claim to have been in the Punjab for as long as their genealogical memory can ascertain.

10. Census data confirm that while significant numbers of Punjabis learn Urdu as a second language, very few Urdu speakers learn Punjabi or, for that matter, Sindhi. The general relationship suggested is that speakers of hotter languages learn cooler languages in order to show greater erudition, gain access to more skilled occupations and identify with literary, urbane pursuits. This linguistic asymmetry is evidenced by the borrowing from Urdu into Punjabi, but not the reverse, of vocabulary, idioms and grammatical forms, as reported by Shackle (1970). Of note, Urdu speakers in Karachi use Punjabi phrases, e.g., curses or *galiyān* in certain contexts in order to convey baser emotions, indicating that differential borrowing may take place.

Neighboring Rājpūt, Jāt, Arain, and Gūjar *qaums* assert similar origins as *desī* Hindus who were conquered and converted to Islam (Eaton 1984). One family in Chakpur is *sayyid*, and villagers note that it was the ancestors of this *ashraf* family who played a part in teaching Islam to the *desī quams* of the region.

The identification, whether based upon "real facts" or "fictional claims" of Urdu-speaking refugees with exogenous forebears, is clearly indicated by a perusal of the surnames of Karachi residents. As Abdullah (1973) has pointed out, the most popular names—Sayyid, Qureshi, Ansari, Siddiqi, Farooqi, Osmani, Alvi, Hussaini, Jafri, Naqvi, Zaidi, Kazmi, Rizvi, Hashmi, Abbassi, Shervani, Shirazi, Isphani, Tirmizi, Bukhari, Barlas, Kirmani, Yazdani—indicate supposed foreign ancestry or origin. Such families typically trace their roots to the Middle East, to Persia, and to central Asia, even if the name of their founding ancestor or the names of intervening ancestors escape them. Some informants in Karachi exhibited written genealogies (*nasab-nāma*), elaborately calligraphed on canvas, and displaying hundreds of relatives for tens of generations. Typically, such genealogies would begin with an ancestor from some city in western Asia.

In Chakpur, family names are clan names, and, in the case of the Nunari, originate with the ancestor who first converted to Islam. The names of these clans—such as Naul, More, Saddan, Vadel—are Punjabi secular names, pointing to the native origins of their ascendents. These key ancestors were conquered by *ashraf* armies and converted by *ashraf pīrs*. In the case of the Nunaris, it is claimed that their ancestor was conquered by the Mughals and his sons converted by Sayyid Jalāl, the Makhdūm-i Jehaniyan (d. 1384) and Sayyid Muḥammad Ghauṣ (d. 1517), or their followers. Unlike the *muhājirīn* of Karachi, Chakpuris do not have written genealogies. Instead, it is a village genealogist (*mirāsī*) who can recite the names of Nunari ancestors for a period of twenty-three generations, starting with the names of those sons of a Hindu Rājpūt who were converted (Kurin 1980).

The significance of such imputed origins, for Karachites and Chakpuris, is not only one of historicity. It is what is made of the tracing of one's origins to a specific type of past. To claim descent from an *ashraf* group, particularly the *sayyids* or *shaikhs* is, for some, to identify with the origins and glories of Islam from the time of the Prophet or thereabouts. It is to be identified with the foundations of Islam, its spiritual grandeur, and the heroes who aided its worldly victories. In contradistinction, to be identified with non-*ashraf*, *desī* peoples is to court identification with

Hindus and Buddhists; idolaters and polytheists who were living in ignorance before being converted by the *ashraf*. Identification with the *ashraf*, also, as pointedly the case with Pathans and Mughals, equates such peoples with the conquest and rule of South Asia and its native-born locals. To be *desī* is to be counted among the conquered and the ruled. To be *ashraf* is to be dominant and controlling; to be *desī* is to be subordinate and controlled (I. Ahmad 1973; Ibbetson 1974: 165–67).

It has been argued that the *ashraf* viewed themselves as the over class in South Asian Muslim society (A. Ahmad 1964; Abdullah 1973). Self-assertedly urbane, sophisticated, cultured, and powerful, the putatively foreign-born elite never seemed to identify strongly with the region they ruled, or with the local groups they converted. Looking westward, primarily to Persian and Islamic roots, the *ashraf* seemed to have a continual problem of identifying with the Subcontinental *des*. Aziz Ahmad, in speaking of these groups, writes:

> Islam in India continued to retain throughout the centuries, despite secondary Indian environmental and ethnic influences, its original foreign character. The Indian Muslim remained . . . on the whole an intellectual exotic who felt he was in India but not of it. Nostalgically, he preserved as much of the original intellectual and psychological heritage of the original form of his culture as he could. Sociologically he considered himself as belonging to the Muslim *úmma*, the great Muslim community which extended beyond the Indian frontiers. (1964:74)

While such a view suggests revisionistic overstatement inspired by the Pakistan movement, the lack of self-identification on the part of the *ashraf* with the land in which they dwelt is corroborated by subsequent and continuing events.

Desī non-*ashraf* Muslims did not have the same problem. Their connection to the land in which they dwelt was less ambiguous. Their families, their roots, and their blood were intimately tied to the land. For example, although the Nunaris "settled" new land with the founding of Chakpur, they still considered themselves to be locals with a strong sense of attachment or belonging to their land and their native country (*des*). As, in their terms, "sons of the soil," they trace their origins to times before the *ashraf* and the present order of things. Recognizing the importance of Islam and their conversion, and the various dynasties of *ashraf* rule (in one form or another), they are nonetheless proud of their own heritage and roots.

Metcalf (1982b), in speaking of the work of Rumi, has suggested that the Hindu was used as a symbol of the *nafs*. The controlling or converting of the Hindu could be interpreted as a victory over *nafs* by the power of *'aql* and *rūḥ*. It is the *ashraf* as the converters who may be equated with *rūḥ* and *'aql*. It is they who are represented as possessing superior qualities of intellect and spirituality. And it is those who were converted, the native people (*desī log*) living without the controls and morality provided by Islam, who can be associated with the *nafs*. Although converted, they may still be represented as being closely connected with the attachments of their *nafs*. Lest they slip back into their ignorant state—characterized by local customs and Hindu practices—they may be regarded, both by themselves and by members of the *ashraf* (Maududi 1975:55–57), as requiring continual and vigilant moral supervision.

Ethnicity, Pakistani Nationalism, and Islamic Identity

The identification of Urdu-speaking refugees with an exogenous nonlocalized heritage, with city life, and with a language valued for its cultural and sophisticated expression contrasts sharply with the identification of Punjabi speakers with an indigenous land-based heritage, with rural life, and with a language valued for its naturalness and simplicity. Yet both groups, or, more precisely, subsets of these groups, consider themselves to be Pakistani. The way in which each of these communities has identified with Pakistan is noteworthy in what it reveals about their differential value orientations about how human beings should live their lives.

For the Urdu-speaking *muhājirīn*, the issue of identification with Pakistan continues to be somewhat problematic. As they formed the great bulk of South Asia's Muslim middle and upper class, as they constituted, in the main, the political, commercial, intellectual, and religious elite of Muslim South Asia, and as they formed the vanguard of the movement for the establishment of Pakistan, this community saw in itself the image of what Pakistan was to be and what it was to represent. To this community, they, the *muhājirīn*, were Pakistan, for Pakistan was, essentially, the apotheosis of a Muslim consciousness that they had originally introduced, nurtured during the period of Muslim imperial rule, preserved in the face of British colonialism, and revitalized when faced with Hindu ascendancy and domination.

Pakistan, literally meaning "land of the pure," was simply their "land," and they, by implication, were the "pure." Significantly, however, "land" did not mean the "soil" or the "fields." The "land" meant the cities, the seats of government and what they represented. Karachi, a flourishing port city and center of trade and finance, was established as the capital, and it was to Karachi that Urdu-speaking *muhājirīn* flocked. When asked why they settled in Karachi, most informants had the same answer: "To us, Karachi was Pakistan." But, more than even this, the "land" represented a place, which could have been any place, where they could maintain and enrich their purity.

The national slogan adopted by *the* Pakistanis, "faith, unity, and discipline," provided a code for how this purity was to be achieved. In so doing, it expressed a single, coherent, and revealing message on two levels—expounding the meaning *muhājirīn* could attach to their mission. The contemporary refugees easily drew parallels between their status and that of the *muhājirīn* of Qur'ānic times who gave up their property and residence in Mecca to flee with the Prophet to Medina. As stated in the Qur'ān (sura 59, verse 8) (Ali 1975):

> Some part is due to the indigent *muhājirīn*
> Those who were expelled from their homes and property
> While seeking grace from Allah
> And his good pleasure, and aiding Allah and his apostle.
> Such are indeed the sincere ones.

In substantive terms, the slogan suggested an idealized course of action for making persons Pakistani. *Faith* in Allāh, the Prophet, and Islam was to provide the spiritual basis of the nation. The requisite *unity*, needed to give Pakistanis a sense of being one people, was to be defined on the basis of a common spiritual identity—the *rūḥ* which all people shared. Finally *discipline* was needed to exert this spirituality—controlled minds would conquer seemingly antisocial, particularistic impulses. Together, faith, unity, and discipline called for persons, defined by their spiritual qualities, to exert their intellectual powers for the purpose of denying their selfish or communal interests and living life as Pakistanis.

In form, the slogan refers to the value of noncorporeal elements. It refers to activities of the mind and the spirit, attaching importance to the *rūḥ* and *'aql* of persons as both the primary means of action and the proper objects of action. To be pure (*pāk*), for this Urdu-speaking, urban, *ashraf* population, has meant the development and cultivation of those aspects of human nature they have historically deemed most important. Pakistan, in this view, will achieve its goals (construed in spiritual and intellectual-moral terms) not by obtaining material things or satisfying physical wants, but rather by acts of conscience through which spiritual potentialities are realized.

In contrast, Chakpuris, in concert with other Punjabis and indigenous communities, tend to view Pakistan in a different way. To them the *muhājirīn* are Pakistanis, but "actually" refugees from India. Ironically, *muhājirīn* are considered to be Hindustanis (Indians), and are often called such by Sindhis, Punjabis, and Baluchis in Karachi bazaars. As refugees, they do not have the intimate tie to the land, the sense of belonging, that indigenous communities have. *Muhājirīn* may sometimes be seen as *the* Pakistanis, although this is probably more likely to mean something like "those people who came here thinking this place was theirs" than it is to mean "those great patriots who sacrificed their homes to make a new nation."

For Chakpuris, Pakistan is a land in which they have a stake. The "land" means the soil, the food grown on it, and the cattle and sheep that graze upon it. The land is something they care for with their labor and sweat and something which nourishes their bodies in return. It is something that belongs to them, and they to it. The Urdu-speaking refugees, without a land of their own, regionless, and homeless, do not belong.

It is worth noting that the Punjab, too, has its refugees. Far greater numbers of Punjabi speakers migrated from East (Indian) Punjab to West (Pakistani) Punjab than all the Urdu-speaking refugees combined. Although the Punjabi *muhājirīn* were technically refugees, they were still considered to be Punjabis. Despite the establishment of somewhat arbitrary boundary lines on a map, such refugees were of a common land and language with those who became their neighbors. As such, they had a place and a land that was theirs. In coming to Pakistan, these refugees settled in rural areas, on lands that had been vacated by departing Hindus and Sikhs. The Punjabi *ashraf* settled in the main in towns and cities such as Lahore, Multan, and Rawalpindi. The integration of the Punjabi refugees into the society and social life of their neighbors has been relatively painless when compared to that of their Urdu-speaking counterparts.

Given this view of their land and their relationship to it, as well as the historical orientations of Punjabis, it is significant that Chakpuris often refer to the saying "women, wealth, and land," when discussing the important things in life. This aphorism is quite popular. It has a latter-day variation, "bread, clothing, housing" (*roṭī*, *kapṛe*, *makān*), a slogan adopted by late prime minister Bhutto and the Pakistan People's Party.[11]

The slogan "women, wealth, and land" refers to what Chakpuris consider the most basic things in life. For Chakpuris, the desire for land, wealth, and women motivates men, for without these things, they cannot survive. The life of the community, the village, and, in Chakpuri eyes, sometimes the whole world, is animated by people attempting to gain these things and guarding against the attempts of others to take them away. In this view, *land* gives food, shelter, and something to work with. *Women* give birth to offspring; they are daughters to exchange; they are wives that give sexual pleasure. And *wealth* gives one power to obtain desired objects and to avoid dependence upon the mercy of others.

In form and substance, this view contrasts markedly with the vision of life as expressed in the national slogan. For Chakpuris, the role of *nafs* in the constitution of persons and the social order is valued. The path to success and honor lies not in acts of will or moral conscience, but rather in concrete, objective activity. The vision of a successful Pakistan, for Chakpuris, requires the fulfillment of recognized human desires and needs. Living close to the earth, Chakpuris remain skeptical of the Pakistan ideology, as expressed in the national slogan. They doubt its applicability as a model for motivations in a harsh and oppressive world. Chakpuris see the world as a hotter place than do Karachites. In such a hot world, men are hotter, and their strategy for living life need take that into consideration. It is not that Chakpuris seek to elevate the importance of *nafs/jism* out of some evil desire: it is rather out of respect for the role the body plays in defining the nature of human beings. Mankind, after all, villagers point out, was created by Allāh out of moist mud. It is Allāh who made man muddy, who gave man his body and psychobiological powers. To deny this constituent of human nature is irreligious—a denial of Allāh's creation.

For Karachites, the world is somewhat cooler, and cooler strategies of living are thought to be more realizable. The salient aspect of creation is that Allāh breathed his spirit into mankind. The proper life, in this view, is lived by orienting one's actions to the characteristics of divinely human or angelic nature. Personal, national, and religious aspirations are to be highly valued when evocative of physically transcendent spiritual, moral, and intellectual actions.

11. According to C. M. Naim (personal communication), this slogan was used by Indira Gandhi before being adopted by Bhutto. Before that, it was the title of a film.

The tension between these two different value orientations, made understandable by a common ancient discourse, defines a central theme of Pakistani culture. Choices about how to best be Pakistani involve choices of how to best be Muslim, and how to best be a human being. And debates and discussions about those choices will continue to occur in forms ranging from the written legal opinions of high court justices to mutterings of villagers sitting around an evening's water pipe.

References

Abdullah, Ahmed
1973 *The Historical Background of Pakistan and Its People.* Karachi: Tanzeem Publishers.

Ahmad, Aziz
1964 *Studies in Islamic Culture in the Indian Environment.* Oxford: Clarendon Press.

Ahmad, Imtiaz
1972 *Caste and Social Stratification among Muslims in India.* New Delhi: Manohar Book Service.

Ali, A. Yusef, trans. and comp.
1975 *The Holy Qoran.* Lahore: Sh. Muhammad Ashraf (first published 1938).

Bailey, T. Grahame
1938 *Studies in North Indian Languages.* London: Lund, Humphries.

Brass, Paul
1979 "Elite Groups, Symbol Manipulation and Ethnic Identity among Muslims of South Asia." *Political Identity in South Asia.* D. Taylor and M. Yap, eds. London: Corzon Press.

Corbin, Henri
1977 *Spiritual Body and Celestial Earth.* Princeton: Princeton University Press.

Dar, Bashir
1971 *A Study in Iqbal's Philosophy.* Lahore: Shaikh Ghulam Ali & Sons.

Eaton, Richard
1984 "The Political and Religious Authority of the Shrine of Baba Farid in Pakpattan, Punjab." In *Moral Conduct and Authority: The Place of Adab in South Asian Islam.* Barbara Metcalf, ed. Berkeley: University of California Press.

Ewing, Katherine
1984 "Malangs of the Punjab: Intoxication or Adab as the Path to God?" In *Moral Conduct and Authority: The Place of Adab in South Asian Islam.* Barbara Metcalf, ed. Berkeley: University of California Press.

Gankovsky, Y. V.
1971 *The Peoples of Pakistan: An Ethnic History.* Lahore: People's Publishing House.

Geertz, Clifford
1960 *The Religion of Java.* New York: The Free Press.

Ghazālī, Ibn
n.d. *Haqīqī Rūḥ Insānī*. Lahore: Sang Mail Publications.

Government of India.
1923 *Census of India—1921*. Vol. 15. Punjab and Delhi. Lahore: Office of Government Printing.

Government of Pakistan
1963 *Population Census of Pakistan—1961*. District Census Reports: Karachi, Lahore, Hyderabad. Karachi: Manager of Publications.
1973 *Population Census of Pakistan—1972*. Housing, Economic and Demographic Survey—Punjab. Karachi: Manager of Publications.

Hashmi, Sultan
1964 *The People of Karachi*. Karachi: Karachi Institute of Development Economics.

Hermansen, Marcia
1984 "Shāh Walī Allāh of Delhi's Arrangement of the Subtle Spiritual Centers." Unpublished ms.

Hughes, T. P.
n.d. *Dictionary of Islam*. Lahore: Premier Book House (reprint of 1885 edition).

Hujwiri, Ali bin Uthman al-
1976 *The Kashf al-Mahjub: The Oldest Persian Treatise on Sufism*. Reynold A. Nicholson, trans. Lahore: Islamic Book Foundation (reprint of 1911 London edition).

Ibbetson, Denzil
1974 *Punjabi Castes*. Lahore: Shaikh Mubarak Ali (reprint of 1883 edition).

Inden, Ronald B., and Ralph W. Nicholas
1977 *Kinship in Bengali Culture*. Chicago: University of Chicago Press.

Johnson, B. L.
1979 *Pakistan*. London: Heinemann.

Krishna, Lajwanti
1977 *Panjabi Sufi Poets*. Karachi: Indus Publications.

Kurin, Richard
1980 "Doctor, Lawyer, Indian Chief." *Natural History* 89 (November):6–24.
1981 "Person, Family and Kin in Two Pakistani Communities." Ph.D. dissertation, University of Chicago.
1984 "Personhood, Morality and the Exemplary Life: Muslims in Paradise." In *Moral Conduct and Authority: The Place of Adab in South Asian Islam*. Barbara Metcalf, ed. Berkeley: University of California Press.

Lapidus, Ira M.
1984 "Knowledge, Virtue and Action: The Classical Muslim Conception of Adab and the Nature of Religious Fulfillment in Islam." In *Moral Conduct and Authority: The Place of Adab in South Asian Islam*. Barbara Metcalf, ed. Berkeley: University of California Press.

Levy, Reuben
1962 *The Social Structure of Islam*. Cambridge: Cambridge University Press.

Marriott, McKim
1976 "Hindu Transactions: Diversity without Dualism." In *Transaction and Meaning: Directions in the Anthropology of Exchange and Symbolic Behavior*. Bruce Kapferer, ed. Philadelphia: ISHI.

Marriott, McKim, and Ronald B. Inden
1974 "Caste Systems." In *Encyclopaedia Britannica.* 15th edition. Chicago.
1977 "Toward an Ethnosociology of South Asian Caste Systems." In *The New Wind: Changing Identities in South Asia.* Kenneth David, ed. The Hague: Mouton.
Maududi, S. Abul A'la
1972 *Purdah and the Status of Women in Islam.* Lahore: Islamic Publications.
1975 *Fundamentals of Islam.* Lahore: Islamic Publications.
Mehta, Ved
1979 *Mamaji.* New York: Oxford University Press.
Metcalf, Barbara Daly
1982a *Islamic Revival in British India: Deoband, 1860–1900.* Princeton: Princeton University Press.
1982b "Islam and Custom in Nineteenth-Century India." *Contributions to Asian Studies* 17:62–78.
Nyrop, R. F., et al.
1971 *Area Handbook for Pakistan.* Washington, D.C.: U.S. Government Printing Office.
Platts, John
1968 *A Dictionary of Urdu, Classical Hindi and English.* Oxford: Oxford University Press (first published 1884).
Qarshi, Alama
1974 *Mukhtasar al-Kūlīyāt.* Lahore: Ashraf Press.
Razi, Imam
1969 *Ilm-e-Akhlaq.* S. Maumi, trans. Islamabad: Islamic Research Institute.
Richter, William
1980 "Regionalism in Central Pakistan: The Bahawalpur Suba and Seraiki Movements." Paper presented at the Annual Meetings of the Association for Asian Studies, Washington, 23 March.
Sayeed, Khalid
1967 *The Political System of Pakistan.* Boston: Houghton Mifflin.
Schimmel, Annemarie
1975 *Mystical Dimensions of Islam.* Chapel Hill: University of North Carolina Press.
Shackle, Christopher
1970 "Punjabi in Lahore." *Modern Asian Studies* 4:239–67.
Siegal, James
1969 *The Rope of God.* Berkeley: University of California Press.
Sirani, Maḥmud
1928 *Punjab me Urdu.* N.p.
Streefland, Pieter
1979 *The Sweepers of Slaughterhouse: Conflict and Survival in a Karachi Neighborhood.* Assen: Van Gorcum.
Yadegari, Muhammad
1980 "Islam: A New School of Thought." *Al-Ittihad* 12:9–18.

12

A Case of Honor among the Oasis Baluch of Makran: Controversy and Accommodation

CARROLL McC. PASTNER

Among the Oasis Baluch of Makran,[1] the delineation and maintenance of honor (*'izzat*) are a central concern. The basic themes of Baluch culture can be described in terms of kinship, social hierarchy, sex roles, and religiosity. The delineation of honor evokes each of these themes and the ideals surrounding them, for to have honor one must (1) live up to the obligations (*ḥaqq*) of kinship; (2) act with proper demeanor as dictated by the social status hierarchy; (3) behave correctly according to one's sexual status; and (4) live up to the moral ideals defined by both Muslim orthodoxy and by Baluch custom. The concept of honor thus subsumes a range of social and ethical issues.

Antoun (1968) suggests that the difficulty in analyzing systems of honor is in deriving their sources, differentiating the ideology of honor from its acting out, and pinpointing accommodations between ideology and action. I would argue that it is largely an academic exercise to seek ultimate origins for systems of honor; rather, the everyday accommodations that individuals make between ideology and action are the actual sources of honor. As Bourdieu has demonstrated, honor is more clearly lived than conceived (Bourdieu 1966). Practically, the maintenance of

1. Field work in Makran District, Baluchistan was conducted with Stephen Pastner in 1968–69 under the aegis of the National Institute of Mental Health. In 1976–77 we worked among coastal Baluch west of Karachi, and were funded by the American Institute of Pakistan Studies. Of those commentators and discussants of an earlier version of this paper, Katherine Ewing, Vincent Crapanzano, Dale Eickelman, and Barbara Metcalf are to be especially thanked.

honor involves a continual evaluation of behavior, an ongoing personal and public tabulation of debts and credits. The calculation of honor involves vigilance over one's self and over those upon whom one depends for the attribution of honor. But this calculation may be complicated by the interplay of social honor on the one hand and personal honor defined in moral terms on the other. The individual needs an alter—namely God—in order to achieve honor on a personal, moral level. Similarly, he needs an alter in the social world, and he depends upon his consociates for the attribution of honor.

We can focus on how ideology is manipulated, adjusted, and accommodated to action by examining the dynamics of establishing honor in a specific situation. The Baluch do conceptualize honor in ideal, normative terms and strive to enact these ideals, thus maintaining their normative cogency. Nevertheless, the evaluation of specific actions may be subject to debate as participants use different frames of reference in their calculations. The issue of honor prompts frequent controversy because in specific circumstances participants in the controversy may calculate honor in a variety of contradictory ways. One can be regarded as *be-ghairat*—without honor—on the basis of deviance from any of the not entirely consistent ideals which shape and define the basic themes in Baluch culture. There is a potential for contradiction, for instance, between kinship and stratificational values, or between religious egalitarianism and social hierarchy. Within the sphere of kinship itself is a significant source of contradiction: to engage in the network of reciprocity demanded by kinship is to risk becoming caught among divergent rights and obligations. Therefore, despite the possibility for the expression of ideals in decontextualized, absolute terms, accommodation and compromise must characterize the attempt to deal with divergencies between custom and orthodoxy, familial and nonfamilial interests, egalitarianism and hierarchy, and male and female spheres.

Case material collected more than a decade ago on an oasis in Makran District, Baluchistan, provides a forum for analyzing controversy generated by the need to define and implement honor. It illustrates how male and female vantage points and pragmatic interests affect specific calculations of honor, as well as how individuals draw upon contradictory rights and obligations defined by kinship. Examination of a moment of controversy such as this also highlights some of the sources of tension in Baluch society and the accommodations that are made in the face of the exigencies of everyday social life.

Social Structure of the Oasis

The social structure of Makran oasis Baluch is based upon the recognition of status differences between genealogically defined social groupings. These groupings are broadly organized into a small aristocratic elite, a large middle layer, and a category of ex-slaves. There is some potential contradiction between the functioning of the stratificational system and the espousal of Islamic egalitarianism, but this can be resolved by situational definitions of publicly recognized honor. Thus, a person high in the secular status hierarchy may be accorded secular deference, but he or she may not be accorded honor on the basis of adherence to morality or ethics as these are defined religiously. Likewise, someone low in the secular status hierarchy may be accorded little or no secular deference but be regarded nonetheless as especially honorable or ethical. Stratification so dominates the social structure of the Oasis Baluch that it minimizes the broader organizational capabilities of kinship. True lineages are absent, and marriage, while endogamous in the stratificational sphere, is largely exogamous in the kinship sphere. Traditional political and economic organization is oriented around the maneuvering for power among members of the elite stratum who contract patron-client ties with members of the lower strata.

Kinship, however, provides the dominant mode of articulation between households within strata and the basis for recruitment to parties in familial disputes. Kinship is defined by material and nonmaterial rights and obligations (*ḥaqq*) between persons related through either blood or marriage. "Delayed reciprocity" is the operative procedure through which kin linkages are maintained, and while debts to kin are easily accumulated, this is the only way one can be assured of reciprocal support at some inevitable future date. Conflict and cooperation over time mark such fundamental dyads as father and son, sister and sister, brother-in-law and brother-in-law, and so on, and everyday life among the Baluch is easily characterized by the push-pull atmosphere in which kinship functions. Conflict can arise between the demands of kinship and the demands of the stratificational system. One may have to choose, for example, between loyalty to a kinsman and loyalty to a non-kin patron or client, and the decision may in one way or another affect one's *'izzat*.

Importantly, kinship defines those male kin, consanguineal and affinal, who are responsible for and dependent upon the correct conduct of women. The position of women in the society is central to any discussion of honor and accommodation. The complex community structure of the Oasis Baluch requires the most formal means of observing *parda*, including mud-walled compounds, male guest rooms, and heavy veiling. Segregation is facilitated by an economic division of labor in which women do not participate in the public aspects of the economy. The ideology of sex roles and the manipulative tactics of women in a "patriarchal" social system are a consistent characteristic among Baluch populations.

A contradiction arises in the attainment of male honor, since it is defined to a large extent by the behavior of women. While men are dependent upon correct female behavior, especially sexual behavior, the physical and social isolation of men from women—resulting from segregation and the economic division of labor—minimizes the ability of men to supervise women and maximizes the potentiality of women to behave independently. One of the causes of this problem of maintaining the correct behavior of women is also its solution: the physical mobility of women is severely restricted by the institution of *parda*. Oasis Baluch rely on architectural and sartorial accommodations in the implementation of *parda*. Female behavior relevant to the sphere of women, for instance, is not always correct according to public (male) tenets of honor (Pastner 1974). Among themselves women may be quite deviant, but as long as deviant behavior does not come to public (male) scrutiny, it is not likely to disrupt the system as a whole. An example is bawdy language and sexual joking among women. Such behavior is regarded by both men and women as deviant, dishonorable, and irreligious, but it is "harmless" as long as it remains in the female sphere and does not intrude into the public sphere.

Interestingly, Baluch men appear to be more prudish among themselves than are Baluch women among themselves. Men are not only dependent upon the correct behavior of women, they also have the added burden of acting correctly themselves in public. Family honor depends on such correct male conduct as well as the suppression of incorrect female conduct. Nevertheless, men remain dependent upon the "correct" behavior of women in order to maintain honor.

The Case of Guli

The case presented here illustrates how questions of honor can arise out of conflict between men and women, and between natal and conjugal kin, over the question of the disposal of women. It also illustrates the kind and content of debate generated by a question of honor. Finally, the case indicates the accommodation and compromise arrived at in resolution of cases of honor.

I had become well acquainted with Guli, a young woman who resided with her widowed mother, her son, her mother's brother, and his wife and young children. Guli spent a good deal of time at the home of our cook, another of her mother's brothers. Guli's husband had killed his adulterous sister, and as a consequence had been in jail in Khuzdar (several hundred miles away in eastern Baluchistan) for eight years. While at our cook's house, Guli would often express to me—or to anyone else who would listen—intense hatred of her husband. Her physical and emotional mistreatment of her son, which I witnessed, could be interpreted as a displacement of her feelings about her husband. One day, word was received that Guli's husband had been released from jail and he wanted his wife and son to join him immediately in Khuzdar. Distraught, Guli refused to go, saying she wanted to remain with her mother. Since her father, her father's brother, and her own brothers were dead, the only close male consanguines who could intercede on her behalf were her mother's two brothers. Every day for a week, intense discussion and eventual shouting matches ensued between, on one side, the mother's two brothers and, on the other, the women: Guli, her mother, and her mother's brothers' wives.

The women were adamant that the mother's brothers had an obligation to Guli, and that they should not force her to join her husband. Initially in the week-long discourse, the women emphasized three areas of male responsibility: that they had an obligation to Guli, their kinswoman; that they should behave as "proper" Muslims; and that they should fulfill the ideal of *aṣli* (true) Baluch-ness. As the week progressed the women continued to stress these points, but, as the situation escalated, a derisive tone was added in which the masculinity of the men was (almost *sotto voce*) being mocked.

The men insisted all along that it was the right of Guli's husband to claim his wife and son. They also emphasized that to override the husband would result in conflict not only with him, but with his male kin resident on the oasis. Guli's uncles were clear in their desire to avoid such conflict.

In desperation by the end of the week, the women refused to cook, but their efforts were to no avail. Guli's husband's brother fetched her and her son and escorted them on the bus to Khuzdar. For several days after the departure the women continued crying and bemoaning Guli's fate.

Her mother told me that the women had done all they could, but that "God wanted things to work out the way they did." The men, meanwhile, were silent. Little was said by anyone about Guli thereafter.

Modes of Discourse

That Guli's case is one involving *'izzat* was clear from the beginning. Her husband had the right to claim his wife and son, but her uncles also had the right to intercede on behalf of their niece. In both instances, honor resided in the capability of retaining control over the disposal of a woman. For the uncles, the conflict was between their obligation (*ḥaqq*) to a consanguine and their accession to male affines. They could have refused to send Guli to Khuzdar on the grounds that they had been her protectors over the past eight years and were continuing to look out for her interests. They did not do so. The primary reason for their refusal, I suspect, was because they wished to avoid an imbroglio with affines which could have been protracted and whose outcome was difficult to predict. Moreover, the cycle of material and nonmaterial reciprocity, or network of indebtedness, which characterizes Baluch kinship (Pastner 1981) provides a deterrent to conflict. If the uncles had defied their affines, not only would conflict have been threatened, but they would have been opting out of otherwise already useful, or potentially useful, kin linkages. In their calculation, therefore, the uncles chose to sacrifice their obligation to a female consanguine in the interest of avoiding disharmony with male affines. There may also have been a connected economic motive for the men. While Guli's mother was an intermittent seamstress, she and Guli were to some degree dependent on the uncles for support. If Guli did not go to her husband, this burden would continue. Thus sending Guli to Khuzdar was an economical move by the uncles, though certainly this did not constitute their only motivation.

The women, on the other hand, had no overt interest in the politics of male affinal linkages. Nevertheless they were aware that they had to rely upon men (consanguines in the case of Guli and her mother, and affines in the case of the mother's brothers' wives) to intercede on Guli's behalf. This, not atypically, did not prevent them from putting up a good fight. They, too, may have had pragmatic as well as other concerns: Guli was a hard worker and did much cooking and housework, not only for her mother but for her aunts as well. Several means were used by the women to influence a decision made ultimately by the men. First, they called upon the men to live up to their obligation (*ḥaqq*) to a kinswoman and to live by the tenets of Islam and Baluch custom (*riwāj*). The problem for the women was that the issue was not clear-cut: the men could (and did) maintain that their acceding to the right of a husband to demand the presence of his wife was in accordance both with their obligation to a male affine and with the ethics of Islam and *riwāj*. After all, Guli had not been mistreated by her husband; his "abandonment" of her was simply the result of correct civil legal action. That Guli did not want to be with her husband provided a motivation for the women, but it carried weight only in the domestic sphere. From the uncles' point of view—that is, the public sphere in which these values operated—this was insufficient grounds for intervention.

At this point in the debate, men and women were using the same repertoire of values—namely, *ḥaqq, riwāj*, and religiosity—but in relation to different goals and as perceived from different spheres. The "rules of discourse" were also shared, with no explicit ambiguity in the meaning of the terminology being used. Subsequent female tactics, however, were not perceived as "legitimate" and were not shared by the men. Questioning of the masculinity of the men and refusing to cook for them were final-hour attempts to shame the men and to affect their decision. As accommodations to male dominance, such tactics (and others such as hypochondria and the refusal of sexual relations) are frequently used by Baluch women (Pastner 1974), though they are not always successful, as the present case demonstrates. Women are not powerless in such patriarchal settings, but they often must revert to non-normative means to exercise power. At this point, the mode of discourse diverges, since men—in a stronger position structurally—need not utilize such an alternative mode. Men and women are no longer playing by the same rules.

Accommodation

In the event, the men "lost" a kinswoman but prevented conflict with male affines and maintained their honor by doing the legitimate thing. The women also "lost" a kinswoman, but remained honorable by finally acceding to the decision of men. Thus, at the outcome, male and female modes of discourse reconverged. The fatalistic attitude of the women, in seeing God's will as prevailing, was acceptable to the men as well. Though they could have used it to bolster their claim to proper Muslim moral behavior, the men did not need to explicitly stress this point, given that the outcome had been under their control. The religious mode, then, was shared by both sexes, serving as an after-the-fact justification, explicit in the case of women and implicit in the case of men. This is not surprising, since, for the Baluch, one function of religion is to provide a cognitive framework of seeming determinism and inevitability. If all else fails, the religious mode offers an explanation of why things are the way they are: the more irremediable the situation (such as the death of a child), the greater the reliance on what an outsider might regard as fatalism. Religion also provides moral authority for otherwise secular areas of concern. Sexual segregation, for example, can be justified according to textual prescriptions, just as political hierarchies can be explained by God's overall scheme for mankind and His bestowal of differential endowments. In this case, the ultimate decision-making power of the uncles could be similarly explained.

And what of Guli? Were there other options open to her which could have altered her fate? One option she did not have, but which otherwise might have strengthened her case, was intercession by patrilateral kinsmen. While kinship among the Baluch groups with which I have worked is bilateral in character and function (Pastner 1979), there is some patrilateral bias to the notion of obligation (*ḥaqq*) to kin. Thus, for example, widowed or divorced women revert to the care of their fathers, brothers, sons, or other available patrikin. Guli's need to rely on her mother's brothers was an accident of fate and may have prejudiced her chance to remain with her mother. A second and open option for Guli would have been to seek refuge in the household of a member of the aristocratic stratum on the oasis. Known as "throwing one's self," this traditional right is used by a woman of a lower than aristocratic status who, usually in marital discord, seeks the intercession of a politically powerful man who can speak on her behalf with a religious judge or a civil magistrate. There is no guarantee, however, that such a woman will not be returned to her husband. I do not know why Guli did not attempt to seek refuge; perhaps she felt that her case was not otherwise strong enough to warrant such a gamble. After Guli left, I asked her mother why refuge had not been sought, but by then her mother had fully assumed the fatalistic position that God's will had been operative all along.

By the time the case of Guli concluded, all participants had effected accommodations in a situation which demanded debate and resolution because it involved the *'izzat* of all participants. We might ask to what extent each was engaging in calculated, "maximizing" behavior. It oversimplifies the case to say that all parties simply calculated their behavior in self-serving terms. This agrees with the position taken by Canfield (1979:422), who notes of the Pathans: "People are capable of truly moral behavior and truly maximizing behavior, but rarely is their behavior purely one or the other." Thus Guli's uncles may have been maximizing their relations with their male affines (or, at the very least, avoiding conflict with them), as well as decreasing their economic responsibility for Guli, but they were also engaging in moral behavior. That they were willing and able to debate with the women for a week, and that they justified their action in moral terms, makes this clear. Similarly, Guli's female allies engaged in maximization on her behalf, and as well perhaps on their own, even though ultimately they had to accede to male authority and rationalize the outcome on the moral basis of God's will. It might be argued that Guli herself was quite definitely behaving in a calculating fashion in her desire to remain with her natal kin. Surely this cannot be denied, but in the end she did do the "right thing" in joining her husband. Ultimately, all participants retained honor, but they were only able to do so by bringing about accommodation between behavior which we as observers separately categorize as maximizing and moral behavior. While it is analytically convenient for us to make such a distinction, we must also realize that the participants in this system of honor need not conceptualize behavior in such sharp, dichotomous terms.

Conclusion

An important reason for focusing on the accommodation between the ideal normative and the pragmatic components of honor is that this is the best means of depicting both male and female participation in the system. Most discussions of honor focus on how female behavior reflects upon the honor of men, but this is an incomplete, skewed portrayal. Men are dependent upon women because women possess the power to act upon the honor of men. Essential to men for moral reasons, women embody "the counter-principle to the male-ruled society, antithetical to it and complementary" (Pitt-Rivers 1977:118).

The definition of what is male and what is female in Baluch social life is clear-cut and allows little in the way of deviation. The strict physical segregation of men and women, and the attendant, strict sexual division of economic labor delineate a social system in which the sexes can to a great extent live mutually dependent but separate lives. This necessitates in part a male and a female version of society. Men interact in both public and domestic spheres, and thus in a behavioral sense the burden of family honor rests more heavily on men than on women. By their acquiescence to the men's ultimate decision-making power, women recognize this added burden.

Despite the final outcome of Guli's predicament, it should not be assumed that all such conflicts among the Baluch inevitably result in what was, after all, a male victory. Women are not totally passive victims of patriarchal ideology; if they were, elaborate means of attempting to control women (namely, *parda*) would not have been developed, and women would not have accumulated such powerful tactics as "going on strike" and refusing to participate in sexual relations. It is not that women do not themselves subscribe to the tenets of honor—for they certainly do—but like men they try to manipulate the system for their own advantage. Manipulation takes different forms for men and women because male and female play different roles in the acting out of the ideology of honor. In the case of Guli the female attempt at manipulation simply did not work.

Speaking of Bengali Muslims in this volume, Carol Prindle indicates that indigenous models of the "social" and the "religious" when juxtaposed can be placed in a relation of conflict and ambiguity. While the Baluch do not possess such clearly labeled, dichotomous models with which to categorize behavior, they similarly face pragmatic situations in which values are juxtaposed and become capable of generating conflict. In their attempt to reconcile pragmatic concerns (such as the disposal of women) with values of religiosity, *riwāj*, and *ḥaqq*, they share repertoires or idioms with which they can both talk about conflict and justify behavior in conflict situations. The rules of discourse stem from bringing the above values to bear on questions of honor. That is, proper conduct during debate is necessary in order for participants to maintain honor. The rules of conduct are shared by men and women up to a certain point. Beyond that point women engage in behavior considered deviant from the male point of view. Such behavior is, however, consistent with the structural position of women in Baluch society, since women need not be as subject as men to the constraints imposed in the "public" sphere of society. When necessary, they will use tactics effective in their domestic sphere, and will be relatively free of the value judgments imposed in the public sphere.

In the discourse between men and women generated by the case of Guli, the debate focused on whether the participants were living up to appropriate moral principles. Thus, in both "legitimate" and "nonlegitimate" ways, the women were demanding that the men behave correctly as proper kinsmen, proper Baluch, and proper Muslims. This forced the men to attempt to reconcile social calculation with morality as defined by kinship, religiosity, and Baluch custom. The women, too, were constrained in their accommodation by the exigencies of the situation. Convergence emerged at the point at which the sexes assumed their correct roles in the moral division of labor which characterizes the Baluch social order.

References

Antoun, Richard T.
1968 "On the Modesty of Women in Arab Muslim Villages: A Study in the Accommodation of Traditions." *American Anthropologist* 70, 4:671–97.

Bourdieu, Pierre
1966 "The Sentiment of Honour in Kabyle Society." In *Honour and Shame*. J. G. Peristiany, ed. Chicago: University of Chicago Press.

Canfield, Robert L.
1979 "On Maximization, Charisma and Pathan Personality." *Current Anthropology* 20, 2:420–22.

Pastner, Carroll McC.
1974 "Accommodations to Purdah: The Female Perspective." *Journal of Marriage and the Family* 36:408–14.
1979 "Cousin Marriage among the Zikri Baluch of Coastal Pakistan." *Ethnology* 18, 1:31–47.
1981 "The Negotiation of Bilateral Endogamy in the Middle East: The Zikri Baluch Example." *Journal of Anthropological Research* 37, 4:305–18.

Pitt-Rivers, Julian
1977 *The Fate of Shechem or the Politics of Sex*. Cambridge: Cambridge University Press.

13

Occupation and Orthopraxy in Bengali Muslim Rank

CAROL PRINDLE

The Muslims of contemporary Chittagong in Bangladesh emphasize a distinctive Muslim identity which they are concerned to distinguish from a Hindu identity.[1] They also wish to align personal practice with Islamic precepts defined by *sharī'at*, the canon law of Islam. Although Chittagonian Muslims acknowledge that Hindu-Muslim syncretism has been pervasive in the Bengali past and is still reflected in regional custom, they are anxious now to exclude or at least explain and justify practices which fall outside the limits of acceptable conduct defined by *sharī'at*.

One topic which is of great concern to many Chittagonian Muslims is rank or social hierarchy. For historical reasons relating to the impact of the nineteenth-century Islamic reform movements and domination by groups outside the Bengali Muslim community, these Muslims are explicitly and consciously concerned with rank and its contradictions, particularly potential contradictions in the relation between Islamic

1. In Islam there is a strong commitment to a moral community and to a common set of normative practices, the Five Pillars. W. Cantwell Smith (1957:28) has suggested that in the Islamic case it is perhaps more appropriate to speak of "orthopraxy" (or the commonality of practice) than of "orthodoxy" (or the commonality of belief). He points out that there is no word meaning "orthodox" in any Islamic language. He writes: "The word usually translated 'orthodox,' *sunni*, actually means rather 'orthoprax,' if we may use the term. A good Muslim is . . . one whose commitment may be expressed in practical terms that conform to an accepted code." Following Smith, then, I have chosen to use the term "orthopraxy."

and alternative South Asian values and moral emphases. One important area of contradiction arises from the juxtaposition of the Islamic doctrine of the equality of all men and the existence of social hierarchy, something which is associated by many Chittagonian Muslims with Hindu influence.

In this essay I investigate Chittagonian Muslim discourse on rank, focusing specifically on the context of work. Work and rank are closely associated in Chittagong. The Chittagonian Muslims use two modes of discourse—one connected with Islam and the other with the world—to talk about work and rank. When figuring relations of rank *within* the Bengali Muslim community, people accept and often exploit the ambiguity which exists in the relationship between religious and social values associated with the two modes of discourse. Yet these Muslims are also concerned with establishing consistency between doctrine and practice. Through their attempt to align personal practice with *sharī'at* and exclude un-Islamic practices, they reiterate and reinforce the boundary *between* the Muslim and Hindu communities.

In their concern to minimize perceived contradictions between Islam and the world, and more specifically between the Islamic doctrine of equality and the existence of social hierarchy, Chittagonian Muslims employ different rhetorical strategies. One strategy involves the application to work relationships of an hierarchical love paradigm drawn from family relationships. A second strategy delimits the significance of the meanings of "high" and "low" to refer to wealth only. Work provides a context in which questions of rank are central and in which the modes of discourse and mitigating strategies can be fruitfully analyzed.

History, Identity, and Rank

Factors such as religion, regional origin, nationalist ideology, and changing politico-economic fortune have all been important in determining the rhetoric of identity assertion and the place of rank in it. The most significant events having an impact on the form of identity assertion in eastern Bengal have been the nineteenth-century reform movements, the Pakistan movement, and the Liberation War which ended in the creation of Bangladesh.

Islam was spread to Bengal from the thirteenth and fourteenth centuries primarily by Sufi missionaries and saints. Up through the medieval period of Bengali history, Islam converged with and was assimilated to the local cultural milieu, a milieu at least nominally

Hindu in orientation. Bengali converts to Islam were mainly low caste Hindus. Thus, a distinct popular Islam evolved with the cultural fusion of Hindu and Muslim belief and practice. At this time Islamic concepts were often deliberately "diluted" with indigenous material by the Muslim elites to bring religion in line with the existent cultural traditions of the people and hence make it acceptable (Roy 1973:23, 30–32).

According to Rafiuddin Ahmed (this volume), it was not until the nineteenth century that the Islamicization of the average Bengali Muslim began. This was the result of the impact of the Islamic revivalist movements which swept through India at this time. Leaders of the revivalist movements not only instructed ordinary people in Islamic laws and practices. They also tried to purify Islam through the exclusion of non-Islamic accretions or elements of belief and practice having no foundation in *sharī'at*. In India this meant mainly the exclusion of Hindu beliefs and practices.

As a result of the reform movements, Bengali Muslims began to be aware of their distinctive Muslim identity. This helped to foster a sense of community solidarity that had not previously existed. There has traditionally been a pervasive cultural dichotomy in Bengali Islam between Muslim culture foreign to Bengal (and imported to Bengal by an immigrant elite) and the culture of Bengali converts. As Rafiuddin Ahmed also points out in this volume, the *ashraf*, or foreign-born nobility, were distinguished from and ranked above the mass of local converts to Islam. Hierarchic distinctions, such as caste and the ranking of a foreign (non-Bengali) elite over commoner Bengali Hindu converts to Islam, had been central to the organization of Bengali communities. During the nineteenth century, as a result of the reform movements, there was an important change in self-identification as large numbers of ordinary Bengalis adopted a non-local ancestry (in the form of titles like *shai<u>kh</u>*) and the higher status which went with it. In opposition to the hierarchical practices associated with Hindu social organization, Muslim reformists emphasized the equality of all men and saw this equality as a principle rooted in Islamic doctrine or *sharī'at*.

The eventual attainment of community solidarity was accompanied by a shift from Hindu-Muslim syncretism to the elimination of ambiguity through the sharp delineation of Hindu and Muslim. As Ewing notes in the introduction to this volume, eliminating Hindu beliefs and practices became an important strategy for drawing a clear boundary around the Muslim community to reinforce Muslim identity. And emphasizing a distinction between Hindu hierarchy and Muslim egalitarianism was a central way of distinguishing the two communities.

Though Chittagong was not a center of reformist activity, the reform movement nevertheless had a profound impact on Chittagonians' ways of talking about themselves. But even today Chittagonian Muslims tend to distinguish "Bengali custom" (*des achār*) from Islam as an alternative code of behavior that has been heavily influenced by Hinduism but now is followed by Bengalis of all religions. While an emphasis on Muslim identity and Hindu/Muslim difference led to the creation of the Islamic state of Pakistan in 1947, an emphasis on a common Bengali identity led to the liberation struggle and the creation of the secular state of Bangladesh in 1971. Emphasis on either the Bengali or on the Muslim component of identity has been an important political and economic response to domination by religious or ethnic groups defined as outsiders and has represented also a program for change beneficial to Bengali Muslim group interests. The shifting stress on being Bengali or being Muslim, in other words, has been pragmatic. Indian Muslims agitated for a Muslim homeland largely as a response to former Hindu domination of governmental, entrepreneurial, and other central roles in East Bengal during the British period. East Pakistani Muslims' emphasis on a Bengali identity reflected opposition to West Pakistani domination of many of these same roles, as well as anger at West Pakistani attempts to institute Urdu as the sole national language.

It is against this backdrop that we must understand the modern Chittagonian Muslims' concern with assertion of a Muslim-yet-Bengali identity, with the drawing of a sharp boundary between Hindu and Muslim communities, with the alignment of personal practice and the *sharī'at*, and with an emphasis on the equality of men as part of Islamic doctrine. These concerns have their roots in the nineteenth-century reform movements and have been rekindled as a result of more recent political and economic domination by groups from outside the Bengali Muslim community.

Contemporary Discourse on Rank

In asserting their identities as Muslims, modern Chittagonians often speak of Hindus. They tend to define a Muslim self in opposition to a Hindu "other." The definition and assertion of Muslim group identity, in Chittagong as elsewhere in Bengal, has often included ideological formulations and injunctions concerning rank. Concern with bringing personal practice within the limits defined by *sharī'at* is evident in a discomfort that many people feel about social hierarchy. Hierarchy is seen as a value and mode of social organization identified with the caste system of Hindus. Nevertheless, different kinds of hierarchy are recognized and some are seen as more legitimate than others. Many Chittagonians are aware that Islamic doctrine itself, especially in its Sufi varieties, condones certain kinds of hierarchic distinctions.[2] In discussions of identity and rank, however, they downplay the kinds of distinctions which occur within the Muslim community, emphasizing instead the similarity and solidarity of Muslims. They stress the emphasis in Islam on the equality of all believers before Allāh and the brotherhood of men. The injunction to treat all men as equals is taken to be part of *sharī'at*, enshrined in the Qur'ān itself.

This attitude toward hierarchy is essentially a reformist attitude. It emphasizes the formal or exoteric aspects of Islam (i.e., *sharī'at*) and is concerned with aligning personal practice consistently with Islamic doctrine. An emphasis on *sharī'at* has been used to strengthen the boundary between the Muslim and Hindu communities where previously ambiguity in the relation between practice and Islamic doctrine blurred the lines of social division (Ewing, this volume).

Though in religious terms all Muslims are seen to be equal, it is generally recognized that social hierarchy does exist in Bengali society. Informants sometimes see this as an example of the inconsistency which exists between ideals and actions due to "Hindu influence." Chittagonian Muslims are explicitly and consciously concerned with reconciling social inequality in everyday life with the emphasis in Islam on equality. They do this by distinguishing religious and social frames of reference. The distinction between religion and the world is a common one in Islam. It allows for ambiguity in community organization and for flexibility in the application of religious doctrine to personal practice. The result is that social divisions and ranks within the Muslim community appear to be loose and flexible. In contrast, Muslims portray Hindu caste ranking as rigid and immutable.

2. For instance, it is widely believed that the *sayyid* should be respected because of his descent from the lineage of the Prophet. Those who believe in Sufi saints or *pīrs* hold that the *pīr*, because of his esoteric knowledge, is higher than his disciple and should therefore be given respectful submission and devotion. Many informants note that although women are given many rights in Islam, men are ranked over women because of their greater duties and responsibilities. All agree that the good man is closer to Allāh and more beloved by Him than the evil man.

People refer to this distinction in terms of opposed "religious" (*dharmik*) and "community" (*sāmājik*) modes of discourse. The *dharmik* mode is rooted in Islam, especially *sharī'at*, and employs an Islamic vocabulary. When it is used, people and their actions are evaluated as good (*bhalā*) or bad (*khārāp*). There is concern with egalitarianism and action or practice. The focus of discourse is on the question of what people *do* and whether or not what they do falls within the limits of proper conduct as defined by *sharī'at*. Thus, even though people are not the same and equal in all socio-economic respects, they should be treated as equal humans. In the *dharmik* mode of discourse, consistency in everyday Muslim practice and the exclusion of alien values and practices are of paramount importance. Use of this mode results in reiteration and reinforcement of the boundaries between the Muslim and Hindu communities.

In the *sāmājik* or "community" mode of discourse there is concern with social difference, hierarchy, and identity as these are reflected in the everyday lives of Bengali Muslims. The focus of discourse is on the question of what or who people *are* by birth or through achievement. When this mode is used, people are evaluated as high (*uchha*) or low (*nimna*), big (*baṛā*) or little (*chhoṭā*). When Chittagonian Muslims use the *sāmājik* mode, they rely heavily on ambiguity. The result is that diversity is encompassed and ranks *within* the Muslim community appear indeterminate, flexible, nonconsensual.

Both modes may be used to refer to Muslim identities and practices. But when Hindu and Muslim identities and practices are distinguished and juxtaposed, the *sāmājik* or community mode becomes associated with the Hindus, while the *dharmik* or religious mode is reserved for Muslims. The result is that Muslims are portrayed as egalitarian and action-oriented (i.e., concerned with social practice), while Hindus are viewed as hierarchical and substantivist (i.e., concerned with such things as birth status and descent). It should be noted here that Chittagonian Muslims view Hindu caste as a system of rank which is based on notions of the unequal birth and differential bodily purity of persons.

People use these two modes of discourse, then, to refer to the distinction which they perceive between religious authority and the world. The modes are simply ways of talking about everyday practices. Each mode involves postulation of a distinct and potentially conflicting set of moral principles and values. Chittagonian Muslims express tension between the two modes when figuring relations of rank. Informants distinguish between the modes by saying such things as "According to religion [*dharmik dike*] all men are equal, but in the community [*sāmājik dike; sāmāje*] men are not equal," or, "Men are equal before Allāh; they are not equal among themselves."

Though there seem to be no clear-cut rules for the contextualized use of the modes, some general observations may be made. When informants point to the disjunction between Islam and the world, they often use both modes of discourse at once, in the same sentence or phrase (as above). When they discuss Hindu-Muslim differences, they draw on the religious mode of discourse and use its Islamic vocabulary to reinforce the boundary between the two communities. And when they discuss everyday practices, often seen to be part of "Bengali custom" (*des achār*), they tend to use the community mode of discourse. As noted, Bengali custom is described as regional custom which has been heavily influenced by Hinduism. Reference to Bengali custom is common when people try to explain or justify the practice of something which seems to have no foundation in *sharī'at*, for instance the practice of touching the feet of elders or superiors as a gesture of deferential respect. Like "Hindu influence," "Bengali custom" is a way of explaining the inconsistency between Islamic ideals and actual practices.

Work as Seen through the Two Modes

The two modes of discourse are clearly operative in the context of work. Various social criteria become important to the evaluation of work when the *sāmājik* mode is employed. These are criteria such as income, education, power, and prestige. While the religious mode of discourse uses a vocabulary of good/bad to evaluate rank, the community mode of discourse uses a vocabulary of high/low or big/little. The tenets of Islam constrain the way work is talked about when the *dharmik* mode is utilized: emphasis is placed upon the treatment of all kinds of workers as if they were equal. Despite the existence of disparities in occupational prestige, income, and power, all Muslim workers are equal as members of the Islamic community (*ummat*) and are equal before Allāh. Workers should not be evaluated as high or low on the basis of their occupational identities and roles alone. Rather, they should be evaluated and ranked only on the basis of assessment of their character (*chāritra*) and behavior (*baebohār*) and the accordance of these with Islamic precepts. The important distinction is not whether a man is rich or poor or whether he is a doctor or manual laborer but rather whether he is a good person (and therefore a good Muslim).

Chittagonian Muslims hold that a Muslim can engage in any kind of work which is lawful (*ḥalāl*) according to Islam. This includes all occupations except those involving usury (*riba'*) or dishonesty, both of which are forbidden by Islam.[3] Informants often distinguish Muslim and Hindu work in religious terms. They hold that a Muslim, as opposed to a Hindu, is not bound to a particular kind of work by either birth or ancestry. In their view Hindus are constrained by birth and ancestry to perform or at least be identified bodily with particular kinds of work. Caste names often refer directly to various occupational specializations of which the higher caste varieties are preferable, say informants.

Chittagonian Muslims often cite the Qur'ān and *ḥadīs̤* when talking about work. The *ḥadīs̤* state that Allāh has given men the means and ability to work, and that work is both the right and the duty of the Muslim man. Every profession which is lawful is also honorable. In addition, the followers of all occupations are equal before Allāh and according to Islamic law. These Muslims often say that there was no work that the Prophet Muḥammad considered too lowly to do himself. Therefore, the Prophet is taken to be the exemplary model for the ideal worker. A *ḥadīs̤* (Karim 1970:236) states that "the Prophet was sent by Divine Wisdom as a model for every man or every profession in the world." However, the Prophet is often cited in Chittagong as the model for the ideal businessman but is not generally cited as the model for other kinds of workers.

According to an Islamic proverb cited by Hughes (1977:52), " 'All facilities are not created to [*sic*] the same person'; everyone is not qualified for every profession, but each for a particular one." Each man is created with a different set of qualities, abilities, and desires which qualify him and give him the means—when properly channeled and refined through education, practical training, or experience—to do a particular kind of work. A person should do that kind of work for which

3. Muslim engagement in trade involves the taking of interest, which some Muslims have identified with usury, something forbidden by Islam. There is evidence that Muslims of early twentieth-century Bengal may have been reluctant to engage in business in part because of their attitude toward interest. Articles in the Bengali press of the time declared that to create capital for modern economic ventures, the practice of taking interest had to be sanctioned (Islam 1973:208). More recently, Papanek (1972:7) and Mines (1972:62) have made it clear that elsewhere Muslim business communities accept a view of Islam that sees the injunction against usury as inapplicable to ordinary interest, which is necessary to economic success. Modern Chittagonian Muslims also feel no contradiction between taking interest in business ventures and being good Muslims.

he is inclined and which lies within his sphere of competence.[4] All kinds of workers are considered to be important and necessary to the proper functioning and harmonious order of society. An informant put this point in the following terms: "Each person's *gun* [attributes] are different. Some become doctors. Others become laborers. If Allāh gives good *gun*, one will do good work, if one tries. Bad work is one's own fault. All kinds of work are good. If all are doctors, who will do the labor?"

When Chittagonian Muslims employ the community (*sāmājik*) mode of discourse, they point out the fact that all occupations are not seen as equally honorable in Chittagonian society. Some kinds of work are considered to be unpleasant, dirty, undignified, or unremunerative, while other kinds of work, requiring more education or offering better pay, command respect. Educated or well-paid workers are seen to be more powerful and are ranked higher socially. The people are quick to point out, however, that prejudices against certain kinds of work are purely social in nature. They have no religious justification.

It should be noted that Chittagonian Muslims, like other Bengalis, have shared many of the prejudices common to Hindus concerning work. (A significant exception is the positive view of business held by Chittagonian Muslims and the negative view of business traditionally held by Bengali Hindus. This will be examined below.) Both communities denigrate manual labor and other "menial" service/artisan work. These Muslims say that there are social bars to their engagement in such occupations as sweeping, barbering, or laundering because these occupations involve dealing with other people's dirt and are therefore unpleasant and undignified. They stress the point that a Muslim who did such work would be subject to gossip and criticism, and his family honor could be tarnished as a result. Sweepers, barbers, washermen, blacksmiths, and potters in Chittagong are almost exclusively either lower caste Hindus or Christians who are believed to have converted from low Hindu castes. Unwilling to concede the existence of a prejudice against these kinds of work, Chittagonian Muslims end up translating a social bar into a religious bar. Occupations such as sweeping and barbering are considered appropriate work for certain Hindu (or former Hindu) castes and are, therefore, not appropriate for

4. In the *Dictionary of Islam* there is a discussion, under the heading "children," of the relation between profession and character of personal competence: "The best course is to ascertain, by examination of the youth's character, for what science or art he is best qualified, and to employ him accordingly. . . . When a person is adapted to a profession, he can acquire it with little pains; when unadapted, the utmost he can do is but to waste his time and defer his establishment in life" (Hughes 1977:52).

Muslims. This is then turned around when it is argued that Muslims may do any kind of work except certain kinds of "Hindu" work. As a result of the translation of social to religious bar, the boundary between the Muslim and Hindu communities is reinforced.

Thus it is evident that in the context of evaluating kinds of work and types of workers, a relation of potential ambiguity and contradiction exists between the community and religious modes of discourse. On the one hand, kinds of work and types of workers can be ranked as high or low on the basis of various social criteria. On the other hand, the social criteria are not the important factors to be considered when ranking a person as good or bad.

The Businessman/Service-holder Distinction in Chittagong

Occupational identity is particularly important in Chittagong. And work provides a central context for the differentiation and evaluation of people. The primary way people are identified and with respect to work in Chittagong is as "businessmen" (*baebsae*) and "service-holders" (*chākrijībī*) or "those who live by serving." The two categories of work—business and service—are defined and discussed in opposition to each other. Together they can encompass virtually all kinds of work performed to earn a livelihood (*jībikā*) in the city of Chittagong.[5] Though the business/service distinction is also made by people of other districts of Bangladesh, it is especially important in Chittagong. Chittagonian Muslims take pride in identifying themselves as successful businessmen with an old and respected tradition of trade. And while Chittagong is presently the main port of the country, it has never been a major governmental service center.

The main way in which businessmen and service-holders are distinguished is on the basis of the concept of "independence" (*sadhīnāta*). The basic difference is that while the businessman is self-employed and

5. Whether cultivation (*chāsa karā*) comprises a third category of work is open to some dispute. Many Chittagonian city dwellers say that agricultural work falls into the categories of business and service. When the cultivator owns the land he works and when a person owns land but finds others to till it for him, each is said to be a businessman. But if a person works on someone else's land for wages, he is described as a service-holder. More research needs to be directed to the rural people's views on work. It may be that they view cultivation as a third category of work, distinct from both business and service. In any event, cultivation is distinguished from business and service as a wholly rural kind of work and is, therefore, not seen to be especially relevant to a discussion of city work.

often the employer of others, the service-holder is an employee of some sort. And self-employment is seen as critical to the attainment and exercise of independence.[6] Thus, the businessman is more independent than the service-holder, who may even be seen as dependent.

Independence or lack of independence is manifested and discussed in a number of ways. First, the businessman's work hours are unfixed. He can come to work and leave when he pleases. The service-holder, on the other hand, works a fixed period of time which is predetermined by his boss or *mālik* (master). Second, the income (profits or fee payments) of the businessman is unfixed. In contrast, the income (salary or wages) of the service-holder is fixed and limited. While the businessman can earn more by working harder, the service-holder earns only that same, fixed amount, no matter how hard he works. Thus business is considered to be an avenue for more rapid social mobility through wealth. Third and most important, the businessman is independent in the sense of not being bound by externally imposed sets of rules and regulations, except for the laws of the nation and Islam. Submitting to no controlling authority in the work place, he is free to exercise his reason and will as he wishes. The service-holder's freedom of action, in contrast, is constrained by his required submission to a boss or employer, who sets circumscribing rules and regulations. Service-holders are described by businessmen (and even by other service-holders) as having no will of their own. This is supposed to be especially true of the clerk class of service-holders. A service-holder informant who occupied a managerial position told the following story: "We call them '*māchi mārā kerānī*' or 'fly-killing clerks.' Why? An officer said to the clerk, 'Go copy this paper.' The clerk copied it. But a fly was squashed on the paper. He worried and worried about how to copy the fly. Finally he caught a fly and then squashed it on the paper." The informant explained the point that the clerk, if he had the capacity to think on his own and make reasonable decisions, would not have bothered to try to copy the fly.

Chittagonians relate the concept of independence to the concept of

6. In a study of Muslim merchants of Tamil Nadu, Mines (1972) shows that for these Muslims, also, independence and self-employment in business are closely associated. Mines notes that "in general Muslim Tamils stress independence as an ideal and envision self-employment as critical to its attainment" (p. 26). Employees, including shop assistants, are seen to have a dependent, even servant, status. Tamil Muslim merchants value business for many of the same reasons as Chittagonians. They value their freedom from supervision and order-taking and claim that working for another not only limits this freedom but also conflicts with the Islamic value of egalitarianism (p. 68). They also value the economic potential of business, of course.

power (*shakti*). While businessmen have the "power of money" (*ṭākār shakti*) or the power that comes with wealth, service-holders have the "power of position" (*pāder shakti*) or the power that is associated with position. Insofar as the power of money can be freely exercised in many contexts outside the occupational sphere, the power is said to be in the *person*. The service-holder's power, in contrast, can be legitimately exercised only while he occupies his position. As people often say of one kind of service-holder, "The power of the government servant is in the *chair*, not in the person."[7]

Differences in education and income are also important aspects of the distinction between these two kinds of work. In the Chittagonian view, service-holders are collectively more educated than businessmen and value education more highly. While service-holders often taken formal technical training or obtain an education, businessmen mostly learn through practical experience. Chittagonians often say also that businessmen as a group are richer than service-holders and value money more highly.

To summarize, then, businessmen and service-holders are distinguished in terms of their independence, power, education, and income. Businessmen and service-holders are two different kinds of people insofar as they hold alternative sets of values which are associated with their occupational roles and to the extent that they follow variant courses of everyday life.

The Big/Little Distinction and Degrees of Power

Significant differences also exist *within* each of these categories, the most important difference being that between big and little workers. The ranking of kinds of workers within each category is based on differing degrees of power. Chittagonians distinguish between "big" (*baṛā*) and "little" (*chhoṭā*) workers on this basis. Big workers, obviously, have more

7. Discussion of alternative views of power helps to clarify the ways in which businessmen and service-holders define themselves in opposition to each other. Businessmen hold that the collectivity of government service-holders controls the government. A businessman who has to cajole and even bribe a low-paid government service-holder in order to obtain a business license or export permit often feels that his pride has been hurt. He may be angry that a man who is much poorer than he has the power (of position) to make him dependent and powerless in such a situation. The businessman may also view the service-holder's bribe-taking as a gross misuse of his power of position. On the other hand, service-holders maintain that the collectivity of businessmen controls the economy. In their view, businessmen make service-holders with fixed and limited incomes feel dependent and powerless by manipulating prices and hoarding needed goods.

power than little workers. Big and little businessmen are differentiated in terms of their wealth or income. In contrast, big and little service-holders are distinguished on the basis of the prestige of the positions they hold, the education necessary to perform their occupational roles, and the level of skill entailed by their work. Bigger workers of both varieties have more authority and independence than littler workers.

Wealth is important, however, to both businessmen and service-holders. Both want to feed, clothe, and house their dependents as adequately as possible. In addition, both maintain that public recognition of high status is dependent on certain expenditures. It is important to help the poor; to fulfill Islamically enjoined norms of hospitality by feeding guests well with costly sweets and rich, sustaining foods; to offer a good sacrifice at the *ʿīd* festival; and to celebrate calendrical festivals, marriages, and other family celebrations as grandly as possible. In Chittagonian society those who can spend more on these occasions are respected as both rich men and good Muslims. The social honor of the lavish giver is defined and perpetuated in relation to others who cannot afford to give as much. Activities such as supporting a family, feeding the poor, entertaining guests, and giving big celebrations all require money. As will be seen, it is thought to be easier for the businessman, with his greater wealth, to perform these activities without suffering financial hardship. But within each of these categories some are more able than others to live up to the ideal. Hierarchical arrangements *within* each group may lead to certain ambiguities when efforts are made to establish ranking *between* the two groups.

Minimizing Contradiction: The Paradigm of Hierarchical Love

When religious and community modes of discourse are juxtaposed in discussions of the ranking of kinds of workers, attitudes toward hierarchy and ranking are inconsistent and contradictory. To bring personal practice within the limits of *sharīʿat* and to reconcile the two modes of discourse, informants employ two strategies. The first is the use of a paradigm of hierarchical love. This paradigm is shared with other Bengalis but is taken by Chittagonian Muslims to fall within the limits of proper conduct (*adab*) and custom prescribed by Islam.[8] Social

8. Kinship and family organization for Hindu and Muslim Bengalis are quite similar. These domains can be seen as part of "Bengali custom," which, though influenced by the Hindus, is also acceptable to the Muslims.

relations, including family relations, are hierarchical in nature. According to Inden and Nicholas (1977:26–29), for Bengalis those of "one's own people" who are junior in generation or younger in age are related to people who are senior in generation or elder in age by a hierarchical form of love. The love of elder for junior is called parental love (*sneha*) and the love of junior for elder is called filial love (*bhakti*). The code for conduct in parental love enjoins elders to care for juniors by supporting, protecting, nourishing, commanding, guiding, and punishing them in order to maintain their well-being. In contrast, the code for conduct in filial love enjoins juniors to show respect to elders by obeying and serving them. Differences in generation and age are also seen to be the source of other differences in power, wealth, knowledge, and respect.

This paradigm of parental and filial love serves as a model for all other relations of dominance and subordination, including those in the work context. For instance, Kakar (1978:119), pointing out that the principle of hierarchical ordering of social dependencies reaches beyond the extended family to all other institutions in Indian life, notes that the ideal superior is viewed as a person who acts in a nurturing way. According to him, "the mode of the relationship is characterized by an almost maternal nurturing on the part of the superior, by filial respect and compliance on the part of the subordinate and by a mutual sense of highly personal attachment."

A central concept for any discussion of the social relations of work is the concept of the *mālik*. For Chittagonian Muslims a *mālik* is the "master" of a household, the master of land, and the master of a business. As a master of a business, he is an employer who has the authority to direct the work of others who are dependent on him, who serve him, and who are willing to show deference to him.[9]

Within the work context of Chittagong, distinction between kinds of workers is seen as inevitable due to the asymmetrical nature of the authority structure. Because complete equality and balance of power are not possible in the employer-employee relation, Chittagonian Muslims say that *mālik*s should treat their employees as younger brothers

9. Hindus generally use the term *kartā*, rather than the term *mālik*, to refer to the head of a household. Writing on late eighteenth-century Bengal, Curley (1980:113–14) describes the usage of the title *kartā bābu*. By analogy with the head of a household, the *kartā bābu* is a person who directs the work of others. These others can be seen as dependent on him. They must show deference to him. The term *mālik* could be substituted here. The translation of the term *mālik* to mean "master" is taken from the work of Thorp (1978) on conceptions of power associated with mastery of land in rural Bangladesh.

while employees reciprocate by treating their *mālik*s as elder brothers. Though in terms of the paradigm of hierarchical love the relationship between elder and junior brother parallels that between the parent and child, it is significant that these Muslims speak in terms of a brother-brother relationship rather than in terms of a parent-child relationship. The "brotherhood" of all men is a central doctrine of Islam.

Chittagonian Muslims point out that at work a *mālik* cannot treat his employees as equals in all respects because this would impede his maintenance of the order, discipline, and efficiency which come as a result of the exercise of control and authority. In the sense that he relies on the *mālik* for his job and wages, the employee is clearly a dependent and a subordinate. Like an elder brother the *mālik* should give *sneha* to the employee and should receive *bhakti* in return. In addition to the difficult tasks of commanding, guiding, and disciplining employees, the *mālik* should also take care of them by protecting, nurturing, and sustaining them in the work situation, a situation which is much more personalistic than is presently the case in the United States. Many *mālik*s of shops and other small businesses in Chittagong provide food, housing, and even clothing for their employees. It is common to find employees who sleep in the *mālik*'s shop, partake of his ordinary cooked food on a regular basis, and may even receive gifts on Islamic festival dates and invitations to family functions such as weddings.[10]

The *mālik* may also train his employees to be bosses themselves by teaching them how to run a business. When the employee is ready to start his own business, the *mālik* may help with loans and personal contacts. Writing on Muslim merchants in Tamil Nadu, Mines (1972:94) states that "Muslims claim that it is good to be a merchant, since it is only in this capacity that a man can be his own boss, and so avoid the servant status of an employee." He also notes that employment in business, as opposed to other types of employment, is seen to be good from the perspective of "egalitarianism." In Chittagong, also, independence and equality are often associated, with business being seen as allowing more potential for equal social relations than government service.

In return for the things that the *mālik* does on the employee's behalf,

10. In their essay on caste systems Marriott and Inden (1974:989) note that servants of a landholder and followers of a village headman express their subordination by taking ordinary cooked food from him. Similarly in Chittagong, the employee's taking of ordinary cooked food from his *mālik* can be seen to express his subordination.

the employee must work efficiently and honestly. He must submit to guidance, obey commands, give service, and show proper deference to his *mālik*. If he fails to do these things, he may be fired. When the employee no longer wants to submit to the *mālik*'s authority, he can terminate the relationship by quitting his job. The fact that the relationship can be terminated is important because it shows that the employer-employee relation is not completely analogous to the elder brother–junior brother relation insofar as the latter cannot be terminated. Nevertheless, the paradigm of hierarchical family love is used to ameliorate the exercise of power within the employer-employee relationship.

Chittagonians are concerned to soften the impact of this power relationship. People stress the point that recognition of differences in rank and power, even in the context of work, should not result in the treatment of the subordinate as an inferior person. Drawing upon religious values, they say that one should act with *adab* (propriety) in all kinds of social relations. The acceptable model of hierarchic family relations provides rules of proper behavior which are seen to be within the limits of discourse prescribed by Islam.

Finally, it is often said in Chittagong that distinctions of rank and power in the work situation are invalid outside of that situation. Away from work the *mālik* and his employee are considered to be (at least theoretically) equals. As one service-holder said, "At the time of work all men are not equal. When all go home and sit as men, all are equal." Similarly, a bookstore salesman commented, "I am a salesman. He is a customer. When I get up and leave I don't remain a salesman. I become a passenger in a rickshaw or just an ordinary man." In other words, a person's role as superior or subordinate is context-specific and does not confer on him a total identity.

This model for hierarchical social relations may be further extended such that people who are not involved in a direct authority relation but occasionally interact, such as rich and poor people, should treat each other as elder and younger brothers, not as superior and inferior humans. When Chittagonian Muslims speak of the relation between superior and subordinate position holders as a relationship between brothers, they are able to minimize the tension resulting from the contradiction between social ranking and religious values. This allows them to discuss rank and power differences and yet avoid the apparent conflict between the community and religious modes of discourse.

Another Mitigating Strategy: Delimiting the High/Low Distinction

A second strategy used by people to avoid or minimize the contradiction between values expressed through community and religious modes of discourse involves the delimitation of the significance of the high/low distinction to wealth: people are high or low in terms of wealth but not in terms of any human qualities. Through this strategy, Chittagonians can acknowledge the fact that objective inequalities of wealth exist in society and people may be ranked accordingly, but they can simultaneously reiterate the point that *as humans* and *as Muslims* all men are equal.

These Muslims share an understanding of the components and dimensions of this wealth-based rank system and agree on the criteria for assignment of ranks. The word most commonly used when people are categorized in hierarchical rank terms is actually a suffix which means "wealth, riches, or property" (*-bitto*). It is qualified by the designations "high" (*uchha*), "middle" (*madhya*), or "low" (*nimna*). It is common for the people to specify *-bitto* or wealth category membership by listing kinds of workers, because there is a correspondence between occupation and income which is often assessed through examination of style of everyday life.

In ranking kinds of workers in *-bitto* categories, wealth or power of money is the main criterion for both businessmen and service-holders. But while wealth is an appropriate criterion for the ranking of kinds of businessmen, it is not always sufficient for ranking service-holders, particularly not in the case of service-holders who hold respected positions but do not earn much money. The power of position (and the education which goes along with it) functions, therefore, as a subsidiary criterion for ranking.

In terms of the Chittagonian value system, the wealthy man is the most respected man. Because there is an esteemed local business tradition, because businessmen value money highly and are the richest men, money is the main criterion for rank, and businessmen who are rich are ranked highest.[11] There is a high degree of agreement concerning the

11. "Big" businessmen such as industrialists, exporters, factory owners, and other rich men are ranked in the *uchha-bitto*, or high wealth, category. Often certain respectable service-holders—high government officers; employed engineers, lawyers, doctors; and professors—are also included in the high category, but just below the businessmen. The *madhya-bitto* category includes middle-level businessmen such as shopkeepers, middle-level service-holders for the government (especially what we might call "white collar"

placement of kinds of workers in *-bitto* categories. Yet the ambiguity that exists between wealth and position as criteria for rank facilitates some variation in individual rank assessments and placements. Chittagonians themselves view this system of social rank as a loose and flexible system which allows for individual social mobility. They also emphasize that this rank system based on wealth is something different from a caste system, based on birth and descent.

The wealth-based rank system exists side by side with the Islamic system (based on evaluation of character and behavior) without contradicting the doctrine of equality. Though all men are equal before Allāh, they are not necessarily equal (in wealth) among themselves. Socioeconomic differences, especially differences in wealth, are inevitable and should not be confused with differences in human qualities. There are always the examples of the poor but good man and the rich but evil man to remind one of this point.

Thus, delimitation of the significance of the meanings of high and low is an important strategy which Chittagonian Muslims use to try to minimize the contradiction that exists between social and religious values. Tension is reintroduced, however, when the criteria for rank which are used in the community mode of discourse (i.e., power of money and power of position) are juxtaposed with the criteria for rank which are used in the religious mode of discourse (i.e., character and behavior). Actual rankings made by individual Chittagonians clearly reveal this tension.

Worker Evaluations

In an occupational categorization and evaluation exercise, informants were asked to distinguish and rank a number of kinds of workers commonly found in Chittagong.[12] Below are two examples of worker

---

workers), skilled artisans, and others who earn an average but adequate income. In the *nimna-bitto*, or low, category are found small businessmen like hawkers, small service-holders like peons and drivers, unskilled laborers and others who earn a small and inadequate income.

12. For the occupational categorization and evaluation exercise I wrote the names of sixty-four common types of workers on flash cards in Bengali and numbered the backs of the cards to facilitate quick recording of results. The cards were shuffled and presented in random order. In cases where informants were illiterate, I read the names of the workers aloud to them. The informants were asked first to categorize the particular kinds of workers as businessmen, service-holders, or other. There was also a "no opinion" category. In the second part of the exercise—the evaluation and ranking of

evaluations. These case studies reveal the ways in which alternative rules and ranking strategies are used by Chittagonian Muslims. They also illuminate the manner in which the community and religious modes of discourse are used simultaneously in the context of worker ranking. As will be seen, social and religious values are juxtaposed, with the high/low (or big/little) and good/bad distinctions being alternately employed.

The first case study focuses on Khālid, an educated, middle-aged Chittagonian service-holder who works in a managerial position. Khālid has a high regard for education and he respects educated people. But as a service-holder with a fixed and limited income, he feels that he cannot afford to live the way he would like to live. He worries about supporting his large family adequately. He complains that he lacks the funds necessary to perform Islamic rites and festivals properly and cannot give much to the poor. As a good Muslim, he feels that he should be able to do more to help those who are poorer than himself.

Though he has always been a service-holder, he thinks business is better than service for both socio-economic and religious reasons. Emphasizing social values, Khālid stresses the point that business is better than service because businessmen can earn more money, support a family more easily, and live more comfortably. When he employs the religious mode of discourse, he argues that business is the highest profession for reasons associated with Islam. Some of the reasons he gives are the following: the Prophet Muḥammad was a trader and it is good to follow the practices of this exemplary leader; honesty in business is difficult and therefore it is good to test one's moral strength by engaging in business; and there is more scope in business to help the poor and serve the nation because businessmen are richer.

When Khālid evaluated particular kinds of workers, he referred alternatively to the criteria of wealth and education, on one hand, and service to humanity or the nation, on the other hand. With respect to the latter, he ranked higher those kinds of workers who can help people and improve the nation by bringing prosperity. For example, he ranked doctors, lawyers, engineers, and businessmen high for these reasons.

---

kinds of workers—informants were asked to rank workers in terms of three categories: high or big, medium, and low or little. Again there were "no opinion" and "other" categories. In both stages of the exercise the informants were free to discard these categories and replace them with other categories that they believed might better reflect the system of occupational categorization and evaluation. During the exercise I recorded all the informant's questions, comments, consultations, and changes of mind. I also discussed particular categorization and evaluation decisions with them.

Though Khālid ranked low those kinds of workers who are generally thought to be low caste Hindus, he emphasized both their low level of education or skill and their minimal contribution to humanity as reasons for the low rank. His wife objected, thinking that he meant that a low profession was a bad profession. He explained to her that *nimna pesa* (low profession) was not meant to be a degrading label.

Khālid spoke in the religious mode when he evaluated the money-lender (*mahajan*) as low because his profession is bad. He noted that though a moneylender may be very rich and therefore might be ranked as high on a social scale, his work (interest taking) is bad because it is absolutely against Islam. Rather than rank the kinds of workers who perform religious functions, Khālid put them in a separate "no opinion" category. He did so because they do not earn much money and are not highly educated except by *madrasa* or Islamic school standards. He felt that he could not rank them as high but he did not want to rank them as low either.

The second case study features Anwar, a young businessman and commerce student who is a member of an old Chittagonian town-based business family. He prefers business to service because of the greater possibility for earning a lot of money. Like Khālid he believes that power of money is necessary for living a comfortable life and for helping the poor. Unlike Khālid he put more emphasis upon income and position than on education in ranking kinds of workers. He also mentioned service to humanity or to the nation as a component of high rank.

In the worker evaluation exercise Anwar included all Muslim religious functionaries in the high category, saying that religious people are good (not high or low) and that therefore you cannot really rank them in terms of such mundane, secular criteria as wealth or position. He did not describe any kinds of workers as low caste Hindus. For him the largest category was the "no opinion" category. He said, "In general all the occupations I put here [in the "no opinion" category] are treated as low. But they shouldn't be treated as low. They are human beings and must be treated as human beings, not as what they do." He went on to criticize those people who treat bearers and laborers as low because they are poor and perform kinds of work which are not socially respected. When he put the sweeper in the "no opinion" category, he noted that though the sweeper's work was considered to be low, you can't say that the sweeper *as a person* is low.

Anwar employed power of money and power of position as two

criteria for social rank. He juxtaposed to this social mode a religious mode of discourse which referred to such things as service to humanity, goodness, and the treatment of people as equal humans. His reluctance to rank any kinds of workers as low, despite his willingness to rank people in higher categories on the basis of the criteria of income and position, reflects his concern with being a good Muslim who treats people as if they were equal.

In both of these cases the community and religious modes of discourse are alternately employed and juxtaposed. The relation between the two modes is one of ambiguity and contradiction. The result of the juxtaposition of the two modes is that ranks appear to be relatively unfixed and variable. Boundaries within the Muslim community which might become more impermeable if rank were unambiguous remain fluid and permeable. Saying that rank is unfixed and changeable makes it easier to stay within the limits of discourse prescribed by Islam.

Conflicting Values in Ranking

Another way to speak of rank and to justify it in an Islamic mode is to use the vocabulary of good and bad. In describing people as good or bad, Chittagonian Muslims focus upon the presence or absence of certain character traits or personal attributes and on the performance of particular activities. Attributes or qualities which are considered to be good are those which help to maintain feelings of solidarity, harmony, order, justice, and brotherhood among people in social life. Good attributes and qualities also uphold Islamic codes of behavior. A good person (and a good Muslim) is generous, humble, industrious, and honest. In contrast, a bad person is miserly, inhospitable, proud, lazy, or dishonest. The source of these character traits is ambiguous. They are variously spoken of as fated or God-given, inherited from the ancestors, or acquired through proper training and personal effort.

People believe that if one properly follows the Islamic codes for conduct one will be a good person as well as a good Muslim. Failure to follow Islamic codes properly is one of the most common explanations given for the existence of non-equal social relations in Chittagong. People observe that the rich man often does not treat the poor man as a dependent junior brother. He becomes proud and treats him as an inferior person. He does not give sufficient alms or service to the poor because he becomes miserly. People *salām* (give a greeting of peace) to the rich man but not to the poor man, even though he may be a more observant Muslim than the rich man. On the other hand, the poor man becomes jealous or envious of the better economic condition of the richer man and ceases to show respect to him. If each person treated all others as if they were elder and junior brothers, the argument goes, then just, balanced, brotherly social relations would be an experienced reality.

According to this argument, social ranking and religious equality are not incompatible in principle. However, it is felt that in day-to-day social life this compatibility is seldom maintained. Though possession of wealth is socially respected in Chittagong, what counts in religious terms is the proper use of money and not its mere possession. The proper use of money according to the religious mode is to fulfill Islamic ends. The person who misuses money (through miserliness, inhospitality, pride, laziness, or dishonesty) should not be respected, no matter how rich he is. People are aware of the corruptive power of money, the tendency for wealth to lead people from the path of Islam. They also recognize that insufficient money is also dangerous, as it can result in thievery or bribe-taking. Interestingly, possession of money is also thought to be necessary for the proper performance of one's Islamic duties. By contrast, when the community mode of discourse is drawn upon, emphasis is placed on the social respectability and high rank that are associated with the mere possession of much money, as well as on the power of money in Chittagonian social life.

Because the two modes of discourse cannot be made fully congruent, it is especially significant that Chittagonians see proper Islamic values and practices as having become attenuated in Bangladesh. The reasons given for this attenuation include the experience of former colonial domination, the forces of modernization and Westernization, and the influence of Hinduism. These forces—considered challenging and at times dangerous—are often blamed for the existence of a "class mentality" and for the selfish concern with personal well-being and success over the concern with community well-being, solidarity, and brotherhood. In particular, "Hindu influence" is used as an explanation for both the attenuation of Islamic practices and the inconsistency between Islamic doctrine and social practice. Chittagonians maintain that if all people acted with propriety in their social relations, true brotherhood could be established. Some said that if Bangladesh were an Islamic state this would be easier because there would be a way to enforce Islamic practice and punish deviations from doctrine.

Putting the Two Modes Together: Ranking Business over Service

Despite the Islamic emphasis on ranking all kinds of work as equally good, Chittagonians consider business to be better than service. They use either or both modes of discourse to justify the ranking of business over service. When the community mode of discourse is employed, business is ranked over service for reasons relating mainly to wealth, but people also argue their position in terms of Chittagonian character, tradition, and history. When the religious mode of discourse is drawn upon, business is ranked over service for reasons relating to Islam and the following of Muslim codes for conduct. People are often unwilling to concede that business is better for purely pragmatic reasons, because that would sound un-Islamic. Instead, they also emphasize religious reasons for the preference for business.

Probably the most important reason for the higher ranking of the businessman in the community mode of discourse is his wealth. The independent businessman can become rich and powerful. People even say that you don't find rich service-holders. Thus, when the community mode is employed, Chittagonians make it clear that they want to be independent, rich, powerful, and highly ranked—as only businessmen can be.

Business is thought to be an appropriate kind of work for Chittagonians, particularly suited to the qualities, character, abilities, and inclinations of the Chittagonian as a kind of person. Chittagonians regard themselves as a distinctive kind of person, possessing a fierce independence. They associate independence with self-employment in business and view it as critical to the accumulation of wealth. It is common to hear Chittagonians say such things as "People here don't like to serve under anyone," and "Each person wants to be his own boss."

Business is the traditional work of Chittagonians. In contrast, service is held to be the work of "foreigners" (*bidesi*) or non-Chittagonians who come from other districts. The people say that more Chittagonians do business than service. This emphasis on a business identity and positively evaluated tradition of commerce occurs within a special historical context. Since the fourteenth century, travelers and traders of various nationalities have visited Chittagong, describing it as a great port and important commercial center. Today Chittagong is the main port and import-export center of Bangladesh. The antiquity of their port, and the trading activities which have occurred there for so long, had conditioned Chittagonians to perceive business as possessing a historically legitimated respectability. There seems to be no comparable local tradition of business elsewhere in Bangladesh. Nor is there a comparable tradition valuing service in Chittagong itself. As contrasted with the capital city of Dhaka, Chittagong has never been a major administrative or governmental center. A non-Chittagonian service-holder informant summarized the business-oriented viewpoint of Chittagonians and set it in its historical context:

> In Chittagong the service tradition is not respected. There is a history of trade. Chittagong is a port city. Since before the Arabs the Chittagonian people have been a seafaring people who have spread over the world. Traditionally they are families with businesses. Chittagong is not a bureaucratically important city in any way, as even Dhaka was in the Pakistan days. There is not much of local administration here. . . . Bureaucracy is run from Dhaka. . . . People in Chittagong must see trade, business, and petty officials. The few [government] service-holders here are sent from headquarters elsewhere. . . . Big bureaucrats wield much power. But people don't see them here. . . . In Dhaka high [government] service is highly respected. . . . "Why service?" they ask here. They have never seen the power and prestige of service, as it can only be seen in Dhaka.

The Chittagonian people are very much aware, then, of the antiquity of their port and business tradition. The perception that business has a historically legitimated respectability allows people to note proudly that they belong to a "business family," that business has been the work of their ancestors.

Chittagonians speak in terms which suggest that the city has always been a pre-eminent port and that local Muslim businessmen (sometimes referred to as Saudagars) had always dominated the trade of the port. In fact, Chittagong's commercial importance was surpassed by first Calcutta's and then Karachi's importance in recent history, and the trade of the port came to be dominated by outsider groups. During the British period, Hindus became an entrepreneurial force in East Bengal. The Pakistan period brought domination of the new industrial concerns and large-scale commercial enterprises by Muslim business communities, traditionally in trade, from western India and the Punjab.[13] Over time a stereotype evolved of the Muslims, and especially the Bengali Muslims, as people who were both averse to and inept at commercial activity. The stereotype occasioned Hindu and later West Pakistani Muslim contempt

13. Many have written on the Bengali business experience during the British and Pakistani periods. For a more detailed discussion see, for example, Papanek (1971, 1972), Kling (1969, 1976), and Timberg (1978).

for Bengali Muslim business skills. Not surprisingly, this contempt annoyed Bengali (including Chittagonian) Muslims.

The contemporary Chittagonian Muslim assertion of a successful businessman identity is at least in part a response to this recent experience. It is a proud response to both the previous domination of the trade of the port by outsider groups and to the negative stereotype. It is important to note that the identity asserted is a *Chittagonian Muslim* business identity. Traditionally it has been said that there is an "anti-commercial ethic" which characterizes Bengali regional identity. Significantly, then, Chittagonian Muslims emphasize a positively valued *district-based* business identity in opposition to the negatively valued regional view of commerce. Here again Chittagonian Muslim informants associate regional culture with Hindu values. They maintain that the Hindu religion does not highly rate trade and ranks trading castes low. In contrast they note the positive injunctions for trade associated with Islam. Thus, emphasis on a Muslim business identity is another way to reinforce the boundary between Muslims and Hindus, once again excluding Hindu values.

When speaking in the religious mode of discourse, Chittagonians again refer to their distinctive character and history. First, they characterize themselves as very observant (*khub dharmik*) Muslims and also as hospitable and generous people. Second, they historically associate trade and religion, emphasizing both their Arab ancestry and their Islamic orthopraxy. They associate both with the belief that Chittagong was first colonized by Arab traders and Muslim saints and missionaries who came in the wake of the traders.[14] They further hold that Islam, having been brought to Chittagong first, was then spread to the rest of what is now Bangladesh. In addition to being an old port and business center, Chittagong is known as the land of the twelve (Muslim) saints (*bāra aulia*). The result of this emphasis is that there is an important association of orthopraxy with occupation in the case of business which seems to be lacking in the case of service.

Chittagonian Muslims also believe that business is better than service because it is through honest business that one can best fulfill the injunctions of the Islamic codes for conduct. Business is the main type of

14. The influence of the early Arabs on Chittagonian life is held to be extensive. Modern Chittagonian Muslims point to evidence of this in the Arab appearance of many people; the proliferation of family titles which indicate Arab ancestry; the predominance in the local dialect of words from Arabic and Persian; place names in and around the city which are associated with the Arab world; the strong Islamic orientation of the people; and the business tradition.

work that allows the worker to guide himself independently, according to his own reason and will. Informants say that only truly independent people can fully exercise reason and control will in a self-disciplined way. Business is also a good place to test one's moral strength, because remaining honest in business is considered to be extremely difficult. The words of an informant corroborate these points: "In service there is limited scope for self-improvement and there is guidance by others. In business the scope is unlimited and you are your own guide. . . . Business is a place to check your temptation. It is honest work. In business there is much room to help others."

In the view of this Muslim informant, it is the wealth of businessmen which allows them to better fulfill Islamic codes of behavior. These codes include such enjoined activities as nourishing and sustaining a family properly, helping the poor, serving the nation, extending hospitality to guests, and celebrating Islamic festivals. All of these activities require money. Moreover, the donation of large sums to the local mosque and the giving of a lavish function on the occasion of an Islamic festival or rite provide public recognition of status as a good Muslim, in addition to recognition of status as a rich and therefore "big" man.[15] For all these reasons, then, it is thought that businessmen, with their greater wealth, can be good Muslims more easily. Another way to look at this is to say that without money the proper performance of a Muslim's religious duty is impossible, a view voiced in the Bengali press in the early part of the century (Islam 1973:211).

Nevertheless, in the religious mode of discourse power of money or wealth is important to the fulfillment of Islamic duties and to one's recognition as a good man. In this way the religious mode shares with the community mode a high valuation of the power of money. There is a kind of merging of piety and wealth such that service to humanity is associated both with being a good businessman and pious Muslim.

Finally, Chittagonians feel that it is not only lawful but recommended that a Muslim do business, and they refer directly to various Islamic texts when giving reasons for preferring business over service.[16] They

15. Mines (1972:41) noted that Muslim Tamil merchants can gain merit in the eyes of God and prestige in the community by giving large donations to mosques.

16. Religious sanctions for trade among Bengali Muslims are not new. Examination of articles from the Bengali press of the early twentieth century reveals the association of Islam and trade. A 1919 article states the following: "We must totally eradicate such attitudes as worrying what people will think of us if we trade in fish. It should, on the contrary, be regarded as a great sin for Muslims to refuse to engage in religiously sanctioned trade. The Prophet himself especially urges us to engage in trade and

say that trade is *sunnat*, a practice of the Prophet Muḥammad which should be practiced by ordinary Muslims in emulation of the Prophet's exemplary ways. Though people often cite the Prophet as the model of the ideal businessman, they do not cite Him as the model of the ideal service-holder. The Prophet, they say, left mercantile rules for the prosperity of individuals and nations. And they are aware that Islamic works on right conduct (such as the Qur'ān and *ḥadīṣ*) present detailed rules for trade, including injunctions for honesty and fair dealing.

Despite the inherent contradictions and ambiguities in the values associated with the two modes of discourse, Chittagonian Muslims have managed to use both to support their preference for business. They have drawn upon views concerning tradition, character, history, wealth, and religion in this preference for business. It is possible to use the religious mode of discourse to support the community mode for two reasons. First, there are some values (for instance, wealth and independence) which the two modes share. Second, the two strategies—the use of the paradigm of hierarchical love and the delimitation of the significance of the high/low distinction—have the effect of minimizing the contradiction that exists between the two modes.

Conclusion

Chittagonian Muslims make choices among alternative sets of values or moral emphases when they assert their identities and figure relations of rank. The act of ranking businessmen and service-holders reveals a tension explicitly perceived by Chittagonian Muslims between the Islamic principles of egalitarianism and brotherhood on the one hand and the hierarchical nature of South Asian social relations on the other hand. These Muslims manage contradiction between social and religious values by juxtaposing and alternatively employing two modes of

commerce, and bestowed great praise on these activities" (Islam 1973:206). A second quotation not only extolls the virtue of trade but also admonishes Muslims to engage in it: "Buying and selling by you, 'has been declared in the Holy Quran by Allah Himself,' to be permitted. . . . So we must open Muslim shops in every village and market. . . . Unless you do this, you will be a sinner" (Islam 1973:211). The motivation for these articles was the realization that many profitable trades had become Hindu monopolies and the belief that many Muslims shared Hindu prejudices about work, prejudices unsupported by Islamic doctrine. In addition to contemporary Chittagonian Muslims, Muslim merchants of Tamil Nadu also find that religion sanctions trade. According to Mines (1972:83), "Muslims have a very positive attitude about the business occupation. They feel a merchant performs a 'sunnath,' an act of religious merit, because the Prophet was a businessman."

discourse—the *sāmājik* or community mode and the *dharmik* or religious mode.

Chittagonian Muslims are concerned with minimizing or avoiding the impact of this contradiction and with bringing personal practice into line with Islamic doctrine. They employ two strategies to mitigate the contradiction. By providing a code for conduct for power relationships (especially the employer-employee relationship), the paradigm of hierarchical love legitimates a *social* ordering by invoking values such as brotherhood which are acceptable in the *religious* mode of discourse. A similar effect is achieved by the delimitation of the significance of the high/low distinction to refer to wealth, not human qualities. This social system of rank is by these means brought into line with the religious system in which the character and behavior of people are judged as good or bad. The rich businessman who uses his money properly and is evaluated as both a big man and a good Muslim demonstrates the potential congruence of social and religious rankings.

Because the two modes of discourse share certain values and because use of the two above strategies minimizes the contradiction between them, it is possible to use the religious mode in support of the social mode. In the process a partial congruency between the two modes of discourse is achieved; at the same time sufficient ambiguity is retained to assure social fluidity within the Muslim community. The result is that boundaries within the Muslim community, which might become fixed if rank was ambiguous and totally consensual, remain fluid, while the boundary between Muslim and Hindu communities is reinforced through the exclusion of alien values and ranking strategies.

References

Curley, David L.

1980 "Rulers and Merchants in Late Eighteenth-Century Bengal." Ph.D. dissertation, Department of History, University of Chicago.

Hughes, T. P.

1977 *Dictionary of Islam*. New Delhi: Cosmo.

Inden, Ronald B., and Ralph W. Nicholas

1977 *Kinship in Bengali Culture*. Chicago: University of Chicago Press.

Islam, Mustafa N.

1973 *Bengali Muslim Public Opinion as Reflected in the Bengali Press, 1901–1930*. Dacca: Bangla Academy.

Kakar, Sudhir

1978 *The Inner World: A Psycho-analytic Study of Childhood and Society in India*. Delhi: Oxford University Press.

Karim, Al-Haj Maulana Fazlul
1970 *Al-Hadis of Mishkat-ul-Masabit*. Vol. 4. Dacca: I. M. Trust.
Kling, Blair B.
1976 *Partner in Empire: Dwarkanath Tagore and the Age of Enterprise in Eastern India*. Berkeley: University of California Press.
1969 "Entrepreneurship and Regional Identity." In *Bengal Regional Identity*. David Kopf, ed. Asian Studies Center, South Asia series, Occasional Paper no. 9. East Lansing: Michigan State University.
Marriott, McKim, and Ronald B. Inden
1974 "Caste Systems." In *Encyclopaedia Britannica*. 15th edition. Pp. 982–91.
Mines, Mattison
1972 *Muslim Merchants: The Economic Behavior of an Indian Muslim Community*. New Delhi: Shri Ram Centre for Industrial Relations and Human Resources.
Papanek, Hanna
1972 "Pakistan's Big Businessmen: Muslim Separatism, Entrepreneurship, and Partial Modernization." *Economic Development and Cultural Change* 21, 1:1–32.
1971 "Entrepreneurs in East Pakistan." In *Bengal: Change and Continuity*. Robert and Mary Jane Beech, eds. Asian Studies Center, South Asia series, Occasional Paper no. 16. East Lansing: Michigan State University.
Roy, Asim
1973 "The Social Factors in the Making of Bengali Islam." *South Asia* 3:23–35.
Smith, Wilfred Cantwell
1957 *Islam in Modern History*. New York: New American Library.
Thorp, John P.
1978 "Masters of Earth: Conceptions of Power among Muslims of Rural Bengal." Ph.D. dissertation, Department of Anthropology, University of Chicago.
Timberg, Thomas A.
1978 *The Marwaris: From Traders to Industrialists*. New Delhi: Vikas.

14

Divination and Ideology in the Banaras Muslim Community

JUDY F. PUGH

The history of the interaction of Islam and Hinduism in north India is nowhere better illustrated than in the city of Banaras.[1] Famous as the sacred center of Hinduism, Banaras came under Muslim domination in A.D. 1194, when Muḥammad of Ghur, also known as Shihāb al-Dīn, expanded his control of north India, and his general Quṭb al-Dīn Aibak invaded the city and established a Muslim kingdom (Smith 1961:210; Cohn 1962:314; Sukul 1974:5). For the next five centuries Banaras was ruled by Muslim kings who were subordinate to the Nawāb of Oudh and to the Mughal Emperor himself (Cohn 1962). During these centuries a sizable segment of the Hindu population converted to Islam. With the death of Aurangzeb in 1708, Mughal rule was virtually at an end, and in 1739 Balwant Singh, the son of a local Hindu official, became Rājā of Banaras (Cohn 1962:314). The autonomy of the Hindu kingdom was short-lived, however; the East India Company took over the administration of Banaras in 1775 (Smith 1961:509). The family of Balwant Singh retained and continues to hold the hereditary position of Rājā of Banaras.

Throughout these eight centuries Banaras has witnessed the full spectrum of Hindu-Muslim relations. The well-known destruction of Hindu temples by Muslim rulers in pre-Mughal and Mughal times and

1. I would like to thank the Social Science Research Council for the award of a dissertation fellowship which supported my research on astrology and divination in Banaras, from January 1975 to June 1976.

the construction of mosques from the very stones of the temples form an infamous chapter in the city's history.[2] On the other side of the coin, Kabīr's poetic vision of a syncretistic union of Hinduism and Islam and the scholarly collaboration between Dārā Shikōh, Shāh Jahān's eldest son, and the *puṇḍit*s (Hindu scholars) and *sannyāsī*s (ascetics) of Banaras stand as evidence of the kind of attenuation of group boundaries that was also a common feature of these earlier centuries.[3] A similarly balanced picture characterizes the twentieth century, with intercommunity tensions and conflicts counterposed to the quiet, commonplace routines in which Hindus and Muslims intermingle without notice or incident. An inspiring legitimation of the more mundane expressions of peaceful coexistence comes daily in the sounds of Muslim *shahnā'ī*[4] players joining in the *ārṭī*[5] of Hindu temples, including the *ārṭī* of the most sacred Vishvanath Mandir.

Today the Banaras Muslim community has a population of 153,000, thus constituting one-quarter of the city's 606,000 residents (*Census of India* 1971) and placing Banaras third among India's major cities in terms of the percentage of its population which is Muslim (Siddiqui 1976:93). The community's role in the local and regional economy is significant, especially in the production of the famous gold- and silver-threaded Banarsi silk saris and other woven goods.

The continuing stability of religious life is indicated by the mosques, *maktab*s and *madrasa*s which dot both Muslim and mixed Hindu-Muslim neighborhoods and also by the annual round of religious celebrations. The high point of the year comes at the end of the fast of *ramaẓān*, when the city's parks are transformed into *'īd-gah*s where crowds of celebrants await a joyous first glimpse of the moon of *'īd*. While Sunnis greatly outnumber Shī'as,[6] both groups maintain schools and mosques and boast of their past and present scholars.

Social customs in the Banaras Sunni community form markers for ideological perspectives which Geertz (1968) has termed traditionalism

2. Eck (1982) and Sukul (1974) contain accounts of these incidents.

3. The *Uttar Pradesh District Gazetteer* for Varanasi (1965:55–56) discusses these cooperative endeavors. The gazetteer's history of the city notes that although temples were destroyed, there were at least some periods when imperial *farmān*s protected the rights of priests to discharge their religious duties.

4. A *shahnā'ī* is a reeded, clarinet-like instrument.

5. *Ārṭī* is a worship ceremony in which lighted lamps are moved in a circle before the image of the deity.

6. In 1901, Sunnis comprised 90.7 percent of the city's Muslim population, Shī'as 4.4 percent, and Wahhābīs 0.5 percent (*Uttar Pradesh Gazetteer* 1965:89). The remaining 4.4 percent is not accounted for.

and scripturalism. Traditionalism draws on authoritative texts *and* on customary practices in order to delineate legitimate codes for conduct. It reads its sources more expansively than does scripturalism, which follows a strict interpretation of the Qur'ān, *ḥadīṡ*, and other texts. Scripturalists typically reject many forms of customary behavior which lie outside the narrow compass of textual edicts. The eclectic, custom-rich perspective of the traditionalists contrasts, then, with the puristic, doctrinal approach of the scripturalists.

Scripturalism in Indian Islam culminated in the reform movements of the nineteenth and twentieth centuries. By the turn of the twentieth century, both Banaras and the nearby towns of Jaunpur and Ghazipur had *madrasa*s affiliated with the school at Deoband and its reformist teachings (Metcalf 1982:134). The Ahl-i Ḥadīṡ movement, which shared with the Deobandīs a sense of urgency in freeing Islam of its accretions of traditional customs, had important followers in Banaras, and, according to Metcalf, the city was actually a center of the Ahl-i Ḥadīṡ for a number of generations (1982:276). However, the winds of scripturalist reform that moved through at least some quarters of the community did not really sweep clean the maze of social custom: today tombs (*mazār*s) of Muslim saints are actively maintained in the city itself, festivals in honor of *pīr*s are celebrated in the towns and villages of the Banaras hinterland, and a host of other traditional practices persist as well.

These two positions—the scripturalist and the traditionalist—tend to take on an appearance of clarity and uniformity when they are described in the context of social movements and the formalized doctrinal oppositions on which they hinge. In the popular domain, however, these counterposing positions are not always quite so sharply etched and not always and in every way mutually opposed. At a popular level the codes for conduct which are emphasized in each of these perspectives have several different modes of expression, and the significances articulated in one mode do not necessarily parallel the significances articulated in the other modes. From this point of view, neither the scripturalist nor the traditionalist positions can be assumed *a priori* to comprise a set of internally consistent principles; rather, each of these ideological positions is constituted by several axes or positions which only partially reinforce one another and which may in fact show contradictions in the particular moral outlook that they express.

Conceptually, the point is Foucault's (1972): the analysis of discourse—here Islamic ideology—should not search heedlessly for unities, congruences, and continuities, but rather for discontinuities and contradictions which define the dynamic structuration of a field of relations. Determining ways in which both scripturalism and traditionalism comprise internally differentiated perspectives may help to pinpoint aspects of moral ambiguity and moral flexibility in popular codes for conduct. In turn this may facilitate the identification of underlying similarities between doctrines which might at more formal levels seem to express completely antithetical ideologies.

Moral Issues and the Religion-Science-Magic Interface

Today in the narrow, winding lanes of Banaras, traditionalism and scripturalism are engaged in a dialogue over many of the same issues which have been debated since the rise of Islam. Two of the most prominent issues center on the nature of the relationship between God and other powerful beings and on questions about the proper conduct of human inquiry and the limitations on human knowledge. The first problem centers on the doctrine of *tauḥīd* (the unity of God) and on definitions of polytheism and idolatry. It asks essentially whether powerful beings other than God can be considered to influence the course of human events. The Qur'ānic world includes Satan, angels, and *jinn*; Middle Eastern and north Indian tradition adds saints, ghosts of the dead, stars and planets, and a multitude of local spirits and godlings. Which of these beings should be recognized and how should their relationship to God be defined? What modes of interaction with these beings are considered proper and legitimate?

The second issue involves questions about acceptable modes of human inquiry and the nature of their limitations. What kinds of phenomena can be comprehended by man and what kinds are essentially unknowable? What sorts of processes are valid for inquiring into the causes of events and the future course of men's personal circumstances? These questions are fundamental to the epistemological groundwork of Islam, comprehending the structure of inquiry not only in the field of theology proper, but also in the fields of science and occult science.

The discourse in which these two ideological issues are embedded is a discourse which poses and re-poses relationships among the fields of theory and practice which are commonly known as science, religion, and magic. The issues of the unity of God and the legitimate conduct of human inquiry are often expressed through understandings about the science-religion-magic interface and its manifestations in codes for conduct. Banaras Sunnis tend to share a broad agreement on the basic features of each of these domains. What they disagree about are the specific kinds of customary practices which fall within each of the three categories and the ways in which one should or should not participate in these areas.

The categories of religion, science, and magic are locally delimited as follows:

1. Religion (*dīn*) deals with God, the Qur'ān, and the Prophet. Proper religious activities for *maulawīs* (learned men) include conducting prayers, performing life-passage ceremonies, interpreting religious texts, and counseling. For lay Muslims, participation in these activities and support of the five pillars of Islam (profession of faith, prayer, almsgiving, pilgrimage to Mecca, and observance of the fast of *ramaẓān*) set the framework of a proper religious life.
2. Science (*'ilm*) involves the rational study of the natural world, including the heavens, the earth, and human life. Since the phenomena which science investigates are part of God's creation, religion encompasses science and provides an orientation for its inquiries. Mathematical calculation (*ḥisāb*) is the primary method by which scientific work is conducted.[7]
3. Magic (*jāḍū*) centers on the manipulation of words and substances in order to gain control over powerful forces, including an array of malevolent beings. Magic is usually a negatively valued category. In the opinion of some Muslims, it is patently false and illusory in its efforts to effect human control over powerful forces. In the views of other Muslims, it is believed to involve actual contact with Satan and other evil beings and hence to emphasize their power rather than the power of God. Sorcery, soul-calling, and hypnotism are often given as examples of magic.[8]

Scripturalist and traditionalist perspectives on the religion-science-magic complex manifest themselves in two modes: (1) a mode of classification which evaluates a whole range of social customs by categorizing them as either religion, science, or magic; (2) a mode of participation which specifies patterns of actual engagement in each of these domains. The mode of participation is rather more complex than the mode of classification since it contains several different levels: (1) engagement by virtue of "knowledge"; (2) engagement by virtue of "belief"; and (3) engagement by virtue of "practice."

These two modes and the definitions of religion, science, and magic

7. See Nasr (1976, 1978) on the rational sciences in Islam, and Peters (1968) on the historical debate between theology and philosophy.
8. Sharif (1972) describes magical practices among the Muslims of India.

given above derive from concepts discussed and enacted by Banaras Sunnis in the realm of social custom. Methodologically, the derivation of analytic constructs from indigenous understandings avoids the use of abstract and external distinctions between science, religion, and magic, while its cultural orientation places aside "the problem of belief" discussed by Needham (1972) and highlights instead "the culture of belief and practice."

Analysis of these two ideological axes—the axis of classification and the axis of participation—identifies the movable positions of the subject within both scripturalist and traditionalist ideology. As we shall see, the ways in which scripturalists classify certain social customs are not fully coincident with their modes of engagement in these customs, and the same holds true for traditionalists. Disjunctions mark the internal organization of both traditionalism and scripturalism, while at the same time these disjunctions constitute certain areas of congruence between these two seemingly opposed ideologies.

If issues centering on the oneness of God and the structure of theological and scientific inquiry are basic to the expression of morality and faith in Islam, they take on added significance because they also represent ways of conceptualizing the boundary between Islam and Hinduism. The ideal of a pure, rigorously monotheistic Islam contrasts sharply with the image of an amorphously polytheistic Hindu way of life, and this set of contrasting images is conducive to the ideological construction of Hinduism as the "antithetical other." Thus the centrality and controversiality of these issues is double-edged: the problem of tension and ambiguity in the realm of moral principles is simultaneously a problem in the relationship between the Muslim and Hindu communities in Banaras, between the historically constructed reservoirs of north Indian traditions and their contemporary interpretations, and, even more broadly, one might argue, between Hindus and Muslims in a secular Indian society. For these reasons, then, these issues of the unity of God and the limitations on human knowledge form subtle but powerful symbolic themes among the Sunnis of Banaras.

Divination and the Movable Positions of the Subject

These two moral issues in the Banaras Sunni community are cast into radical relief in the area of divinatory counseling. *Maulawīs* provide counseling services which constitute an important source of aid and advice for an array of situations from illness and family conflict to problems involving livelihood, education, court cases, and many other concerns. *Maulawīs* may sometimes use divination in their counseling sessions in order to clarify a client's circumstances, identify causes, offer advice, prescribe remedies, and predict future outcomes.

Historically, divination was widely practiced in both India and the Middle East,[9] and in the Islamic world it was a subject of rather pointed controversy. Luminaries such as Ibn Khaldūn, Al-Bīrūnī, and Ibn Sīnā wrote on a range of divinatory practices.[10] Al-Bīrūnī authored a study of astrology which provides a detailed, ostensibly sympathetic account of the system, while Ibn Khaldūn devoted pages of the *Muqaddama* to a description and refutation of many varieties of divination. Why was divination such an intellectually and theologically controversial topic?

Dominant forms of divination such as numerology and astrology were often classified as part of the rational sciences,[11] and astrology's sibling link with astronomy helped support its claims to legitimacy.[12] These perspectives were buttressed by the patronage of regional rulers and other high-level officials and by the expansive construction of Ismā'īlī and Hermetic cosmologies. On the other hand, both theological and rational arguments were marshaled against divination. Theologically, divinatory practices seemed to enhance man's own powers of comprehension and to cultivate the potent influences of evil spirits, celestial bodies, and other occult forces—the same arguments put forward today by Banaras scripturalists. Rationally, it was noted that astrologers could not provide empirical proof that celestial configurations actually had the influences which they claimed for them, and that diviners could not meet the "advance challenge" (*taḥaddī*) of making an accurate prediction in advance of the actual event or occurrence.[13] The fact that critics felt compelled to present such systematically argued positions suggests the very real persistence of divinatory practices in various quarters of the Muslim world.

9. On divination and omens, see, for instance, Westermarck on Morocco (1926, vol. 1: 119–31, 356–59; vol. 2: 126–29, 162–69); Masse on Persia (1954:239–53); and Sharif on India (1972:218–63).
10. Nasr (1978) describes the cosmological doctrines of Ibn Sīnā and Al-Bīrūnī.
11. Nasr (1976:15–16; 1978:passim) and Peters (1968:105–20) list classifications of the branches of knowledge in Islam.
12. Nasr (1976:91–134) presents an overview of Islamic astronomy and astrology. Pugh (1983a, 1983b, 1984) analyzes the contemporary meanings and uses of astrology and related forms of divination among the Hindus and Muslims of Banaras.
13. Ibn Khaldūn (1958:passim) makes this point about the advance challenge.

Systems of divination which are found today in the Banaras Sunni community include the following:

1. the Qur'ān, which is opened at random in order to obtain guidance on a particular problem;
2. numerology (*abjad*), a system by which calculations are made on the basis of the numerical values of the letters of the alphabet;
3. dice (*ramal*), a system of calculating the face values of dice through a series of permutations to yield a final ideogram, which indicates the presence of specific afflictive forces and the likely outcomes of situations;
4. labeled tokens, which are selected blind from a dish in order to identify current influences on the client, such as ghosts, evil spirits, and stars;
5. cowrie shells (*kauṛī*), which are thrown and their "open" and "closed" values calculated in order to answer questions;
6. astronomical/astrological tables (*zīj*) showing celestial positions which indicate auspicious times for important undertakings;
7. horoscopes (*janam kuṇḍalī, patrī, za'icha*) which show configurations of planets and constellations for a specific time and place;
8. palms (*hāth ki lakīr, hasta rekhā*), where lines and mounts indicate a person's character traits and a trajectory of important life-events.

These forms of divination do not all involve the same structure of inquiry or embed the same assumptions about the influences of powerful forces on the human world. Divination still is not a value-free form of inquiry but rather one which is infused with ideological import. In Banaras, present-day disagreement over legitimate forms of divination constitutes a point of refraction of underlying differences and similarities between scripturalist and traditionalist interpretations of moral principles. The movable positions of the subject show up in traditionalist and scripturalist differences in the classification of divinatory practices and also in their differences at the level of actual participation in these customary systems.

The Classificational Position

Both scripturalists and traditionalists express their more conservative orientations through their classifications of divinatory systems (figure 14.1). The two groups agree that consulting the Qur'ān for guidance on personal problems falls within the realm of religion, thus making it the most legitimate mode of inquiry. Its surety lies in the power of God, and thus man as diviner is not considered an agent who actively influences the outcome.

Figure 14.1

Modes of Classification and Symbolic Evaluation of Divinatory Systems

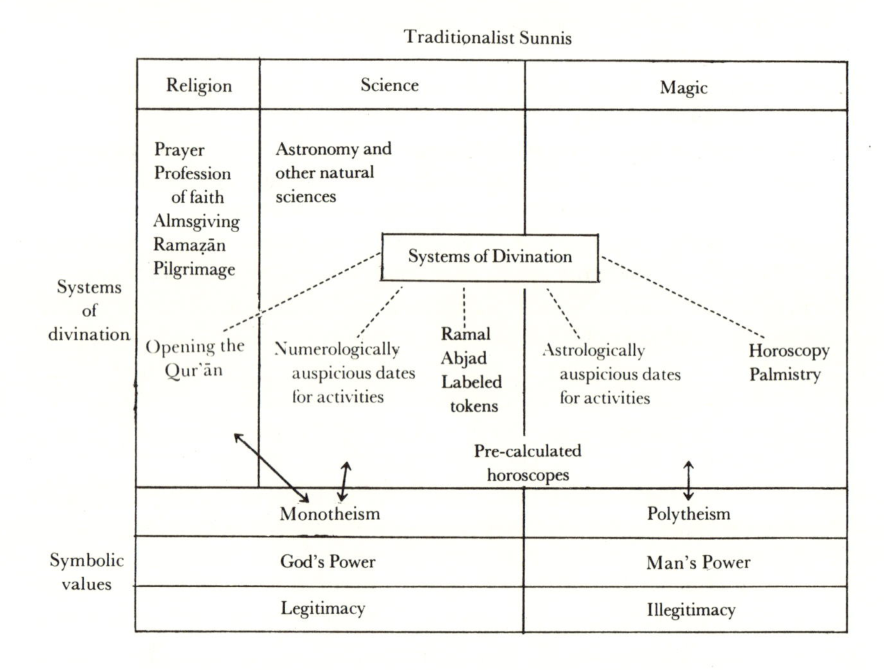

Differences in classificatory perspective are evident in the categories of science and magic. The differences hinge on the interpretation of a key reference point for most of these systems—the traditional field of astronomy and astrology. The field comprises the following areas:

1. the study of the structure of the heavens, including observation and calculation of planetary and stellar movements, time-reckoning, and location of cardinal directions for purposes of prayer and travel;
2. the analysis of influences of the heavens on the earth in the form of natural events such as earthquakes, floods, droughts, and eclipses;
3. the assessment of auspicious periods of time for scheduling important activities;
4. the determination of heavenly influences on the person and the prediction of future events in his or her life.

The first two areas—the study of the structure of the heavens and the nature of celestial influences on the earth—have historically been considered legitimate scientific pursuits in Islam, and today Banaras Sunnis label these activities as science. The *Mishkātu'l Maṣabīḥ*, a source of *ḥadīṣ* for Indian Sunnis, refers to several Qur'ānic suras which are taken to indicate the purposes for which the heavens may be used: as an ornament to the heavens (sura 67, verse 5); to stone the Devil with (sura 67, verse 5); to direct travelers through the forests and on the sea (sura 15, verse 16) (*Mishkāt* book 12, chap. 3, pt. 3; quoted in Yasin 1974:82n). Some Sunnis feel that these suras restrict the study of the heavens to these three purposes only, and hence forbid all other aspects of celestial study.

Selecting auspicious times (*sā'at*) for special undertakings marks the beginning of controversy. On the one hand, it is true, as both scripturalist and traditionalist Sunnis know, that Mughal rulers and other Muslim leaders often followed this practice, and that Urdu almanacs include lists of auspicious times for performing a range of activities. On the other hand, the custom of using auspicious times is intimately associated with Hinduism. One solution which some Sunnis regard as legitimate and scientific, rather than illegitimate and magical, is the custom of reckoning auspicious periods of time numerologically in terms of dates in the Islamic lunar month, rather than astrologically in terms of the positions and qualitatively differentiated influences of the heavenly bodies. Traditionalist Sunnis consider the 3rd, 13th, 23rd, 8th, 18th, and 28th to be unlucky days in the lunar month, and they avoid scheduling important activities such as marriages on those days.

Scripturalist Sunnis who do not follow these customs nonetheless do not find anything particularly objectionable in their use by other Sunnis. What they do find objectionable, however, is the use of astrologically auspicious dates, which they consider to fall within the general category of magic. What they are rejecting, first of all, is the idea that the heavens have influences powerful enough to affect the course of daily life; second, they are also rejecting the symbolic parallel between Hinduism and Islam which the use of astrologically auspicious dates would work to establish. In this light, it is interesting to note that one of the most commonly reported "Hindu" customs that Indian Muslims have abandoned in the ongoing process of Islamization is the use of astrologically auspicious dates for scheduling important activities (see, for instance, Aggarwal 1969).

It is in the fourth area—the area of divination involving personal fortunes—that conflicting classifications come noticeably into play. Scripturalist Sunnis classify as magic all forms of divination except consulting the Qur'ān. This classification is based textually on certain passages in the Qur'ān and the *ḥadīs̤*. As we have seen, the Qur'ān contains several suras which scripturalist Sunnis take to limit the study of the heavens and to forbid fortunetelling. The *Mishkāt* (book 22, chaps. 2–3) states that taking evil omens and consulting diviners are forbidden. It also states that "taking evil omens is polytheism" (book 22, chap. 2, pt. 2). Scripturalist Sunnis, while often admitting that the heavens have natural power (*qudrat*), say that the stars do not have any significant impact on events in the person's life—the only effective power is God. They disapprove of divination because it assumes that heavenly bodies have special power over men. Scripturalist Muslims may also reject divination because they see it as recognizing and cultivating the powers of Satan. Finally, scripturalists see divination as involving man's assumption of a position of insight and potency which goes beyond their human limitations; they say that diviners give clients their own personal opinions, rather than giving them insight into some ultimate form of reality.

In contrast, traditionalist Sunnis construe the category of science quite broadly while they include in the category of magic a significantly smaller number of divinatory systems than do scripturalists. Traditionalists use alternative interpretations of the Qur'ān and the *ḥadīs̤* as the basis for labeling several kinds of divination as science (and hence as legitimate and falling within the compass of religion), while labeling other kinds of divination as magic (and hence as illegitimate and falling outside the compass of both science and religion). They cite the Qur'ānic emphasis on the signs and portents of God's will, and they stress the fact that the heavens are part of God's creation and hence must naturally reflect His will. They believe that the planets and stars have natural power which influences terrestrial life and the life of the person. They consider the legitimate sciences to include numerology (*abjad*), dice (*ramal*), and selections of labeled tokens. Each of these divinatory methods may include the identification of planetary influences, through links with numbers, letters, and planets, through associations between *ramal* ideograms and planets, and through token labels marking planets and stars.

For traditionalist Sunnis, the legitimacy of these forms of divination is enhanced, first, by the fact that they are commonly considered to be of Middle Eastern origin and hence part of Islamic tradition, and second, by the fact that the divination procedure itself typically uses framing devices, such as invoking the name of Allāh and asking for divine guidance, in order to ensure its scientific and hence religious status. These procedures reaffirm the proper hierarchical relationship between God and man and de-emphasize the powers of man as diviner; coordinately, traditionalists favor these forms of divination because they do not allow undue leeway for human manipulation or error.

Traditionalist Sunnis tend to label horoscopy and palmistry as magic. These procedures involve a much more influential role for the diviner, a role seen as abrogating the power of God. Because these interpretative procedures are seen as highly subjective and, in the case of horoscopy, mathematically complex, they appear to offer more scope for human error and deception than do other forms of divination. To take these objections into account, some *maulawīs* read horoscopes printed in Urdu almanacs because they regard these horoscopes as correctly calculated and because they require no calculations on their own part. Finally, because horoscopy and palmistry are widely prevalent Hindu customs, they inhere in an image of the "other" which both scripturalists and traditionalists symbolically oppose to their own images of self and community.

These classificatory schemes underlie certain choices which scripturalists and traditionalists make in dealing with problem situations. They appear to influence the choice of particular *maulawīs* as counselors, and they also inform the etiological assessments of their situation which they will consider as acceptable and the remedial procedures which they will follow.

In examining these conflicting classifications as expressions of ideological positions, one must ask how fully and adequately the evaluative scheme which each position constructs fits with the sheer reality of social life in the Sunni community. How do we understand a situation in which Sunnis recognize the existence of two at least partially contradictory interpretations of reality within their own community, and in an oblique and perhaps half-formed fashion, the contingent character of their own particular view of the situation? These are important questions, especially for scripturalists, since the classificatory scheme which they use has the effect of drawing a significant divide between groups of Sunnis, and also of being patently at odds with the customary life styles of many members of the community, including well-known *maulawīs*, whose divinatory customs they label as magic. It seems, however, that classifications based on the moral significance of facts can never completely obscure the existence of the facts themselves. In this situation, then, it is essential to ask whether there are other ideological positions which provide a different ordering of these facts, perhaps an ordering which offsets some of the disjunctions reflected in these classificational perspectives. In the following section, I suggest that a second position—one marked by modes of participation in divinatory systems—reflects a different, less disjuncture image of the Sunni community itself and also of its relationship to its Hindu neighbors.

The Participational Position

This ideological position works through the manipulation of the juncture between theory and practice. Banaras Sunnis themselves express this position as a conjunction or disjunction between the factors of "belief," "knowledge," and "practice" within each of the domains we are discussing—the domains of religion, science, and magic. This position, then, takes as problematic the unity of any given domain of theory and practice.

These three modes of participation together constitute a matrix of separable categories whose permutations organize levels of engagement in the fields of religion, science, and magic. This position of participation organizes a flexible strategy for assessing customary practices in a complex sociocultural environment. Banaras constitutes an environment where sometimes negatively valued customs, such as certain features of divinatory counseling, form part of a historical ensemble of traditions with a visible presence in the community.

I take these three forms of participation from the terms which Sunnis use to discuss divinatory counseling:

1. belief	*mānnā* (to accept as true or valid)
2. knowledge	*jānnā* (to know)
	jānkārī (knowledge)
	'ilm (knowledge)
3. practice	*istĕ'mal karnā* (to use)
	karnā (to do, to act)
	kām karnā (to work, to do work)

In this framework, belief assumes knowledge: one has some knowledge of the principles or details of those things which one accepts as true or valid. However, knowledge does not assume belief: one may know many things which one does not actually believe or accept as true. Finally, belief and knowledge may exist without practice: one may know or believe a variety of things which one does not put into practice. Conversely, practice exists without apparent belief or knowledge, as in cases in which Muslims read their horoscopes in the local newspapers out of curiosity or just for fun, as they say. In this context "amusement" and "curiosity" as modes of engagement do not assume that the person believes in the validity of the horoscope reading, and they carry only an implicit assumption that he or she has any substantial knowledge of the system.

Sunnis have several different ways of organizing their modes of participation in the fields of religion, science, and magic (figure 14.2). In the domains of religion and science, both scripturalist and traditionalist Sunnis see belief, knowledge, and practice as naturally conjoined. Belief in God goes hand in hand with at least some knowledge of religious precepts, which in turn receive their full confirmation through participation in religious practices. Knowledge of the natural world, if it is genuinely scientific, may be accepted as true, and practices based on this knowledge are considered legitimate. Scripturalists, then, actually practice the few forms of divination which they classify as religion or science. Traditionalists, as we have noted, classify a larger number of divinatory systems as science, which implies that they not only know these systems and accept them as valid, but that they also practice them and see practice as natural to them.

The domain of magic provides the interesting case, however, since it shows the existence of real disjunctions between belief, knowledge, and practice for both groups of Sunnis. Scripturalists, who classify all

Figure 14.2
Modes of Participation in Divinatory Systems

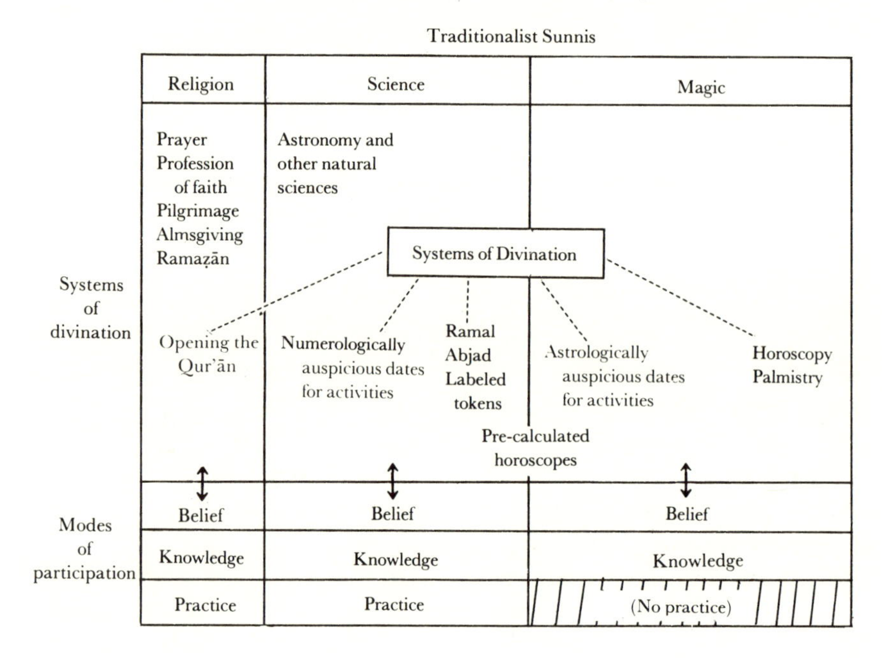

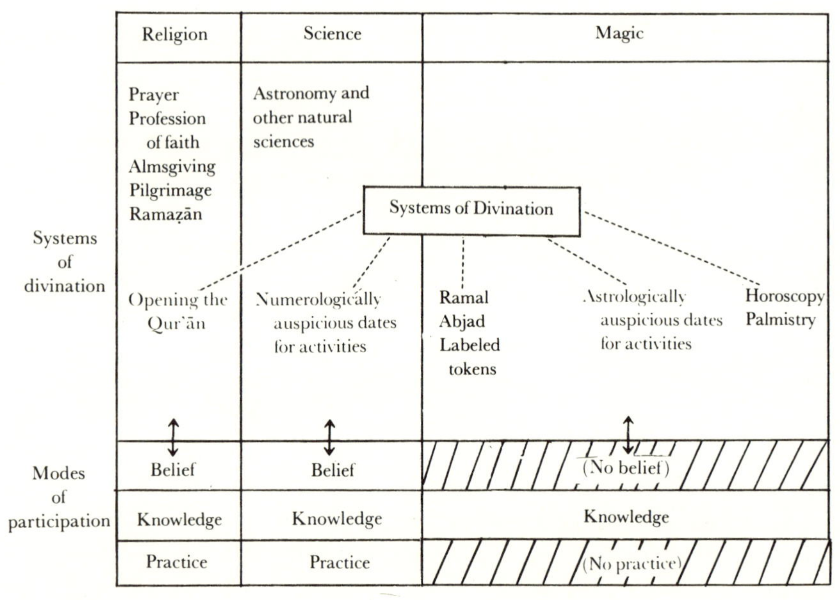

divinatory systems except consulting the Qur'ān as magic and hence as illegitimate, say in another vein that both the *maulawīs* whose advice they follow and they themselves, at least to some extent, know the basic details of these "illegitimate" systems, but that they do not accept them as valid nor do they practice them. Traditionalists say that they know and believe in various forms of divination, including some which they classify as magic. But while they know and believe in the principles of these systems, they say that they do not actually practice (and actually seem not to practice) or follow advice based on these principles.

Common examples include the fact that some traditionalists say that they know about and believe in the power of Saturn, Mars, and other malevolent planets and that they believe in the special powers of days governed by these planets, but that they do not (and seem actually not to) adhere to any practices associated with these beliefs. They say that they do not (and actually seem not to) worship or make offerings to planetary powers, nor do they alter their schedules because of the power of the planets on certain days of the week or during other time periods. As a rule they do not wear stones or gems selected specifically for protection against these planets, and they do not have birth-horoscopes cast. The practices which they rule out are those which seem to provide full confirmation of the existence of independent celestial powers. They see divinatory practices in which they do participate as scientific practices which preserve the proper hierarchical relationship between God and man and which naturally conjoin knowledge, belief, and practice.

Thus the factors of knowledge, belief, and practice constitute levels of engagement in the domains of religion, science, and magic, and in the historically accumulated reservoirs of customary systems in South Asian society. And, as separable levels of participation, they are arranged by Banaras Sunnis into several different configurations, each of which expresses an ideological perspective on these customary systems. What is striking about these two different configurations of participation—the scripturalist and the traditionalist—is that they are less absolutely and monolithically defined and more internally differentiated than the configurations based on classification. When scripturalists acknowledge that they know the details of a system of divination which in another mode they label as magical and illegitimate, they also implicitly acknowledge that they participate, at least on one level, in north Indian cultural traditions which they share with eclectic Sunnis and, indeed, with Hindus as well. And the fact that traditionalists refuse participation in numerous "magical" practices which scripturalist Sunnis also refuse, indicates another level of participation—or rather, refusal of participation—which is shared by both groups of Sunnis.

Conclusion

Divinatory counseling refracts important ideological differences between scripturalist and traditionalist Sunnis on the issues of the nature of divine power and the proper conduct of human inquiry. The present analysis shows that the framework of ideological debate among Banaras Sunnis cannot be accounted for by positing two monolithically consistent and irretrievably opposed perspectives. Instead, the analysis first indicates that each ideological perspective is itself a composite entity formed around two enunciatory positions—a position of classification and a position of participation—which may be significantly discrepant from one another. Second, the analysis shows that these two positions organize a flexible symbolic field which allows both scripturalists and traditionalists to construe the divisions within the Sunni community, and the boundaries between the Sunni community and the Hindu community, in several different ways. The classificational position represents a more conservative, concisely defined perspective for both scripturalists and traditionalists, while the participational position organizes a more liberal perspective which mediates some of the oppositions articulated by the classificatory axis.

The existence of these movable positions on basic moral principles attests to the complexities of Muslim life in the Indian context. The process of Islamization, as described, for instance, by Ahmad (1976), has occurred historically and continues to occur today in a cultural environment which often poses contradictory requirements—the old and common dilemma between adjustment and assimilation, on the one hand, and exclusion and boundary maintenance on the other. One might suggest that the existence of both more conservative and more liberal enunciatory positions within the ideologies of scripturalists and traditionalists alike has served to reflect and sustain a certain amount of flexibility in Hindu-Muslim relations.

A more comprehensive view of Indian Islam might discover ways in which these enunciatory positions organize an inner dynamic in the debate between scripturalists and traditionalists on other moral issues and in other realms of social custom. This analytic perspective might also provide a different reading of similar debates in other parts of the

Islamic world, such as the debacle over the Javanese funeral discussed by Geertz (1973). Looking at enunciatory positions which animate ideological debates in complex societies allows an exploration of the construction of images of self and others, not as West describing East, a process which Said (1978) has so eloquently analyzed, but rather as East describing East, through the informally parlanced routines of everyday life and the reticulately expressed moral underpinnings of the customary practices of self and other. A broadly cast symbolic perspective offers a useful vantage point for examining the situational contexts and subjective complexities of cultural identity and customary practices in the Islamic world.

References

Aggarwal, P. C.
1969 "Changing Religious Practices: Their Relationship to Secular Power in a Rajasthan Village." *Economic and Political Weekly* 4, 12:547–51.

Ahmad, Imtiaz
1976 "Exclusion and Assimilation in Indian Islam." In *Socio-Cultural Impact of Islam on India*. Attar Singh, ed. Chandigarh: Punjab University Publication Bureau.

Census of India
1971 Pt. II-C. Social and Cultural Tables. Uttar Pradesh.

Cohn, Bernard S.
1962 "Political Systems of Eighteenth-Century India: The Banaras Region." *Journal of the American Oriental Society* 82, 3:312–20.

Eck, Diana L.
1982 *Banaras: City of Light*. New York: Alfred A. Knopf.

Foucault, Michel
1972 *The Archaeology of Knowledge*. New York: Harper & Row.

Geertz, Clifford
1968 *Islam Observed: Religious Development in Morocco and Indonesia*. Chicago: University of Chicago Press.
1973 "Ritual and Social Change: A Javanese Example." In *The Interpretation of Cultures*. New York: Basic Books.

Ibn Khaldūn
1958 *The Muqaddimah*. 3 vols. New York: Pantheon Books.

Masse, Henri
1954 *Persian Beliefs and Customs*. New Haven: Human Relations Area Files (first published 1938).

Metcalf, Barbara Daly
1982 *Islamic Revival in British India: Deoband, 1860–1900*. Princeton: Princeton University Press.

Mishkātu'l Maṣabīḥ
1963–65 4 vols. James Robson, ed. and trans. Lahore: Sh. Muhammad Ashraf.

Nasr, Seyyed Hossein
1976 *Islamic Science: An Illustrated Study*. N.p.: World of Islam Festival Publishing Co.
1978 *An Introduction to Islamic Cosmological Doctrines*. Boulder, Colo.: Shambala (first published 1964).
Needham, Rodney
1972 *Belief, Language, and Experience*. Chicago: University of Chicago Press.
Peters F. E.
1968 *Aristotle and the Arabs: The Aristotelian Tradition in Islam*. New York: New York University Press.
Pugh, Judy F.
1983a "Astrology and Fate: The Hindu and Muslim Experiences." In *Karma: An Anthropological Inquiry*. Charles F. Keyes and E. Valentine Daniel, eds. Berkeley: University of California Press, pp. 131–46.
1983b "Astrological Counseling in Contemporary India." *Culture, Medicine and Psychiatry* 7:279–99.
1984 "Concepts of Person and Situation in North Indian Counseling: The Case of Astrology." In *South Asian Systems of Healing*. E. Valentine Daniel and Judy F. Pugh, eds. *Contributions to Asian Studies* 18:85–105 (special issue).
Said, Edward W.
1978 *Orientalism*. New York: Random House (Vintage Books).
Sharif, Jafar
1972 *Islam in India: The Customs of the Musalmans of India*. William Crooke, ed.; G. A. Herklots, trans. Delhi: Oriental Books Reprint Corporation (first published 1921).
Siddiqui, Nafis Ahmad
1976 *Population Geography of Muslims of India*. New Delhi: S. Chand & Co.
Smith, Vincent A.
1961 *The Oxford History of India*. Percival Spear, ed. Oxford: Clarendon Press (3rd edition).
Sukul, Kuber Nath
1974 *Varanasi down the Ages*. Patna: Kameshwar Nath Sukul.
Uttar Pradesh District Gazetteers (Varanasi)
1965 Esha Basanti Joshi, ed. Allahabad: Government Press.
Westermarck, Edward
1926 *Ritual and Belief in Morocco*. 2 vols. London: MacMillan & Co.
Yasin, Mohammed
1974 *A Social History of Islamic India, 1605–1748*. New Delhi: Munshiram Manoharlal.

Glossary of Selected Terms

abjad — numerology, a system by which calculations are made on the basis of the numerical values traditionally assigned to the letters of the alphabet.

adab — etiquette, proper deportment.

Aga Khan — the title originating in Iran given to modern Nizārī Ismā'īlī *imāms*.

agama — religion (Malay).

ahl-i ḥadīs̤ — "People of the Traditions," a reform group originating in the nineteenth century.

ahl-i zubān — masters of the language.

ajlāf — common people, the lower social orders.

akal — reason, intellect (Malay; Urdu: *'aql*).

akhara — a physical fitness group.

'ālim — (pl. *'ulamā*) a scholar of Islamic jurisprudence; a learned man.

'ām log — common people.

amīr — a person of rank or distinction, a noble.

'aql — reason, reasoning, intelligence.

ashraf — (sing. *sharīf*) respectable class (see *sharīf*).

aṣli — true, fundamental.

ātrāp — the lowly born (Bengali).

avatār — incarnation of a Hindu deity.

bābū — an elder; a noble.

baebsae — businessman (Bengali).

baḥas̤ — religious disputation.

barādarī — "brotherhood," kinsfolk.

barakat — spiritual power, blessing, auspiciousness.

bāt̤in — inner or esoteric meaning of Revelation.

be-adab — lacking *adab* (see *adab*).

be-ghairat — lacking honor.

be-shar' — unlawful; in violation of *sharī'at*.

bhakti — filial love.

bi'dat — innovation.

-bitto — property, wealth (Bengali, suffix).

chākrijībī — service holders (Bengali).

chālāk — clever, cunning.

chalweshti — armed supporters (Pashto).

chillag — extended fasting (literally, "forty days") (Baluchi; Urdu: *chillā*).

chimcha — patronage politics (literally, "spoon") (Baluchi).

dālān — a hall; bathing place attached to a mosque.

dargāh — a royal court; a shrine or tomb.

dasā avatāra — the Vaishnavite Hindu doctrine of the ten descents of Vishnu; among the Ismā'īlīs the name came to be applied to a mythopoeic *ginān*.

des — country.

desī — native.

dharma — religion.

dharmik — religious.

dīn — faith, religion.

dolass kassi — a group of twelve men (Pashto).

du'ā — prayer or supplication, which among the Nizārī Ismā'īlīs came to refer to a daily ritual form of prayer.

dunyā — the present world.

faqīr — a Muslim ascetic.

farmān — decree; directive or guidance from the Ismā'īlī *imām* to his followers.

fātiḥa — prayers for the dead.

fatwā — (pl. *fatāwā*) formal legal opinion; a notification of the decision of the law with respect to a particular case.

fiqh — Classical Muslim jurisprudence.

firqa — sect.

garm — warm, hot.

ghaṭ-pāṭ — a ceremony of initiation refered to in the Ismā'īlī *ginān*s.

ghazal — an ode.

ginān — the traditional indigenous literature preserved among the Nizārī Ismā'īlīs of the Subcontinent.

gun — qualities.

ḥadīṣ — Traditions of the Prophet of Islam.

ḥājī — one who has performed the pilgrimage to Mecca.

ḥajj — annual pilgrimage to Mecca.

ḥalāl — lawful.

ḥaqā'iq — (pl. of *haqīqat*) truths, a technical term in Ismā'īlī thought denoting the ultimate sense and meaning of divine revelation.

ḥaqq — personal moral duty; right, obligation.

ḥarām — forbidden.

hati — intuition (Malay).

Hindustani — pertaining to north India; also refers to the Urdu language.

'īd — a holiday marking the breaking of the fast kept during the month of *ramaẓān*.

'īd-gah — enclosed area where *'īd* services are held.

ijmā' — consensus of opinion.

ijtihād — the use of individual reason.

'ilm — knowledge; science.

imām — leader, generally referring to the person who leads others in prayer. In the past the term was used interchangeably with Caliph, for the head of the state, and occasionally as an honorific title for very learned religious scholars. Among Shī'ās, the *imām* is a divinely appointed leader, succeeding the Prophet. He possesses spiritual knowledge and guides Muslims to an understanding of the inner meaning of revelation as well as implementing Islamic values according to changing times and circumstances.

imāmat — the office of an *imām*.

īmān — faith; refers to faith in the unity of God and the prophethood of Muḥammad.

insān — human being.

insānīyat — humanity.

iqta' — an assignment of land.

īshwar — a Hindu term for God.

Islam — submission to the will of God.

islāmīya — precepts of Islam.

'izzat — honor.

jāḍū — magic.

jāgīr — a land grant from the government, either attached to an office or a reward for services.

jamā'at — a society, congregation, assembly.

jamā'at-khāna — houses of assembly and the centers of communal, religious, and social activity among Nizārī Ismā'īlīs.

janglī — a person living in the wild.

jāti — community.

jībikā — livelihood (Bengali).

jihād — holy war.

jinn — a spirit, demon.

jirga — council of elders; village council of adult men (Baluchi, Pashto, Urdu).

jism — the body.

kāfir — infidel, unbeliever.

kalma — the Muslim profession of faith.

khalīfa — a successor; the spiritual successor of a *pīr*.

khāliṣ — pure.

khānaqāh — a religious establishment for Sufis, where a *pīr* teaches his disciples.

khāṭib — orator.

khilāfat — deputyship.

khōjkī — the Indian script in which the Ismā'īlī *ginān*s were preserved.

khuṭba — an oration recited by the *khāṭib* from the mosque during Friday prayers.

kuroh — a measure of distance of approximately two miles.

madrasa — school, originally attached to a mosque; traditional Muslim school of learning.

mahdī — future deliverer, ultimate restorer of the true Islam.

majlis muzākara — public council of debate (Malay).

maktab — Qur'ānic school, usually attached to a mosque.

malang — a Muslim dervish, whose behavior is typically *be-shar'*.

mālik — master; among the Pukhtuns, a traditional political leader.

maulānā — title given to the head of a religious group.

maulawī — learned man.

mazār — tomb of a saint, mausoleum.

maẕhab — the four acknowledged schools of jurisprudence in Islam; religion.

meshuarat ulama — council of *'ulamā* (Malay).

miḥrāb — the niche of a mosque, which shows the direction of Mecca.

mīlād — religious ceremony marking the birth anniversary of the Prophet.

miyān — a respectable person; descendant of a holy man.

mu'aẕẕin — one who chants the call to prayer.

mufaṣṣal — subordinate division of a district.

muftī — a jurisconsult.

muḥājir — (pl. *muḥājirīn*) refugee.

muḥarram — first month of the Islamic year, during which the death of Ḥusain is commemorated, especially by Shī'ās.

mullā — a learned man; Persian for the Arabic "*maulawī*"; in South Asia it usually refers to a class of rural priests.

muqallid — a follower, one who adheres to a particular school of law.

murīd — follower of a *pīr*.

murshid — spiritual preceptor.

Muslim — one who is in submission to God's will.

nabī — a prophet who has received commands from God.

nafs — the lower or "animal" faculty of the human soul.

nafsu — emotion, especially base emotion (see *nafs*) (Malay).

najas — dirt, impurity.

namāz — prescribed prayer of Muslims.

nasl — progeny.

nasp — soul (see *nafs*) (Baluchi).

naṣṣ — text, often from the Qur'ān, as evidenced in legal argument.

nūr — radiant light; a Qur'ānic term of central significance in Ismā'īlī and Sufi thought.

pāk — pure.

pakar hadis — specialist or expert in the study of *ḥadīṡ* (Malay).

pānchāli — narration of events in verse (Bengali).

parda — seclusion of women.

pāṭhsālā — traditional vernacular elementary school in Bengal.

pīr — saint, either living or dead; in Sufism, the spiritual leader and teacher; among the Nizārī Ismā'īlīs, the teacher representing the *imām* and acting on his behalf.

pīr-zāda — the son or successor of a *pīr*.

pondok — traditional religious school (literally, "hut") (Malay).

pra-bhāt pherī — morning procession.

punḍit — a Hindu scholar; the traditional Bengali scholar.

pūthi — a type of Bengali literature written in verse.

qaṣba — a town dominated by a family of Muslim administrative elite.

qaum — tribe, people.

qāẓī — a Muslim judge.

qiyās — analogy (as a source of Islamic jurisprudence).

rābiṭa — connection, bond of union.

ramaẓān — the ninth month of the Islamic year, during which fasting is practiced from sunrise to sunset.

rasūl — a prophet receiving a book from God.

riba' — usurious interest; usury.

risāla — written report, pamphlet.

rishtadār — a relative, kinsman.

riwāj — popular custom; normative custom.

riwāj-i 'ām — district records of tribal customs, compiled by the British.

rōz-marra bōlchāl — ordinary speech.

roza — obligatory fasting in Islam during *ramaẓān*, the ninth month of the Islamic calendar.

rūḥ — the spirit.

sajjāda-nishīn — successor to the leadership of a shrine and its following.

salām — a salutation, a greeting.

salām karnā — to give deferential respect to.

ṣalāt — formal ritual prayer in Islam (*namāz*).

sāmājik — community (adj.; Bengali).

sardār — chief.

satpanth — the "true way".

sayyid — a descendant of the Prophet Muḥammad.

shāh — a title meaning king, monarch.

shaikh — an elder; a reputed saint; the head of a Sufi order; a title taken by descendants of the Prophet.

shaiṭān — a satan; the devil who misguides human beings.

shakti — power.

sharī'at — the concept of the right way in Islam, embodied in the divinely established body of law and code for conduct, encompassing beliefs, practices, rituals, public and personal law. In Ismā'īlism, it is complemented by the *haqīqat*.

shar'ī — pertaining to the law.

sharīf — (pl. *ashraf*) of good family; a descendant of the Prophet.

shirk — polytheism; infidelity.

siasat shariah — administrative regulation (Malay; *siyāsat sharī'at* has a technical meaning in Islamic jurisprudence different from this local meaning).

sīdhā-sādhā — simple, artless.

silsila — genealogy, chain of succession.

sīmiyā — magic; numerology.

sneha — parental love.

sunnat — The practices and sayings of Muḥammad as handed down by tradition (*ḥadīṣ*).

suwār — horse.

taḥṣīldār — a sub-collector of revenue.

talfīq — selective and combinative employment of the schools of law.

talkin — giving instruction to the dead before burial (Malay; Arabic: *talqīn*).

taqdīr — fate.

taqīya — pious dissimulation, practiced particularly by Shī'as as a precaution against persecution.

taqlīd — unquestioning adoption of past authority.

tārīkh — chronicle; history.

ṭarīqa — Sufi brotherhood.

tāṣīr — temperament (Arabic: "effect").

tauḥīd — Islamic concept of the unity of God.

ta'wīẕ — a talisman.

ṭhanḍā — cool, cold.

ṭheṭh — pure, genuine.

'ulamā — see *'ālim.*

ummat — the Muslim community.

'urs — the anniversary of a *pīr*'s death; the annual gathering of disciples of a living *pīr.*

wadera — a village chief (Baluchi).

waqf — endowed property designated in Islamic law as held in trust for the benefit of the community.

wazīr — a minister of state.

ẓāhir — outer, external, or literal sense, particularly of Revelation.

zaildār — leader of a *zail*, a local unit of administration, consisting of roughly ten to forty villages.

zakāt — the compulsory alms payable by a Muslim; one of the "Five Pillars" of Islam.

zamīn — land.

zamzam — a sacred well near the Ka'ba in Mecca.

zan — women.

zar — gold.

ẕāt — tribe, caste.

ẕatī ta'alluqāt — tribal and caste connections and loyalties.

ẕikr — recollection of God, often through the repetition of specific formulae associated with one of the Sufi orders.

Index

Designer:	Sandy Drooker
Compositor:	OUP Delhi
Text:	11/13 Baskerville
Display:	Baskerville
Printer:	Braun-Brumfield
Binder:	Braun-Brumfield